The Cambridge Companion to Herodotus

Herodotus' *Histories* is the first major surviving prose work from antiquity. Its range of interests is immense, covering the whole of the known world and much beyond, and it culminates in a detailed account of the Persian Wars of the early fifth century BCE. Moreover, recent research has shown that Herodotus is a sophisticated and at times even ironic narrator, and a pioneer and serious practitioner of historical research at a time when the Greeks' traditions about their past were still the fluid transmissions and memories of a largely oral society. This *Companion* provides a series of up-to-date and accessible chapters, written by distinguished scholars, illuminating many aspects of Herodotus' work: his skill in language and his narrative art; his intellectual preconceptions; his working methods and techniques; his attitude towards nature and the gods; his attitude towards foreign cultures and peoples; and his view of human life and human history.

THE CAMBRIDGE
COMPANION TO
HERODOTUS

EDITED BY
CAROLYN DEWALD
Professor of Classics and History, Bard College

and

JOHN MARINCOLA
Professor of Classics, Florida State University

CAMBRIDGE
UNIVERSITY PRESS

CAMBRIDGE UNIVERSITY PRESS
Cambridge, New York, Melbourne, Madrid, Cape Town, Singapore, São Paulo

Cambridge University Press
The Edinburgh Building, Cambridge CB2 8RU, UK

Published in the United States of America by Cambridge University Press, New York

www.cambridge.org
Information on this title: www.cambridge.org/9780521536837

© Cambridge University Press 2006

First published 2006
Reprinted 2007

Printed in the United Kingdom at the University Press, Cambridge

A catalogue record for this publication is available from the British Library

ISBN-13 978-0-521-83001-0 hardback
ISBN-13 978-0-521-53683-7 paperback

CONTENTS

CONTENTS

MAPS

NOTES ON CONTRIBUTORS

EGBERT J. BAKKER is Professor of Classics at Yale University. His publications include *Linguistics and Formulas in Homer* (1988) and *Poetry in Speech: Orality and Homeric Discourse* (1997). He is co-editor of *Brill's Companion to Herodotus* (2002).

CAROLYN DEWALD taught for many years at the University of Southern California, and is now Professor of History and Classics at Bard College. She has written extensively on Herodotus, including the Introduction and Notes to the Oxford World's Classics translation of Herodotus (1998). Her latest publication is *Thucydides' War Narrative: A Structural Study* (2006). She is currently co-editing (with Rosaria Munson) a commentary on Herodotus 1 for the Cambridge Greek and Latin Classics series.

MICHAEL A. FLOWER is a Lecturer in the Department of Classics at Princeton University. In addition to articles on Greek history and historiography, he is the author of *Theopompus of Chios. History and Rhetoric in the Fourth Century B.C.* (1994) and (with John Marincola) of *Herodotus, Histories, Book IX* (2002). His current project is a book on the role of the seer in archaic and classical Greece.

SARA FORSDYKE is Assistant Professor of Greek and Latin in the Department of Classical Studies at the University of Michigan. Her publications include a number of articles on Herodotus and Greek political ideology, as well as a book, *Exile, Ostracism and Democracy: The Politics of Expulsion in Ancient Greece* (2005).

ROBERT L. FOWLER is H. O. Wills Professor of Greek in the University of Bristol. He is author of *The Nature of Early Greek Lyric: Three Preliminary Studies* (1987), *Early Greek Mythography* I: *Text and Introduction* (2000), and articles on early Greek poetry and prose and the history of scholarship. He is preparing *Early Greek Mythography* II: *Commentary*, and has edited the *Cambridge Companion to Homer* (2004).

RACHEL FRIEDMAN is an Assistant Professor of Classics at Vassar College. She wrote her Ph.D. thesis, 'Home and Displacement in Herodotus' *Histories*', at Columbia University. She is interested in ancient cultural studies and has written articles on Homeric poetics and on the use of myth in Euripides. Her current projects include an expansion of her dissertation and work on the Caribbean poet Derek Walcott.

JASPER GRIFFIN retired in 2004 as Professor of Classical Literature at Oxford University; he is a Fellow of Balliol College. Amongst his numerous publications are *Homer on Life and Death* (1980), *Virgil* (1986), and *Latin Poets and Roman Life* (1985). He is currently working on a book about the relation between Attic tragedy and contemporary history.

ALAN GRIFFITHS is Senior Lecturer in Greek and Latin at University College London. He is editor of *Stage Directions: Essays in Ancient Drama in Honour of E. W. Handley* (1995), and has published in the areas of archaic and Hellenistic poetry and Greek vase-painting. His main field of interest is the typological study of Greek accounts of the mythical and historical past. He is preparing an edition of Herodotus Book 3, and a series of studies on Herodotean narrative for a book, provisionally titled *Herodotos His Stories*. He proselytises tirelessly for the (free, but priceless) Linux computer-operating system.

SIMON HORNBLOWER is Professor of Classics and Ancient History at University College London. He is writing a large-scale commentary on Thucydides (in progress, two volumes published, 1991 and 1996), and has published articles and book-chapters on both Thucydides and Herodotus. He edited and contributed to *Greek Historiography* (1994). His most recent book is *Thucydides and Pindar: Historical Narrative and the World of Epinikian Poetry* (2004).

RACHEL KITZINGER is the Matthew Vassar Professor of Greek and Latin Language and Literature at Vassar College. Her work on Sophocles includes articles, productions of plays, and a translation of the *Oedipus at Colonus* with the poet Eamon Grennan (2005). She also does recitals of ancient Greek and Latin poetry using restored pronunciation.

NINO LURAGHI has taught at the Universities of Parma, Freiburg, and Toronto, and is now Professor of Classics at Harvard University. He is the author of *Tirannidi arcaiche in Sicilia e Magna Grecia* (1994; English edition forthcoming), and has edited *The Historian's Craft in the Age of Herodotus* (2001) and (with S. A. Alcock) *Helots and their Masters in Laconia and Messenia* (2003).

JOHN MARINCOLA is Professor of Classics at Florida State University. He is the author of *Authority and Tradition in Ancient Historiography* (1997), *Greek Historians* (2001), and (with M. A. Flower) *Herodotus: Histories Book IX* (2002). His current project is a book on Hellenistic historiography.

ROSARIA VIGNOLO MUNSON is Professor of Classics at Swarthmore College. She is the author of *Telling Wonders: Ethnographic and Political Discourse in the Work of Herodotus* (2001), several articles on Herodotus, and *Black Doves Speak: Herodotus and the Languages of Barbarians* (2005). She is currently co-editing (with Carolyn Dewald) a commentary on Herodotus Book 1 for the Cambridge Greek and Latin Classics series.

CHRISTOPHER PELLING is Regius Professor of Greek at Oxford University. He has published widely on Greek and Latin literature and history. His latest books are *Literary Texts and the Greek Historian* (2000) and *Plutarch and History* (2002).

JAMES ROMM is the James H. Ottaway Jr. Professor of Classics at Bard College, and author of *The Edges of the Earth in Ancient Greek Thought* (1992) and *Herodotus* (1998). He is currently preparing an edition of Arrian's history of Alexander's campaigns for the Landmark Series of Ancient Historians.

TIM ROOD is Fellow and Tutor in Classics at St Hugh's College, Oxford. He is the author of *Thucydides: Narrative and Explanation* (1998) and *The Sea! The Sea! Xenophon and the Modern Imagination* (2004), as well as several articles on Greek historiography.

SCOTT SCULLION is Fellow of Worcester College and Faculty Lecturer in Classical Languages and Literature, University of Oxford. His principal interests are Greek religion and Greek literature, especially tragedy, and he has published a number of articles on these subjects. He is author of *Three Studies in Athenian Dramaturgy* (1994), and is presently at work on an introductory monograph on Euripides for Blackwell.

PHILIP A. STADTER, Falk Professor in the Humanities Emeritus at the University of North Carolina at Chapel Hill, is author of many articles on the Greek historians, and of *Arrian of Nicomedia* (1980) and *A Commentary on Plutarch's Pericles* (1989) and has edited *The Speeches in Thucydides* (1973), *Plutarch and the Historical Tradition* (1992), and (with L. Van der Stockt) *Sage and Emperor: Plutarch, Greek Intellectuals, and Roman Power in the Time of Trajan (98–117 A.D.)* (2002).

ROSALIND THOMAS is Fellow in Ancient History at Balliol College, Oxford. She has written extensively on literacy and orality in the ancient world, and is the author of *Oral Tradition and Written Record in Classical Athens* (1989), *Literacy and Orality in Ancient Greece* (1992), and, more recently, *Herodotus in Context: Ethnography, Science and the Art of Persuasion* (2000). She is currently working on Greek historiography.

LAWRENCE A. TRITLE is Professor of History at Loyola Marymount University, Los Angeles. His most recent books are *From Melos to My Lai. War and Survival* (2000) and *Crossroads of History: The Age of Alexander*, co-edited with W. Heckel (2003). He is currently writing a book on the Peloponnesian War, and editing another on Alexander the Great.

PREFACE

Arnaldo Momigliano remarked of Herodotus nearly forty years ago that 'the secrets of his workshop are not yet all out', and this is still the case; paradoxically, new approaches to the ancient world and to the writing of history in general have shown more clearly how little we understand the genesis of this great work and Herodotus' own accomplishment.

From the variety of approaches that one can adopt in studying Herodotus, ours in this volume has been primarily literary. It is certainly not the case that we consider Herodotus *only* or even *primarily* a literary artist – far from it. Despite his shortcomings, flaws and errors, he is manifestly the first historian of the Western tradition, and in writing history he needed to undertake travels and engage in research before he had any work to offer the public. But since we do in fact consider him an extraordinary writer and artist who shaped the raw material of his history into a monument *aere perennius*, we also believe that this volume's more detailed treatment of his work as an artist is amply justified as part of our understanding of him as a historian.

In producing this volume we have been greatly assisted by many people, beginning with those at Cambridge University Press: Anne Sanow, formerly of the Press' offices in New York, first suggested a number of years ago the idea of a *Companion* to Herodotus; Pauline Hire in Cambridge was our guide for a time, and her successor there, Michael Sharp, has seen us through to the completion of the volume with his customary kindness, interest and support. Our copy-editor, Tony Rainer, helped us greatly in working through the manuscript, and our Production Editors, Jackie Warren and Anna-Marie Lovett, assisted quickly and courteously with our many inquiries and requests. To each of these we offer our thanks.

CJD thanks Thomas Habinek, Donal Manahan, and the University of Southern California Zumberge Fund that made possible her participation in this volume, and Deborah Boedeker, Donald Lateiner, Rachel Kitzinger and Rosaria Vignolo Munson for bibliographical and editorial advice generously given.

JM thanks Michael Flower, Laurel Fulkerson, Christopher Pelling, Scott Scullion, and Mark Toher for advice and assistance along the way (and along so many previous ways). He is also grateful to Florida State University for a semester's teaching relief.

Finally, we wish to thank our contributors who have made the volume possible, and who have made our task so very pleasant from start to finish. Not the least of their virtues was an admirable patience with their editors, each of whom engaged in a major *metoikēsis* as the volume was being completed.

ABBREVIATIONS

Ancient authors and their works are cited according to the abbreviations of H. G. Liddell and R. Scott, *Greek-English Lexicon*, 9th edn, with revised supplement (Oxford 1996) and (for Latin authors) P. G. W. Glare, ed., *Oxford Latin Dictionary* (Oxford 1982).

CAH	*Cambridge Ancient History*
CEG	P. A. Hansen, *Carmina Epigraphica Graeca, Saeculorum VIII-V a.Chr.n.* (Berlin and New York 1983)
CHI	*Cambridge History of Iran*, vol. II: *The Median and Achaemenid Period* (Cambridge 1985)
EGM	R. Fowler, *Early Greek Mythography* (Oxford 2000–)
F or FF	Fragment or Fragments
FGE	D. L. Page, ed., *Further Greek Epigrams* (Cambridge 1981)
FGrHist	F. Jacoby, et al., *Die Fragmente der griechischen Historiker* (Berlin and Leiden, 1923–58; Leiden 1994–). Authors are cited by the number they are given in the collection, followed by either the testimonium (T) or fragment (F) number(s)
FHG	C. and F. Müller, *Fragmenta Historicorum Graecorum*, 5 vols. (Paris 1841–7)
GGM	C. Müller, *Geographi Graeci Minores*, 2 vols. (2nd edn) (Paris 1861)
IEG	M. L. West, ed., *Iambi et Elegi Graeci*, 2 vols. (2nd edn) (Oxford 1989–92)
PMG	D. L. Page, ed., *Poetae Melici Graeci* (Oxford 1962)
T or TT	Testimonium or Testimonia
TGF	A. Nauck, ed., *Tragicorum Graecorum Fragmenta* (2nd edn) (Leipzig 1889)
TrGF	B. Snell, R. Kannicht and S. Radt, eds., *Tragicorum Graecorum Fragmenta* (Berlin 1971–)
VS	H. Diels and W. Kranz, *Die Fragmente der Vorsokratiker* (6th edn) (Berlin 1951–2). Authors are cited by the number they are given in the collection, followed by either the testimonium (A) or fragment (B) number(s)

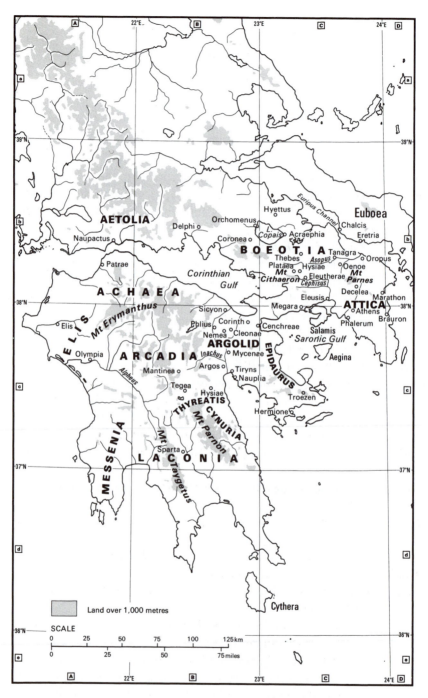

Map 1: Central Greece and the Peloponnese

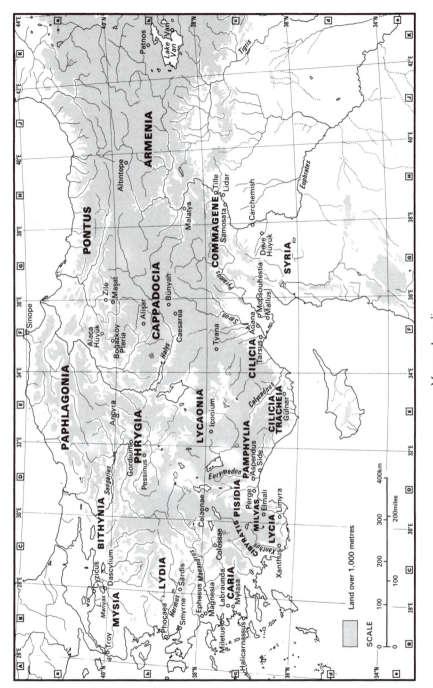

Map 2: Anatolia

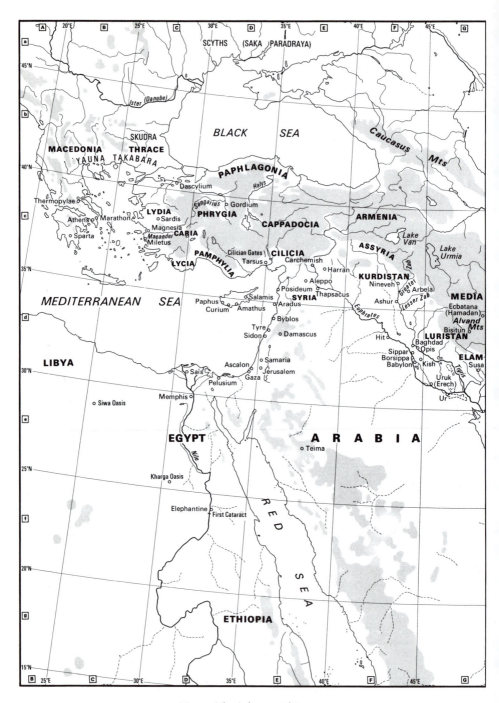

Map 3: The Achaemenid Empire

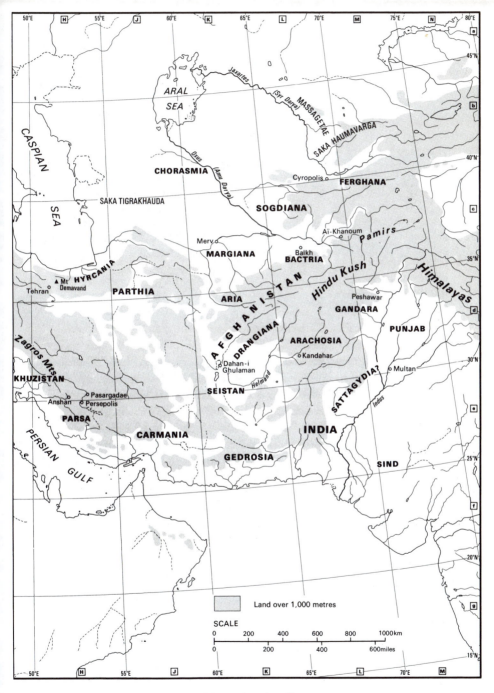

Map 3: (continued)

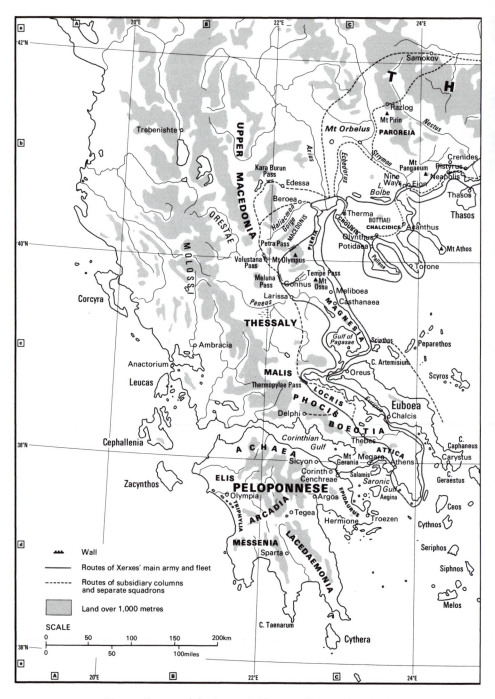

Map 4: Greece and the Aegean (with route of Xerxes' invasion)

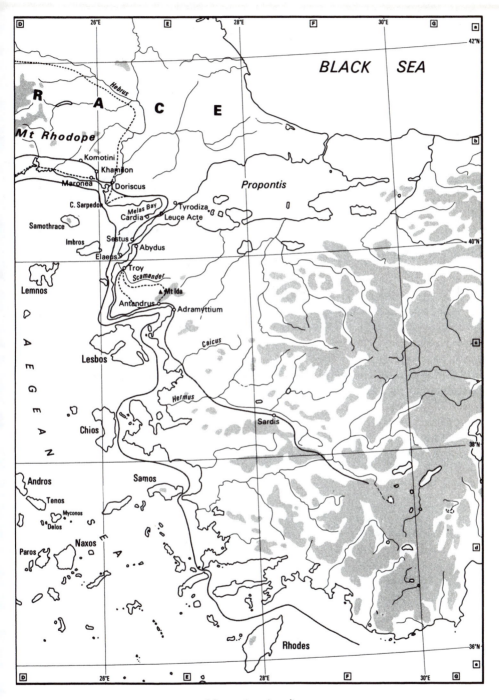

Map 4: (continued)

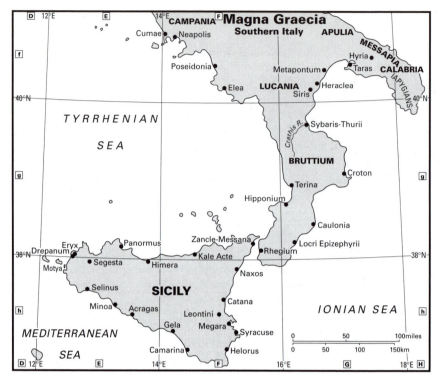

Map 5: Southern Italy and Sicily

CAROLYN DEWALD AND JOHN MARINCOLA

Introduction

Few historians, indeed few writers, of any era have been subjected to such widely divergent evaluations as Herodotus of Halicarnassus. Throughout antiquity we can detect two schools of thought about him, one seeing him as the 'father of history', the first person to put together an accurate account of the past and to infuse it with meaning by giving causes, consequences, and the intentions of the participants. But there was also a persistent strain of criticism that took Herodotus to task for his stories of the fabulous and the improbable, for the accuracy of his reports of non-Greek lands, and for his portrayal of a quarrelsome and disunited Greek force. Herodotus continued to be read, however, because of the beauty of his style, his obvious gifts as a narrator, and because enough people saw in him an appropriate predecessor for what they themselves were trying to achieve.

Like Herodotus' *Histories*, this *Companion* is a product of its time and place. The ways in which scholars view Herodotus today have arisen from dependence on, but also debate with, those who have preceded them. In this Introduction, we first survey briefly the various strains of Herodotean scholarship (with special emphasis on more recent trends), and then discuss the various contributions to this volume, trying to situate the work to be found here in the larger context of contemporary Herodotean studies.

I

Although the nineteenth century, that great period of the systematic study of antiquity, produced important work on Herodotus, it is no exaggeration to say that the modern study of Herodotus depends directly and indirectly on one man, the great German scholar Felix Jacoby (1876–1959). His 1913 'article' on Herodotus for the massive German encyclopedia known as Pauly-Wissowa comprised 316 closely-printed columns, in which he treated every aspect of Herodotus: his style, his dialect, his sources, the structure and content of his work, the manuscript tradition, and the influence he had on later antiquity. It is impossible to do justice to this landmark of scholarship, but suffice it to say that Jacoby illuminated every aspect of Herodotus that he touched, even if one might disagree with some of his individual interpretations. After Jacoby, several issues seem to have dominated much of the scholarship on Herodotus.

Of particular interest was the question of how Herodotus had come to write this work, the first Greek history, and whether the work could be viewed as an artistic whole. Jacoby argued that Herodotus had started out in the same tradition as his predecessor, Hecataeus of Miletus (born c. 560/550 BCE), who wrote works (now lost) entitled *Genealogies*, which sought to bring order to the various and at times conflicting Greek genealogies, and *Circuit of the Earth*, in which Hecataeus described the coastal areas of the Mediterranean, and the lands, climates, customs, and marvels of the individual settlements. It was this tradition of Ionian inquiry that initially shaped Herodotus' investigations. What changed Herodotus into an historian, argued Jacoby, was above all the Persian Wars, because through them Herodotus saw Persia as a connecting thread binding together the destinies of other lands and the Greek city-states. Just as important and influential was Athens and in particular its leading statesman in the mid-fifth century, Pericles. Jacoby believed (against some earlier scholars) that Herodotus' work was written roughly in the order we have it, that is, the Persian Wars narrative of Books 5–9 came last.

Jacoby's developmental view of Herodotus has had profound consequences, not least because he saw in Herodotus' progression from geographer and ethnographer to historian a personal evolution that was of profound importance not only for the historian himself but for the development of the entire genre of Greek historiography: indeed, Herodotus' development *was* the development of Greek historiography. For Jacoby Herodotus had no real predecessors and no real contemporaries; Hecataeus provided only a starting-point which Herodotus vastly transcended. That viewpoint has held sway for almost a century now, and only recently have some doubts about it been expressed.

The compositional question remained one of great interest for the early and mid-twentieth century, and scholars continued to debate how Herodotus came to write his history and which parts of it were written first. Jacoby's view found several adherents (who sometimes made minor changes to his schema), but other scholars argued against his developmental notion. For these scholars, Herodotus was from the beginning the historian of the Persian Wars, and it was in consequence of this initial interest that he examined the lands and customs of those nations which had been subjugated by the Persians. This debate was related to the larger question of whether

Herodotus' history was part of a unified plan or was rather a collection of accounts, written at different times and with different aims, that were eventually 'stitched together' into a whole. This discussion (already in full swing before Jacoby) was clearly influenced by the debate then raging about the Homeric poems, where 'separatists' or 'analysts' had been arguing with 'unitarians' as to the genesis and nature of the *Iliad* and *Odyssey*. (Jacoby was clearly an 'analyst' as his developmental thesis indicated.)

The 'unitarian' interpretation, which argued for the essential unity of the *Histories*, was first decisively stated by Otto Regenbogen (1930), who related the individual stories within the *Histories* to the purposes of the larger whole. His work was taken up and expanded by Wolfgang Schadewaldt (1934) and then by Max Pohlenz in his *Herodot: Der erste Geschichtschreiber des Abendlandes* (1937). In the English-speaking world the unitarian viewpoint culminates in Henry Immerwahr's important and influential study *Form and Thought in Herodotus* (1966); here Immerwahr examines the structure of individual episodes and how these episodes are integrated into the entire work, arguing that the key to understanding Herodotus' intentions and view of history is to be found in its carefully articulated structure. A few years later Charles Fornara, in a short but immensely influential book, *Herodotus: An Interpretative Essay* (1971a), argued that the approaches of unitarians and analysts were complementary, not contradictory (p. 13): 'The one describes what we possess, the other attempts to explain how what we do possess could have come into the world.' Recent scholars, nonetheless, have definitely tended more towards a unitarian view of Herodotus.

Another issue with which twentieth-century scholarship was much concerned was the relationship between Herodotus and Athens. Jacoby had seen this as crucial for the historian's development, but he was careful not to make Herodotus the mouthpiece for Athens. Later scholars, however, eagerly made this leap, portraying Herodotus as a spokesman for – indeed in some cases a panegyrist of – Athens and its empire. Hermann Strasburger, however, in an influential article (Strasburger 1955) argued convincingly against these ideas, and scholars today are very reluctant to ascribe to Herodotus unalloyed praise of Athens. Here again Fornara's work played an important role, since he emphasised Herodotus' contemporary audience as the key to a proper understanding of his work: the *Histories* could not be read apart from the time in which Herodotus was actually writing – the years before the Peloponnesian War when Athens and Sparta were moving towards open conflict – and this context allowed us to see in Herodotus' work an ironic or dramatic detachment, in which the 'glories' of the Spartan and Athenian achievement in the Persian Wars had to be read against the backdrop of Athenian imperialism and the movement by the erstwhile allies towards war.

Indeed, scholars have now come almost to the opposite view from their predecessors, namely that Herodotus is critical of Athens and his portrait of the Persian empire is meant to serve as a warning to the Athenians of the dangers of imperialism.

Jacoby's work was also influential in the matter of Herodotus' trustworthiness. The late nineteenth century had made many attacks on Herodotus' honesty and ability, and although Herodotus had his defenders, it was not until Jacoby's article that most scholars accepted the basic reliability of Herodotus' account. Jacoby saw Herodotus as an honest practitioner whose account was based on the historian's own inquiries and examination of oral sources from a wide variety of local informants (for these, and not written sources, were the basis of his account). Where Herodotus had made errors, these could be explained without impugning his good faith; he was naïve or had failed to understand what he had been told, or he was at the mercy of not always scrupulous informants. For most of the twentieth century this view held sway, and though doubts continued to be voiced about Herodotus' reliability, most scholars were content to accept Jacoby's picture of Herodotus' inquiries. The most striking challenge to this picture came with Detlev Fehling's 1971 book. Fehling focussed on Herodotus' source-citations, the numerous places where the historian reports that 'the Persians say' this or 'the Spartans say' that, and he attempted to show that these remarks followed predictable and unvarying rules in their deployment by Herodotus. He concluded from this that they were not the transparent and straightforward statements of a 'scientific' historian, but were rather the devices of a writer of fiction, chosen to give the *appearance* of reliability, while they were in fact the free invention of Herodotus himself. Perhaps not surprisingly, this work has been much criticised (although not always sensibly), and sits astride one of the great divides in modern Herodotean scholarship. There is, at least at the present, little dialogue between the two camps, although newer approaches have given this issue and others a different complexion.

In more recent decades, a number of intellectual developments, both in the field of classical studies and in the larger culture of which it is a part, have come together to reframe how we read the text of Herodotus. Four of them, briefly listed here, give some idea of the range of issues whose influences can be seen to be very much still at work in the study of Herodotus and in the chapters of this volume. Together they go some distance towards negotiating the split between analysts and unitarians, and between those who see Herodotus as a source-based historian and those who consider him little more than a fabulist.

First, by 1980 history itself as a discursive rhetoric was under investigation, as postmodernist thinkers and historiographers such as Roland Barthes,

Michel Foucault, and Hayden White were beginning to redefine the goals, aims and nature of 'history'. For them and others like them, any historian was no longer someone carefully collecting, assessing and recording facts from the past, to tell us 'what really happened', but was rather viewed to be almost in the position of a novelist, selecting and arranging material from the past that would produce a story that was by definition also an interpretation of that material. The genre of historical narrative now came to be viewed as deeply ideological, since the tacit assumptions shaping the historical text were at least as significant as the accuracy of the 'facts' presented in it. Obviously Herodotus, the father of history, was very much implicated in this project, as was his immediate heir, Thucydides, and the intellectual connections linking them to each other as co-creators of a new genre increasingly seemed significant.

The second development influencing Herodotean studies had to do with the growing sophistication of cultural studies and the application of anthropological and sociological modes of analysis to ancient Greek culture. The year 1980 saw the publication of François Hartog's groundbreaking *Le miroir d'Hérodote*, a structuralist reading of Herodotus' text. Hartog was deeply influenced by the anthropologically-trained classicists, especially in France, who had created a radical reassessment of the culture of the late archaic and early classical period in Greece. Louis Gernet, Jean-Pierre Vernant, Marcel Detienne, Pierre Vidal-Naquet and others had substantially redrawn the outlines of early classical culture, depicting it through the lens of a sociology and anthropology whose codes and objectives were not at all those of a nineteenth-century European historiography. Work by contemporary anthropologists such as Jan Vansina on orality also led to a reassessment of the quality of Herodotean historiography, by emphasising the distinctiveness of oral ways of transmitting and preserving memories of the past. As Oswyn Murray saw, Greek society remained largely oral at least through the Hellenistic period, and Herodotus' relation to his (mostly oral) informants and material needed to be rethought, to play an important part in our changed understanding of his text. Herodotus' text was now seen to be the repository of ways of thinking, speaking, and writing that came out of a complex and interlocking set of traditional Greek cultural codes.

This trend in Herodotean studies was closely linked to a third development. With the advent of the postcolonial studies of Edward Saïd and others came a growing understanding of how deeply Eurocentric were the traditional ways of viewing classical Greece and its great early historian. Although the claims of scholars arguing that Greek culture largely came 'out of Africa' were not ultimately sustained, it became increasingly clear how many of the cultural roots of the classical Greek experience lay in the larger world of East Mediterranean culture that Herodotus inhabited. Herodotus' interest in and awareness of Egypt, Scythia, Lydia, Babylon and other lands were now seen not as incidental to the purposes of his text (there only to explain who these enemies were that came to attack Greece in the early fifth century BCE) but deeply central to its meaning, and to contemporary Greek definitions of and ways of understanding themselves.

And finally, as ancient Greek history and its historians were now viewed as much more connected to an archaic Greek past and a non-Greek contemporary world, paradoxically they were also being viewed as more intimately connected to the world of a mid-fifth-century Greek culture and politics. In contrast to an earlier view that depicted Herodotus as an old-fashioned purveyor of an 'archaic' world view, new studies emphasised his deep connections to the thought world of the great figures of the fifth-century intellectual revolution such as Protagoras and Gorgias. The political representations of his text, moreover, were increasingly seen as embedded in the issues emerging in Athens, its enemies, and the cities of its empire, in the years leading up to the Peloponnesian War, in ways that Jacoby and his followers could not have envisioned. Work on the intellectual milieu and politics of democratic Athens has argued that much of Herodotus' depiction of early fifth-century political dynamics was framed by but also tacitly critiqued the political and social problems of contemporary mid-century Athens.

From all these viewpoints a new question has emerged, as Robert Connor observed in 1987: 'just what sort of text is this and how does it work?' Part of his answer is worth quoting as a summation of what was now opening in Herodotean studies (Connor [1987] 261):

> When we read Herodotus we move in a world of unexpected outcomes. Great powers become small; poor states defeat grand and mighty ones; mythic patterns are contraverted; oracles have hidden layers of meaning. In such a world there are no laws of history, no neat lessons or maxims, no sure way to success or even survival. That leaves little room for advice or sermons in historical writing. But if one wrestles enough, the result may be a certain alertness and suppleness, a readiness for the unexpected that is the condition for survival in such a world.

This 'new' Herodotus may at first sight seem to have little in common with the historian constructed by Jacoby and his immediate successors, although many of those early concerns continue to be represented in recent work. What has changed is that older assumptions about the writing of history and how it is managed have been complicated by the various methodologies mentioned above, that is, by the recognition that historiography is neither a straightforward and transparent activity nor a matter merely of recording unproblematic 'facts'.

II

All of the following chapters have incorporated some aspect of this new attitude into their reading of Herodotus. Some issues, expressed in the chapters of this volume in different ways, strike us as especially prominent and interesting, although each reader will of course come up with others on his or her own. And yet, as we shall see at the end of this essay, a distinctive feature of Herodotus' prose is that it can be read in a multiplicity of ways, depending on what interests each reader brings to the task.

Regarding Herodotus' deep engagement with mid-fifth-century Greek culture, Rosalind Thomas, James Romm, and Scott Scullion consider the complexities of his engagement with contemporary Greek intellectual issues, especially in the realms of biology and geography, often expressed in the language of the argumentative rhetoric prevalent in mid- and late-fifth-century Athens. Although Romm and Scullion approach the issue from different directions, both emphasise that Herodotus sees the world that human intelligence understands and manipulates as connected to larger questions of cosmic balance and order. Romm connects Herodotus' interest in the natural sciences to his deep-seated moral and ethical concerns, while Scullion sharply distinguishes Herodotus' belief in an abstract, enduring cosmic order from his occasional mention of names and features of specific Greek and foreign divinities, respected by Herodotus rather as aspects of human culture than as independently powerful individual personalities. Interestingly enough, both Romm and Scullion have read Herodotus' depictions of bridge building not as involving the hubris of boundary transgression, but rather as his acknowledgment of positive achievement, in the realm of human *sophiē*. By their readings, Herodotus plays an active part in the generation of the fifth-century Greek enlightenment, and is alert and engaged in making sense of his world very much like that of his contemporaries, the first sophists.

Thomas deepens this connection still further, pointing out that Herodotus' interest in *nomos*, law or custom, pervades the *Histories*. Both Thomas and Robert Fowler emphasise the degree of Herodotus' engagement with other intellectual figures of his day, although Thomas sees a subtle, courteous disagreement among colleagues, while Fowler points to a mélange of competitive, argumentative positions, in what he calls the 'gallimaufry' that makes up the *Histories*; Herodotus' competitive voice is particularly apparent in

Book 2. Sara Forsdyke also considers Herodotus' political philosophy as an engagement in issues of contemporary importance; Herodotus' exploration of the nature of imperialism, the value of political freedom, and the relation between geography, climate, and political culture, though expressed in the context of the Persian imperial adventures of the early fifth century, are pointedly if tacitly relevant to the Athenian imperialism of his own day as well. It is not just an Athenian issue, either: Philip Stadter comments on how many sons of Greek leaders from the Persian Wars, from different cities, are mentioned in Herodotus' narrative. For both Forsdyke and Stadter, there is considerable irony in Herodotus' picture of the united Greek effort that expelled the Persians, since the various cities that helped one another in the near past had in his own time become hostile and competitive instead. Stadter emphasises how distinct and sharply differentiated Herodotus' portraits of the major Greek cities are from one another; Lawrence Tritle makes the same point about his account of the major battles that formed the Persian Wars, from Marathon through Mycale. Clearly part of Herodotus' own engagement with contemporary Greek material entailed recording information from the past that was specific and as accurate as possible, in this way resembling, as both Thomas and Fowler point out, a contemporary Hippocratic discourse. As Marincola puts it: 'Herodotus relishes the individual, the contingent, the unforeseen.' In this, his goals are different from those of the doctors.

But Herodotus was not only interested in Greeks and contemporary Greek issues and ideas. A number of the chapters in this volume investigate Herodotus' interest in, and portrait of, other cultures than his own, with a new and more nuanced appreciation that stems from our growing awareness of the problems and interpretive limitations of our own more recent colonialist and Eurocentrist assumptions. Both Michael Flower and Tim Rood consider Herodotus' interest in the *nomoi* or customs of others as a fascination with gridding the specific details of cultural distinctiveness, and also in investigating the more general phenomenon of foreignness. Flower makes the point that Herodotus, though limning a Greek victory, does not write a triumphalist history but rather builds underlying thematic parallels that enable a Greek audience to understand and make sense of the Persian experience of the war; for instance, Herodotus emphasises the pervasiveness of human suffering (e.g. the suffering endured by the Persian dinner guest in 9.16). He does not create a simple-minded dichotomy or clichéd portrait of the hubris of autocratic kings; both retribution for the sacking of Sardis and the needs of an expansionist imperialism are in play in the Persian war effort, as well as a code of Achilles-like military honour that the Greeks themselves less consistently embody. In sketching out Herodotus' broader understanding of foreignness, Rood sees a number of the (foreign) actors in the *Histories* as stand-ins for Herodotus' own authorial efforts to encounter 'the other'. Croesus, after all, undertakes a *historiē* or investigation of his own, in exploring which of the Greek cities to invite to be his ally (1.56); Darius actively explores the problem of cultural relativism, and himself becomes king through the manipulation of Persian custom (3.38, 3.72 and 84–7). Herodotus' interest in ethnography is unusual, moreover, in that it is not undertaken from the point of view of the imperialist aggressor (as, say, more recent nineteenth-, twentieth-, or twenty-first-century efforts have been), but rather from the point of view of the invaded people, the Greeks. Perhaps for that reason, he gives special attention to the ethnographic descriptions of other peoples who actively resist the Persians (Egypt, Scythia), but he also emphasises the multiple ironies implicit in the mindset of the Persians that might explain their decision to invade Greece as an especially valuable source of new resources (see, for instance, Pausanias' contrast of the Spartan and Persian dinners in 9.82, discussed in the chapter by Christopher Pelling).

Rosaria Vignolo Munson and Rachel Friedman both contemplate some of the ironic complexities of Herodotus' stance as an Asiatic Greek transplanted to the west, writing about a war that took place mostly between mainland Greeks and Asians. Munson's focus is on the Greek West, Italy and Sicily; she points out that Herodotus resists assimilating the narratives about the western Greeks, in particular the Greek tyrants, to those about the cities of central Greece and the Peloponnese, but rather renders the western experience exotic, even somewhat foreign, by using the traditional language and tropes of Greek colonialist discourse to depict the harshness of the early fifth-century western tyrannies. Friedman emphasises Herodotus' own status as an itinerant savant, his corresponding interest in other Greek *dēmiourgoi*, or travelling experts, and the tension between home and away that the career of the travelling Greek expert entails. Both chapters consider the massive dislocations that the political crises of the Persian Wars engendered, Munson to emphasise the harshness of the western Greek tyrants, Friedman to emphasise the degree to which Herodotus problematises the issue of cultural identity and its connections to specific geography.

Many of the chapters already mentioned include an anthropological or structural component in their reading of Herodotus. Forsdyke and Rood consider the effects of social memory in the *Histories*, and the confrontation with Greek or foreign information that is necessarily transmitted by oral tradition, refracted through what fifth-century Greek audiences needed to remember. Tritle also comments that the war reports that formed the backbone of Herodotus' accounts in the last five books of the *Histories* were of necessity somewhat vague as regards military *technē* because (unlike Thucydides) Herodotus was dealing not with reports from the various war planners and chiefs-of-staff, but with memories retained for decades by men who would have been young foot-soldiers or sailors in the wars of the 490s and 480s. What he got right and transmitted accurately was the 'fog of war' experienced by all combatants, and the brutality that war entailed. Both Carolyn Dewald and Alan Griffiths discuss more generally the way that the *logoi* that provide the substance of Herodotus' narrative have been shaped originally as (retold) stories; oral repetition creates story, either by giving it a humorous point relevant to an ongoing local political context or, more generally, by smoothing it out and creating out of memory an anecdote with a particular narrative shape that guarantees its later preservation.

Nino Luraghi considers the implications of oral transmission as the basis for Herodotus' *historiē* or investigation, and he analyses at length the processes through which the *logoi* or oral reports might have been collected and formulated. It is worth noting that, since Hartog, not only has it proved fruitful to analyse Herodotus through anthropological or structuralist lenses, but it has also seemed increasingly necessary to acknowledge the sophistication of Herodotus' own deep interests in culture as a sphere where politics intersect with religion, geography, ethnography, and law. As we have already seen, many of the chapters in this volume move easily among these different spheres of concern and consider the intersections between them; Jasper Griffin, Forsdyke, Marincola, and Scullion in particular focus on the extent to which various tropes of a conventional Greek value-world fall under Herodotus' tacitly relativist, if not actively ironic, ongoing examination.

Perhaps the area that involves some of the most interesting advances in our understanding of Herodotus' achievement has to do with his skills as a writer, and the genre of writing of which he seems to have been the first practitioner. A number of chapters in this volume deal with Herodotus as a literary craftsman. History as a genre and mode of discourse influenced by other Greek genres, is discussed by Marincola, in the context of its dependence on the legacy of earlier Greek poetry, especially epic, by Griffin for the themes and some of the habitual tropes of Attic tragedy, by Fowler for Herodotus' engagement with contemporary and previous prose authors, and by Griffiths for motifs and ways of patterning narrative often found in storytelling. Taken together, all of these chapters make clear how generously Herodotus drew on the formal opportunities available to him from the literary past of his own culture, and what excellent use he made of them.

Herodotus is also analysed more particularly as a wordsmith, shaping his *logoi* or stories into an elaborately patterned, lengthy, ongoing text. Luraghi looks at the authorial 'I' of the Herodotean text, and his employment of *gnomē*, judgement, and *opsis*, eyewitness investigation, to critique *akoē* or the material he has gathered from oral accounts (2.99). Both Luraghi and Fowler stress the enormous achievement of Herodotus' *Histories* in using his melange of *logoi* from distant times and places in effect to grid the extent of contemporary Greek knowledge both about the period of Persian expansion and about the world in which that expansion occurred. Several pieces, notably those of Egbert Bakker, Fowler, Luraghi and Marincola, analyse the originality of Herodotus' prose accomplishment, making use of previous material and generic expectations in order to produce a new genre of his own from it. Bakker stresses Herodotus' peculiar ability to weave together into a single 'syntax' or intricately structured, dovetailed narrative what had originally been extremely heterogeneous material. As Bakker puts it, in a most basic sense, the text that results, that we read now, performs – in one sense, *is* – itself the accomplishment of Herodotus' *historiē* or investigation. Forsdyke comments that the thematic patterns grow in subtlety and complexity as we follow them from one *logos* to another; Griffiths shows us how carefully each individual story is positioned in order to achieve a particular effect through placement within the ongoing whole.

The investigation of the constructedness of Herodotus' text, finally, leads us back again to Herodotus as a thinker, able now to be viewed as something of a poststructuralist himself. Pelling explores how complex is Herodotus' understanding of the potential of *logos*; the *logoi* or stories that people tell within Herodotus' account are also actions undertaken, with consequences that sometimes quite ironically undercut the overt or simple meaning of the text. Dewald and Rachel Kitzinger also explore this line of thought analysing the story of the woman who chose to save a brother instead of a husband or son that is found both in Herodotus and in Sophocles' *Antigone*. Griffiths shows how the arrangement of *logoi* in the text is itself an act of interpretation, refusing a single or simple, linear interpretation of causal connection or indeed of meaning. Herodotus, more than any other ancient historian, is aware of the competing claims and interpretive demands made of his text, and indeed, makes these a central concern. Simon Hornblower demonstrates how actively Herodotus' text continued to challenge and indeed shape later Greek and Roman historiography; it is clear that each generation responded to this text by finding in it elements that suited its own needs.

Certainly one cause of the resurgence or renaissance of Herodotean studies in the past few decades lies in Herodotus' own recognition of the complexity and multivalence inherent in accounts of the past and in his assumption – indeed, his encouragement – of an audience that will also take its part in reconstructing and interpreting *ta erga ex anthrōpōn*, the world of human achievement. We are pleased to bring you this rich collection of contemporary responses to a remarkable ancient text.

I

JOHN MARINCOLA

Herodotus and the poetry of the past

When Herodotus came to write his history sometime in the mid-fifth century, the medium of prose was a relatively new phenomenon: it was poetry that had dominated discourse for centuries, and had done so in a variety of genres: narrative and didactic epic, personal and choral lyric, hymns, drinking songs, oracles, and epinician odes in praise of victorious athletes. The poet in the archaic world was not usually an isolated 'artistic' figure, but instead often intimately involved in the life of his city, and he used poetry to teach and persuade, among other things.[1] That the poet was primarily a teacher was assumed in the intellectual revolution of the sixth century, when writers such as Heraclitus and Xenophanes began to question and criticise Greek traditions by focussing especially on Homer and Hesiod – sometimes even using poetry in their own attacks.[2] And if the biographical tradition is true, Herodotus may have known intimately about historical poetry from his uncle Panyassis who wrote a long verse epic on the foundations of Ionian cities.[3]

The Greek word for poetry, *poiēsis*, means simply 'making', and the poet (*poiētēs*) is a 'maker'. Only when the new medium of prose became common did it become necessary to distinguish poetry from prose.[4] Although it can hardly be denied that prose sought to distance itself from poetry, it is also the case that the first great prose writer of the Greek tradition, Herodotus, is deeply indebted to his poetic predecessors both for the presentation of his work and for the themes to be found in it. That he knew the work of the major poets is beyond doubt, and he cites or quotes more than a dozen of them in the course of the *Histories*.[5] It is clear, however, that Herodotus was not equally influenced by all poetic genres. Given his own topic and interests, narrative epic was the predominant influence, especially Homer, as the ancients recognised in calling him 'most like Homer'.[6] But Herodotus was almost certainly also influenced by the numerous poems recording early events such as foundations of cities or more recent events, especially the Persian Wars.[7]

Homeric influence on Herodotus is an enormous topic, and I cannot do justice to it here; I shall not treat, for example, Herodotus' evocation of Homer by the use of 'poetic' language, even though it is abundantly clear that he was familiar with, and often employed, this language.[8] Herodotus' original audience would not have failed to hear Homeric echoes when Artemisia tells Xerxes to 'put away in your heart this thing also' (8.68γ.1 ∼ Il. 1.297), or when Psammenitus weeps for his friend 'on the threshold of old age' (3.14.10 ∼ Il. 22.60).[9] It is more difficult, of course, to know how one should interpret such echoes, though they certainly seem to invest the scenes in which they appear with solemnity or at the very least suggest a sense of something extraordinary or noteworthy. However that may be, I shall in what follows focus on other, more conceptual areas where Herodotus is indebted to, but also distinguishes himself from, his poetic predecessors. For Herodotus did not radically break with his poetic predecessors so much as take their legacy in a different direction.

Telling the story

The poets before Herodotus told stories in many different ways, but the acknowledged master of all was Homer. In both Iliad and Odyssey Herodotus found an authoritative narrative voice that recounted deeds, as well as a more 'mimetic' voice that used speeches and represented characters in action.[10] The use of direct speech, common in Homer, was taken over by Herodotus, who added to it the frequent use of indirect speech as well. Just as Homer by means of flashbacks and anticipations (what narratologists term analepses and prolepses) fills out the story beyond the temporal boundaries of his main narrative, so Herodotus frequently employs digressions (temporal and spatial) to give necessary or important background or supplementary information.[11] Here particularly the Odyssey, with its sophisticated manipulation of time, demonstrated how one could maintain forward movement of the plot while narrating events that occurred outside the time frame of the epic.[12]

Both Homeric epics also gave Herodotus some sense of worthy subject matter. The Iliad, as an epic of war, set the terms for later historiography, not only for Herodotus, but also for Thucydides and nearly all the historians who followed. Brave deeds, conquest, courage in the face of death – all these are the subjects of epic and history alike. The influence of the Odyssey is more indirect, but can be perceived, in Herodotus at least, in the historian's interest in travel and exploration, in wandering, in craftiness, and in the discovery of marvels of all kinds. Like Odysseus, Herodotus goes through the 'cities of men'[13] examining and testing them, and telling their stories.

Herodotus as narrator differs, however, from Homer in important ways. The first is in the organising presence of the Herodotean narrator, for, unlike Homer who only rarely speaks in his own person, Herodotus' 'I' is ubiquitous in the *Histories*, either on or just below the surface, even if it is not intrusive in equal measure throughout the work.[14] Yet even in his adoption of an overtly manipulative narrative voice, Herodotus had a predecessor in Pindar, who in his victory odes uses his 'I' as a guiding force in the poem, calling attention to his own act of narration, speaking explicitly of his opinions, or offering advice.[15]

Another important area of Homeric influence is in the narrator's relationship to his subject matter. Andrew Ford has pointed out that although Homer's heroes are presented as having existed a long time before the poet and his audience, Homer nonetheless portrays himself as an 'immediate' narrator of events, recognising no intermediaries in the handing on of the tradition.[16] Herodotus has a more complicated narrative stance: on the one hand, unlike the effaced Homeric narrator, Herodotus presents himself as the person who has collected different accounts, which has made possible the preservation of the story; he also recognises previous treatments of some of the material he narrates, especially by engaging in polemic with predecessors. Yet on the other hand, it must be admitted that despite this feature, Herodotus in most of his narrative has, like Homer, 'erased' his predecessors and for the most part presents himself as wrestling *directly* with the sources themselves – that is to say, for most of his work he portrays himself implicitly as the first to write up these events.[17] Now it may well be that for much of his work Herodotus *was* the first and had no predecessors: that, at least, has been the common wisdom among scholars for over a century now, although doubts have begun to be expressed.[18] But it is important to realise that this impression of priority might be the effect that Herodotus, imitating Homer, desired to create in the minds of his audience: a directly mediated account in the sense that the narrator, as he attempts to construct the history of the past, is engaged not with other chroniclers but with the *logoi* themselves.[19]

Herodotus differs from Homer, however, in that he is not an omniscient narrator. Whereas the poets rely for their authoritativeness on the god or muse who is invoked at the beginning of their poems,[20] Herodotus has no appeal to the Muses, and consequently informs his audience of the restricted parameters of his knowledge, often expressing uncertainty, conjecture, or outright ignorance.[21] Herodotus' consistent authorial intrusiveness reminds the audience of the inquiring presence responsible for the account before them. This is a crucial distinction between poetry and prose, namely, that the former invests the narrator with truth and authority from some external sources who are presented as inspiring and/or instructing the poet, while the narrator of prose must win his own authority by human means, the construction of an account that is inherently probable and based on reliable and accurate reporting.[22] The consequence of this is that despite the 'assurance' of the Herodotean narrator, there is still a place in the prose historical narrative for the reader to be actively engaged in a joint search for the truth about the past; Herodotus does not pretend to have the final word.

Past and present

No audience of Homer's epics could fail to perceive that the men who are the subjects of his poems all lived long ago, and an unbridgeable gulf separates them from the poet's audience: men and deeds of olden times are bigger, greater, more splendid.[23] In Hesiod's poetry the same gulf is evident in his presentation of the ages that decline from gold to silver to bronze to the current wretched race – today's men – of iron (*Works and Days* 109–201).[24] Herodotus' *Histories* takes as its subject, however, the men of his own day and the immediate past. When Herodotus extols Pausanias' victory at Plataea as 'the most splendid of all those we know' (9.64) or says of Xerxes' armament that it was 'incomparably larger than the armies which the stories tell us Agamemnon and Menelaus led to Troy' (7.20), he is implicitly rejecting the notion that greatness resided in the past alone. Herodotus, therefore, cannot have looked to Homer or Hesiod for his notions of past and present.

Where he could and did look was to praise poetry, where Pindar, Bacchylides and Simonides (to name only a few) chose contemporary men and events as the subjects of their poems. In epinician poetry the poet praises a victorious athlete, but does so in a way that connects him with his ancestors, or with some hero whose exploits often form the central myth of the ode. This is best seen in Pindar, where transitions between past, present, and future suggest continuity and stability, not decline and unpredictability.[25] Yet it was not Pindar alone who pointed the way for Herodotus here. Simonides in his poem on Plataea began with an invocation of the heroes of the Trojan War before he moved on to his narration of the Spartans' march out of the Peloponnese, thereby making a clear connection between the heroes of the Trojan War and those of the Persian Wars.[26] Herodotus thus learned particularly from praise poetry how to see continuities of behaviour and outlook between generations.

Even so, there is a difference, for in Herodotus' hands the movement back and forth through time becomes more than simply the assertion of stability, similarity or continuity. In the hands of a historian, it becomes a way of recognising and delineating *causal* connections between past and present, of emphasising the role that earlier actions play in later ones. In Herodotus there is a direct line drawn from the opening figure of Croesus, the first man to conquer Greeks, to the final battle of Mycale, the last historical incident in Herodotus' work: for Croesus eventually yielded his power to Cyrus, and from then on the Greeks' destiny became entwined with that of the Persian empire. Moreover, Herodotus has emphasised this line of causation by cutting off for the most part what might be called 'mythical' time and basing himself mainly on events for which there are human sources and evidence.[27]

This recognition of causal continuity allows the historian to isolate the consistent patterns of *historical* behaviour that can be perceived when one takes the wide compass of actions over several generations or even centuries. In this regard the fact that Xerxes resembles his ancestors who preceded him on the throne not only indicates part of his personality but also explains the weight of history that drives him forward, as he himself explains to his fellow Persians (7.8α.1–2):

> Men of Persia, I am not introducing a new custom here but using the one that I inherited. I have learned from my elders that we have never been inactive since the time when Cyrus deposed Astyages and we took over from the Medes the sovereign power we now have. So God leads us on, and by following we have prospered. . . . (2) Now I myself, ever since I gained the throne, have been thinking how not to fall short of those kings who reigned before me, and how I might add as much as they did to the power of Persia.

It is that 'likeness' to his predecessors Cyrus, Cambyses and Darius that Herodotus has been at pains to sketch up to this point, so that we see clearly *how* the past has come to be present in Xerxes. Herodotus is not the first to compare past and present, but he is the first to connect the present with the past in an *analytic* manner, showing how causes – here, human desire, national character, and the forward logic of empire – intertwine in a complex way.

Glory and renown

It has long been observed that Herodotus' remark in his preface that he has written his history so that the 'great and marvellous deeds' of Greeks and barbarians 'not be without glory (*aklea*)' intimately links his work with Homeric epic and praise poetry, where the desire for glory (*kleos*) is paramount.[28] That the poet guarantees the immortality of his subject is also a common motif in archaic poetry, even if the nature of this immortality differs according to the context, and the immortality promised by Theognis is not necessarily the same as that promised by Pindar.[29] Now it is clear that well before

Herodotus poets were praising the men and actions of the Persian Wars, and indeed this began shortly after the victories of 480 and 479. Simonides, as we saw above, already adopted it, and the idealised portrait in Aeschylus' *Persians* (produced 472) of the confident, aggressive Greeks sailing against the Persians with the cry of 'liberate your country, your children and wives, the dwelling-places of the gods and tombs of your ancestors' (403–5) suggests a force collectively warding off that 'day of slavery' (*doulion ēmar*) that Hector had promised to keep from Andromache (*Il.* 6.463). Even clearer evidence was on display in the Painted Stoa, where the battle of Marathon was surrounded by paintings of Theseus fighting the Amazons and Greeks fighting Trojans. There are also the contemporary epigrams from (probably) the mid-fifth century, in which Athenian actions in the aftermath of the Persian Wars are linked explicitly with Athenian excellence at Troy.[30] Thus, Herodotus by himself will not have been responsible for the 'Homeric' cast to the Persian Wars.[31]

A clue to Herodotus' real accomplishment lies in the preface itself, where he makes clear his desire to accord glory to the great and wonderful *erga* both of Greeks and non-Greeks. There are two new aspects here. First, the conferral of glory on *erga* ('deeds' or 'works'), a word that often suggests great or martial deeds, but in Herodotus also comprehends anything done or made well: so on Herodotus' reckoning the pyramids of Egypt are *erga* worthy of renown, as are the ways in which the Indians get gold from ants (4.102–5), or even the witty remarks that revealed the intense self-confidence of Dieneces before the battle of Thermopylae (7.226).[32] Second, *kleos* is to be conferred on Greeks and non-Greeks alike. Herodotus, in other words, will not be parochial but will bestow glory beyond the Hellenic world wherever it is seen as deserving. Herodotus' conception of his task, therefore, derives from poetry, but represents a broadening of, and challenge to, narrower 'poetic' and parochial conceptions of what is worthy of glory and renown. He has not rejected a poetic notion so much as harnessed it to a different purpose.

Moreover, because Herodotus' purpose is understanding as much as, if not more than, commendation, he is particularly careful in the matter of praise (and its opposite, blame), which is often wedded to a historical context that helps to explain his judgement: a particularly good example is his praise of Athens as the saviour of Greece (7.139), a passage that expounds the reasons for such a view. It can also be seen in Herodotus' treatment of Ephialtes of Malis, whom he identifies as the betrayer of the pass at Thermopylae (7.214), giving two reasons why he, rather than some other suspects, was the guilty one. The terms of praise and blame are not simply dependent on the speaker's authority, but part of a larger debate in which the informed reader may take part. Indeed, Herodotus makes clear elsewhere that he will not assign praise or blame with abandon, and in fact cautions his audience that such things must be contextualised (7.152.1–2):

> I cannot accurately say whether Xerxes did or did not send the messenger to Argos; nor whether Argive ambassadors went to Susa and discussed friendship with Artaxerxes. I express no opinion on the matter other than what the Argives themselves say. (2) One thing, however, I do know: if everyone in the world met and brought his own evils with him to exchange with somebody else's, there is no one who, having looked at his neighbour's evils, would not happily return home with his own. So then the Argives were not the worst offenders.

Closely related to this is the incident at Darius' court where the burial practices of Greeks and Indians are compared (3.38): here Herodotus shows how beliefs about appropriate behaviour are culturally conditioned. Herodotus' recognition that each society praises its own customs (*nomoi*) as best both shows his far-reaching view of culture and custom, and simultaneously removes the privileged position from which one can 'neutrally' pass judgement on others. So although Herodotus cites specific actions for praise or blame, he has nevertheless contributed in an important way to problematising the idea of such judgements, for he has broken through the insularity presupposed by a single value system. Whereas the praise poet labours intensively to make sure that his praise is not devalued because of jealousy,[33] the historian allows praise, like everything else, to be examined and debated.

Wisdom and measure

Much of early Greek poetry, epic and otherwise, is concerned with the inculcation of wisdom and with reflections on human success and failure in the world. The *Iliad* features a major wisdom figure, Nestor, who encourages the men into battle, warns them when they are shirking their duty, and attempts to make peace among warring factions. In the *Theogony* Hesiod sets himself up as one empowered by the Muses to instruct men about the cosmos, and in the *Works and Days* he addresses to his brother Perses a vision of the just human community and the place of human beings in the larger world of nature and the immortal gods. In all archaic poetry, human wisdom requires both knowing one's place in the world (in relation to both the gods and one's human community), and having a sense of limits, in recognising the frailty of human life, the tenuous nature of success, and the hostile or indifferent forces arrayed against humankind.

Herodotus, like Homer and the archaic poets, often has his characters use maxims, fables and 'exemplary' narratives to convey a positive or negative warning, usually to some figure in authority.[34] Herodotus' use of these 'warning figures' puts him closer to the poets than, for example, to his successor Thucydides, whose speakers employ a different and more directly political form of argumentation. Nevertheless, the gaining of wisdom for the characters in Herodotus' history is a complex and elusive process – one that often turns out to have results contrary to what might have been expected. Even when good advice is followed, the result is not always success. The difficulty is well seen in the interchange between Croesus and Cyrus during the latter's attack on Tomyris, the queen of the Massagetae (1.206–7). Croesus introduces his advice by emphasising that his experiences, although unpleasurable, have brought him learning,[35] and he instructs Cyrus to remember that he is mortal, and that as such he is subject to the 'cycle of human affairs' (*kuklos tōn anthropēiōn prēgmatōn*) that forbids the same people always to be prosperous. The advice he then proffers is strategic, namely that Cyrus should fight on Tomyris' side of the river, so that if he is defeated he will not leave the way to his empire open to the Massagetae. Cyrus in fact does take this advice, and although there is no reason to doubt the soundness of the counsel, Cyrus nonetheless is defeated – in part because those who offer advice and make decisions often do so in ignorance of other factors and of the actions of other characters.[36]

Success in Herodotus, as Carolyn Dewald has pointed out, comes to those who have a practical wisdom, an adaptability that at times looks very much like that of the trickster figure of folklore – or, to take the obvious Greek example, like Odysseus.[37] The 'wisdom' of a successful character may appear as the trickery whereby Themistocles manages to get the Greeks to fight the Persians in the advantageous setting off Salamis: as Herodotus presents it, the idea was not Themistocles' own, but borrowed from a certain Mnesiphilus – yet it was Themistocles who actually made it happen (8.57–63). The historian, therefore, is interested not simply in the possession of wisdom but also in the ability to put it into *action*. That is what counts in history; understanding the situation but being unable to affect it is, as one of Herodotus' characters says, 'the most grievous pain of all for human beings' (9.16).

Truth and revisionism, historical and poetical truth

The early Greek poets had an extremely sophisticated understanding of the relationship between lies and truth, as can be seen, for example, in Odysseus' lying tales throughout the second half of the *Odyssey*, or, more directly and more famously, Hesiod's encounter with the Muses at the beginning of the *Theogony* in which they say, 'we know how to speak many falsehoods similar to the truth, but we can also, when we wish, utter true things' (27–8).[38] Although the Muses give no indication of how one may know truth from things that sound like truth, it is clear that Hesiod, like the early poets in general, knew that not everything that claimed to be truth was in fact truth.[39] It is precisely because archaic poetry had a very sophisticated understanding of truth and lies and the difficulty of telling one from the other that a character such as Odysseus could flourish in the world and have ultimate success. We often refer to his tales on Ithaca as false, but this is not quite accurate, since the stories are true in ways that those loyal to Odysseus – his household and those who think like him – can understand.[40] Indeed, sometimes early Greek literature seems to look at truth as a closed system, available only to the initiates who listen to it and (in a circular procedure) will understand because they already know it.[41]

Very often in archaic poetry the poet's truth brings with it a certain revisionism, the replacement of a previous story with a new or different one that is by implication better.[42] A particularly wonderful example is the opening of the *Homeric Hymn to Dionysus* (1–7):

> Some say you were born in Dracanus, others in windy Icarus,
> Others in Naxos, O divinely-born one, Eiraphiota.
> Others say that by the deep-whirling Alpheius river
> Semele conceived and bore you to Zeus who delights in thunder.
> Still others say that you were born as lord in Thebes.
> They lie. The father of men and gods bore you
> Far from men, concealing you from white-shouldered Hera.

The laying-out of variant versions here would not be out of place in a history, indeed in Herodotus' narrative (although he never gives as many as five!). And indeed one might ascribe to this author a type of 'revisionism', whereby earlier versions are rejected and a new one substituted.[43]

Yet if we compare this with Herodotus' rejection of the Homeric story of Troy in Book 2 of his *Histories* the difference is immediately visible. There Herodotus wishes to argue that Helen never went to Troy, but was in Egypt during the whole time of the war. Now the poets Hesiod and Stesichorus had both told something similar: Hesiod mentions a 'phantom' of Helen at Troy, and Stesichorus in his famous 'Palinode' stated that Helen never went to Troy.[44] For all the similarity of content, however, Herodotus' version is a world away in method and approach. To argue (not merely assert) that Helen was never at Troy, Herodotus employs: (a) the evidence of the Egyptian priests who tell him a story they claim is from Menelaus himself, namely, that the Greeks found no Helen or treasure when they sacked Troy (2.118); (b) passages from the *Iliad* and *Odyssey* that show that Homer knew of Paris and Helen's sojourn in Egypt (2.116); and (c) his own detailed argument, based on probability, that the Trojans would never have allowed such devastation to their people if peace could have been made merely by the return of a single woman to the Greeks (2.120).

Herodotus' remark that Homer knew but rejected this version because it was not as attractive (*euprepēs*, 2.116.1) as the one he did use indicates a belief that poetry has different criteria from other genres, and we may see here the kernel of that criticism of poetry that was to play so large a role in ancient literary criticism. In the historians, as we can see from Thucydides (1.22.4), the criticism often concerns the exaggeration and improbability of poetic stories. In fact Herodotus treated at least one story that was known from a previous poetic account, namely the end of Croesus. In Bacchylides' version (3.23–62), Croesus upon the pyre is miraculously rescued by Zeus who then sends Apollo to escort Croesus to the land of the Hyperboreans. Herodotus' version, by contrast, maintains human probability: Croesus calls upon Apollo to deliver him, and a rainstorm immediately springs up to douse the flames. Herodotus is careful not to say that the rainstorm came as the direct consequence of Croesus' plea, and he maintains a critical distance by ascribing the account to what 'the Lydians say' (1.87; cf. 7.189.2–3 for similar reticence). So in these cases of Helen and Croesus, the historian's procedure differs from the poet's, for the historian either gives reasons for preferring one version over the other or replaces a supernatural mechanism with one that is centred on natural or human probability.[45]

Nor is it the case that the historian always asserts a single or certain truth. The choice is frequently left open; or the truth might be irrecoverable: not everything is or can be known.[46] In his discussion of the annual inundation of the Nile, Herodotus summarises previous hypotheses and then gives his own argued interpretation of the 'true' nature of this phenomenon (2.20–27), marshalling evidence and argument. Even so, much – not all – of the truth Herodotus offers *is* provisional and possibly can be bettered in the future: an eyewitness of the sources of the Nile could presumably answer many questions about that river once and for all, as could explorers who go beyond the known portion of the world. In historical matters, however, the solution might be more complicated. Herodotus suggests that the truth about the battle of Lade can never be known because all the contingents blame one another (6.14), and so one must simply live with such uncertainty. And one might compare Aeschylus' 'poetic' picture of the united and single-hearted Greek advance against the Persian navy at Salamis with Herodotus' account of the fractious quarrels that preceded the battle, to say nothing of the different possibilities he offers for how the battle actually began (8.84).[47]

Yet one well might ask, then, what kind of truth, if any, the historian is proffering. That is not an unreasonable question, for there continues to this day a vigorous debate concerning the truth value of narrative history. And is there a historical truth that is somehow different from poetic truth? In a famous passage of the *Poetics*, Aristotle distinguished between history and poetry, pronouncing the latter 'more serious and more philosophical' because it aimed at the general or probable ('the things that would happen in accordance with probability or necessity'), whereas history was about particulars ('what Alcibiades did or had done to him'). Made up of disparate and not necessarily related facts, history lacked the kind of causative structure that the poet could impose in tragedy.[48] G. E. M. de Ste. Croix has pointed out, however, that Aristotle's use of 'more' (*mallon*) indicates that he was not denying to history the possibility of being philosophical and serious, but only noting a general tendency of historical works.[49]

Indeed, Herodotus, while pursuing a different kind of truth, in no way abandoned or thought unimportant traditional poetic conceptions of truth, and it is clear that he saw not only the particular but also the universal. On the one hand, he exhibits a love of details. He relishes the individual, the contingent, the unforeseen, and sometimes even the improbable. It is the *particular* unfolding of events that he tries to capture. Herodotus' preface emphasises *wonder*, and this is one of the keys to understanding his history. As with the rest of his poetic legacy, wonder is not new with Herodotus: 'a wonder to behold' is a stock phrase of epic vocabulary. But whereas poetic wonder is the strong sense of admiration for something that already exists, the wonder of Herodotus is an *investigative* wonder, the inquirer marvelling at the enormous particularity of the world and of human life within it.[50] This wonder can reveal itself in nearly infinite ways, from Herodotus' habit of noting the small mistakes made by historical actors or the unpredictable courage of individuals, to the way in which Babylon was built, or fascination with the particular marriage rites of a remote tribe in the deserts of Africa. On the historical level, the historian is interested not only in the rise and fall of states but also in the different ways that each empire rises and falls. Xerxes is very much like Cyrus, Cambyses and Darius, but he is not *exactly* like any of them, and his own story is unique. What fascinates the historian in these cases is not so much the general rule, as how that rule works out in the real world. Mnesiphilus had the understanding, but Themistocles had the craftiness precisely at the right moment and under the right circumstances to make it happen (8.57–63). The contingent events of history are not created by the historian (as they are by the poet, who has a freer hand),[51] but the historian revels in them, and seeks to explain and contextualise them. Precisely because the historian seeks to record an external and already existent particularity, history presents a unique challenge for those seeking to understand events as more than simply an agglomeration of facts.

On the other hand, although Herodotus narrates *particular* events and customs, he nevertheless shows the patterns in history, and he suggests that these are of *universal* significance, whether it be the rise and fall of empires, the ubiquity of retribution (*tisis*) in the world, or the stark choice that men face either to rule or be ruled. Herodotus might well say that these things happen 'in accordance with probability and necessity'. In this way, at least, he is indeed a poet, constructing a world-view and reading a pattern from (or into) the events that he chronicles. Yet any history that aspires to be more than an agglomeration of disparate facts must have some level of poetic creation, some aspiration, to use Aristotle's terms, towards the universal. Herodotus, after all, wants it both ways: he wants his audience to recognise both the staggering particularity of the world and the way that certain constants play out on the historical stage. He wants to lay claim to an older poetic truth while mapping out a place for his newer conception of historical truth.

*

Herodotus, then, was profoundly influenced by the subject matter, the concerns, and at times even the methods of his poetic predecessors. Simultaneously, his work represents a movement away from the poets, from their omniscience, and from their freedom to construct a persuasive, but not necessarily accurate, i.e., real, story. Herodotus says at the outset that his work is the result of his research (*historiē*), his human attempt to understand the world in all its particularity, and he displays throughout a willingness to reveal to his audience the fractured and incomplete nature of his own knowledge. In accepting this imperfect truth with all its gaps, suppositions, and best guesses, Herodotus may be said to inaugurate a new method of learning and understanding.[52]

FURTHER READING

A full treatment of Herodotus' engagement with his poetic predecessors remains a desideratum. Most scholars understandably concentrate on Herodotus' debt to Homer, for which one should consult: Strasburger (1972); Huber (1965); Fornara (1983) 62–3, 76–7; Woodman (1988) ch. 1; Griffin (1990); Erbse (1992) 122–32; and Marincola (forthcoming). Boedeker (2002) and (2003) are insightful and sensitive treatments of the similarities and differences between poetry and history. Nagy (1989) 215–338 is a full discussion of the intersection of interests between Pindar and

Herodotus, although much remains to be done on the relationship between these two authors.

On the more general debates about the differences between poetry and history, nearly all of which begin with Aristotle's remarks at *Poetics* 9, see: Gomme (1954), Ste. Croix (1975), Rosenmeyer (1982); Calame (1995) 58–96; Goldhill (2002) 10–44; and Halliwell (2002) 164–7, 193–9.

ENDNOTE: POEMS ON HISTORICAL THEMES

Following is a list of poems that pre-date or are roughly contemporary with Herodotus and whose theme can be described generally as historical. Much is uncertain about these poems, both in terms of form and content. For treatments see Bowie (1986) and (2001); Dougherty (1994).

1. *Early History of the Samians* (*Archaiologia tōn Samiōn*) by Semonides of Amorgos (mid-seventh century). Possibly 4,000 verses in length; most likely dealt with the foundation and early events in Samos' history.

2. *Smyrneis* by Mimnermus of Colophon (mid- to late-seventh century). This work contained an elaborate preface in which the Muses were invoked (*IEG* F 13) and a full narrative with speeches (FF 13–13a); a fragment about the settlement of Colophon (F 9) might also be from this poem.

3. *Foundation (Ktisis) of Colophon and Colonisation of Elea* by Xenophanes of Colophon (late sixth/early fifth century). This poem is supposed to have been 2,000 verses in length.

4. *Iōnika* by Panyassis of Halicarnassus (early fifth century). Panyassis was said to be the uncle or cousin of Herodotus. According to the *Suda*, the *Iōnika* was 7,000 lines long, written in elegiac couplets, and treated (i.a.) the Ionian colonies: see further Matthews (1974) 26–31.

5. *Battle of Artemisium* by Simonides of Ceos (late sixth/early fifth century). Said by the *Suda* to be in elegiac couplets, although two fragments survive (*PMG* 533) in lyric metre. This may not have been a poem separate from the *Battle of Salamis*: see Rutherford (2001) 33–8.

6. *Battle of Salamis* by Simonides of Ceos. According to the *Suda* this was in lyric metre though that has been doubted. Possibly this and the preceding comprised a single poem; the *Suda* also refers to a *Sea Battle of Xerxes*, which could have comprehended both.

7. *Battle of Plataea* by Simonides of Ceos. For the text and translation of this poem, together with a series of essays, see Boedeker and Sider (2001).

8. *Foundation (Ktisis) of Chios* by Ion of Chios (mid to late fifth century). It is not certain that this was a poem: Jacoby (1947) 4–7 argues that it was in prose; cf. Bowie (1986) 32 n. 104.

NOTES

1. On poetry and poets in the archaic age see Gentili (1988); Nagy (1989).

2. On these figures and the intellectual revolution in general see Lloyd (1987).

3. See Rösler (1990) 236; for Panyassis' fragments see Bernabé (1988) 171–87; for treatments, Huxley (1969) 177–88; Matthews (1974).

4. Good remarks on this in Goldhill (2002) *passim*.

5. Aeschylus (2.156); Alcaeus (5.95); Anacreon (3.121); Arion (1.23); Aristeas (4.13–16); Hesiod (2.53, 4.32); Homer (2.23, 53, 116, 4.29–32, 7.161); the Homeric Hymns (5.67) and the Epic Cycle (2.117); Pindar (3.38); Sappho (2.135); Simonides (5.102, 7.228); and Solon (1.29–34, 86, 2.177, 5.113).

6. [Long.] *Subl.* 13.3: *Homērikōtatos*; an inscription from Halicarnassus (see Isager [1999]) refers to him as 'the prose Homer of history'.

7. On narrative epics treating 'historical' events, see Huxley (1969); Lasserre (1976a) 121–42; Bowie (1986) 27–34; (1993) 8–20; (2001); Dougherty (1994). A list of these may be found in the Endnote.

8. For the influence of Homer on Herodotus see above all Strasburger (1972); also Huber (1965); Fornara (1983) 62–3, 76–7; Woodman (1988) ch. 1; Griffin (1990); Erbse (1992) 122–32; Boedeker (2002); see also Griffiths in this volume.

9. For Homeric language in Herodotus see Aly (1921/1969) 266–71, and the works cited in the previous note; for other poets, Schmid-Stählin (1934) 553–4. Murray (2001b) 322 wisely cautions that Homeric influence on Herodotus should not be limited to such verbal reminiscences.

10. On the Homeric narrator see Richardson (1990); de Jong (2002); Bowie (2001) 65 suggests that speeches in historical elegy may also have influenced the historians.

11. On Herodotus' digressions see Cobet (1971).

12. See de Jong (2001a), who notes (221) that what is distinctive about the *Odyssey* is the scale on which such manipulation of time is deployed.

13. Hdt. 1.5.3, *astea anthrōpōn*, echoing *Od.* 1.3; for the influence of the *Odyssey* on ancient historiography in general see Marincola (forthcoming).

14. See Dewald (1987) and (2002); Calame (1995) 75–96; de Jong (1999); further references at Marincola (2001) 40 n.90; on the narrator of Book 2 see Darbo-Peschanski (1987) 108–12; Marincola (1987).

15. For Pindar see Lefkowitz (1992), especially 1–71 and 161–8; more generally see Slings (1990) for the 'I' of the lyric poet; cf. Mackie (2003).

16. Ford (1991) 90–130.

17. The only prose writer with whom he engages by name is Hecataeus, and only once for an account of the Athenian expulsion of the Pelasgians (6.137, but cf. 2.143). Polemic by name is most common in Book 2: see Fowler in this volume.

18. Fowler (1996); Marincola (1999).

19. One would never guess from Herodotus' account of Egypt that Hecataeus had treated some of the same material. And although Herodotus names poets (above, n. 5), he never makes reference to poetic treatments of events he also narrates, such as Aeschylus' account of the battle of Salamis in his *Persians*, or Simonides' accounts of some of the major battles of the Persian Wars, though it is hardly likely he was ignorant of such works.

20. See Calame (1995) 77–8, although cf. 51, where he notes that the Muse in epinician is subordinated to the poet himself; Mackie (2003) 47–54 treats the contrast between Homeric and Pindaric invocation of the Muses. On Hesiod's narrative voice in the *Theogony* see Stoddard (2004). It is noteworthy that Mimnermus in his poem on the battle of Gyges with the Lydians seems to have begun with an invocation of the Muses (*IEG* F 13).

21. Lateiner (1989) 69–72 for those passages where Herodotus claims ignorance. Yet cf. Pindar, *Paean* 6.51–8 for the belief that some things cannot be known.

22. Note, however, Mimnermus, *IEG* F 14.1–4, where the speaker (perhaps the narrator) says that he learned of things from men of former times who had themselves seen the events. Such remarks as these might provide a poetic link with Herodotus.

23. Ajax picks up a stone in one hand that 'a man of today could not hold with two' (*Il.* 12.382–3), and Aeneas hoists a boulder that 'not two men of today could lift' (20.284).

24. Even the race of heroes, sandwiched between the bronze and iron races (they have probably been inserted into an original sequence based on metals: see West [1978] 173–4), do not arrest this decline.

25. See Mackie (2003) 39–47, 55–67, who speaks of 'the rhetorical priority of present to past' (67) in epinician.

26. *IEG* F 11; for discussion, see Boedeker (2001); cf. Bowie (2001) 57.

27. For different interpretations of the opening passage see the literature cited at Marincola (2001) 25 n. 24. On Herodotus' separation of a 'mythical' time from an historical one see van Leyden (1949–50); Vannicelli (1993) and (2001).

28. For the importance of glory to the Homeric heroes see Griffin (1980) 81–102.

29. For a wide-ranging analysis of how context determines the nature of poetic *kleos* see Goldhill (1991) 69–166.

30. Plut. *Cimon* 7.4–6 = *CEG* 2–5; for discussion see Wade-Gery (1933) and Jacoby (1945).

31. See Erskine (2001) 61–92 for the development of the Trojan–Persian comparison; he sees it as first appearing among the Aeginetans.

32. On *ergon* in Herodotus see Immerwahr (1960).

33. See Bulman (1992).

34. See, above all, Aly (1921/1969), and Griffiths in this volume. For the 'warner' figure in Herodotus see Bischoff (1932); Lattimore (1939a).

35. Croesus with a pun says (1.207.2) that his *pathēmata* (experiences) have become his *mathēmata* (learnings).

36. Croesus cannot foresee that Cyrus will capture Tomyris' son, or that the son will commit suicide and thereby goad the queen to vow vengeance upon Cyrus (1.212–14). For the complications of advice and decision making in Herodotus see Dewald (forthcoming).

37. Dewald (1985), especially 53–5.

38. Discussions of this passage are legion: for summaries of viewpoints see Svenbro (1976) 46–9 and Neitzel (1980); cf. Scodel (2001) 114–15.

39. On this topic see especially Pratt (1993).

40. Austin (1975) 179–238. Odysseus' 'truth' is acceptable because it furthers a social good, namely his return and reintegration into Ithaca; for the importance of context and truth see Scodel (2001) 110–11, and for Odysseus especially 118–19; for the more general problems encountered by Homeric characters in detecting truth see Mauritsch (2000).

41. The thought is nicely elucidated in Theognis 681–2: 'Let these be my riddling words with hidden meaning for the noble, / but one who is wise can recognise the evil.' For archaic poetry and truth see (i.a) Cole (1983); Puelma (1989); Pratt (1993); and for New Testament parallels, Kermode (1979) 1–47.

42. Even Homer, who never as narrator calls attention to a different version from his own, shows that he is aware of the phenomenon: see Bowie (1993) 11–20; Pratt (1993) 29–30.
43. Scodel (2001) 120–1 suggests that the poet here is implying that these places have invented false traditions that promote particular interests.
44. Hesiod F 358 Merkelbach-West; Stesichorus, *PMG* 192: 'This story is not true; / neither did you go on the well-benched ships / nor did you arrive at the citadel of Troy.'
45. I cannot here enter into the complicated question of Herodotus' attitude towards religion, but my view is very close to that of Scullion in this volume.
46. For a list of Herodotus' variant versions see Lateiner (1989) 84–90; on the procedure of ancient historians in general when dealing with variants see Marincola (1997) 280–6.
47. The Athenian account makes Ameinias of Pallene the first to ram an enemy ship; the Aeginetans claim they started the battle; and a popular belief held that a phantom voice faulted the Greeks for backing water and urged them on. There is also the story that the Corinthians sailed away at the beginning of the battle, although Herodotus says that only the Athenians claim this.
48. See *Poetics* 9, 1451a36–b11. Discussions of the passage are legion; for some representative views see Gomme (1954) 49–72; Ste. Croix (1975); Halliwell (2002) 193–8.
49. Ste. Croix (1975) 49–53, with important remarks on the importance to history of 'the as a general rule' (*to epi to polu*).
50. On the historian's wonder see the full treatment of Munson (2001a); cf. Goldhill (2002) 21: 'For the historian . . . wonder provokes a desire to know, followed by research, hypothesis and argument.'
51. A point that Lucian recognises when he denies invention to the historian because the material already exists: *de hist. conscr.* 51.
52. I am grateful to Carolyn Dewald, Robert Fowler, Richard Rutherford, and Kathryn Stoddard, who read earlier versions of this chapter and suggested many improvements. They do not, of course, necessarily agree with the views here expressed.

2

ROBERT FOWLER

Herodotus and his prose predecessors

Herodotus being so miraculous, and the Herodotean urge to seek origins still being so strong with us, the desire to historicise him remains irresistible. Knowing what lay around and behind him could make clearer what was unique about him; it could, assuming an agreed definition of history, tell us whether he really was its Father. It happens that we do have a certain amount of information – desperately fragmentary, permitting only the smallest number of verifiable hypotheses – about his predecessors and contemporaries. But in truth, if one wishes to know what relationship exists between Herodotus and his colleagues, it is best to look first in Herodotus' own text.

Herodotus is frequently argumentative and judgemental. From the very first chapters he rejects foolish opinions, weighs up conflicting evidence, makes firm pronouncements on method: were it not for his winning charm, one could find all this very irritating (as indeed some readers have). For all its prominence, however, scholars have only recently begun to relate this feistiness to Herodotus' conception of himself as an historian. For it is obvious (now) that he must be arguing *with* someone, and a close study of the intellectual terrain over which these battles and negotiations are being conducted can do much to illuminate Herodotus' situation as a writer.

The word *historia* (or *historiē*, in Herodotus' dialect), which he uses in his first sentence to describe his amazing gallimaufry, is the first important clue. It does not mean 'history' until well into the fourth century.[1] Until then the noun and its associated verb *historein* have a more general meaning of 'inquiry', 'question', 'investigate'; related is the noun *histōr* meaning 'judge', 'expert', or 'witness' (i.e., 'one who investigates / knows / sees').[2] These words are used in a relatively unmarked way by Herodotus and other early writers, as their narratives happen to involve people asking questions or making judgements. But they are also used in a marked and self-conscious way to denote intellectual activity. The philosopher Heraclitus of Ephesus (c. 500 BCE) is the first, who in his usual enigmatic style tells us that 'philosophers really have to know (*historas einai*) a lot of things well'.³ 'Philosophers' in this period could mean any intellectual or scientist. The remark need not be complimentary: in another place, Heraclitus dismisses Pythagoras, who 'cultivated inquiry (*historiē*) more than any other man, and from out of his books put together his wisdom (*sophiē*), his manifold learning (*polymathiē*), his pernicious expertise (*kakotechniē*)'.⁴ His comment about philosophers knowing a lot of things could, then, be sarcastic: their knowledge is uselessly diffuse, focussed on the wrong object (not the Heraclitean *logos*), and acquired by risible methods. On the other hand, given the right methods and goals, Heraclitus might well embrace the notion of *historiē*, and the comment could be sincere. In another place, he claims to have 'asked himself';⁵ he learned everything by introspection, and had no teacher (contrast Pythagoras). However that may be, *historiē* in these passages plainly denotes self-conscious intellectual activity: 'asking questions' raised to professional standards, which must imply some thought about methods and goals, aspirations of expertise, and a public profile, i.e. publication of findings (whether in oral or written form). Yet, curiously, there seem to be no restrictions as to the object of inquiry, which could be anything; among the witless polymaths scorned by Heraclitus there is an ethnographer *cum* geographer, a cosmologist *cum* moralist, a mythologer and a mystical mathematician. All these things are *historiē*. It is as though people have suddenly realised that the world holds an infinity of secrets awaiting discovery, and that we have the wherewithal to discover them all, if only we make the effort. Parallels with the Enlightenment are tempting.

Among other examples of this unrestricted sense of *historiē*, it is most helpful to cite the proem of *On the Medical Art*, one of the oldest treatises in the Hippocratic corpus:

> There are those who have made a profession (*technē*) out of reviling the professions; in so doing they think they are producing a display of their personal researches (*historiēs oikeiēs epideixis*), though this is not my assessment of their activity.⁶ For me, finding out something which is better for being discovered, is what intelligence should wish to do, and make it its task to do; similarly bringing partial discoveries to completion. To wish to use one's skill (*technē*) in abuse (*logoi kakoi*) to scorn what others have found out, while making no improvements of one's own, and slandering to the ignorant the discoveries of the learned, cannot be the inclination and task of intelligence; rather it is a proclamation of one's own mean nature, or a lack of professional skill (*atechniē*). As for those who may attack other professions in this manner, let those concerned with those professions fend them off as best they can; this treatise shall oppose those who so proceed against medicine, taking

courage from the very people it finds fault with, drawing its resources from the profession it seeks to help, and finding strength in the wisdom education imparts.

One infers that these non-professionals (or 'unprofessionals') are to be found dogging honest practitioners of all the *technai*. Not that the author of this treatise would, on another day, be loath to advertise his own *historiēs epideixis*; after all, *historiē* is about finding out, and he has much to say about discovery in this passage. It is a matter, he says – somewhat lamely – of the right kind of discovery (just as Heraclitus desiderates the right kind of inquiry). The rhetoric is palpable, and bespeaks a highly competitive environment, in which authors are as much concerned to discredit rivals as to persuade audiences of their own views. Herodotus is thoroughly at home in this environment, as Rosalind Thomas' recent book has shown in detail.[7]

Herodotus' first words provide a close parallel to the doctor's turn of phrase: 'This is the publication of the inquiry (*historiēs apodexis*) of Herodotus of Halicarnassus, so that human events (*ta genomena ex anthrōpōn*) should not fade from memory in the course of time, and that great and marvellous deeds (*erga*), whether of Greek or barbarian, should not be without their meed of glory; in particular, the reason why (*di' hēn aitiēn*) they fought each other' (*praef.*).[8] *Historiē* being a general term, the writer must specify the scope of his particular inquiry, as Herodotus does here. The first part, 'human events', is in Greek more generally 'what has come about as the result of human agency': close to 'history' in our sense, but still broad enough to include ethnography, the description of foreign customs. The second part is *erga*, which as many commentators have pointed out includes not only actions but monuments (such as the pyramids, Polycrates' tunnel, and many other engineering marvels in the *Histories*). Between them these two clauses encompass much of the work, but not quite everything: they exclude geography, and inquiry into natural phenomena such as the cause of the Nile's annual flooding. Yet there is a sense in which these subjects are implied by the proem. In the final clause Herodotus states the special focus of his book, the cause (*aitiē*) of the Persian Wars. Since he shares the contemporary view that the natural environment helps to shape human behaviour,[9] geography is a logical part of his ethnography. Moreover, the notion of cause, here produced with all emphasis, is an essential part of *historiē* in the writers of this period.[10] Herodotus has much to say about causes in the course of his inquiry.[11] He is entitled to take a generous view of relevance, given his clear inclination to get to the bottom of everything. The work is encyclopaedic: one way or another, the whole of the known world (and much beyond) is worked into the narrative; every major division of the human race – Greeks, Persians, Egyptians, Libyans, Scythians, various Asian tribes – is traced back to its remotest ancestors. Everything in Egypt depends on the Nile, so it behoves Herodotus to discuss its peculiar flooding. But although he could produce a plausible justification for many of his inclusions, he is nonetheless conscious of stretching the bounds of tolerance;[12] even if the particular focus, the Persian Wars, requires him, on his understanding of his task, to range very far afield, there are times when the reader might think he is in danger of losing his way.[13] The compulsion to be comprehensive, inherited from Homer but reinforced by philosophy and Herodotus' prose predecessors, was too powerful to resist.

This linking of *aitiē* and *historiē* which suddenly appears in the writers of the mid-fifth century must be a contemporary development. The search into the origin of the world had begun in the preceding century, and one can argue that, in essence, the first philosophers were not so very different from their successors, for they too sought causes. But the change in vocabulary – older writers spoke of *dizēsis* and *archai*, 'seeking' and 'beginnings'[14] – marks a change in the tenor of discourse. *Aitiē*, 'cause', is a more abstract notion and one with greater explanatory power than 'beginning'. Although in many of its instances in Herodotus and other writers the word does not go beyond recognised legal or religious usages, there are some passages (e.g. 2.20–7, again on the flooding of the Nile) where the abstract principle of cause and effect is becoming explicit.[15] *Historiē*, as already noted, contains an element of 'judging' – an activity Herodotus dramatises both with regard to his own *historiē* and that of his characters.[16] A greater sophistication of analysis has been attained, and authors foreground the conditions of this analysis in their accounts. Intellectually these writers have grasped that difficulties of method claim priority of consideration. As a matter of rhetoric too, simple pronouncements *ex cathedra*, in the manner of a Hecataeus, no longer persuade an audience. One must give evidence of how one arrived at one's conclusions, weighing pros and cons. One of Herodotus' trademarks is his frequent expressions of uncertainty; he often *declines* to judge between conflicting accounts. This is partly intellectual honesty, but it is also very persuasive rhetorically (unkind critics have called it the trademark of the liar).

So far as our evidence, with all its uncertainties of date and vast gaps, allows us to judge, Herodotus was the first writer to apply this powerful new concept of 'inquiry' to the study of the human past. Indeed he is the first writer to use the word at all, so that the possibility exists in theory that the physicists are the debtors, Herodotus the creditor. Yet most 'inquiry' was, in fact, devoted to physical phenomena (so that occasionally 'inquiry' without specification meant 'scientific inquiry'),[17] and the general sense prevailed for a long time. Neither Thucydides nor Xenophon uses the word to describe what they do; Plato uses the word only its generic sense. Even Aristotle, in his day, continued to add qualifiers such as 'inquiry into nature' or 'inquiry into animals' or, to designate history, 'inquiry into events' (*Rhet.* 1360a36). In his *Poetics*, however, *historiē* without qualification means 'history': possibly the earliest example of the usage.[18] Significantly, his stock example of the historian is Herodotus (1451b2). One wonders whether Herodotus' classic text, which determined the course of all subsequent historiography, was precisely what altered the meaning of *historiē*, at a time when the boundaries of prose genres were finally becoming a matter of explicit definition. But to return to Herodotus himself: his constant foregrounding of the difficulties inherent in conducting 'inquiry' is integral to his self-conception and without parallel in the surviving fragments of contemporary writers of history, or in earlier writers of ethnography or geography.[19] It does, however, find its echo in contemporary 'inquirers' of other kinds, and there are signs of similar concerns with methodology in other historians whose working lives overlapped with Herodotus'. So it is best to see Herodotus as a man constantly engaged in the debates of his day, continually shaping his own *historiē* in conversation with others, over the course of a career spanning perhaps four decades. This in no way underestimates the power of his own voice or the brilliance of his personal achievement.

If we may credit Herodotus with first applying *historiē* to the past, with all that that entails, it is not of course the case that Herodotus was the first to write about the past. Homer and other poets were already historians; the great legends counted as history. Beginning in the late sixth century, Greeks began to write these legends down in prose. Hecataeus of Miletus was the first to do so. The backbone of the narrative was provided by the complicated genealogies of gods and heroes; the poetic foundation document underlying all mythography, as the Greeks came to call this activity once 'myth' and 'history' had been distinguished,[20] was not Homer but the Hesiodic *Catalogue of Women*.[21] Before Herodotus began his career, several major works of genealogy were already in circulation: those of Hecataeus, Acusilaus, and Pherecydes.[22] Over 250 fragments survive from these authors, sometimes in verbatim quotation, more often in paraphrase, with admixture of later material of uncertain extent.

Nor was Herodotus the first to write about foreign peoples and customs. Of Hecataeus nearly 350 additional fragments survive from his *Periodos* or *Circuit of the World*, though the great majority are disappointing one-liners from the epitome of the early medieval lexicographer Stephanus of Byzantium; for instance, 'Esdetes: an Iberian tribe; Hecataeus in the

"Europe"' (i.e. Book 1 of the *Periodos*; Book 2 was 'Asia', which included Egypt and Libya). In this work Hecataeus gives an account of a voyage clockwise around the Mediterranean and the Black Sea (with inland excursions at various points), recording places of interest and importance, distances, oddities, and mythical lore. A few fragments, similar in nature, survive of Scylax's work or works, and his voyage is described by Herodotus (4.44). Euthymenes' views on the cause of tides in the Atlantic and the flooding of the Nile (connected to the Atlantic in his view) were passed to posterity by Theophrastus. Hanno's Phoenician text was translated at an unknown date; something of his exploits might have been known to Herodotus through oral sources (and it is notable that Herodotus' account of Libya shows little contact with the surviving fragments of Hecataeus, suggesting an alternative source).[23] Hecataeus himself figures as a player in the Ionian revolt (Hdt. 5.36, 125–6), and is cited for his version of the Pelasgian eviction from Attica (6.137). He was certainly a major source of the Egyptian *logos* of Herodotus, who pays him the compliment of abuse in a famous passage therein (2.143, to which we will return below).

These two types of book – genealogy and ethnography *cum* geography – are the only ones unequivocally known to predate Herodotus. The evidence that Scylax wrote an historical work on Heracleides of Mylasa is too late to trust. It is not clear that Dionysius of Miletus was more than an ethnographer. *If* he wrote but one book, the *Persica*, and mentioned Mt Haemon in it (as opposed to in a *Periodos*: cf. Hecataeus, *FGrHist* 1 FF 167–9), one infers he related Darius' Scythian campaign (cf. Hdt. 4.49). That he told the story of the false magus (Hdt. 3.61) is unambiguously attested: perhaps this information seemed pertinent at some point in a basically geographical work, but it is curious that in all the fragments of Hecataeus, the geographer, while freely relating myths associated with various sites, never makes a reference to an historical event. Yet if Dionysius' *Persica* was a work moving towards Herodotean history, there is little hint of it in our sources (the book was still known to Apollodorus of Athens in the second century BCE).[24] One could also wish for more information about the local historians. Whether any of them was active before Herodotus is controversial. Dogmatism on the point is unwise when so much is uncertain; it is better to hold options open. One can see certain points of contact between Herodotus and the local historians at least in method. When one recalls that Herodotus was at work for several decades, and accepts that he did not work in a vacuum, it becomes probable that the influence between him and other investigators of the past was not entirely in one direction. His text as it stands is a document of the 430s; its latest datable reference is 430, and many passages yield their richest meaning when read against the background of the Athenian Empire and the brewing war.[25] By 440, the other writers named in the Appendix come into view.[26]

Nevertheless, direct connections are hard to establish. The clearest are between Herodotus and Hecataeus. Porphyry says the former's account of the phoenix, the hippopotamus, and the hunting of crocodiles is lifted word for word, with minimal changes, from Hecataeus (*FGrHist* 1 F 324), though such charges are usually overstated in the ancient lists of plagiarism, and in general one should avoid attributing too much to the absent and unverifiable source: the *Periodos* only extended to two books, after all.[27] Both writers commented on the Nile delta, on the 'floating' island Chemmis, and on Egyptian bread and beer.[28] We sometimes detect anonymous criticism, for instance at 4.36, where Herodotus 'laughs' at 'the many writers of *Periodoi*' who make Ocean a circular stream surrounding the earth, and think Asia and Europe are of equal size. Hecataeus held this view, so he may be the target here, though perhaps not only he.[29] There are, however, two explicit citations, apart from the reports of Hecataeus' role in the Ionian revolt (5.36, 125–6). One of them (6.137) concerns the Pelasgian eviction from Attica, on which Hecataeus had a different version from the Athenians. Although analysis of this passage is profitable,[30] it is the other which I propose to examine briefly here. After his account of the first 341 generations of Egyptian history (2.99–141), as recounted to him by the priests of the temple of Zeus (Amun-Re) at Thebes (Karnak), Herodotus pauses to consider the implications of their vast chronology. He first reckons the sums, and then wheels Hecataeus onto the stage of his history. Hecataeus, he claims, had been there before him, and had recited his own genealogy, which led back through sixteen generations to a god; whereupon 'the priests did for him what they did for me, though I did not recite my genealogy': they showed him the 341 statues erected by each priest before his death, assured him that in every generation a son succeeded a father, and noted that in the entire period no god had trodden Egyptian earth. Consequently they refused to believe that a god had fathered one of Hecataeus' ancestors a mere sixteen generations before.

This is a troubling passage, prompting difficult questions. Did Hecataeus really present himself in such a bad light, or is this Herodotus' malicious gloss? Could Hecataeus have told this story in such a way as to preserve face? Would self-deprecating irony be probable in a text of the period? If he did realise the extreme disparity of Greek and Egyptian chronology, would this not undermine the whole of his genealogical research, to say nothing of obliging him to abandon family pretensions? If he realised the implications, hadn't he already made Herodotus' point for him; is the epigone motivated by mere spite and jealousy?

Scholars have variously answered these questions. A way forward is offered by West's careful discussion, in which she demonstrates convincingly how difficult it is to believe that Hecataeus' encounter actually took place as presented.[31] However, we are not obliged to conclude that the whole is merely invented, or that Hecataeus did not go to Karnak. It is becoming clearer all the time how Herodotus often presents opinions ('the Egyptians say') as fact, when what lies behind the statement is inference: he conjectures that this is what the Egyptians would say, were you to ask them.[32] This is not a fraudulent procedure in his view. Following this principle, I suggest that in the present passage Herodotus *infers* that this was Hecataeus' experience, on the basis of two facts: the 16-generation genealogy, which Hecataeus must have given somewhere in his works; and his belief that Hecataeus had visited Karnak.[33] Hecataeus must therefore have heard the same speech from the priests, who would have rejected his claims absolutely. For Herodotus the implication of the statues was truly staggering; it lies at the heart of his historical vision.[34] The tremendous emphasis placed on this implication is surely his own. He is very proud of his superior insight, and must scorn Hecataeus for having missed it completely. His account implies that his predecessor was utterly wrong-footed by the experience, and left feeling foolish and bewildered. One sees how very subtle and damaging this competition amongst the *logioi* could be.

This reconstruction must, of course, remain speculative. Other connections between Herodotus and his colleagues are even more elusive. Some of his targets of frequent outspoken disagreement on historical and geographical affairs are apt to be names in our Appendix.[35] Since he deals with the relatively recent past, Herodotus avoids almost entirely the terrain of the genealogists, who rarely bridged the gap between the end of the heroic age and their own day.[36] Where he happens to tread on their ground, giving a genealogy from the 'mythical' period, we usually do not have a corresponding fragment in the mythographical corpus for comparison; in one egregious example, the genealogy of the Athenian Philaids (6.35.127–9), he and Pherecydes (F 2) give contradictory versions.[37] Herodotus seems in this case to have got his information from talking to people in Athens.

'Talking' was, in fact, what Herodotus did most of the time. In his own work, though obviously written,[38] he does not distinguish between written and oral sources in respect of reliability. The world he lived in was still predominantly oral in character; books there were aplenty, but they were not privileged over other sources of information. Fleeting points of contact between Herodotus and another author should not predispose one to think that the latter was the former's principal or sole source. Herodotus was always free to supplement his reading with data obtained from oral informants; such informants, indeed, might often be the common source of both writers, who could be entirely ignorant of one another. The general level of talk in the Greek cities of the mid-fifth century BCE is hard to overestimate: open, dynamic, democratic city-states, materially booming and culturally exploding, generated an incessant buzz: political speeches, legal proceedings, military and civilian councils, philosophical conversation, learned expositions, religious aetiology, tales told for casual entertainment or education of the young, fables (and to this list one must add the countless poetic performances). This background must be borne in mind by anyone asking what Herodotus' genre might have been. 'Inquiry' was already a bewilderingly broad term: what are we to do with *logoi*, 'talk'? Yet its importance to Herodotus is obvious; after his opening sentence, he continues 'The *logioi* amongst the Persians say that the Phoenicians were responsible (*aitious*) for the quarrel.' These *logioi andres*, the talkers, are those ready to provide information and opinions on important topics wherever one happens to end up in one's travels. The talk, like the 'inquiry', could in theory be about anything. Like 'inquiry', *logoi* is being used in a marked sense, as its prominence in Herodotus shows. These *logioi* have status; they are expert, informed, meaningful talkers, sociologically apparent, though one would not go so far as to call them an institution.[39] An even more marked term is *logopoios*, '*logos*-maker'; Herodotus applies it three times to Hecataeus (2.143.1, 5.36.2, 5.125), and once to Aesop (2.134.3). 'Maker' appropriates for the talker the activity of the *poiētēs*, the poet; it connotes a more active involvement in the production of *logoi* than mere transmission of reports. Just as the marked use of 'inquiry' implied self-consciousness about one's procedures, so the marked use of 'talk' implies a sense of rules to the game. 'The Persians say', 'the Egyptians say', 'the Corinthians say', and the like, are expressions in constant use in Herodotus. Close study shows that these are artfully employed – so artfully, that they give rise to accusations of fraud; but in fact, Herodotus sees nothing fraudulent about reporting undifferentiated consensus, even when based on nothing more than reasonable conjecture about that consensus.[40] This is the way the *logioi andres* conducted their conversation. It is for this reason that scholars have begun to study closely the dynamics and conventions of this sort of interchange: the arguments, the posturing, the narrative technique, the critical methods of a predominantly oral environment.

In this broader perspective, comparison of Herodotus and his colleagues can be more fruitful than the hunt for specific connections. For instance, the problematisation of *logoi* already in the opening words of Hecataeus' *Genealogies* confirms our general assessment of their importance.[41] Features of discourse which can be usefully studied include: the author's *persona* (e.g. explicit and implicit first-person statements, relation of implied author to text, attitude to others' texts);[42] narratology (e.g. implied audiences and their manipulation; rhythm of fabula vs. story, prolepses and analepses, actorial and narratorial motivations, focalisation);[43] scientific methods such as rationalisation, chronography, etymology, probability (*to eikos*), use of eyewitness (*opsis*) and hearsay evidence (*akoē*), critical judgement (*gnōmē*);[44] attitude to the past;[45] use of sources;[46] deployment of various kinds of argument.[47] The gain for students of historiography is that in every one of these categories Herodotus can be seen to win hands down. He is a far subtler manipulator of his persona and discourse than his predecessors; he is in a league of his own as a storyteller (and that not only with respect to predecessors); he deploys every weapon of the scientific arsenal with greater sophistication; he makes awareness of method an important part of his text; he has achieved greater critical distance from the object of his inquiry; so far from evading the problem of sources, he has in effect discovered it; his enthymemes are proto-Aristotelian. Herodotus' predecessors deserve all credit for their pioneering efforts, and part of the charm of studying them is seeing how often they have been underestimated; but in the end one seeks most to take the precise measure of the difference between them and Herodotus. Moreover, one not only sees the difference in this or that respect, but the difference resulting from the concentration of the entire arsenal on the historian's various targets; the combination of all these methods is as unique as the combination of subject-matter, ethnography and history – a combination not seen on this scale before or after Herodotus, but necessary to his grandiose task as he conceived it.[48] And grandiose it was: though one can see the encyclopaedic spirit thriving in the all-inclusive, panhellenic genealogies, and in the catalogues (ostensibly complete) of every city Greek and barbarian in the known world, no other work had Herodotus' breathtaking sweep, not only of space and time, but of human life from the bathetic to the sublime. That is why Herodotus is Father of history.[49]

FURTHER READING

There is no up-to-date, comprehensive treatment of all the predecessors and contemporaries of Herodotus, but one may usefully consult in English the works of Pearson (1939), (1942) ch. 1 (on Hellanicus), (1987) 11–18 (on Antiochus), and Drews (1973); in German, Lendle (1992) introduces Hecataeus, Acusilaus, Pherecydes, Xanthus, and Ion; von Fritz (1967) is a thorough and authoritative discussion. For Hecataeus, see Bertelli (2001); for Ion of Chios, see West (1985) and Dover (1986); for Hellanicus, see Möller (2001); for Antiochus of Syracuse, see Luraghi (2002). Pertinent in various ways are Thomas (2000), Fowler (2000a) xxvii–xxxviii, (2001), and Raaflaub (2002a).

APPENDIX
WRITERS OF GENEALOGY, ETHNOGRAPHY, GEOGRAPHY, AND LOCAL HISTORY[50]

Active before Herodotus' working life (born c. 485)

Name	Dates	Titles of Works[51]	Edition of Fragments[52]
Hecataeus of Miletus	c. 555–485	*Genealogies* or *Histories*;[53] *Periodos* ('Circuit') or *Periegesis* ('Guide') *of the World*	FGrHist 1; EGM
Acusilaus of Argos	flourished before 480	*Genealogies*	EGM
Pherecydes of Athens	published c. 465	*Histories* (genealogies, in fact)	EGM
Scylax of Caryandra	c. 550–475	*Periplous* ('Circumnavigation') *of the World Outside*[54] *the Pillars of Hercules*; *Circuit of the World*; *Events in the Time of Heracleides King of Mylasa*[55]. Sailed from the Indus to Suez (Hdt. 4.44).	FGrHist 709; for pseudo-Scylax see GGM I 15ff.
Euthymenes of Massilia	end of 6th cent.	none transmitted; a periegete like Scylax; voyaged down west coast of Africa (compare the voyage of Sataspes, Hdt. 4.43)	FHG 4.408
Hanno of Carthage	beginning of 5th cent.	*Periplous* (originally in Phoenician; translated into Greek sometime before the 3rd cent. BCE); voyaged down west coast of Africa	GGM I.1ff.
Dionysius of Miletus	coeval with King Darius (reigned 521–486)	*Persica*; *Periegesis of the World*; *Events after Darius* (or possibly 'in the Time of Darius'); *Troica*	FGrHist 687[56]

(*cont.*)

Active during Herodotus' working life

Name[57]	Dates	Works	Edition of Fragments
Euagon of Samos	flourished before 431	none transmitted; local history of Samos	*EGM*
Dei(l)ochus of Proconnesus[58]	flourished before 431	*On Cyzicus*; *On Samothrace*	*EGM*; *FGrHist* 471
Democles of Phygela	flourished before 431	none transmitted; local history?	*EGM*; cf. *FHG* II.20–1
Eudemus of Paros or Naxos	flourished before 421	none transmitted; local history?	*EGM*
Charon of Lampsacus	flourished c. 450	*Aethiopica*; *Persica*; *Hellenica*; *Libyca*; *Cretica*; *On Lampsacus*; *Lampsacene Chronicles*; *Prytaneis* ('Civic Officials') *of the Lacedaemonians* (emend to *Lampsacenes?*); *Foundations of Cities*; *Periplous of the World Outside the Pillars of Hercules*	*EGM*; *FGrHist* 262
Hellanicus of Lesbos	?480/79– after 407/6	*Phoronis*; *Deucalionia*; *Atlantis*; *Asopis*; *Troica*; *Aeolica/Lesbica*; *Argolica*; *On Arcadia*; *Atthis*; *Boeotiaca*; *Thessalica*; *Cypriaca*; *On the Foundation of Chios*; *Aegyptiaca*; *Expedition to the Shrine of Ammon*; *On Lydia*; *Persica*; *Scythica*; *Origins of Cities and Tribes*; *Barbarian Customs*; *Priestesses of the Temple of Hera in Argos*; *Victors at the Carneia: Set Down in Prose*; *Victors at the Carneia: Composed in Verse*[59]	*EGM*; *FGrHist* 4, 323a, 601a, 645a, 687a

Active during Herodotus' working life

Name	Dates	Works	Edition of Fragments
Xanthus of Lydia	flourished c. 450	*Lydiaca*; *On the Magi*; *On Empedocles*	*FGrHist* 765
Damastes of Sigeum	flourished c. 440–430	*Genealogy of Those who Fought at Troy*;[60] *Catalogue of Tribes and Cities*; *On Poets and Sophists*	*EGM*; *FGrHist* 5
Xenomedes of Ceos	?flourished c. 450	none transmitted; local history of Ceos	*EGM*
Ion of Chios	c. 480–422/1	*Foundation of Chios*; *Epidemiai* ('Visits': reminiscences of his meetings with famous people); poetic and philosophical works	*EGM*; *FGrHist* 392; *TrGF* 19; B. Gentili, C. Prato, *Poetarum elegiacorum testt. et frr.* II.61–9, *IEG* II.79–82; A. Leurini, *Ionis Chii testimonia et fragmenta*
Antiochus of Syracuse	died after 424/3	*On Italy*; *Sicelica* (history of Sicily)	*EGM*; *FGrHist* 555
Simonides of Ceos the Genealogist	flourished before 431	*Genealogy*; *Inventions*	*EGM*[61]
Stesimbrotus of Thasos	flourished c. 430	*On Themistocles, Thucydides and Pericles*;[62] *On Religious Rites*; a book of Homeric problems, title not transmitted	*FGrHist* 107
Hippias of Elis	end of 5th c.	*Names of Tribes* (ethnography); *Victors in the Olympics* (chronography); *Synagōgē* ('Collection'; a work of miscellaneous content); *Trojan Dialogue* (see Pl. *Hippias Major* 286a)	*FGrHist* 6; *VS* 86

NOTES

1. Below, n. 18. On *historiē* generally see Thomas (2000) 161–7.
2. See most recently Munson (2001a), index s.v. *Histor*.
3. *VS* 22 B 35, quoted by Clement of Alexandria (*Strom.*5.140.5). There must remain some doubt whether 'philosophers' is Heraclitus' word. Herodotus uses the verb *philosophein* at 1.30.2 of Solon's curiosity-driven travel.
4. *VS* 22 B 129. For the negative connotation of *polymathiē* in Heraclitus see also B 40 *VS* = Hecataeus T 21 *EGM*: '*polymathiē* does not teach intelligence; if so, it would have taught Hesiod and Pythagoras, Xenophanes and Hecataeus'.
5. Using the verb *dizēsthai* (B 101 *VS*): on this word see below p. 32.
6. Following the text of J. Jouanna (Budé) and others.
7. Thomas (2000); see also her contribution to the present volume.
8. For a close study of the phrase *historiēs epi/apode(i)xis* see Bakker (2002).
9. Most emphatically at the very end of the work, when Cyrus opines that 'soft countries produce soft men' (9.122.3); the Persians took the point, declined to emigrate from their harsh land, and retained their ability to rule. On the theory of environmental determinism in Herodotus and others see Thomas (2000) 102–14, and in this volume.
10. See Bakker (2002) 13–14.
11. Gould (1989) ch. 4; Lateiner (1989) ch. 9.
12. 'My work from the outset has required digressions', he apologises (4.30.1).
13. 'Path' (*hodos*) is in fact one of his metaphors for his narrative (1.95.1; cf. 1.117.2, 2.20.1, 2.22.1). On the cohesion of the various elements in the *Histories* see especially Immerwahr (1966) and Munson (2001a).
14. For early philosophical use see Parmenides, *VS* 28 B 2.2: 'I will tell you the only paths of *dizēsis*', cf. 6.3, 7.2, 8.6. In Herodotus, it a less forceful word than *historiē*, denoting simple seeking for something lost, or desiring: see 1.67.5, 1.94.3 ('seeking' a cure: one might think this example a little more marked than the others), 2.66.1, 2.147.3, 2.156.4, 4.9.1, 4.139.3, 4.151.2 ('asking' for factual information), 5.92.2, 7.16.2, 7.142.1 ('seeking' the meaning of the oracle of the wooden walls). Similarly in earlier writers: Homer, e.g. *Il.* 4.88, 17.221, *Od.* 1.261, 11.100, 16.391 = 21.161; Theogn. e.g. 83, 180; Anacr. *PMG* 360.2; Simon. *PMG* 514, 542.22. It appears to be the ordinary Ionic word for 'seek'.
15. Vegetti (1999).
16. For example, 1.24.7, of Periander's inquiry (resembling a police investigation) into Arion's curious tale; 1.56.1–2, of Croesus investigating the current state of Greece; 2.19.3, 29.1, 34.1, 44.5, 99.1, 113.1 of his own inquiries in Egypt, 4.192.3 of his inquiries into Libyan geography; 2.118–19, of the Egyptian priests' inquiries of Menelaus; 7.96.1, of what the rationale (*logos*) of his inquiry requires him to mention.
17. Eur. *TrGF* F 910.
18. In Isocr. *Panath.* 246 the word might have this meaning, but cf. Aeschin. *In Tim.* 141 where it is equivalent to *paideia*, education; as examples he gives Homer and other poets, who, though they told stories which were historical enough for most Greeks, are cited here for their morally improving *exempla*. 'General knowledge' might be a good translation. Isocr. *Ep.* 8.4 has *historia tēs paideias* which appears to mean 'expertise (expert judgement) in education'.

Dem. *Cor.* 144 speaks of *historia tōn koinōn*, investigation into public affairs. (Wankel (1976) 782–4 would delete this clause; Yunis (2001) *ad loc.* is able to defend it.)

19. Fowler (1996).
20. The word 'mythography' first occurs in the late fourth century: see Fowler (2000a).
21. Fowler (1998).
22. See Appendix.
23. Thomas (2000) 53 n. 53. For a translation of Hanno's text see Cary and Warmington (1963) 63–8 or Carpenter (1966) 83–5.
24. Dionysius is unfortunately missing from the list of early writers in Dion. Hal. *Thuc.* 5, but as John Marincola reminds me, Dionysius does not distinguish ethnography and history in his discussion of the predecessors of Herodotus; perhaps this is the desired 'hint'. Compare Marincola (1999) 297, Moggi (1972).
25. Moles (2002); Fowler (2003a). Raaflaub (2002a) 165 n. 53, citing Hornblower (1991) 83, notes that Hippias' warning to the Corinthians at 5.93 cannot predate 440, when Athens and Corinth were still on good terms according to Thucydides 1.40.5, 41.2. This whole section lies at the heart of Herodotus' work (I should have noticed this point in the article just cited).
26. Space forbids discussion of such interesting close contemporaries as Ion, Charon, Hellanicus, or Xanthus. See 'Further Reading'.
27. Erbse (1992) 172–3.
28. The delta: *FGrHist* 1 FF 301, 306–9, Hdt. 2.13ff.; Chemmis: 1 F 305, Hdt. 2.156; bread and beer: 1 FF 322–3, Hdt. 2.77.4.
29. Hec. *FGrHist* 1 FF 18, 36a, 302; Thomas (2000) 80–3, 215; Boedeker (2002) 107 points out that Herodotus' 'I laugh (*gelō*)' turns the tables on Hecataeus, who sneers at the stories of the Greeks as 'ridiculous (*geloioi*)', F 1. At 2.23 'the man who spoke of Ocean' in connection with the Nile is probably Hecataeus. For other possible connections between Herodotus and Hecataeus see Lloyd (1975–88) I.127–39, II.8–10.
30. See Luraghi (2001b) 159–60; Fowler (2003b); Sourvinou-Inwood (forthcoming). Hecataeus also mentioned Pelasgians in F 119; cf. Hdt. 1.56–8.
31. S. R. West (1991).
32. See below p. 37.
33. As Nino Luraghi points out (private communication), Herodotus' sly 'though I did not recite my genealogy' (why say this at all?) is in fact a forceful renunciation of Hecataeus' whole project of bridging the human and heroic ages. This and the priests' flat rejection of Hecataeus' account, as Herodotus imagines the encounter (either it is imagined, or he elicited their response during his own visit: either way, they are surrogates for Herodotus himself), make it hard to read the tone as other than denigrating. Whether the genealogy was given in the *Genealogy* or the *Periodos* is unknown; I think the former more likely. The latter could be the source of Herodotus' belief that Hecataeus visited Karnak. The wanderings of Hecataeus could also have been the subject of oral tradition (cf. the stories of his participation in the Ionian revolt); but it is extremely unlikely that this story as a whole, including the knowledge of Egyptian chronology so central to Herodotus' historical vision, circulated as an anecdote.

34. Vannicelli (2001).
35. Lateiner (1989) 104–8 compiles a list of passages in which Herodotus is disagreeing with a source, usually unnamed.
36. In addition to Pherecydes F 2 (next note) and Hecataeus T 4 (his own genealogy: above, p. 35), Acusilaus' discussion of the Homeridae (F 2) referred by implication at least to recent history. Writers of local histories such as Charon, Antiochus or Hellanicus are different: they will have started in the age of the founding or autochthonous heroes and brought the story down to their own time.
37. Thomas (1989) 161–73. Ruschenbusch (1995) argued that all the genealogies in Herodotus reaching from the heroic age to recent history derive from Pherecydes; criticism in Fowler (2001) 114 n. 34.
38. Fowler (2001); Rösler (2002).
39. Luraghi (2001b) 157–8. We may view Herodotus in this light, even if it is far from certain that he would have accepted the labels *logios* or *logopoios* for himself (Vannicelli (2001) 214–15); that refusal could, indeed, be part of the characteristic competitiveness of this group.
40. Luraghi (2001b) and in this volume.
41. F 1 *EGM*: 'Thus speaks Hecataeus of Miletus: I write what follows as it seems to me to be true; for the *logoi* of the Greeks are, as it seems to me, many and ridiculous.' For *logoi* in other proems cf. Antiochus F 2 *EGM*, Ion of Chios *Triagmos* (F 20 von Blumenthal = 114 Leurini), Alcmaeon of Croton, *VS* 24 B 1, Diogenes of Apollonia, *VS* 64 B 1, Hippoc. *On Ancient Medicine* 1.1, *On the Medical Art* 1 (above, p. 30), *On the Nature of Man* 1, *Regimen* I.1. Thucydides writes up the Peloponnesian War in the expectation that it will be *axiologōtatos*, most worthy of *logoi* (1.1).
42. Thomas (2000) 235–47; Dewald (2002); Brock (2003).
43. de Jong (2002); cf. Munson (2001a). I shall discuss the narratology of mythography in *EGM* II.
44. For an overview of the first three items see Fowler (1996); more recently, Bertelli (2001), Möller (2001), Raaflaub (2002a) 157–8. *To eikos* possibly already a tool for Hekataios (F 27a); for *opsis, akoē, gnōmē* see especially Hdt. 2.99; discussion in e.g. Lateiner (1989) (index s.vv.), Schepens (1980), Hussey (1990), Thomas (2000) (index s.vv.).
45. Hartog (1989); Bertelli (2001); van Wees (2002).
46. Luraghi (2001b); Hornblower (2002).
47. Thomas (2000) 175–90.
48. On this point Raaflaub (2002a) 181–2 is eloquent. But Dionysius still raises a tiny doubt (above, n. 24).
49. My best thanks to Nino Luraghi, Ellen O'Gorman, and the editors of this volume for beneficial comment.
50. I include only authors for whom there is reasonably reliable information as to their dates. There are others one might suspect were working early enough for Herodotus to have known them. Discussion in Fowler (1996). I do not accept that Hippys of Rhegium is an early writer: see *EGM* I.xxxvi; Pearson (1987) 8–10.
51. As transmitted by various sources; this is not the place to discuss the various problems attending such lists. For authors in *EGM* I, see the forthcoming commentary (*EGM* II). In general one suspects that the lists of works in medieval

encyclopaedias such as the *Suda* have been artificially lengthened by fictitious or duplicate titles.

52. *EGM* I is the most recent edition, but gives only mythographical fragments; where other kinds of fragments survive, these are to be found in the other edition named.

53. None of these early titles is apt to derive from the authors themselves.

54. Some scholars think this a mistake for 'Inside' or even 'Inside and Outside'. Perhaps behind the first two titles lies a single work describing the circuit of the Mediterranean in one roll and of the Indian Ocean in the next; the titles were added later, with predictable confusion.

55. Herodotus mentions this man's role in the Ionian revolt (5.121). If genuine, this title must denote a proto-historical work.

56. See Rusten (1982) 68–74 who shows that *FGrHist* 32 F 42 (*apud* schol. Ap. Rhod. 1.1116), attributed by Müller and Jacoby to Scytobrachion, is certainly by the Milesian. The five fragments appear to give not only geography of Persian-controlled areas, but history (see above p. 34). Of the transmitted titles, if 'Events in the Time of Darius (*ta kata Dareion*)' is a correct emendation, the first three could be alternatives for the same work; *Troica* one suspects is a spurious attribution.

57. The first five names in the list are put in the first, oldest group of writers by Dion. Hal. *Thuc.* 5 = Hec. T 17a *EGM*, who 'lived before the Peloponnesian War'; the next four are a little later, alive 'a little before the war and down to the time of Thucydides'. In some cases we are able to supplement his meagre data from other sources. The last five are not mentioned by him at all.

58. Both forms of the name are transmitted with equal authority.

59. The first thirteen works (assuming all these titles denote discrete works) treat the major branches of the traditional mythical genealogies, but at least in some cases (egregiously, the *Atthis* or 'Attic History') bringing the story down to his own day, seemingly unaware of any difference between 'mythical' and 'historical' periods; the next seven works are ethnographical and geographical; the last three are chronographical.

60. Possibly rather by Polus of Acragas, who was still a young man in 427 BCE (testimonia in Fowler [1997] 27–34). The *Suda* also records a book *On Events in Greece*, but the title seems too vague; corruption is probable.

61. The fragments in *FGrHist* but not in *EGM* are probably to be attributed rather to the famous poet of this name; these record an additional title *Symmicta* ('Miscellany'; cf. Hippias' *Synagōgē*).

62. Although the book displays an active (conservative) political agenda, its title suggests a retrospective published after the death of Pericles in 429, about the same time as Herodotus' work. F 11 refers to the plague. Stesimbrotus has been suggested, somewhat adventurously, as the author of the Derveni papyrus. Janko (1997) 73–4, who believes Diagoras of Melos wrote the Derveni text, dates Stesimbrotus' *On Religious Rites* to the 430s.

3

JASPER GRIFFIN

Herodotus and tragedy

The ancient biographical tradition tells us that Herodotus spent time in Athens, and he was accused by some later Greeks of undue partiality to the Athenians.[1] He is described as especially a friend of Sophocles, who addressed to him, about 445–440 BCE, a poem of which a fragment survives.[2] Certain passages in Sophocles' extant work are clearly related to passages in Herodotus, and it seems certain that it was the tragedian who drew on the historian, not the reverse.[3]

It has been thought that it was his stay in Attica that made Herodotus into an historian, not a mere chronicler or antiquarian, and that the impact of tragedy was responsible for the moral interest of his work: 'Athens was his Damascus'.[4] He appears to emerge suddenly from a much less developed and sophisticated tradition of historical writing. 'Herodotus is an unaccountable phenomenon in the history of literature', says the perceptive Denniston;[5] 'he is in the direct line of succession to the logographers [early historical writers such as Hecataeus and Hellanicus]; but while they, apparently, had no technique at all, he had a technique at once effortless and adequate to any demands he chose to make upon it'. Nor is it simply a matter of style in the sense of arrangement of words, masterly as Herodotus is in that art, but of his conception and his scope.[6]

Some of the most productive influences on Herodotus were not prose writers but poets. A Greek critic famously called him 'very Homeric' ('Longinus' 13.3).[7] Tragedy itself is the daughter of the Homeric epic, and in the fifth century it was the most vital representative of that tradition, which depicted human action emerging from the interplay of divine and human actions and motivations. Tragedy also learned from Homer that heroes and heroines are highly articulate, and that great events cannot be presented and experienced without powerful speeches.[8] So too Herodotus transforms the story of Gyges and Candaules' wife (1.8–12) from a simple folktale pattern, by creating the crucial dialogue between Gyges and the queen: she faces him with a moral decision like that of Agamemnon at Aulis, deciding to sacrifice his daughter, or that of Orestes, confronting his wicked mother,[9] and the story takes on a tragic colour.

We can approach the question of tragedy and Herodotus from several directions.[10] Like the tragic poets, Herodotus starts from the myths; the heroes and heroines appear regularly.[11] He opens his history with reciprocal abductions of mythical heroines from Greece by Asiatics, and from Asia by Greeks: Io, Europa, Medea, Helen; that was the beginning of ill-will between the two continents (1.1–5). Gomme called that a 'humorous little preface', but the stern Felix Jacoby long ago expressed the hope that people would soon stop finding humour there.[12] Three of these mythical princesses appear in extant tragedies, *Prometheus Vinctus*, *Medea*, *Helen* and *Troades*, and the fourth, Europa, appeared in at least one lost play.[13] We find the Argonauts (4.145, 179); the three sons of Temenus, of whom the youngest won a kingdom (8.137–8); Cleisthenes, tyrant of Sicyon, who refused to honour the Argive hero Adrastus, one of the Seven against Thebes, and instituted instead the cult of his enemy Melanippus the Theban (5.67). The Spartans claim the leadership of the Peloponnese as the heirs of Agamemnon (whom Homer never calls a Spartan); they find and bring back the bones of his son Orestes (1.67–8),[14] and they inform Gelon, the great tyrant of Syracuse, that Agamemnon would turn in his grave, if the Spartans were to be under the command of a Syracusan (7.159).[15] Before Plataea the leaders of the contingents from Athens and Tegea dispute for the position of honour in the battleline, and both sides argue from the deeds of their ancestors[16] in the mythical period (9.26–7).[17]

Even the Persians are drawn into the game. Xerxes claims the land once possessed by Pelops the Phrygian (7.8.3), mythical immigrant from the East who gave his name to the Peloponnese; he tours the site of Troy and makes offerings there to Athena of Troy and to the heroes (7.43.1–2). One story told that he wrote to Argos, claiming kin, as the Persians descended from Perseus (7.150, cf. 7.61); as for the Medes, they themselves, says Herodotus, claim to take their name from Medea (7.62.1). An astute Persian takes advantage of a Greek myth to trick the king.[18]

All this points not only to tragedy specifically; the text of Herodotus, like his world, is soaked in the myth. It was worth the while of the Athenians to invoke Boreas before Artemisium, reminding the North Wind that he had married an Athenian princess;[19] it was worthwhile to send a war ship to Aegina before Salamis, to fetch Aeacus and the Aeacidae (8.64, 83.2). Occasionally Herodotus shows signs of a very different attitude, dismissing the people of myth as simply different, or as beyond the reach of proper knowledge,[20] but more usually his attitude seems to be one of acceptance. They were part of reality.

We see also that many of the typical situations of the tragic stage recur in Herodotus' *Histories*. The motif of suppliants begging for their lives[21] is not prominent in early lyric or in epic. It is, however, central to Attic tragedy. It poses acute and inescapable moral decisions. We may compare the plea of the chorus in Aeschylus' *Supplices* ('If you do not defend us – at the risk of war – we will hang ourselves at the images of your gods!' 455–67), with Herodotus' extensive treatment of the story of Pactyes (1.157–61): the god apparently agrees that the people of Cyme should surrender the suppliant – but only so that by this wicked act they may bring on themselves destruction. Homer does not depict suppliants taking refuge at altars. The scene had strong visual appeal, which suited it particularly for the theatre.

The historian shares with the tragedians a liking for other scenes that involve fearful moral choices. One is self-sacrifice to death: Evadne in Euripides' *Supplices*, Iphigenia in *Iphigenia in Aulis*, Menoeceus in *Phoenissae*, noble princesses in *Heracleidae* and *Erechtheus*; and in Herodotus the mutual killing of the people of Xanthus (1.176), the self-immolation of Hamilcar in the sacrificial flames (7.166), Themistocles persuading Eurybiades to stand and fight at Salamis (8.60–3), and, above all, the heroic decision of Leonidas (7.205) and of the seer Megistias (7.219, 221) to die at Thermopylae.[22]

Sacrilege is another theme important in both forms.[23] At a supreme moment of the *Histories* Themistocles declares that the defeat of Xerxes was the work of the offended gods and heroes, who would not allow one man to rule both Europe and Asia, and especially a blasphemer like Xerxes, who treated sacred things just like profane ones, burning and destroying the shrines of the gods, and presuming to brand and chain the sea (8.109.3). Like the cognate theme of the sack of cities,[24] it is weighty also in tragedy, for instance in *Agamemnon*, *Troades*, and *Bacchae*. Madness is another specially favoured theme: mad Cambyses and crazy Cleomenes (3.30; 5.72.3; 6.66.2–3, 6.75.3, 79–81) can stand beside raving Io and Heracles and Pentheus (*Prometheus Vinctus*, *Heracles*, *Bacchae*).

The great theme of revenge, one to which every bosom returns an echo, is pervasive in both.[25] Heaven, we are assured, will punish excessive savagery in vengeance.[26] The gruesome themes of human sacrifice and of cannibalism occur in both; so does that of refusal of burial to the dead.[27] The tragic motif that 'the dead are killing the living!' (*Choeph*. 886; Soph. *Ajax* 661–5, 815–19, 1026–7; *El*.1420–2) occurs at 3.128; 7.137; 9.64; see also 8.114. The Thyestean banquet, in which an unwary victim devours the flesh of his dearest kin, is familiar to Herodotus as to the tragic stage (1.73.5, 1.119; cf. also 3.11). We observe that most of these themes of horror are scrupulously avoided by Homer. Nor are they characteristic of the lyric. It is in fifth-century authors, both dramatic and historical, that we find them prominent. In these anxious themes Herodotus is closely linked with the tragic poets.

The exposure of a baby and his eventual return, not without disastrous consequences, is a regular mythical motif, in tragedy meeting us in *Oedipus Tyrannus*, in the *Alexandros* of Euripides and Sophocles (the exposure and return of Paris), and in *Ion*. Herodotus gives the ancient motif extended treatment in the rise of Cyrus the Persian, who comes from nowhere to overthrow the kingdom of Lydia (1.95–130). His Cyrus sounds like Sophocles' Oedipus when he says 'I consider that I was born by divine chance . . .' (1.126.6): compare *Oedipus Tyrannus* 1080, 'I regard myself as the son of Chance which gives good things.'[28]

Herodotus has an enormous canvas, from Massilia to India and from Scythia to the cataracts of the Nile, from the predecessors of the Persian Empire to the battle of Mycale; but he has also a synoptic view of his theme, and for all his digressions[29] he carries his audience along with one of his central themes: the clash of nations and cultures.[30] But often the political or military outcome is less interesting than its illumination of human character and destiny.

He creates a gallery of men with stories which remain in the memory. Most of them are, in the popular sense of the word, 'tragic': the doom of Polycrates, who – like King Agamemnon – after all his splendour (*megaloprepeiē*) through his own folly met a death so unworthy of him and his aspirations (3.125.2); Croesus, who aspired to be the most blessed of mankind, and who lost his son and his kingdom; Periander of Corinth, who killed his wife and was cursed by his son (3.50–3)[31] – all these stories are grim. The tale of Lycophron, Periander's son, who refused to speak to his father for having killed his mother, and who was driven to an outlaw existence, cut off from human contact (3.50–3), has been compared with the situation of Sophocles' Electra and with that of Shakespeare's Hamlet.[32] The Phrygian Adrestus, who fulfils destiny by inadvertently killing the son of his benefactor Croesus (1.35–45), has been likened to Sophocles' Oedipus.[33]

The fall of Sardis itself is less interesting than the destiny of King Croesus;[34] Samos, which possesses 'three of the greatest works of all the Hellenes' (3.60.1), is overshadowed by the story of Polycrates; the narration of the Persian conquest of Egypt reaches its climax in the moral tale of the testing of Psammenitus and its effect on Cambyses (3.14–15.1): like Cyrus facing the defeated Croesus, even mad Cambyses feels pity (1.86.6; 3.14.11). Crucial to Thermopylae are the resolution and defiance of Leonidas and Megistias (7.219–21). The whole story of the expedition of Xerxes itself is, in one vital aspect, the story of divine temptation, superhuman presumption and aspiration, and eventual defeat and despair (7.17; 8.109.3). That is very Aeschylean. In the *Oresteia* we hear of the compulsion applied by destructive Persuasion, child of Ruin, which plans ahead. That is: the divine impels man, by a temptation too strong to be resisted. We are close here to the world of *Macbeth*.[35] Xerxes' story is completed by a gruesome episode, placed conspicuously at the very end of the *Histories*: a fearful story of sexual crime and disaster within his own family, which will be avenged by his son (9.108–13).[36]

That story centres on the strong and hate-filled figure of Xerxes' queen, who forces her wretched husband to choose between public disgrace and giving her his paramour's mother, perfectly innocent in the affair, to mutilate; her action precipitates further destruction within the royal family. It echoes the opening story of Book 1, in which the strong and angry queen of King Candaules forces the unhappy Gyges to choose between murdering his master and dying himself (1.8–11). In each the man finds himself impaled on the horns of a dilemma, recalling such tragic choices as that forced on King Agamemnon at Aulis (Sacrifice your daughter Iphigenia or forfeit your leadership and betray the mission of Zeus to punish Troy!), and on his son Orestes (Avenge your father – by killing your mother!);[37] while the fearsome queens are akin to tragic women like Aeschylus' Clytemnestra and Euripides' Medea.

Acute observers had noted the resemblance between the story of Candaules' wife and an Attic tragedy. In 1950 a fragment of papyrus, part of a tragic treatment of that very theme, seemed to confirm it: the angry queen relates how she saw Gyges slip out of the room, saw that her husband was awake and unconcerned, understood his plot, 'bridled in silence my cry of dishonour', and after a sleepless night summoned Gyges for the fateful interview. Here, perhaps, was the very play which had served Herodotus as a source.[38] But most scholars now think the piece was composed much later, under the influence of – and largely paraphrasing – Herodotus.[39] That, however, does not dispose of the kinship between the Herodotean narrative and fifth-century tragedy: the concentration in Herodotus on the choice of Gyges, the interplay of free will and compulsion, is surely itself influenced by tragedy.

Some story was needed to explain Gyges' unexpected rise to power. One day, the great Eastern monarch was Candaules; then suddenly it was this new man, Gyges. How did it happen? Two other versions exist. In one, made famous by Plato,[40] Gyges was a herdsman who found a ring of invisibility. So equipped, he killed the king and secured the queen. That is a universal wish-fulfilment motif. The other version goes back to a fifth-century source, the annalist Xanthus of Lydia.[41] It presents Gyges as the trusted servant whom the king sends to fetch his bride. Like Tristan, Gyges falls in love with her himself, but she rejects his advances and denounces him to the king, who plans to put him to death in the morning. A maid-servant, enamoured of Gyges, warns him of his danger, and he kills the king in his sleep.

It is obvious how much simpler these versions are. In the former, Gyges simply acts out a universal fantasy: if only we could at will be invisible! In the second, he is a guilty man who seizes a chance to save his skin. Neither has the moral interest of Herodotus' version, in which Gyges first tries and fails to escape from the king's foolish plan and then finds himself in another moral bind: 'he implored her not to compel him to choose between such alternatives' (1.11.3).

Gyges is essentially innocent, forced – like Aeschylus' Agamemnon or Orestes – to make a disastrous choice. He is an agent in the ruin of his master, which itself is fated, 'since Candaules was destined to come to a bad end' (1.8.2); the judgement, which at one level means no more than 'This is what, in fact, happened to him', at another suggests the more mysterious doom language of tragedy: one might think of *Oedipus Tyrannus*. That interplay of personal responsibility and divine compulsion is central to tragedy. And, finally, the grim reckoning. Gyges' descendant Croesus will pay for his ancestor's sin (1.13.2; 1.91.1). In tragedy we think of the accursed houses of Atreus and of Laius. We are in that world, and the vividness of the snatches of dialogue is not unworthy of the tragic stage.

More extensive and more important is the story of Croesus. Herodotus offers an explanation for its prominence: whatever may be the case with the abducted heroines of myth, Croesus is 'the first man whom I myself know to have initiated aggression against the Greeks', and, emphatically, 'the first barbarian known to us who reduced some Greeks to tributary status while making others his friends . . . Before the reign of Croesus, all Greeks were free' (1.5.3, 1.6.2). It turns out immediately that this is not true. Croesus' predecessors all did the same. Gyges himself attacked Miletus and Smyrna and took the city of Colophon; his successor Ardys took Priene and attacked Miletus; his successor took Smyrna and invaded Clazomenae; and so on (1.14.4ff.). Jacoby speaks of 'a flagrant contradiction'.[42]

Herodotus wants to open his *Histories* with Croesus, and he justifies the transition plausibly ('this is where it all began'). But why Croesus? Because he was great and yet failed, and his failure illuminates the nature of man and his relation to the divine. His success tempts him to go too far, to forget the limits set for human kind; and so he comes to grief. He is, in fact, a precedent for the career of Xerxes.[43] But the story of Croesus, no mere stylistic flourish, should help us to understand the true significance of events. It is a tragedy.[44]

The story of Croesus is full of oracles, and he is a great figure at Delphi. That adds to his attraction for Herodotus, who is familiar with Delphi, keenly interested in oracles, and generous with their introduction.[45] They are also a great feature of tragedy; *Oedipus Tyrannus*, in which the whole action is announced by Delphi in advance, is an extreme instance. Oracular utterances are important in most extant plays. Prophets and prophecies appear regularly, along with dreams,[46] omens, and curses. All these supernatural devices, both in tragedy and in Herodotus, have a two-fold function. On the one hand, they establish the actions depicted as significant: not just something that happened, they were predicted, dreaded, evaded, and in the event came ineluctably to pass. Secondly, they show the interest of the divine and illuminate its workings.

The life story of Sophocles' Oedipus, predicted, foreknown, and (as far as humanly possible) evaded, is a fearful revelation of the working of the world and the fragility of human life: the point is made explicitly by the chorus.[47] The oracular predictions that accompany the career of Croesus bring out the same point. He is secure 'until a mule shall foal'; by attacking Cyrus he will 'destroy a great kingdom': and the oracles are fulfilled, and he and his kingdom are ruined. In the tragedy of *Ajax*, it is predicted that if he could survive this present day, all would be well; to mortal vision that seems to mean that he can be saved, but in the divine perspective it means that his doom is fixed for today, and we are not surprised that the next scene is that of his suicide.[48] In the *Trachiniae* Heracles has received a prediction that 'this present season' will release him from his labours; that turns out to mean his death.[49]

So in Herodotus Cambyses expects not to die until he reaches Agbatana, and assumes that means the city in Media; discovering that the place of his sickness is actually called Agbatana, though in Syria, he understands[50] and accepts his death (3.64). So King Cleomenes of Sparta had a prophecy that he would take Argos; at war with that city, he burned a grove sacred to a hero whose name turned out (too late!) to be Argos, and immediately cried 'Apollo of prophecy, how you have deceived me, saying that I should take Argos! I understand that the prophecy is fulfilled.' And he marched his men back to Sparta; and he was prosecuted for sparing the city of Argos for a bribe; and he told this story, with another about a supernatural omen, 'whether truly or falsely', says Herodotus, 'I cannot reliably make out'; and his account seemed to the Spartans credible and reasonable; and he was acquitted by a large majority (3.74–82). Such a story is highly suggestive for the world of Herodotus. It remains true and important that the historian brings a cultural and rational approach to such a story; that marks his treatment off from the normal style of tragic poetry.

Croesus is magnificent, he honours Delphi more splendidly than any man. Naïvely he tells the wise Greek Solon that he believes himself to be supreme in felicity, disregarding the fact that, as Solon tells him, the divine is jealous and destructive; the days of man's life are many, and any one of them may bring something quite new; and 'man is altogether a matter of chance' (1.32). Xerxes, too, who flogged the sea and insulted it with 'words barbaric and monstrous' (7.35.2); Xerxes, who aspired to rule both Europe and Asia, and who laughed when he was told that the Greeks would not run away at the sight of his magnificent army (7.105): he too, in the end, will have to learn the hard lesson of humility. Look to the end of the story before you pass judgement, call no man happy until he is dead: the moral spelled out for Croesus by Solon (1.32.9) and only remembered by him when it is too late (1.86), the lesson read to Polycrates by Amasis (3.40), is frequent in tragedy: so speaks the chorus of *Oedipus Tyrannus* (1186–1222), so the wise Odysseus as he contemplates the ruin of Ajax (Soph. *Ajax* 125–6), so the sententious servant of Euripides' *Heracleidae* (865–6).[51]

One of Herodotus' great leitmotifs is the mutability of fortune and the fragility of human life.[52] He states it explicitly at the outset: 'Most of the cities that were once great are now small, while those that were great in my time had been small before. I understand that human prosperity is never constant, and in that knowledge I shall deal with states both great and small' (1.5). That is in line with what Xerxes utters to Artabanus, when he reviews his troops at Abydos and suddenly weeps to think that in a hundred years all those men will be dead. 'But even that', is the reply, 'is not the worst: short as men's life is, there is no man so happy that he does not often wish himself dead while he lives' (7.44–7). So too at dinner before Plataea a Persian notable tells Herodotus' informant with tears that of all that mighty host very soon few will be left alive, adding that divinely ordered necessity cannot be evaded, and that there is no pain equal to that of helpless knowledge (9.16). These Herodotean speakers invoke the gods as the ultimate explanation of this fearful alternation.

Tragic parallels are obvious. That mortals are the prey of divinely motivated reversals is the sad wisdom of *Oedipus Tyrannus*, and of Cassandra as she goes off to death at *Agamemnon* 1327–30. Athena says of the ruin of Ajax, 'Do you see how great is the power of the gods? Have you ever found anyone more far-sighted or more effective in action than Ajax here? . . . One day can bring down all that is mortal, and one day can build it up' (Soph. *Ajax* 118ff.). Herodotus' epitaph for Polycrates (3.125) has the same ring: Polycrates was a man of true grandeur, and he came to a miserable end – which was predicted in general terms by his Egyptian friend Amasis, and in detail in his daughter's dream (3.40; 3.124), exactly as if he were a character in a tragic drama, like Clytemnestra (Aesch. *Choephoroe* 32–41, 523–52), or Hecuba (Eur. *Hecuba* 30–3, 69–78). The fortunes of Euripides' Heracles, in the play named after him, or the laments of Hecuba and Polyxena and

Andromache, princesses of Troy, point the contrast of their past prosperity and present misery.[53]

Is Herodotus influenced by tragedy in the technique of constructing and narrating episodes, as well as in his selection of themes? Sometimes a resemblance can be seen: the story of Gyges and his fatal choice has been analysed in such terms.[54] But the historian, with his larger scale and longer perspective of the connections of events, often interrupts what might have been a straightforwardly tragic narrative by inserting material of other kinds. Thus the history of Croesus is made to include a substantial account of the power of Athens and Sparta (1.53–70), with the link – a thin one – that Delphi told Croesus to ally himself with the two leading Greek powers; he found that they were Athens and Sparta; now, their history . . . So, too, the grim tale of Periander of Corinth is artfully divided between two widely separated contexts (3.48–53; 5.92), both concerned with Spartan and Athenian history. Nothing can be less like the concentrated manner of tragedy, and the historian does not lose sight, in his most engrossing episodes, of the structure and significance of the great whole. And, as Herodotus says himself (4.30), digression is a central part of his technique.[55] Such a manner is far removed from that of the Attic tragedians.

The alternation of conversation and narrative, so central to Herodotus' *Histories*, recalls the style of the *Iliad* and *Odyssey* rather than the division of a tragedy into speech and song; the explicit moral comments and lessons are drawn, not by a chorus, but either by characters (e.g. 1.32, Solon, endorsed by Croesus, 1.86; 1.207, Croesus again; 3.40, Amasis; 7.10, 7.46, Artabanus) or by the historian himself (e.g. 1.5, human prosperity is fragile; 2.3, all peoples have equal insight into religion; 3.38, only a mad man attacks other people's beliefs; 5.78, Athenian history shows the value of democracy; 8.77, I reject attacks on the value of oracles).

Nor is it in the manner of tragedy to offer several explanations and leave the audience to choose (e.g. 3.122.1, downfall of Polycrates; 3.32, death of Cambyses' queen; 3.85–7, Darius' accession). Tragedy likes to juxtapose pairs of contrasting speeches, pro and con, regularly following them with close argumentation in single-line utterances (*stichomythia*);[56] Herodotus never imitates *stichomythia*, he sometimes gives only very short speeches, and he may create a confrontation, not of two, but of three (3.80–2, on the best type of constitution). His technique is more like that of Homer; it is his moral concerns which resemble those of tragedy.

In conclusion, let us consider the one striking case in which we actually have a tragedy on the same theme as a memorable passage in Herodotus.[57] In 472 Aeschylus presented his *Persae*, which includes a vivid account of the battle of Salamis, fought only eight years before (249–531). Herodotus gives a much more detailed account (8.56–96). The historian begins with the Greeks in panic, resolving to abandon Attica and fight only at the Isthmus of Corinth; they must be persuaded to reverse that disastrous decision by the eloquence of Themistocles, using arguments taken (without acknowledgement) from somebody else (8.58.2). Arguments and insults are exchanged (8.61), the Peloponnesians are anxious to sail off home (8.74). In the end Themistocles contrives to induce the Persians, by sending them a tricky secret message, to encircle Salamis, so that the Peloponnesian Greeks cannot leave, even if they want to (8.75–6), and he must get the news announced by Aristides, the only Athenian anyone trusted, for it to be believed (8.80). Even after the battle there were recriminations (8.94).

All this shady stuff, besmirching the radiance of Our Finest Hour, still distressed Plutarch centuries later;[58] no trace of it appears in Aeschylus' play, which presents the Greeks as united, sailing out together for battle in determined mood (Persae 384–411). The wrangling and dissension were too complex for tragedy, too 'political' in the wrong sense; they blurred the clear contrast of Greek and barbarian, and the purposes of heaven.[59] So, too, the Greek ships do not in Persae, as they do in Herodotus, back water and use complex manoeuvres: they sail straight at the foe. Details of individual achievements are not for the austere taste of tragedy, which will not even name Themistocles. Of his message to the Persians we hear that 'an *alastor* or some evil spirit appeared and began the disaster: a man came from the Athenian camp with a message . . .' (353–68),[60] arriving before nightfall in Aeschylus, but after dark in Herodotus (8.75).[61]

The tragic poet presents a simplified and streamlined version of the battle. Herodotus emphasises the role of geography in the general defeat of Xerxes,[62] and in the battle he pays attention to the topography and its effects; that suits his purposes, as Aeschylus' neglect of it suits his. The historian has made the battle one element in a long, complex, and exciting narrative, the whole story of the clash of East and West, from Croesus the Lydian to Xerxes, by way of Cyrus and Darius, of Marathon and Thermopylae, to the crowning mercy of Plataea; it has involved excursuses of every kind, on prehistory, geography, mythology, ethnography, the Nile, the phoenix, the city of Babylon, the history of Cyrene and Sparta and Athens and Egypt. The divine purpose has always been there, but often it has been occluded by material of many other kinds. The narrower focus of Aeschylean tragedy needs only the one crucial encounter to bring out the manifest purpose of heaven. The divine led Xerxes into his arrogant venture; it deceived him (Persae 107, 353–68, 472, 724); and it planned his ruin.

That is a part of Herodotus' story, too, but only a part. As powerful as tragedy, in its own more spacious and apparently leisurely way, it does not pierce the reader with the plangent shrieks and exotic gestures of the *Persae*, appropriate to a short and intense experience in the theatre. But it, too, shows the tricky deception of God, which no man is nimble enough to escape: *Atē*, infatuation, smiles winningly on a man at first, and leads him into the net; once in it, he can never escape (*Persae* 93–100). In that dark vision, tragedian and historian are at one.

FURTHER READING

For the themes and concerns treated here see further Asheri (1993); Chiasson (1980); Fohl (1913); Fowler (1996); Gould (1989); Ostwald (1991); Powell (1939); and Vandiver (1991).

NOTES

1. See Gould (1989) 14-18; Ostwald (1991). It is striking that Herodotus uses a stretch of the Attic coastline as a measure to explain the dimensions of part of Scythia, adding an alternative comparison 'for anyone who has not sailed along this part of the Attic coast', 4.99.4–5; cf.2.7; 6.131; 7.139.
2. *IEG* II.166, F5. On Herodotus and Sophocles see further Dewald and Kitzinger in this volume.
3. Powell (1939) 34; see now West (1999) for a convincing proof in the especially vexed case of *Antigone* 904-24; also Finkelberg (1995) on Herodotus as the source of *Trachiniae* 634–9.
4. Aly (1921/1969) 278. Herodotus only once uses the word *tragikos*, of 'tragic choruses' (5.67.5), performing not in Athens but in Sicyon, in the sixth century. They were doubtless unlike Attic tragedy.
5. Denniston (1952) 5. Compare Fowler (1996) and in this volume.
6. Aristotle in the *Poetics* devotes a chapter, not perhaps his happiest, to arguing that Herodotus is absolutely an historian, not a poet: 1451a36ff. See the penetrating criticism of Gomme (1954) 73–94; cf. Marincola in this volume.
7. On Homer and Herodotus see Marincola in this volume.
8. Regenbogen (1961) 80–91 speaks of the division into speech and action, *Wort und Tat*, inherited from epic and tragedy by Herodotus, which his authority made standard for later Greek and Roman historians. Compare Griffin (2004).
9. Aesch. *Ag.* 192–257; *Cho.* 892–930.
10. Herodotus mentions by name the tragic poets Phrynichus (6.21) and Aeschylus (2.156.6), both of earlier generations.
11. Vandiver (1991).
12. 'The fashion for seeing jokes in these chapters will surely pass', Jacoby (1913) 484.15ff. 'The material of Greek legend, but reshaped against its proper spirit: the tone <is> ironic, not heroic', observes Karl Reinhardt (1960) 152. Contemporaries did see the comical side: Aristophanes burlesques the passage in *Acharnians* 524–9; cf. the treatment of Dewald in this volume.
13. On Aeschylus' *Carians or Europa* see *TrGF* III, F 99.

14. Boedeker (1993).
15. 7.159, closely echoing the wording of a passage in the *Iliad*: 7.125.
16. Thucydides ostentatiously makes his Athenians, in a comparable situation, explicitly disclaim any appeal to 'very ancient events, for which we have only hearsay to go on, not the evidence of our eyes': 1.73.2.
17. We might also mention such episodes as 5.94.2, land claimed by descendants of men who fought at Troy; 7.169.2, Cretans dissuaded from fighting the Persians by Delphi, in the light of their actions at the time of the Trojan War; 7.197, Xerxes hears a long story about the descendants of Phrixus.
18. Artaÿctes (9.116) asks to be allowed to expropriate 'the estate of a Greek who attacked your land' – meaning Protesilaus, who died at Troy.
19. 7.189; cf. F 3 of the new Simonides (*IEG* II.115). The story seems to have been dramatised by Aeschylus: the evidence does make it likely that he composed an *Oreithyia*, cf. *TrGF* III, F 281; a play of the same name by Sophocles seems less likely.
20. 1.5 (mythical heroines, different from 'what I know', namely, events of the sixth century); 3.122, Minos, opposed to 'what is called the generation of men'; 6.53.2, genealogy must stop with Perseus, for whom only a divine, not a mortal, father is named.
21. Compare the classic article of Gould (1973). In Herodotus, e.g. 1.158f., Pactyes; 3.48, Corcyraean boys on Samos; 5.51, Aristagoras; 5.71, Cylon; 6.108.4, Plataeans; 7.141, Athenians at Delphi; 8.53.2, Athenians on the Acropolis. In tragedy: Orestes in *Eumenides*; the family of Heracles in *Heracles* and *Heraclidae*; Polynices in *Oedipus Coloneus*; the choruses of the *Supplices*, both of Aeschylus and Euripides; etc.
22. Compare also 3.75, devotion (despite ill-usage) of Prexaspes.
23. For example, 3.27–30, Cambyses; 5.72.3, 6.66.2, 6.75.3, 6.79–81, 6.84, Cleomenes; 8.32, 33, 53.2, Persians; 9.36–9, attack on Delphi; 9.65, Eleusinian deities. Again, the theme is very muted in Homer.
24. For example, 1.162–5, 169 (cities of Ionia), 4.201–2, 6.101 (Eretria), 6.18–21 (Miletus), 8.53 (Athens); in tragedy, the sack of Troy (*Agamemnon, Andromache, Hecuba, Troades, Helen*); of Oechalia (*Trachiniae*); of Thebes (*Septem*). As with the motif of sacrilege, the bitter experience of the sack of Athens by Xerxes is always in the background.
25. Clytemnestra, Medea, Hecuba, the Danaids, and of course the vengeful deities (especially goddesses): Athena in *Ajax*, Aphrodite in *Hippolytus*, Hera in *Heracles*, Dionysus in *Bacchae*. In Herodotus, Candaules' wife; Phanes, 3.11; Pheretime, 4.202–5; Hermotimus' vengeance on Panionius, 'the greatest vengeance taken by any man we know of', 8.105–6. Compare Gould (1989), index, s.v. 'revenge'.
26. Pheretime, 4.202–5. The endings of Euripides' *Heracleidae* and *Hecuba* make the same point.
27. Soph. *Antigone, Ajax*, Eur. *Supplices*; Hdt. 7.238, Leonidas; 9.75, Mardonius.
28. Immerwahr (1966) 165.
29. 'My History (*logos*) has been on the lookout for digressions from the beginning', 4.30.1; 'The art of Herodotus in the arrangement of material lies in the manner and the placing of his digressions', Jacoby (1913) 380.43f. On digressions see also in this volume Bakker, Griffiths, and Fowler at n. 12.

30. Herodotus was sometimes reproached as *philobarbaros*, too fond of barbarians. Early tragedy, too, had a marked taste for barbarians and the exotic, from Phrynichus' *Phoenissae* and *Egyptians* to Aeschylus' *Persians* and *Choephoroe*; cf. Hall (1989).

31. Sourvinou-Inwood (1988) 167–82 well brings out the mythical patterns in this story.

32. Aly (1921/1969) 94.

33. Carrière (1966) 17–18.

34. Aly (1921/1969) 38.

35. 'All remedy is fruitless, he is like a child chasing a bird in flight', and the result is disaster for the community (*Agam.* 385–98). Compare also *Persae* 93–100. So Macbeth is led on by prophecies and omens into crime, despair, and destruction.

36. 9.108–13, and Wolff (1964). This story and its later sequel, known to Herodotus' contemporary audience, has resemblances to that of Thyestes and Atreus, and to that of Semele, both treated in tragedy.

37. They are not alone in Aeschylean tragedy. We think of the king in the *Suppliants*, forced to accept the daughters of Danaus, at the price of a war in which he will himself be killed; of Eteocles in the *Septem*, choosing to fight the invader of his country, his own brother. In Sophocles we recall the dilemmas of Antigone and Electra; in Euripides, of those who volunteer for sacrifice – Macaria, Menoeceus, Iphigenia; or of the weak Agamemnon of *Hecuba* or *Iphigenia in Aulis*, beset on all sides, like the weak Menelaus of *Orestes*, or the weak Orestes of his *Electra*.

38. So Page (1951), an influential publication; the fragment is now in *TrGF* II, F 664. The editors do not commit themselves on the question of the date: 'You would not be more surprised by the survival till the second or third century of a play from the age of Aeschylus than by that of one by a member of the [Hellenistic] Pleiad', they observe, guardedly.

39. Lesky (1953).

40. Plato, *Republic* 359c-e. On these stories see Schadewaldt (1934) 409–13 = Marg (1982) 112–17.

41. The narrative: Nicolaus of Damascus, *FGrHist* 90 F 47.

42. Jacoby (1913) 338.55. He explains it by assuming that originally Herodotus composed a separate account of Lydia, a Lydian *logos*, only later incorporating it in the present *Histories*. That recalls the fashion in Germany in the late nineteenth century for supposing that the first four books of our *Odyssey* originally were a separate *Telemachy*: an epic poem in which no heroic event occurred. . . . But it is fair to see Herodotus distinguishing mere temporary raids for booty from permanent occupation and regular taxation.

43. Hellmann (1934); cf. Gould (1989) 121–5, who is good on the importance of the resemblance between the Croesus and Xerxes narratives, allowing for the fact that Herodotus has more, and more accurate, information about Xerxes, who is so much nearer his own time.

44. Compare Waters (1971) 86–100.

45. Kirchberg (1964); Asheri (1993).

46. Frisch (1968).

47. *OT* 1186–96: 'O generations of men, how I count your lives as amounting to nothing! . . . . Taking your destiny as a paradigm, poor Oedipus, I call no mortal man happy.'

48. Soph. *Ajax* 748–82; Diller (1950) 10–11.
49. Soph. *Trach.* 1164–72. The oracle is slightly different at 76–81, and 165–70, where it takes the form: at this time, *either* the end of his life *or* delivery from toil. It is noticeable that Sophocles includes many more oracles than were 'necessary' for the plot.
50. Herodotus says he 'sobered up', a rare thing indeed in his account of this maniac king; but we need him to sober up at this moment, or he will not understand the point of the divine trick.
51. Further references in tragedy in Wilkins (1993) *ad loc.*
52. Thus Solon to Croesus, 1.32.4; Croesus to Cyrus, 1.207.2: 'There is a cycle to the affairs of men, which does not allow the same people to be fortunate forever.' Compare Amasis to Polycrates, 3.40.3; Artabanus to Xerxes, 7.10ε, and again at 7.49.3: Events, not men, are the masters.
53. For example, Eur. *Andromache* 109ff., *Hecuba* 349ff., 475ff., *Troades* 577ff.
54. Page (1951) 7–12. Compare above, nn. 3 and 38.
55. See above, n. 29.
56. For example, Duchemin (1968); Lloyd (1992).
57. See Pelling (1997a); Hall (1996) 5–10.
58. Plutarch, *On the Malignity of Herodotus* 37–40 = *Moralia* 869c–71e.
59. Aeschylus does not mention, as Herodotus does, the contingents from Greek states which served in the Persian fleet: Hall (1996) on vv. 21–58.
60. Contrast 8.85, where Herodotus tells us of two Phoenician captains who distinguished themselves against the Greeks; 8.87, a clever exploit of Queen Artemisia of (Herodotus' own city of) Halicarnassus; and so on.
61. Pelling (1997a) 2–3 on Aeschylus' symbolic use of light and darkness.
62. Stated categorically at 7.47.2: Xerxes will have two things most strongly opposed to him – the land and the sea.

4

ROSALIND THOMAS

The intellectual milieu of Herodotus

The scope of the *Histories*, covering anthropology and geography, early origins and the grand narrative of Greek–barbarian relations culminating in the Persian Wars, is not to be found in any writer we know of before Herodotus.[1] The story of the Persian Wars themselves has been called 'the greatest continuous prose narrative in Greek literature, and a literary masterpiece',[2] but of course the *Histories* is more than a narrative, encompassing descriptions of virtually all the peoples of the known world. The *Iliad* and *Odyssey* could provide a model for narrative history, and remained the measure against which Herodotus and Thucydides set their histories. Herodotus opens with a promise to tell of the 'great and wondrous deeds' both of Greeks and of barbarians, to preserve the past before it gets forgotten, and show the cause (*aitiē*) of the conflict. That *aitiē* encompasses the many facets of the past, even the remote past, which could explain the Greek–barbarian conflict, and the past and present achievements, lands, peoples, customs, on either side.

It is not easy to pin down the antecedents of the *Histories*, still less the intellectual background. We can see points of contact between the *Histories* and certain Presocratic natural philosophers of the sixth-century Ionian Enlightenment, and they share a desire to make sense of the world in non-mythical and non-genealogical terms, which we could call 'rational'. Herodotus' contemporary world is also significant. A writer's background involves looking at earlier influences, but this can marginalise the question of interaction with or reaction to his contemporaries. This chapter, then, explores Herodotus' relation to and interaction with the intellectual writers of the generations before and contemporary with him. Because of constraints of space, 'intellectual milieu' is being taken in a fairly restricted sense, to encompass philosophers, intellectuals and sophists, though poets were the archaic *sophoi* of the Greek world, and dramatists in fifth-century Athens often played that role.[3] The *Histories* clearly answered in many ways to various contemporary ideas, fifth-century political and imperial developments, and the use and misuse of the Persian Wars as justification. Developments in 'science' and methods of argument and persuasion from around 450–420 were also highly relevant. Herodotus occasionally declares the truth of something against some unnamed opponent when it is likely that the contrary views are those of contemporaries. He states at 7.138–9 that he has to affirm an unpopular opinion, that the Athenians did most to win the Persian Wars. This gives a fascinating glimpse at his awareness of current conflicts, the political significance of such claims in the mid- and late-fifth century, and his willingness to offer unpopular opinions to a contemporary audience, which at least in this case was not envisaged as primarily Athenian.

Herodotus must have been researching and writing the *Histories* over a long period, perhaps from c. 450 onwards, and the final publication must be as late as the 420s to judge from references to the start of the Peloponnesian War. For instance, he mentions the reawakening of the wrath of Talthybius and the Athenian slaughtering of the heralds in 430 BCE, an episode recounted, with some differences, by Thucydides.[4] He was writing at the height of Athens' power and saw the start of the war. He was in exile for much of this period, a status which seems to help historians in the ancient world. Presumably he visited Athens, but he is also connected with Athens' colony Thurii by the very late *Suda* and by Aristotle; the identification of Herodotus with Athens and her fortunes has probably been exaggerated.[5] His home town was a Dorian city with Carian elements on the edge of both the Persian empire and the Athenian (it fought for the Persians in the Persian Wars under its enterprising queen Artemisia), and it participated in the circle of Ionian cultural and intellectual life, a life which was by no means defunct by the mid-fifth century. Herodotus would have been one of many writers from East Greece who were active in the second half of the fifth century, including the figures whose works were collected under the name of Hippocrates, and Hippocrates of Cos himself. In that respect too, then, he need not have depended on Athens alone for cultural and intellectual stimulation. Many writers, sophists, philosophers and doctors were peripatetic, and many in this period hailed from places across the Aegean – Protagoras of Abdera, Hippocrates of Cos, Oinopides of Chios, for instance. Democritus of Abdera connected his travelling with the search for wisdom: 'I covered more territory than any other man of my time, making the most extensive investigations; I saw the most climates and lands, and listened to many learned men' (*VS* 68 B 299). Though in exile much of his life, Herodotus was hardly a solitary or isolated figure able to encounter new ideas only in Athens.[6]

With his oral traditions, 'wonders' and the prominence of religious elements and explanation, Herodotus seems more rooted in the world of archaic Greece than his immediate successor Thucydides. His search for the distant roots of the confict as well as his voracity for tales of the past of all kinds mean that he had to use oral traditions, and these would inevitably become smoother and more schematic in the telling, not to mention 'deformed' by the later reasons for telling them.[7] He is usually associated by scholars with the earlier world of the late archaic and early classical period and (if at all) with figures such as Xenophanes, Heraclitus, Pythagoras, and the Milesian natural philosophers, as Gould's important study suggests.[8] He mentions Thales and Pythagoras, and the hints of relativism or awareness of relative values might be a legacy of Xenophanes. Xenophanes' criticism of Homer and Hesiod's gods as implausibly anthropomorphic may reappear in 1.131, Herodotus' account of Persian customs.[9] Less convincingly, Herodotus' emphasis on the fluidity and certainty of change in human affairs at the start of the *Histories* (1.5) and throughout has been linked to Heraclitean flux,[10] though awareness of the transience of prosperity was a common feature of Greek gnomic wisdom. His interest in the Nile's source and the explanation for its summer flooding connects with the discussions of the Ionian natural philosophers and Hecataeus, and Herodotus himself criticises a group he calls 'the Ionians' for their theories about Egypt: presumably he means the Milesians and Hecataeus. The comparison of the Nile delta with the flood plain of the Maeander along with the plain of Ilium, Teuthrania and Ephesus (2.10) betrays an Ionian perspective, and we know that Hecataeus discussed sedimentation (*FGrHist* 1 F 301).[11] His observations about fossils as signs that the land was previously sea are paralleled by Xenophanes' discussion of fossils (*VS* 21 A 33), and he may have been following Anaximander.[12] A rational explanation of dreams given to Artabanus (7.16.2) may be linked with Empedocles, though it might equally derive from later medical or sophistic theories.[13]

But he is selective: uninterested in the abstract or cosmological speculations about prime matter, whether Empedoclean or Heraclitean, he homes in on the theories about the physical make-up of the visible world and criticises them if he can. He seems to take considerable pleasure in attacking the more tangible and 'most ignorant' idea that the inhabited world is surrounded by Ocean, and that this explains the Nile flood, a view surely held by Hecataeus (2.21, 23):[14] 'he who talks about Ocean refers the question into the realm of the invisible, which therefore does not admit of refutation. For my part, I know of no river called Ocean.' He thinks 'Homer or some other of the earlier poets' put the name into their poetry. This illustrates beautifully Herodotus' preference for the tangible, the visible, and the empirically verifiable against abstract, 'invisible' speculations, as Lateiner has pointed out,[15] though it should be added that he goes on immediately to attempt his own explanation, admitting that he too has to delve into the realm of 'the invisible' to do so (2.24.1).

Herodotus' long section on the Nile's summer flooding (2.19–26), how-ever, also brings his *Histories* into close connection with later and contem-porary thinkers, one of the most striking examples of where he is explictly engaging in articulate debate with contemporary natural philosophers. For while the theory of Thales (unnamed) is rebutted in 2.20, Hecataeus' in 2.23, it is the theory of Anaxagoras (also unnamed) that the flood derives from melting snow which receives the longest and most careful critique, surely because Anaxagoras' theory, as the newest, was most worth rebutting. How could it possibly be flooding from melted snow, Herodotus asks, when the river would be flowing from hotter parts to colder (Ethiopia being obviously hotter than Egypt), and from a dry country in addition? Herodotus' own explanation involves the idea of the sun 'pulling up' the water and evaporat-ing it (2.24–7), and this has affinities to the theory of Diogenes of Apollonia, active in the late fifth century, and his method of reversing the question resembles that of Oinopides of Chios.[16] The atomist Democritus also had a theory, combining Anaxagoras' melting snow (but in the north) with the Etesian winds (*VS* 68 A 99). The length of Herodotus' own solution suggests that he pursues the problem partly because it aroused contemporary interest, and partly because any intellectual concerned with the natural world had to have a view on it. It is important to recollect that the speculations into the natural world carry on into the late fifth century and beyond, reappearing in the writings of Aristotle. In pursuing these matters, Herodotus was not simply looking backwards to early Presocratics.

Similar questions arise with Herodotus' other forays into describing or interpreting the natural world:[17] his lengthy descriptions of the Scythian rivers, his fascination with the Ister (Danube), which he sees as balancing the Nile; his remarks on the entry into Thessaly and the geography of Thes-saly, which prompts Xerxes' inquiries about rerouting the mouth of the river, and the comment that Thessaly was clearly once a lake, its gorge produced by an earthquake or, 'as some say', Poseidon (7.128–9); his attempt to trace what is known about the desert west of Egypt and into Libya (4.168ff.); and his descriptions of the fauna and flora of various places which he does particularly carefully for Libya (e.g. 4.191–2, 198–9), but equally for Egypt and Scythia. Since Jacoby, it is generally thought that here Herodotus was following the older genre of geography, the researches of previous genera-tions (especially Hecataeus) which belonged to an era before true history was invented.[18] There is something in this: geographical information was a main topic of Hecataeus' *Periegesis*, and of course of certain earlier Pre-socratics. Yet even in Hecataeus, the past, in the form of mythology, was equally important, and Herodotus seems to regard past stories and current geography as equally germane to his inquiries.

There is an interesting twist to this. The oddities of nature, of animals and plants as well as of geographical formations, went on forming a part of the intellectual discussion of the nature of the world, and a perusal of Aristotle's *History of Animals* or the Pseudo-Aristotelian *Problemata* reveals how the fascination with oddities was an important part of the process of explaining how nature worked. In the mid-fifth century too, Anaxagoras was said to have dissected a ram to show a natural, rather than divine, cause for its single horn (Plut. *Per.* 6), and similar lines of thought are prominent in the Hippocratic Corpus (e.g. *On the Sacred Disease* takes the much feared epilepsy and shows that there are natural causes for it; no disease is any more sacred than another). Herodotus has views on oddities of nature that demand an explanation: the Nile flooding is the outstanding natural 'wonder', but Herodotus is also curious about questions which come up in the course of the grand narrative, for instance why the lions of northern Greece only attacked the camels in Xerxes' army, and he has no answer; or about the fact repeated by Aristotle, that lions are only found in this relatively limited area (7.125–6). While these are often seen as symptomatic of Herodotus' naïve credulity or willingness to please his audience by feeding them examples of extraordinary *thōmata*, it is also possible to see these from another angle (and the two are not incompatible). Since it is the wonders which are out of the ordinary, their explanations would be part of the understanding of nature; the Nile flood, on one level a *thōma*, is also a test for successive writers to come up with a rational explanation, one explicable in terms of what was then thought about the workings of nature. There is a serious role, then, to the wonders of Herodotus, *as well as* (I stress) the amusing and pleasing one of giving his audience curiosities to marvel at. When Herodotus tells us that cattle do not grow horns in Scythia – but do in Libya – because of the cold (4.29–30.1), he is effectively using underlying and universal laws of nature to produce an explanation.[19]

A curiosity about nature was shared by early medical writers and even some sophists, and one of the most striking features of this period is the combination of interest in nature and in the human world, with theories to link them, a combination also striking in Herodotus. The *Histories* has links with certain early essays on medicine preserved in the Hippocratic Corpus, and here it begins to be very clear how misleading it is to think in terms of the conventional disciplines as they developed in the next generation or two. Certain areas of inquiry into the world of human society – for instance, customs and the relation between human society and climate – might equally be found among medical work, sophistic or philosophical, and fifth-century medicine was heavily endebted to the methods and ideas of the Presocratics.[20] There are hints at various points in Herodotus that he thought climate and geography had an important effect on the character of a people (though they were mediated in the end by custom and politics). The Ionians are singled out as living in the most beautiful position in the world, oppressed neither by cold and damp, nor by hot and dry (1.142.1–2), and of course they failed to resist the Persians successfully – though later he blames their unwillingness for exertion as their great weakness (6.11). The Greeks, especially the Spartans, had a hard life, and poverty made them hardy, brave warriors, whereas the Persians were initially successful in achieving freedom when they had come from a harsh land, 'for before they conquered the Lydians, the Persians had nothing either luxurious or good' (1.71), and they seem in Herodotus' schema to have become enervated by the luxuries resulting from their empire. Persian luxury is contrasted pointedly in the scene after the battle of Plataea where the victorious Greeks create a Persian banquet and a Spartan one, and then wonder why the Persians had ever bothered to invade Greece (9.82). The moral is important enough to form the final paragraph of the *Histories* (9.122), where Cyrus the Great, founder of the Persian empire, solemnly warned his fellow Persians not to expect to inhabit soft lands and remain rulers of men, for 'soft lands give rise to soft men' (9.122).[21]

In fact Herodotus ultimately emphasised the importance of custom and politics in human success, but such an interweaving of geography, ethnography and implied historical was prominent in Hippocratic theory. A similar combination occurs in the essay *Airs, Waters, Places*, one of the earliest pieces in the Hippocratic Corpus (late fifth century), which argues that human health is linked closely to climate and geography, the 'airs, waters, places' of the title, then links very schematically the ethnic characteristics of 'Europeans' and 'Asians' to the climate and geography of each continent. With breathtakingly broad brush, he claims that the evenness of the climate of Asia, without sudden changes, made 'Asians' (who include the Greeks of Asia Minor) more cowardly and less spirited than 'Europeans' (who include Scythians as well as mainland Greeks). Herodotus shares some ideas also current in an explicitly medical text, then, but it is a text which is probably part of a wider milieu of speculation about the nature of human society and different peoples.[22]

It is difficult to show either that Herodotus borrowed from *Airs* or vice versa, since ultimately they have radically different views of the parts of the world they concentrate upon, Libya, Scythia and Egypt. But perhaps what we are seeing is an area of inquiry into nature and human society that belonged not exclusively to the activities of any one group, but more commonly to the pursuit of 'science' in the sense of knowledge, *historiē* or inquiry, and *sophiē* or wisdom, in the later fifth century. After all, even *Airs* brought way of life (*diaita*) into the equation, and *nomos* too, which seems more characteristic of sophistic thought (*Airs* ch.16). At various points these inquiries into nature and human society touched the primary activities of intellectuals who thought of themselves primarily as doctors, or as 'sophists' or natural philosophers. Herodotus knows of this kind of theory and, I would argue, goes far beyond its extreme schematisation in his detailed descriptions of places and his historian's recognition of the importance of human agency and human motives.

He also shows a remarkable familiarity with a range of theories which can be specifically linked with Hippocratic medicine. He implies that he knows that epilepsy, 'which some call sacred' (3.33), was given natural explanations by some, and *On the Sacred Disease* did precisely this; he mentions the famous Scythian female disease, for which the author of *Airs* offered a natural explanation (1.105.4 and 4.67.2). He affirms that the health of the Egyptians was 'the best in the world after the Libyans' and that this was because of the seasons, not the diet, as the Egyptians claim (2.77.3). This touches two fifth-century Greek medical theories, for the Egyptians' theory that disease arose from food happens to correspond to one Greek medical theory, while the source of Egyptian health, and also of Libyan health, improved by cauterisation to prevent phlegm (4.187.3), corresponds closely to the theories of health explained in *Airs*. Herodotus' mention of phlegm here is the earliest example of phlegm appearing as a humour in Greek literature.[23] Herodotus seems both to be drawing on Hippocratic theory and contributing, or posing as contributing, to such theory himself, when he says that he does indeed think Egyptians were healthy because of the seasons, 'for it is with changes that diseases are most prone to occur, and most especially during changes of the seasons' (2.77.3). We begin to wonder if his interest in Egyptian diet, fasting and purging (2.77.2–4) is part of some wider theorising about human health, and if the 'ethnography of health' in which he has much interest represented a new intellectual trend in which non-Greeks were being brought in as samples to determine the common features crossing all peoples.

Egyptians have only doctors who are specialists (2.84). This comment, not strictly correct, alerts us to a further interesting feature in these apparent interweavings between Herodotus' interests and those of early medicine: the Greeks had known of Egypt as a source of medical lore as early as Homer and many standard ingredients of medical recipes were labelled as 'Egyptian'. It seems plausible, then, that Egypt formed a conventional part of Greek medical lore and that, in addition to its other fascinations, it featured in the late fifth-century speculations of early medical writers (and perhaps others) about the origins of human health. Libya and Scythia also featured in the debates about Hippocratic medicine, most obviously in *Airs*, so when

Herodotus devoted his longest descriptions to Scythia, Libya (both in Book 4) and to Egypt (Book 2), we strongly suspect that he did so partly because these were areas that already formed part of the Greek inquiries into the nature of the world and of human health, part of the world of contemporary science as well as older geography. To judge from later reactions to Herodotus, his accounts surpassed others in depth and thoroughness, and we may suspect that when he laboured a point or gave lengthy descriptions of an area he might be silently correcting contemporaries' misconceptions.[24]

So far it has been most illuminating to see the *Histories* not so much in terms of influence from one specific writer to Herodotus but in terms of intellectual groups and milieux – examining whether his treatment of a topic seems to share affinities or interests with groups of writers like the early medical writers. A similar approach is profitable when we turn to the sophists of the last half of the fifth century. The meagre fragments of the great sophists like Protagoras, Prodicus, or Hippias, leave us with a sense of fitting together many tiny pieces of a jigsaw most of which is missing, and much of the evidence from Plato's dialogues is distorted by his hostility to the sophists. Myres called Herodotus 'the only "Pre-socratic" writer who is preserved in full',[25] and a similar paradox might hold for the sophists, especially when we bear in mind that the very category of sophist in the fifth century was imprecise and that sophists such as Prodicus, Protagoras and Gorgias shared some methods and interests with medical writers and natural philosophers.[26] There are indications that Herodotus had familiarity with certain sophists and, more certainly, that he could use arguments and style that are more usually associated with the early developments of the sophists and that are also found in some of the more sophistic medical writers.[27] These categories are not hard-edged.

Of specific sophists, Protagoras stands out. Herodotus seems to echo the fragment from the opening of Protagoras' work *On the Gods* when he discusses the names and the forms (*eidea*) of the gods and expresses reservations about knowing them in Book 2 (2.3.2, 53.1; Protagoras, VS 80 B 4),[28] and another idea of Protagoras as described by Plato when Herodotus claims that it is by divine foresight (*pronoia*) that timid animals are prolific and fierce animals need have few offspring – though Protagoras' myth attributes the idea to Epimetheus (Hdt. 3.108.2; *Protagoras* 320d7ff.).[29] Protagoras' contribution to political thought was certainly important; there should be something at least behind Aristoxenus' late fourth-century claim that almost all Plato's *Republic* was to be found in Protagoras' *Antilogia*, and Plato's *Protagoras* at least suggests he had theories on the nature and origins of human societies, but without greater precision, we can only speculate how far any of this is reflected in Herodotus. The 'Constitutional Debate' that Herodotus attributes to the Persian conspirators (3.80–83) has often been linked with Protagoras though the links are only suggested by cumulative but rather flimsy evidence.[30] More securely, we know that Protagoras, like Prodicus and Democritus, was interested in the correctness of names, so Herodotus' interest in naming might be an example of his sharing a sophistic concern, or perhaps a fashionable topic that was of interest to both sophistic and medical writers.[31] There may be an echo of Protagoras' famous claim that he could make the weaker argument the stronger when the Persian Artabanus opens a speech with the words, 'O King, it is impossible to make a choice of the best if no arguments are uttered in opposition to one another' (7.10α.1). Similarly, Herodotus comments on Themistocles' speech urging the Greeks to fight: 'His speech throughout, contrasted the greater features which occur in human nature and the human condition with the weaker.'[32] Both vocabulary and expression seem reminiscent of Protagoras, and if they occurred in Thucydides they would surely be considered as referring to this new emphasis on antithetical argument, the Protagorean *antilogia*. Herodotus seems to echo the famous Protagorean development of *antilogiai* and the title of his *Truth or Refutations* (*Alētheia ē kataballontes*) when he affirms, 'I cannot deny (*antilegein*) that there is truth in oracles, not wanting to overturn/refute (*kataballein*) those which express themselves clearly, when I look at the following case' (7.77.1). However, he might also be picking up the new ideas and new methods or vocabulary that were 'in the air' at the time, influenced by Protagoras, and be using in a more general way the language of the *antilogiai*, argument and counter-argument popularised by Protagoras and other sophists.

This is not to suggest that Herodotus shared the extreme scepticism and radical espousal of the demands of Nature (*physis*) that become associated with the more provocative sophists: far from it. What is particularly interesting is the way he sometimes reveals that he knows of a particular extreme theory and makes clear that he rejects it, that is, he is part of the intellectual milieu that knew of at least some of these theories, but he kept his own views and in these was markedly more traditional and conservative than some of his peers (some literary criticism tends to forget that in classical Greece as in any other society there would have been a spectum of views around at any one time, and that not all writers would espouse the most radical). Such an example occurs in Book 2 where he says he does not agree with those who think animal behaviour gives an acceptable model for humans: the fact that animals may copulate in temples should not justify similar human behaviour, 'I do not agree with those who now defend their practice in this way' (2.64). This sounds like a fragment of a sophistic justification via the superiority of *physis*, the kind of argument parodied in Aristophanes' *Clouds*, and Herodotus knows of it but rejects it. Similarly when he declares that the travelling rumour of the Plataean victory across the sea just in time for the battle of Mycale *does in fact show* that the divine is active in the lives of men (9.100–101). He is aware others thought otherwise – we might think of the sceptical opening of Protagoras' *On the Gods*, or the parodies in the *Clouds* again – and he signals his disagreement.

It is above all in Herodotus' exploration of customs or *nomoi* and the specific contribution of *nomos* to human society that his *Histories* seem most sophistic, and he surely shares the wider sophistic interest in human society, its components, and the mechanisms which keep it together. The role of *nomos* and *physis* and their antithetical relationship were explored by almost all the main sophists. Here too, Herodotus has his feet placed more firmly in the realm of reality, actual (or supposed) *nomoi* rather than speculative, abstract argument. He does not play with the antithesis of *nomos/physis* to suggest the absolute moral or amoral superiority of one over the other. But he points out that *nomos* is crucial to the ordering and creating of human society, a rather Protagorean view, and we can surely conclude that in the end it is *nomos* rather than *physis* which does most to determine a people's character. This is brought out most spectacularly in the exchange between the exiled Spartan Demaratus and Xerxes (7.101–5), though it is emphasised implicitly, of course, by the way Herodotus describes each people's *nomoi* when he reaches them. Xerxes believes his forces will win in the ensuing conflict through strength of numbers and fear, but Demaratus counters this by stressing the Spartans' poverty and also their *aretē*, asserting that the *aretē* is 'acquired' from wisdom (*sophiē*) and *nomos*, above all their *nomos*, their way of life and discipline: '*their* ruler is *nomos*'. Since Xerxes had claimed fear would make his subjects 'stronger than their nature (*physis*)' (7.103.4), Demaratus' stress on *nomos* as the determinant is implicitly drawing up the contrast in terms of *nomos* and *physis*: as the force which works on the whole society, *nomos* here gives the whole exchange a distinctly sophistic flavour.[33]

Similarly, the Persian king Darius is portrayed earlier in the *Histories* as conducting the kind of inquiry (*historiē*) Herodotus does: in a well-known passage, Herodotus claims that Darius asked some assembled Greeks how they treated the corpses of their parents.[34] Upon learning that the Greeks burned them, he asked some Indians, who said they ate theirs; each group is horrified at the others' habits, and Herodotus takes this to show that all people adhere to their own customs: 'And I think Pindar was correct to say that *nomos* is king of all' (3.38.4). The importance of *nomos* is upheld here with Pindar's authority, but it is particularly interesting that both the citation and the sentiment itself seem to have been fashionable among certain thinkers of the late fifth century. The Pindar quotation is also cited by Callicles in Plato's *Gorgias* (484b), but for the very opposite conclusion. The idea of *nomos* as tyrant was attributed to the sophist Hippias (*Protagoras* 337d1–e2), and the claim 'Nomos governs all' begins the Hippocratic work *Generation/Nature of the Child*. All these writers share a fascination with the power of custom and it is illuminating to see a poet cited to back up a view developed in a way quite different from the poet's. Sections like this one imply strongly that Herodotus' awareness of the value and role of *nomoi* may have been sharpened by the sophistic debates about *nomos* and *physis*. He did not take the extreme antinomian view, however, and it seems likely that his inquiries into ethnography were at least made sharper, more focussed, perhaps even propelled by contemporary interest in *nomos*.[35] The anonymous work called *Dissoi Logoi* shows most acutely how easily some of Herodotus' ethnographic data could be slotted into sophistic exercises designed to explore the problem of relative values and differing customs across the world. In what now seems a pedestrian manner, this author attempts to show that there are two sides to every question, the 'double arguments' of the title. Chapter 2 uses Herodotean examples among others to show how quite contradictory ideas about correct behaviour can be found: cannibals consuming deceased parents appear again (2.14; cf. Hdt. 3.38), the Egyptians do not think in the same way as anyone else (2.17; cf. Hdt. 2.35–6), and so on, a schematic and deliberately shocking list. Herodotus' ethnography is so susceptible to this kind of sophistic argument partly, I would suggest, because he gathered and described his material with such sophistic ideas at least partly in the background. They might also have encouraged his use of variant versions.

Herodotus is not a relativist in the full sense that he abstains from judgement. He observes and describes customs of different peoples, apparently reserving judgement much of the time, yet he is clear that certain customs are wise because they promote endurance and military success. Once the Athenians became free, he says, they became successful in war because they were fighting for themselves rather than for others (5.78), an idea also favoured by *Airs* (ch.16). The Scythians have discovered one thing which is 'the greatest of all human achievements which we know', for they make it impossible for the invader to escape while they themselves are entirely out of reach (4.46.2). This is, of course, ethnography in the service of political and historical analysis rather than moral relativism. Similarly, he expressly commends certain customs, the Babylonian marriage market for instance, which is their 'wisest' custom (1.196), or Amasis' rather crude method of ensuring full employment (2.177.2). The importance of *nomoi* also allows him to part company with the current theories of environmental determinism visible in *Airs*; environment, climate or continent are just not enough for historical explanation, not to mention his research into the historical forces and human motivations of the past. Here we see the historical thinker rather than the sophist playing with paradoxical opposites. Perhaps too, as a Greek from Asia Minor, he was acutely aware that it was not enough to be Greek in the fight against the Persians, and while geography was important, the Asiatic Greeks could hardly accept that as inhabitants of Asia they were different by nature from the mainland Greeks. The new sophistic stress on *nomoi* perhaps offered Herodotus conceptual terms in which to express some reasons for the longer-term confict between Greeks and Persians and the surprising success of the Greeks.

Herodotus' method of presenting his material reveals something more of his intellectual milieu. Here I do not mean the subtle ways of structuring and creating his narrative which have been much discussed and owe debts to the epic narrator and the oral storyteller.[36] For our purposes here, it is his manner of explicitly commenting on his sources, on his method, his emphasis on autopsy or eyewitness accounts, and indeed his very presence in the narrative as an active inquirer[37] and commentator, which reveal his relation to very recent and contemporary intellectual trends; these are elements which are new, which Thucydides had to answer in his own way, and which are all too easy to take for granted as part of the Herodotean persona. Yet, as Fowler has recently suggested, his very habit of mentioning his sources, however infrequent, is probably itself new: 'he invented the *problem* of sources'.[38] Stressing your source of knowledge or inference is a prominent part of the new methods visible in the early medical writings, and they remain our best way into the details of late fifth-century methods of argument. This would suggest it was the now fashionable and proper method to generate credibility for the author, whether or not the evidence was itself credible! Moreover, in contrast to most natural philosophers, Herodotus seems to prefer visible and physical evidence, and for that reason he has been tentatively called 'the father of empiricism'.[39] The early medical writings, however, give by far the richest contemporary or near-contemporary evidence for the building up of complete theories with arguments and evidence, and these suggest a somewhat more complex picture. Lateiner has shown that Herodotus shares with these essays a wide range of words for method and evidence, and he argued that they basically shared the same 'epistemological response', preoccupation with physical and visible data, providing proofs and signs, rather than with the more abstract processes of deduction of the Presocratic type.[40]

The comparison can also work in a rather different direction, for while some Hippocratic works are preoccupied with visible evidence, some are just as concerned with philosophical deductions to make up for lack of empirical evidence. Others are highly rhetorical, argumentative and flamboyant (*On the Art, Breaths*), and the claims to provide proofs and evidence can be seen partly as a rhetorical ploy to claim authority, the persuasiveness lying in style and argument rather than any profound or extensive observation of facts and the visible world. Herodotus seems on occasion to have affinities with these too; rather surprisingly, he can be a master of logical deductive arguments, he can claim to produce 'proofs' (*tekmēria*) at precisely the point where he has to resort to complicated argument and deduction to make up for the lack of any clear empirical evidence; and he is capable of just the kind of first-person interventions and competitive, argumentative, polemical style which is familiar from the more rhetorical essays in the Hippocratic Corpus (e.g. 4.36.1–2 on the Hyperboreans). These sometimes occur at interesting junctures where he is criticising ill-founded or false ideas.[41]

Is this sophistic, or something less well defined? What is clear from the medical works is first, that there is a spectrum of styles even within the same discipline, the emerging discipline of medicine, and second, that a highly rhetorical, polemical and 'sophistic' style was evidently used more widely for conveying theories about the nature of the world and the nature of health, that is, for the fledgling early stages of Greek 'science'. New methods of argument were developing simultaneously for the art of rhetoric and for the propagation of new theories of 'science', and many of these could be found in the new, rather sophistic style used for the performance piece, the *epideixis*. This was a serious vehicle for oral performances about various spheres of knowledge, as well as for teaching the art of persuasion, though it was to become one of the main display methods of the later sophists. There were oral contests on subjects like the nature of man (Hippocrates, *On the Nature of Man* chs. 1-2J). The striking parallels in style with Herodotus in certain passages when he is being controversial or polemical, or criticising opponents and predecessors, indicate that he too partook of this world. This was a world of scientific inquiry which shared some methods and style of presentation with some of the rhetorical and sophistic displays and certainly used the new methods of argument and display of evidence, but was still firmly rooted in serious 'scientific' inquiry into nature – far from the rhyming antitheses of display pieces by teachers of rhetoric such as Gorgias. Thucydides may be objecting to this kind of display when he stresses that his work is no *agonisma*, no competition piece for the immediate pleasure of the listeners (Thuc. 1.22.4).[42] It is an intellectual style, not simply a style of oral display lectures; by using this style, Herodotus in the generation before was signalling his participation in this intellectual milieu.

But of course Herodotus' subject was also the past, and this seems to be unparalleled in any of these other writers. His marriage of the methods and style of contemporary science to the subject of past history was the product of his own originality. How does this intellectual milieu affect our interpretation of Herodotus as an historian? In this period before disciplines were properly separated, it seems that Herodotus could (and did) pose both as a rival and emulator of Homer, and as a writer who was familiar with the new methods of the various areas we call for convenience 'science'. He points to this in the very opening where he makes clear reference to the Homeric preservation of fame (*kleos*) at the same time as he uses the fashionable language of scientific inquiry, calling his work an *histories apodexis* (*praef.*).[43] Irene de Jong has pertinent remarks about the danger of imposing modern conceptions about 'unity' upon Herodotus, when ancient literary criticism showed 'a greater tendency towards the episodic, ecphrastic, and digressional',[44] and when we recall that even a sophist like Protagoras could offer his theory of society in Plato's *Protagoras* as either a myth or a *logos*, we perhaps should not be overly concerned to find different modes of exposition in Herodotus – the argumentative style alongside the narrative. The fact that he poses as aware of his methods and often overtly critical of what he has heard should remind us that his account of past history may not always have been as innocent as he sometimes makes out. Since remarks about evidence and method are a fashionable part of intellectual inquiry, and can have a fairly barbed rhetorical purpose, we may suspect that some of Herodotus' remarks about past history may have more sting in them than at first appears, and that they may subtly remind the audience of the problems of ascertaining the truth. One thinks particularly of the way he says, with apparent naïveté, that 'I am bound to repeat what has been said, but I am not bound to believe everything, and this principle holds for every tale (*logos*)': this is said when he deals with the shocking question of Argos' medism and what is more, of later Athenian negotiation with the Persians. It cannot possibly be as innocent and neutral as it pretends to be (7.152.2–4). Such distancing from the *logoi* appears from the start.[45]

But Herodotus is also the *sophos* and wise adviser through his narrative and the speeches within this narrative, and here, while we can point to such and such an idea or concept – e.g. justice, expediency, the growth of the state – as familiar in sophistic discussion, some of the larger problems of historical explanation may well have had a wider currency among his politically acute contemporaries.[46] I would like to end by suggesting that the sophistic display piece and the historical-political analysis come together in certain of Herodotus' speeches. The debate between Xerxes and Demaratus (7.101–5) dramatises the abstract qualities that may or may not make a people great and emphasises the assumptions of Xerxes which will lead to his defeat. The 'Constitutional Debate' (3.80–83) dramatises the political decision to be made for the Persians' future, the routes not taken, and does so in a form familiar in late fifth-century rhetorical contests. Both are just as much set pieces as Thucydides' 'Melian Dialogue' (5.84–111), with an equally problematic relationship to what might really have happened, and both perform a crucial analytical role in the historical narrative.

NOTES

1. Fowler (2001) 101–3 on Hecataeus, and his chapter in this volume, for prose predecessors; also Momigliano (1966); Fowler (1996).
2. Murray (2001b) 322.
3. See Marincola on Homer and Griffin on tragedy in this volume. Compare Loraux and Miralles (1998).
4. Hdt. 7.137; Thuc. 2.67. For evidence for date of publication, Fornara (1971b).
5. See Fornara (1971a); Strasburger (1955); Moles (2002); and the subtle article by Fowler (2003a). Murray (2001b) emphasises the significance of Thurii.
6. Further details, Thomas (2000) 9ff.; cf. also Montiglio (2000), and the chapters by Fowler, Friedman and Munson in this volume.
7. See the chapters of Luraghi and Griffiths in this volume. Note that even Thucydides is markedly Herodotean when dealing with traditions about Pausanias and Themistocles in Book 1.
8. Gould (1989) 7–8; A. Lloyd (1975–88) I, esp. ch. 4; Corcella (1984). For fullest treatment of Presocratic and sophistic links see Nestle (1908) with Thomas (2000) 16–17.
9. Raaflaub (2002a) 157.
10. A. Lloyd (1990); also Nestle (1908).
11. See also A. Lloyd (1975–88) II.60 (comm. on 2.10), and 36–7.
12. As A. Lloyd (1975–88) *ad loc.* suggests; Xanthus of Lydia also mentions fossils, *FGrHist* 765 F 12.
13. Hdt. 7.16.2, Empedocles, *VS* 31 B 108: Raaflaub (2002a) 157; but a rational explanation also appears in *Sacred Disease* ch.17, and Democritus, *VS* 68 A 77. Compare also Romm's chapter in this volume.
14. With A. Lloyd (1975–88), comm. on 2.21.
15. Lateiner (1986); cf. also Raaflaub (2002a) 158–9, and Scullion's chapter in this volume.
16. See Thomas (2000) 182ff., on the method of argumentation.
17. See Romm's chapter in this volume.
18. Jacoby (1913).
19. Thomas (2000) 139, and Corcella (1984) 80–81; Thomas (2000) ch. 5 for wonders as part of the study of nature.
20. For medicine's debt to philosophy see especially G. Lloyd (1979), (1987), Jouanna (1992) 366–403.
21. See Thomas (2000) 103 ff., especially 104–9. For doubts, see Flower and Marincola (2002) 15–16, 312.
22. Bibliography and discussion of *Airs* at Thomas (2000) 86–98.
23. Thomas (2000) 36, and generally 37–9; Althoff (1993); Demont (1988).
24. See Dorati (2000) for recent study of the scope and language of his ethnography.
25. Myres (1953) 43.

26. See, e.g., G. Lloyd (1987) 92–3; Guthrie (1971); Kerferd (1981), especially 39–40 and ch. 4. Note especially the remarks in Plato's *Sophist*, to the effect that sophists concern themselves, as the Eleatic stranger puts it, with matters divine, the visible objects of earth and heavens, being and coming to be, laws (*nomoi*) and all matters of politics, every *technē*, as well as the art of argument (232b11–e2).

27. For Herodotus and the sophists, Dihle (1962a), (1962b); Nestle (1908); Thomas (2000).

28. Burkert (1985) 131, and Thomas (2000) 280–1.

29. Thomas (2000) 147–9 for further references; Nestle (1908); Demont (1994).

30. See especially Lasserre (1976b); Raaflaub (2002a) 161 for caution. Most recent discussion of the debate in general, Pelling (2002).

31. See Thomas (2000) 230ff. for details; Harrison (2000) App. 2 on Herodotus' 'names of the gods'.

32. 8.83.1: *ta de epea ēn panta <ta> kressō toisi hēssosi antitithemena, hosa dē en anthrōpou phusi kai katastasi engignetai.*

33. See Dihle (1962a); also Dihle (1981); Heinimann (1945); Thomas (2000) 109ff.

34. See also Rood and Romm in this volume.

35. See Thomas (2000) 129–31 for some possible examples; note also 7.152.2, with *Dissoi Logoi* 2.18.

36. See especially de Jong (2002) and (1999); Lang (1984), and numerous small scale studies; Aly (1921/1969) and Erbse (1992), for stories and folktales, and for the idea of Herodotus as an Ionian storyteller see Murray (2001a) with modifications in Murray (2001b) 318, and Griffiths in this volume; on tragedy see now Saïd (2002) and Griffin in this volume.

37. Note now the important discussion of the authorial 'I' in Dewald (2002).

38. Fowler (1996) 86.

39. Müller (1981).

40. Lateiner (1986).

41. Full evidence in Thomas (1997) and (2000) chs. 7–8.

42. See previous note and cf. Demont (1993) on the *epideixis*; G. Lloyd (1979) and (1987) for medical writers' use of rhetoric.

43. Thomas (2000) 267–9.

44. de Jong (2002); quotation, p. 246.

45. Dewald (2002), especially 270–71.

46. Raaflaub (2002a) 164–83, stressing similarities to Thucydides; cf. also Moles (1996).

5

NINO LURAGHI

Meta-*historiē*: Method and genre in the *Histories*

I, Herodotus

In general, ancient historiography consists of extended narratives in the third person, with the author only rarely intruding in the first person. Herodotus' *Histories*, at the very dawn of ancient historiography, represent a conspicuous exception. The presence of Herodotus the narrator[1] in his text is stressed almost continuously by the occurrence of statements in the first person. They range from the rather nondescript kind, such as 'Those of the barbarians who returned [*from a raid against Delphi*] said – as I have been told – that they had seen other divine signs besides these' (8.38), or 'I cannot write down exactly which of the Ionians were cowardly or brave in that naval battle' (6.14.1), to extremely specific ones, such as 'This is what I heard from the priests in Thebes' (2.55.1). At times, the Herodotean narrator intrudes in his text to express a judgement, and more often to formulate an opinion. Most of the time, however, he raises his voice, as in the examples above, to refer to the process of gathering information, with its successes and failures.

Especially to readers accustomed to modern historiography, it does not seem strange that a historian should spend time talking about his activity as a researcher. After all, one of the first things a history student is trained to do is precisely to buttress his or her every statement, in so far as it goes above absolute banality, with a reference, usually telling where the corresponding information comes from. However, seen against the background of common practice in ancient historiography, Herodotus' presence in his text is highly peculiar. Other ancient historians rarely dealt with the question of how they gathered information, usually confining it to preliminary statements at the beginning of their works. They more commonly used the first person to pass judgement, especially in moral terms, as Polybius liked doing, or they disappeared completely from their texts, as Thucydides did most of the time. There is no real parallel among the Greek and Roman historians for the enormous frequency of statements about the process of finding and assessing information that is typical of the *Histories*.[2] It seems that the characteristics of the Herodotean narrator should not simply be taken for granted.

Or should they? After all, authorial statements in Herodotus are rather straightforward, their meaning is not ambiguous, and on the whole they seem to lend themselves to a satisfactory interpretation. Why not take them at face value and use them as evidence for Herodotus' methods as a researcher?[3] That is the question that will be explored here.

Herodotean footnotes

First-person statements are not the only passages that refer to the narrator's activity as a researcher. To come clean as to the provenance of the stories assembled in the *Histories* seems to be a paramount concern of the Herodotean narrator.[4] Besides occasionally specifying the person by whom he himself was told something, he refers very often to other speakers, rarely individuals, usually groups, as vouching for portions of the text that may vary in length from a single piece of information to a whole story. Such references usually take the form of statements like 'the Spartans/Athenians/Egyptians say'. Taken together, first-person statements on the process of collecting and assessing information and 'they say' references form a sort of meta-discourse, running parallel to the narrative surface of the *Histories* and commenting on its nature and origin. Since Herodotus in his proem calls the activity he is engaging in *historiē*,[5] the statements about such activity could be called meta-*historiē*; they form the core of modern reconstructions of Herodotus' historical method.

This method has three cornerstones, different in nature and relevance: first and most important, oral information, called by Herodotus *akoē*; second, his personal eyewitness testimony, called *opsis*, more powerful than *akoē* but subject to obvious restrictions, especially when talking about the past; third, Herodotus' own reasoning, called *gnōmē*. The three come together in a famous passage in Book 2, at the point where Herodotus moves from a more or less synchronic presentation of Egypt and Egyptian culture to the narrative of Egyptian history from the earliest times (2.99.1):

> Up to this point, it is my own autopsy (*opsis*), judgement (*gnōmē*), and inquiry (*historiē*) that have spoken these things. Henceforth I will go on recording Egyptian stories as I have heard them; they will be supplemented by a certain amount of my autopsy.

The strange way that *opsis*, *gnōmē* and *historiē* are presented as the subject of the action of uttering the text has captured less attention than it perhaps deserves;[6] it will be necessary to return to this point later. For now, it should be observed that the relationship between *opsis*, *gnōmē* and *historiē* in the passage above is not completely straightforward. Apparently, *historiē* means here a process of inquiry quite separate from seeing and reasoning. Obviously autopsy and historical reasoning cannot be entirely divorced from the *apodexis historiēs* announced in the Herodotean proem.[7] Yet *opsis* and *gnōmē* are never an end in themselves in the *Histories*, but appear to reinforce and complement the primary activity of research called *historiē*.

Opsis or lack thereof, the ultimate proof of truth, becomes especially relevant when things are described or mentioned that go beyond what can be counted upon as the audience's personal experience. Occasionally, however, it can also prove or disprove a plausible story collected by *akoē*.[8] 'Some people' – presumably Egyptians, but Herodotus does not specify – say that, after Pharaoh Mycerinus raped his own daughter, her mother punished the maidens who had allowed this to happen by having their hands chopped off (2.131). To confirm the story, the handless statues of these maidens were pointed to, but Herodotus is not convinced:

> As far as the above is concerned, these people talk nonsense, as it seems to me, especially as regards the statues: for in fact we ourselves have seen that the hands had fallen off through age, and they were still to be seen at the feet of the statues in my time.

Herodotus is here addressing a characteristic phenomenon of oral tradition, called iconatrophy, whereby a monument becomes the focus of stories that explain its features, with a rather loose connection to the real circumstances of its construction.[9]

Gnōmē applies to natural phenomena, as we see most famously in Herodotus' discussion of the Nile's floods (2.19–27), but it is also very often brought to bear on genuinely historical problems, as when Herodotus refuses to accept the story that the Alcmeonids had been prepared to betray Athens at the time of Marathon because he cannot see any plausible reason to explain such alleged treason (6.121–4). In general, Herodotus' reasoning is omnipresent in his narrative, and logical arguments, often deployed to rationalise and cut down to size mythic stories of the epic tradition, are the most powerful weapon of his hermeneutic arsenal – unsurprisingly, since, after all, early Greek historiography was born as a rationalising rewriting of myths based on the authors' marshalling arguments of plausibility.[10] One of the most distinctive methods of Herodotean *gnōmē* is analogical reasoning, the use of conjecture about phenomena on which no direct evidence is available – the course of the Nile, that Herodotus assumes to be similar to that of the Danube, provides the best example (2.33–4).[11]

In striking contrast to *gnōmē* and *opsis*, Herodotean *akoē* does not necessarily guarantee the truth of the statement involved. On the contrary, Herodotus explicitly says a couple of times that his task is to report what is said, regardless of whether he believes it or not. One of these statements is found embedded in the discussion of Argos' behaviour at the time of Xerxes' invasion of Greece. Again, the wording is slightly puzzling (7.152.3):

> As for myself, I am bound to tell what is told, but I am absolutely not bound to believe it, and let it be understood that this statement applies to every story I report. For it is also told that it was the Argives who called in the Persian against Greece, because their struggle with Sparta was not going well and they were ready to take anything instead of their present sorrow.[12]

The generalising tone of this statement should not divert attention from the fact that the narrator here is voicing his doubts about the credibility of the Argive complicity with the Persian invader. This was no doubt a highly contentious issue in Herodotus' own lifetime. Nevertheless, the narrator's insistence on this disclaimer as well as on its general applicability has to be taken seriously.

The cognitive instruments used by Herodotus, while setting him apart from later Greek historians, closely associate him with other thinkers involved in explaining the world and looking for the truth in a rational way. Traditionally, emphasis has fallen on the relationship with the methods and arguments of the early Presocratic philosophers of the late-sixth and early-fifth century, a relationship that is shown in the clearest way by a fragment of Heraclitus of Ephesus (*VS* 22 B 55), according to which Heraclitus' interest extended to all that falls into the range of *opsis*, *akoē*, and *mathēsis* (learning).[13] The obvious resemblance to the Herodotean statement at 2.99 should not be taken, however, as a sign that Herodotus, who after all was active during the third quarter of the fifth century, was an old-fashioned fellow harking back to a previous cultural phase. Especially in the variety and complexity of logical arguments he uses, Herodotus is definitely a contemporary of his times, well aware of the developments in philosophy and rhetoric associated with the sophists, and abreast of the new turns taken in the investigation of nature, documented by Hippocratic medical treatises.[14] An incipient contemporary discussion about nature and culture, or *physis* and *nomos*, is visible both in his cultural relativism and in his readiness to take on its own terms the coherence of patterns of behaviour different from those of the Greeks.[15] However, Herodotus devoted himself largely to the investigation and recording of the past, a field markedly different in nature from those explored by contemporary Hippocratic writers, natural philosophers and rhetoricians, and *gnōmē* and *opsis* can account only for a limited part of the impressive display of information comprised in the *Histories*. It is in the realm of oral inquiry that the true secrets of Herodotus' workshop have to lie.

Herodotus as oral historian

Statements that fall into the broad range of *akoē* have been foremost in capturing the attention of scholars interested in Herodotus' historical methods and ultimately in the reliability of his stories.[16] With their deceptive similarity to modern practice, statements of *akoē* have conjured up the image of Herodotus collecting information, carefully comparing different versions, assessing the trustworthiness of his informants, and keeping track of the process and inscribing it into his final text for all to see. The story of the foundation of the Greek colony of Cyrene in North Africa seems to provide a particularly good example of such a way of operating. It begins with a narrative of how Thera, Cyrene's mother-city, had been colonised by the Spartans – a story told by Spartans and Therans in agreement with each other (3.150.1). Then the circumstances are recounted that induced the Therans to plan a colonial expedition to Cyrene and the actual foundation of the city, according to the Therans (3.154.1: 'This is what the Therans say'). However, Herodotus adds, the people from Cyrene, while agreeing to some extent with this story, had something different to say about their founder, the Theran Battus, and added that the Therans had compelled the original colonists, fellow-citizens of theirs, to sail away, repelling them with stones when they tried to return to Thera.

The image of Herodotus the oral historian remained a rather sketchy one as long as scholars had to use only the narrator's own statements and a few passages from other fifth-century authors to give it substance. A turning point finally seemed to be reached once some scholars started adopting a comparative approach, looking for parallels into empirical research in living oral traditions, which represents one of the most distinct developments in the study of history in the second half of the twentieth century.[17] Rather accidentally, what ended up being a template for students of Herodotus was not, e.g., oral history as practised by left-wing scholars in Western Europe and America, but rather the research on the transmission of knowledge by word of mouth that had been carried out by historians of pre-colonial Africa.[18] In the decades after World War II, in a political climate dominated by the search for a new political identity in many new-born African states, a group of scholars, and especially the Belgian historian Jan Vansina, had started looking for hermeneutic instruments that could break through the chronological boundary represented by the written records of the colonial powers and reach back into an African past.[19] Vansina was a medievalist by training, with a strong philological background. He was familiar with the essentially Romantic idea that complex texts could be transmitted in a faithful way by word of mouth, but he was also sceptical. His solution to the problem of how to create a history of pre-colonial Africa was to work out a methodology to evaluate orally transmitted information and turn it into the foundation of a historical narrative that could satisfy the standards of twentieth-century professional historians. In so doing, he developed a typology and phenomenology of oral traditions that he intended to be generally applicable to other cultural contexts,[20] which made it all the more attractive for ancient historians to use his method to investigate oral tradition in Greece.[21]

Although the original reason for thinking of Herodotus as a historian working from oral tradition was the meta-*historiē* embedded in the text, the real strength of this new direction of research has been the ability to show that Vansina's principles on transmission and function of the oral tradition could be applied to narratives on archaic Greek history in the *Histories*, providing a number of insights into the origins and meaning of such narratives.[22] This seemed to confirm that the knowledge about the past and about foreign lands and customs that forms the substance of Herodotus' *Histories* is best understood as originating from oral communication and transmission. In this process, it should be noted, Herodotean meta-*historiē* with its insistence on the oral nature of the inquiry allowed scholars to bracket the question of Herodotus' use of written sources and more generally to bypass the hotly debated problem of the relative importance of oral tradition and written texts in fifth-century Greek culture.

One thing has become clearer since Herodotean scholars first turned to oral tradition research: the comparative evidence provided by African oral tradition, while extremely relevant to the problem of the ultimate nature and provenance of Herodotus' stories, was not, however, helpful in advancing an understanding of Herodotus' own methods, that is, of answering the question of how precisely he had gathered oral traditions. Vansina's method presupposed direct access to knowledge about the past in its social context by way of fieldwork, that is, by way of interaction between the carriers of oral traditions and the historian, who was supposed to use rigorous methods to collect testimonies without contaminating them. From this point of view, the risk of anachronism in reconstructing Herodotus' own activity was high. It was still necessary to take meta-*historiē* literally, as a truthful description of Herodotus at work.

However, the narrator's references to collective informants could not possibly be taken in a strictly literal way. This problem, which had been recognised already in the early twentieth century,[23] was originally dealt with by build-ing on a small number of passages in which Herodotus defines some groups as *logioi*, obviously alluding in some way to their particular competence as informants. One of these passages comes right at the beginning of the *Histo-ries* (1.1.1), where 'those of the Persians who are *logioi*' relate the sequence of abductions which they regarded as the origin of the hatred between Greeks and barbarians.[24] The assumption was that references to a group as saying something should be taken as a kind of shorthand for 'the *logioi* among the relevant people,' whom Herodotus supposedly sought out and consulted.[25]

In a very general way, this theory cannot be wrong, for Herodotus doubt-less looked for learned and knowledgeable informants, but taking collective *akoē* statements as shorthand for the interview of experts is a less than sat-isfactory solution, because the attribution of stories and various versions thereof to collective informants turns out to be highly artificial. Basically, this kind of *akoē* statement in Herodotus obeys two simple rules: first, that any human group is cited for events which happened or happen in their own country or, more rarely, happened to their ancestors elsewhere, and second, that a group, whether people or *polis*, will have a version of the past that puts the group itself in a good light.[26] The example of the foundation story of Cyrene, discussed above, shows both rules in action: it is the Spartans and Therans who speak about the foundation of Thera, and the Therans and Cyreneans who speak about the foundation of Cyrene. Where the latter two disagree, the Therans have a version that implies a non-traumatic sepa-ration of the would-be colonists of Cyrene from their metropolis, while the Cyreneans remember how their ancestors had great difficulties in founding their new city in an unknown land, and that the Therans had been distinctly unhelpful in that connection.[27] The second rule emerges most clearly when a conflict or controversy is narrated in two opposing versions, attributed to the two opposed parties, as in the case of the Athenian fiasco on the island of Aegina, which the Athenians attributed to divine intervention and the Aeginetans to themselves and their Argive allies (5.85–6).

On the whole, it seems reasonable to conclude that Herodotean refer-ences to collective informants are too good to be true, i.e., to be taken as a literal depiction of how Herodotus collected information. Otherwise we must believe that he never met, say, some very knowledgeable Milesian somewhere in the Aegean who had some interesting story to tell about Samos or Mytilene, or that he never took any story or piece of infor-mation from a written source – except for the story of the Pelasgians he attributes to Hecataeus (6.137.1–2). It should also be emphasised that meta-*historiē* in general and *akoē* in particular do not have a word for a category of informants that modern scholars increasingly recognise behind Herodotus' stories, i.e., storytellers.[28] The consequence that should be drawn from these observations, however, is not that Herodotus forged his *akoē* statements to cheat his audience and feed it stories he had really concocted himself.[29] Such an interpretation would be anachronistic and misleading. But perhaps taking Herodotean *akoē* statements as source references is no less anachronistic. To be sure, it was almost inevitable that modern scholars should do so. Since the ancient historians have very often been seen as the founding heroes of historiography, attributing to the Father of History a practice typical of modern historiography is a very strong and almost subliminal temptation. Nonetheless, the temptation should be resisted, because the analogy between Herodotean *akoē* statements and modern historical source references is misleading in too many ways. Most conspicuously, the Herodotean narrator very often uses such statements to distance himself from a particular piece of information or from a story, not to lend it credibility by pointing to genuineness.[30] Indeed, in the case of the alleged treason of the Argives, quoted above (p. 79), he even suggests that such statements in general should be taken as disclaimers. Also relevant is the fact that the narrator apparently uses interchangeably *akoē* statements that would seem to us very different in quality, for instance, general references to collective informants and quite specific ones implying personal contact with a specific group of people (2.91.3–5; 4.14). This in turn calls our attention to the fact that after all it is not very clear why some stories or details are provided with an *akoē* statement while others are not.

In spite of the new and fruitful avenues of interpretation opened up by oral tradition research, taking meta-*historiē* literally, as if it were a realistic description of how the *Histories* came about, is problematic – witness the ongoing scholarly controversy on the trustworthiness of Herodotean *opsis* and the true extent of Herodotus' travels.[31] But if meta-*historiē* is neither the giveaway of a grandiose literary forgery nor a straightforward depiction of Herodotus' historical method and an implicit autobiography of Herodotus of Halicarnassus, what can it be?

A map of knowledge

To answer this question, it may be helpful to dwell a little longer on the collective *akoē* statements, the so-called source references. They represent a reasonably well-defined group, and their meaning is not beyond explanation, especially once the notion is set aside that they refer in a realistic way to the process of gathering information. As pointed out above, the logic of the connection between the speakers and what they say is extremely clear. The collective *akoē* statements sketch a map of knowledge, based on the principle that the locals are the most competent informants about

NINO LURAGHI

themselves and their own land. This does not mean that they are not interested in their neighbours: when he reaches the borders of the world, the
Herodotean narrator sometimes conveys a sense of distance by referring
to the last people but one, as it were, as saying something about the very
last (3.105; cf. 4.32), but these are the only exceptions to the rule. In other
words, one of the functions of these statements is to define the limits of
possible knowledge, both in space and in time – a topic the narrator is very
interested in.[32] They are based on the assumption that a community's memory will start at the community's birth and last as long as the community
itself exists.[33]

Besides that, the collective *akoē* statements simply reflect what may be
expected to be the conventional interests and viewpoints of those who utter
them. A very striking example is provided by the causes for the madness
and untimely death of King Cleomenes of Sparta (6.75.3). According to
the Athenians, this was a case of divine retribution because Cleomenes had
plundered an Athenian sanctuary at Eleusis, while the Argives referred to a
similar episode that had taken place at Argos and had involved also a treacherous massacre of Argive soldiers who had sought refuge in the sanctuary.
According to the majority of the Greeks, however, Cleomenes' madness was
a punishment for having corrupted the prophetess of Apollo in Delphi. As for
the Spartans, they refused any supernatural explanation and preferred one
that connected the fate of their king to alcoholism brought on by drinking
wine not watered but neat, Scythian-style: a break of Spartan temperance
(6.84) – an explanation that reinforced the normative value of the Spartan behavioural code. Clearly, locals are depicted as invoking local motives,
while 'the majority of the Greeks' refer to a panhellenic transgression.

It is important to underline that the perfect overlap between collective
akoē statements and local communities with their views and interests cannot have been any less obvious to an ancient audience than it is to a modern
reader. This strongly suggests that Herodotus did not intend such statements
to be taken as realistic depictions of the process he went through in gathering
information, but as something different: recurring reminders of the nature of
the knowledge assembled in the *Histories*. With the terminology of modern
anthropology, the collective *akoē* statements can be seen as references to the
social surface of such knowledge, that is, to the several groups that consider
each single story or piece of information to be true and significant.[34] More
appropriately, these statements form a part of the Herodotean narrator's
attempt to explain his work to his audience in an understandable way, playing on their latent perception of knowledge about the past and about uses
and customs as a shared possession of the community. This, incidentally,
may help explain why there are no references to other early historians as

sources in the *Histories*: for a late-fifth-century audience, a written text did not yet carry an intrinsic authority that would have made it more valuable than what a given community thought of its past.[35] In the only case in the *Histories* where another historian is quoted (6.137), the reason is probably that the group whose viewpoint would have had to be called upon did not exist any more.[36]

Author and authority

Reflecting about audience expectations seems a fruitful way of advancing our understanding of meta-*historiē*. This brings us back to the problem of genre. If we adopt a rather loose and pragmatic definition of genre as a set of historically and culturally specific expectations with which an audience approaches a text, it may be profitable to regard meta-*historiē* as an attempt at meeting and at the same time shaping those expectations, at activating notions of genre already existing in the cultural context while self-consciously creating a new genre.

The need to articulate the rules of a new genre and communicate them to the audience are the most satisfactory explanation for some extremely peculiar statements of meta-*historiē*, in which the narrator tells the audience what he is or is not supposed to do – as if inviting them to take part in a game whose rules they do not yet know exactly, while at the same time showing himself bound by those rules. For instance, after reporting some rather imaginative stories told by the Egyptians about the Pharaoh Rhampsinitus, Herodotus comments (2.123.1):

> Let whoever considers trustworthy stories like these take for good the things told by the Egyptians. As for myself, my task in the whole *logos* is to write down[37] what everybody says, as I hear it (*akoēi*).

This attitude is voiced explicitly elsewhere in the *Histories*. A story qualified as less credible 'has to be reported, too, since it is told' (3.9.2). As we saw above, the Herodotean narrator is expected to report what is said, but he is not expected to believe it (7.152.3). He is not bound to mention the names of all the Persian fleet commanders at Salamis (7.99.1). On the other hand, when a *gnōmē* seems right to him, he is compelled to tell it, regardless of whether his audience will like it or not (7.139.1). As Deborah Boedeker aptly put it, 'Herodotus is free but not entirely free': the rules of his *logos* are above him.[38] They also dictate the rhythm of the text, as it were, pushing the narrator forward towards the next stage of a story, or back to a topic he had started addressing (e.g. 5.62: 'but on top of this, I must come back to the story I intended to tell . . .').[39] In general, his *logos* not only admits but positively requires digressions (4.30). However, such digressions have to be justified (3.60.1).

In some cases, the Herodotean narrator defines the genre he is practising in an implicit and oblique fashion, pointing to ways of dealing with the past that are acceptable in other genres, but not in his. The best example is the discussion of the 'true' story of the abduction of Helen and of the Trojan War. Based on *gnōmē*, it is incredible that Priam and the Trojans might have chosen to be massacred by the Greeks rather than return Helen (2.120); if they did, it means that returning Helen was impossible and the Egyptian priests are right to say that she had been kept in Egypt by their king Proteus, and Menelaus had found her there after the war (2.113–19). Homer, according to Herodotus, had known the true story, but preferred the other one – that is, the *Iliad*! – because it was more appropriate for epic poetry (2.116). This, we are expected to understand, is the kind of liberty the author of the *Histories* would not claim for himself. The statement that Aeschylus had 'stolen' a story from the Egyptians (2.156.6) may have similar implications, pointing indirectly to the Herodotean narrator's practice of letting the audience know where his stories originate.[40]

A number of statements regarding the gods, normally understood as expressing the narrator's stance in matters of religion, may also have implications for the definition of the genre of the *Histories*. Exclusively in Book 2, Herodotus repeatedly voices his unwillingness to deal with religion in depth. He would not report what the Egyptian priests told about the gods, except in so far as he is compelled to mention them by his *logos* (2.3.2). Explaining Egyptian rituals and the iconography of the gods is not something he is inclined to do (2.46.2, 47.2, 48.3); in general, he tries to avoid as far as possible talking about divine matters (2.65.1). While all such statements define an attitude to religion itself, they also separate *historiē* from other fields of knowledge and literary genres which dealt precisely with such topics.

These observations point to a central aspect of the problem of genre. Crucial to the definition of a genre is the drawing of borders towards other genres, all the more so when the subject matter does not of itself identify the genre. Herodotus' account of the Persian Wars and of their causes competed most directly with tragedy, elegiac poetry, and epic, and in some ways with encomiastic poetry, too. However, the problem was from the outset inherent in what is usually called early Greek historiography, which before Herodotus to a large extent had been mythography in prose, thereby dealing with the traditional subject matter of epic.[41] In Greek culture, the past had been for centuries the province of poetry, especially but not only epic poetry, and the discourse of authority that traditionally applied to the past was based on privileged access to knowledge by virtue of what we might call a charismatic predisposition, that is, direct inspiration from a superior entity, the Muse(s).[42] Establishing a new way of dealing with the past implied the creation of a new kind of authority. The problem is already obvious in what is for us the very beginning of Greek historiography, the first sentence of Hecataeus' *Genealogies* (see n. 10 to this chapter). However, Hecataean *gnōmē* and the rationalist criticism of myth could only go so far, and were potentially problematic: once the stories had been purged of all implausible details, the problem of what authority vouched for the stories themselves was bound to come up.

Meta-*historiē* can be seen as a way to mark the differences towards other genres and carve out a niche for the *Histories*. To some extent, it avails itself of the discourse of authority developed by philosophy and the incipient natural sciences – hence the insistence upon *gnōmē* and *opsis*. More importantly, however, meta-*historiē* tackles headlong the problem of the provenance of the knowledge about the past and about foreign lands the author draws upon. Obviously, not all such knowledge could be validated by the critical scrutiny of *gnōmē* and *opsis*, yet on the other hand, excluding all that did not fall under that category meant the renunciation of the project altogether. Meta-*historiē* solves the problem by introducing multiple speakers to tell the several stories, and by generally bracketing the question of their truthfulness. By stressing that he is repeating things that are said already, independently of his retelling them or not, the Herodotean narrator in a sense hides his own activity and minimises it. The narrator may speak out for or against the truth of this or that story, but the stories exist of themselves and it is ultimately up to the reader to believe them or not. This tendency to put at the forefront the voices of other speakers comes to the fore with almost paradoxical clarity in the statement we have discussed earlier, where the narrator names his *opsis*, his *gnōmē* and his *historiē* as the entities that utter the text.[43]

Both the *akoē* statements and source-references of later historians serve to legitimise the historian's narrative. The radical difference between the two pertains to the contexts in which this function is discharged. Before the emergence of historiography as a branch of knowledge and a literary genre, the set of techniques and assumptions that make it possible did not yet exist. The very concept of a 'source' is a product of this development, of which meta-*historiē* represents an early stage. Meta-*historiē* bears testimony to a cultural context in which a narrator cannot lend authority to his narrative by referring to the written works of a predecessor, as later Greek and Roman historians will do. Short of being able to assess a story based on consistency and autopsy, the Herodotean narrator can only step aside, letting the human groups whose past he relates take the stage and tell the story, in a way that is most likely intended to mirror the audience's perception of its own knowledge of its past.

The approach sketched above has implications for the vexed question of the problematic status of the *Histories* between history and literature. Contemporary professional historians are often unwilling to see historiography as a genre. Writing in a genre means saying certain things because the norms of the genre require so, whereas pre-postmodern historians like to think that by and large the only laws that govern their writing are the old ones of Cicero, 'not to say anything untrue and not to leave out anything true' (*de orat.* 2.62). The notion of an implied author in a modern work of history is bound to create uneasiness, yet its appropriateness cannot be seriously denied. The same ambiguous relationship between genre and method applies to ancient historians. The texts of the ancient historians are not straightforward reflections of extra-textual 'true facts', but complex cultural artefacts, whose correct interpretation requires an understanding of their social logic.[44]

Understanding meta-*historiē* is not the same as adjudicating the question of Herodotus' reliability. The claim that meta-*historiē* is more a literary strategy than a genuine depiction of the historian at work should not be taken to imply that Herodotus, the real author of the *Histories*, was not interested in a truthful reconstruction of the past. The amount of external confirmation that is available for countless pieces of information contained in the *Histories* should of itself show that indeed he was. However, fifth-century Greek culture had its own ideas on the nature and proper textual form of truth. Herodotean meta-*historiē* is shaped by such ideas, while at the same time attempting itself to shape them.

FURTHER READING

For detailed discussions of Herodotus' historical methods see especially Darbo-Peschanski (1987) and Lateiner (1989). Lloyd's commentary on Book 2 is also helpful. Jacoby's works (1913, 1949) are still worth reading, not only for their influence on later scholarship. Murray (2001a) remains the best study of Herodotus in the light of research on oral tradition; see also his retrospective comments, Murray (2001b). For an illuminating case-study see Forsdyke (1999). Research on oral tradition and the diffusion of knowledge about the past in societies ancient and modern have gone a long way after Vansina; see especially Fentress and Wickham (1992) and Assmann (1992), and the essays collected in von Ungern-Sternberg and Reinau (1988). On the circulation of information in Greek society see Lewis (1996). Herodotus' use of written sources is a matter for controversy, because of his own silence on this point and general lack of parallel evidence. Parallels in Book 2 with fragments of Hecataeus have long since convinced most scholars that he did indeed use written sources of different kinds, but the extent of such usage is hard to assess. Fowler (2001) gives a sense of the amount of evidence that would have been available to Herodotus. Recent works by Giangiulio (2001 and forthcoming) show by way of sophisticated case-studies how we can imagine Herodotus weaving together a plurality of written and oral sources, generally undisclosed. Calame (1986) offers a rigorous framework to investigate Herodotus' presence in his text. Finding the bugs in the extremely subtle arguments of Fehling (1989) is a very instructive exercise.

NOTES

1. Throughout this chapter, 'the narrator' or 'the Herodotean narrator' refers to the textual *persona* of the author of the *Histories*. On Herodotus' authorial *persona* see especially Dewald (1987), (2002) with further references in n. 13.
2. Fowler (1996) 76; Marincola (1997) 10.
3. The disposition to read Herodotus for what he says, instead of interpreting his work in the light of categories derived from a scrutiny of ancient historiography as a genre, has often marked the dividing line between historians and philologists – a dividing line across which communication has not always been easy. As is always the case, lack of communication has damaged both sides.
4. Marincola (1997) 8.
5. On the meaning of this word see Fowler's contribution to this volume.
6. It is noteworthy that most translations cancel this oddity with renderings such as 'up to this point I have spoken based on, *etc*'. See Schepens (1975) 260–1.
7. The meaning of this announcement is explained by Bakker (2002) 20–8. See the discussion of 2.99.1 by Lloyd (1975–88) I.81–2.
8. On *opsis* and its limits see Darbo-Peschanski (1987) 84–90; on its use to confirm odd pieces of information, Dewald (2002) 278–9.
9. The term 'iconatrophy' was coined by Jan Vansina; see Vansina (1985) 10. See pp. 80–82 for the relationship of Herodotean method and oral tradition.
10. Herodotean *gnōmē* is a key topic of Darbo-Peschanski (1987). The fact that for Herodotus *gnōmē* carries more weight than *akoē* is highlighted in Luraghi (2001b) 142–3. The superiority of the historian's reasoning over tradition comes strikingly to the fore in the first line of Hecataeus' *Genealogies*, *FGrHist* 1 F 1a: 'Hecataeus the Milesian says thus: I write what follows according to what I think is the truth, for the stories of the Greeks are many and ridiculous, in my opinion.' On Hecataeus' rationalism see Corcella (1984) 48–54 and Bertelli (2001).
11. On analogy in Herodotus see Corcella (1984) and Thomas (2000) 200–11, who shows connections between Herodotus' reasoning and contemporary trends in philosophy and medicine.
12. The other passage is 2.123.1, on which see below. Compare also 3.9.2: after giving what seems to him the most credible version of how Cambyses was able to cross the Arabian desert with his army, Herodotus adds a second version, that

he considers less credible, because, after all, 'it is told'. On these passages see Lateiner (1989) 79.

13. See the contributions of Fowler and Thomas in this volume.

14. On Herodotus' intellectual affinities see especially Thomas (2000) and in this volume, and in brief Raaflaub (2002a) 155–64.

15. For an exploration of Herodotus' attitude to cultural difference see Munson (2001a), correcting the excessive rigidity of the classic Hartog (1991).

16. Compare Jacoby (1913) 395.46–50: among the sources of Herodotus' knowledge, *opsis* and *gnōmē* need no further explanation.

17. This development is outlined in Luraghi (2001a).

18. On the politics of oral history and oral tradition research see Prins (2001) 120–6, 138–9.

19. For the development of the history of pre-colonial Africa and especially for the origins of Vansina's methods and concerns see Vansina (1994).

20. See especially Vansina (1985), although ancient historians have been more influenced by Vansina (1961) – note the subtitle: *Essai de méthode historique*. On the difference between the two see Murray (2001b) 321.

21. Studies of oral tradition in Greece inspired more or less directly by Vansina's works include Murray (2001a), Flower (1991), Thomas (1989), Evans (1991), Raaflaub (1988), Cobet (1988).

22. Murray (2001a).

23. Jacoby (1913) 412.

24. The meanings of the Greek word *logios* range from 'important, illustrious', with implications of social prestige, to 'learned, competent'. On its meaning in Herodotus see Vannicelli (2001) 214–15 and Luraghi (2001b) 156–9, with references to the relevant passages.

25. Jacoby (1949) 215–16, followed by Murray (2001a) 26–7; cf. also 40. For different versions of the *logioi*-theory see Nagy (1987), revised in Nagy (1990) 221–7 and Evans (1991). Criticism thereof in Luraghi (2001b).

26. See Fehling (1989) 87–108 and Darbo-Peschanski (1987) 91–4.

27. For an illuminating discussion of Herodotus' narratives on the foundation of Cyrene, highlighting the impossibility of taking Herodotean *akoē* statements at face value, see Giangiulio (2001).

28. See Griffiths in this volume.

29. This interpretation, first put forward by Plutarch in his pamphlet against Herodotus (*de Her. mal.* 40), has been argued extensively in recent years by Detlev Fehling: see Fehling (1989). For an excellent discussion of Fehling's approach see Fowler (1996) 80–5.

30. See Shrimpton (1997) 245–6 and the discussion in Hornblower (2002) 374–80.

31. The main actors and their works are discussed in Luraghi (1994b).

32. On Herodotus' ideas about the limits of possible knowledge of the past see Darbo-Peschanki (1987) 25–38 and Vannicelli (1993).

33. Note Darbo-Peschanski (1987) 93–4: distance in time does not seem to affect local memory as depicted by Herodotus.

34. For the notion of social surface see Moniot (1970) 134–5.

35. This notion would also help make sense of Herodotus' peculiar attitude to written documentary evidence, whose existence is acknowledged without it being used

as a source for specific statements; see the perceptive observations of Darbo-Peschanski (1987) 95–6, and West (1985) on inscriptions.

36. Luraghi (2001b) 159–60.
37. Interestingly, the Herodotean narrator refers a number of times to his activity with the verb *graphō*, 'to write'; see Rösler (2002) 88–90.
38. Boedeker (2000) 109; Boedeker's excellent discussion of the genre of the *Histories* forms the starting point for the considerations that follow.
39. See Boedeker (2000) 108–11, Dewald (2002) 274–5 and Brock (2003).
40. See Darbo-Peschanski (1987) 99–100.
41. See Fowler's edition of the early mythographers and his forthcoming commentary (*EGM*).
42. Calame (1986) explores thoroughly the problem of the construction of authority in Greek literature, from the archaic age to Herodotus. See also two recent and excellent articles, Scodel (1998) and (2001).
43. See Dewald (2002).
44. See Spiegel (1997), especially 3–28.

6

EGBERT J. BAKKER

The syntax of *historiē*: How Herodotus writes

He invested his style with all the qualities that his predecessors
had failed to acquire.
Dionysius of Halicarnassus, *De Thuc.* 5

Herodotus is an unaccountable phenomenon in the history of literature.
J. D. Denniston, *Greek Prose Style*

Herodotus' *Histories* is a work of startling originality; there are no pre-existing categories that capture the work's multifaceted nature. It can be read as historiography (tragic and epic, universal and local), ethnography, geography, oracular warning, and much more. To see the work in terms of any of these genres to the exclusion of others would be an arbitrary reduction of the whole to one of its component parts. And to see it as an 'early' instance of any of them would create a retrojection of modern assumptions that would exclude much of the living text's multifaceted reality. What would be lost is the context for which it was originally designed. Herodotus may write for posterity, but he practises *historiē* – his own unique kind of investigation into the world he inhabits – on his own terms.[1]

What applies to the context of Herodotus' ambitious project of *historiē* is no less true of its style. Herodotus' own term for his discourse is *logos*. Epic and prosaic, colloquial and elevated, oral and literate, Herodotus' discourse defies categorisation just as much as content does. Indeed, to make a distinction between the context and its 'style', or between Herodotus' investigations and their linguistic articulation, is misleading. *Historiē*, the quest for the 'cause' of the conflict between Greeks and barbarians, is achieved in and through the *logos* that Herodotus presents to us.

This chapter seeks to discuss the 'style' of the *Histories* as a complex, adaptive response to the demands of Herodotus' *historiē*. Herodotus sought to capture the experience of the entire known world in one long, complex and continuous *logos*. He did so by making use of the *logoi* of others and integrating them in various ways into the texture of his own huge *logos*.

From style to performance

Herodotus' style is often characterised as 'early prose'. This is both ancient and modern practice. Aristotle uses the term *lexis eiromenē*, the 'strung-on way of speaking' for the style of 'previous generations', within which he includes Herodotus.[2] He contrasts this older style with *lexis katestrammenē*, the 'turned-down way of speaking' that produces 'periods', sentences with a beginning, middle, and end that give a sense of finitude and closure. A modern version of the contrast would rephrase it as the difference between parataxis and hypotaxis: a co-ordinating style that presents all its elements on one and the same level is opposed to a style organised to subordinate the less important to the more important idea.

The concept of the paratactic style is not confined to the way in which the single sentences of a discourse are structured. In works called 'paratactic' in their organisation, it is claimed that only a limited organic unity is found. Two ideas seem to interfere with one another here. First, there is the idea that stories or episodes are linked to one another in a structure that has been compared to the beads on a string.[3] Second, there is the (sometimes implicit) idea that such stringing reflects the author's proclivity to digression: any item in the string can be linked as a parenthetical comment only loosely attached to what precedes or follows.[4] The structural necessity of returning to the main line of the story, thus the marking of the 'end' of the digression, has given rise to the term 'ring composition': a paratactic unit comes to a close in referring back to its beginning.[5]

The most detailed application of this stylistics to Herodotus is that of Henry Immerwahr (1966). On the assumption that both larger and smaller units obey the same principles in the paratactic style, Immerwahr discusses Herodotus' discourse in terms of the way in which sentences and phrases are linked to each other. According to Immerwahr, 'early literature' is stylistically characterised by two types of linkage: parataxis, essentially articulated by the particle *kai* ('and'), and antithesis, as expressed by *de* (commonly translated as either 'and' or 'but'). 'Antithesis' in the paratactic style is for Immerwahr not a true alternative between two ideas, but only the addition of a new member in a longer chain, one that stands 'in opposition to the main sequence in a list or an argument'.[6]

Immerwahr holds that Herodotus 'inherited' his paratactic style from predecessors such as Hecataeus, 'among whom it flourished by virtue of its appropriateness for lists of geographical names and for the description of animals and human customs'.[7] Such a wording implies that 'style' is somehow autonomous, pre-existing the author who 'uses' it. It also may imply that style has an autonomous development: from being 'early' it may mature and become 'classical' or some such characterisation. Without minimising the importance of style or aesthetics *per se*, I suggest that any discourse, regardless of its place in a stylistic development, will have features in accordance with the communicative tasks it is meant to perform. This is particularly appropriate for the *Histories*, whose communicative purpose was unprecedented in the history of Greek literature, and was not followed by his successors in the historiographical tradition. The important question to ask here is what communicative demands the peculiarities of Herodotus' prose style were meant to satisfy.

The ancient historian and literary critic Dionysius of Halicarnassus (first century BCE) in his treatise on the style of Thucydides (ch. 5) sets Herodotus apart from those before him, on the grounds that Herodotus' aims and subject matter were fundamentally different. Instead of writing the history of one single city, Herodotus chose to present the history of the entire known world, from the Lydian empire all the way to the failure of Xerxes' attempt to invade Greece. Dionysius saw no 'early prose' here, but an entirely new project, one calling for a new way of putting things into language. Dionysius uses a suggestive term for Herodotus' project. In combining many lines of action encompassing many different places and many different times, Herodotus has managed to transform the history of the entire known world into 'one single *suntaxis*' (*en miâi suntaxei*).[8]

Borrowing Dionysius' term, I propose here to speak of 'syntaxis' as a general characterisation of Herodotus' style. Syntaxis cuts through the contrast between parataxis and hypotaxis mentioned earlier. The *Histories*' 'syntactic' style is neither paratactic nor hypotactic, and the *logoi* that make up the *Histories* are neither beads on a string nor strictly hierarchically ordered. Moving from one *logos* to the next may involve a shift in time or space, and so a 'putting together' ('syntaxis') of two different places or two different times: different times are linked to one place, or different places to one time, as the historian moves backwards and forwards, from the cause of the conflict of Greeks and barbarians to the events that transpired from it.

In the fifth century BCE, Herodotus did not have ways, as we do, to visualise relationships textually, with subheadings, indentations, footnotes, etc. on the printed page. Nor was it possible to create cross-references between apparently independent *logoi* (such as the history of Croesus of Lydia, or of Cyrus of Persia, etc.); this would diminish meaning and impede explanation. The only way to make clear the causal relations between various lines of actions was to integrate into one continuous *logos* all the single *logoi* he could find that would help explain the conflict between Greeks and barbarians. This task involves 'syntaxis', an integration of disparate action strings into the ongoing progression of one single, heterogeneous, *logos*. The efforts at integration are most visible at the 'joints' of the work, the beginning and end of individual *logoi*, since it is there that the work's listeners can be most easily led astray, but also where the historian's orienting voice – the voice of the narrator specifying what has just finished and what is to come – can be of most help.

This leads to another important point about Herodotus' prose style: it has a 'performative' quality. This means, first, that the text is structured by the needs of a listening audience. But even more important is the fact that the *Histories* itself, whether in actual oral delivery or in the fictional orality of the act of reading, performs and enacts the speaking historian's research.[9] The text is the very accomplishment of the researches and investigations that led to its existence; the *logos* itself 'seeks out' its subjects, leading us to the goals it indicates.[10]

The *Histories* as syntaxis

For illustration of how Herodotus' style works in practice, let us turn to the beginning of the *Histories*. The proem informs us that the *historiē* to be accomplished in the act of reading will above all provide the cause (*aitiēn*) of the conflict between Greeks and barbarians. This is less an act of reference than an announcement: a goal is indicated that provides direction and long-range orientation to the reader.[11] This looking ahead is continued in the first sentence beyond the proem, which gets the project of *historiē* under way:[12]

Περσέων <u>μέν νυν</u> [*men nun*] οἱ λόγιοι Φοίνικας αἰτίους φασὶ γενέσθαι τῆς διαφορῆς.

(1.1.1)

Now the chroniclers of the Persians claim that it is the Phoenicians who have been responsible for the conflict.

This is the introduction to the account of mutual bride-stealing that is concluded as follows:

ταῦτα <u>μέν νυν</u> [*men nun*] Πέρσαι τε καὶ Φοίνικες λέγουσι. <u>ἐγὼ δὲ</u> [*egō de*] <u>περὶ μὲν τούτων</u> [*peri men toutōn*] οὐκ ἔρχομαι ἐρέων ὡς οὕτως ἢ ἄλλως κως ταῦτα ἐγένετο, <u>τὸν δὲ οἶδα</u> [*ton de oida*] αὐτὸς πρῶτον ὑπάρξαντα ἀδίκων ἔργων ἐς τοὺς Ἕλληνας, τοῦτον σημήνας προβήσομαι ἐς τὸ πρόσω τοῦ λόγου ... (1.5.3)

<u>Now this</u> <is what> the Persians and Phoenicians say; as for myself, about <u>these matters</u> I am not going to say that these events happened this way or some other way, <u>but whom I know</u> myself to have started acts of injustice against the Greeks, that man I will indicate and get underway with my *logos*.

These two extracts mark the beginning and end of a *logos*. But is it a separate *logos* that is arranged paratactically, as Immerwahr would argue? Let us look more carefully at the connections, which involve the particles *men* and *de*. In accounts of Greek grammar and style, these particles are usually described in terms of 'antithesis', and contrast is in fact what seems at first sight the principle that drives these extracts: contrast between the Persian chroniclers and Herodotus himself, and contrast between the stories of bride-stealing and the real agent of injustice as uncovered by Herodotus' own researches.

But this is a contrast that goes beyond items arranged like beads on a string; rather, it extends into the very flow, the syntax, of the *logos*. In some antitheses between an 'a' and a 'b' it does not make much difference which member is mentioned first; the contrast would be the same if the order were reversed.[13] The *men ... de* that frames the *logos* of bride-stealing, by contrast, is very different. Owing to the original function of *men* as a discourse particle signalling that the phrase it modifies needs the next phrase in order to be properly understood, I propose to see the *men*-member as *preparatory* with respect to the *de*-member: the former creates an expectancy that will be fulfilled by the latter.[14]

A phrase marked by *men* constitutes a stepping-stone to the point (*de*) the speaker wants to make. This can take the form of a concessive relationship between the two ('although it is true [*men*] that A; still, [*de*] B'); but often the relation is syntactically less specified. In any case, parataxis does not seem to be an appropriate concept here. Nor does hypotaxis work as a descriptive term, in the sense of subordinating syntactic relation. Instead, there is a strategy of complex signposting, which Herodotus exploits to the full: moments in discourse time are linked simultaneously both to what precedes and to what follows, to the past and the future.

A prime example of this discourse strategy is the *men* with which Herodotus' *logos* takes off: 'Now (*men*) the chroniclers of the Persians claim that ....' This *men* looks ahead and is for any reader or listener an unmistakable sign that the account of the Persian chroniclers will not be the last word on the matter of the *aitiē* ('cause') of the conflict between Greeks and barbarians. After the earlier mention in the proem of Herodotus and his *historiē*, we can surmise that here begins the stepping-stone to Herodotus' own investigation, or rather to the positive results of the investigation, since the account of the Persian scholars is part of his *historiē*, too. The *de* that 'answers' the *men* of the first extract is the *egō de* 'as for me ...' of the second one. The distance between the two members, or, alternatively, the 'discourse scope' of the first *men*, is so great that a repetition of the *men*-member, in the form of an anaphoric recapitulation ('now this is [*tauta men nun*] what the Persians and Phoenicians say') has been inserted to remind the reader of the nature of the investigation underway. Herodotus here does what many speakers do when they move from phrase to phrase in their speech: repairing things that have gone wrong, or providing extra orientation to keep the listener on the right track.

When we compare the two instances of *men* that frame the *logos* of the Persians, we note that the first is purely preparatory, for the simple reason that at this point at the very beginning of the first *logos*, the discourse does not have a past yet, only a future. The second, on the other hand ('this [*tauta men nun*] is what the Persians say'), is first of all recapitulative. It captions the previous account, but it also prepares *transition* to what follows: even when *men* looks back to the discourse's past, it does so in order to facilitate a step into the future.[15]

Nor is the present neglected. The two instances of *men* are both accompanied by the particle *nun* 'now': *men nun*. This unaccented discourse marker has to be distinguished from its accented counterpart *nūn* 'now'. Accented *nūn* is the particle of discourse-external 'now': it points to the present moment within which the discourse is presented or to a present created by the discourse. Unaccented *nun*, by contrast, is discourse-internal. It points not to the 'now' within which the discourse is presented, but to the 'now' *of* the discourse, a 'now' that is present as long as the discourse is listened to or read. This is the 'now' of the joints of Herodotus' *logos*, a 'now' that ensures the presence of a speaker, even millennia after Herodotus himself presented his work in real discourse contexts; this is the 'now' of anyone's encounter with Herodotus' work.

It is worth pointing out that the combination *men nun*, exceedingly frequent in the *Histories*, never occurs in Herodotus' successors Thucydides and Xenophon: a major difference, not just in 'style', but in the way the speaker is present in the discourse. Instead, the combination is found in the tragedians (although not in comedy).[16] Apparently its register is too formal for the comic stage, yet too dialogic to be of interest to Thucydides. Herodotus uses it profusely for the many joints in his *logos* that are required by the 'syntactic style'. Not only does the element *nun* point to the discourse's internal present; it also testifies to the speaker's continuous presence. The plus-value added with *nun* to the pair *men . . . de* is the speaker's presence in the act of guiding the listener or reader through the transitions and exchanges between the many tracks of the *Histories*: many times the transition is either to the historian himself or to material on which he has a strong opinion.[17]

The path from the Persian chroniclers to the 'I' of the historian immediately leads to a new *men . . . de* contrast within the space opened up by *egō de*: from 'Persians versus Herodotus' we now move to 'stories from the remote past versus Croesus'. The first mention of the Lydian king as 'the man whom I know to have started acts of injustice against the Greeks', however, is less an arrival than a new goal. After a programmatic introduction to Croesus and his annexation of the Ionian Greeks (1.6) the narrative veers away to the story of how the Lydian dynasty prior to Croesus' came to an end, and to the *res gestae* of the kings of the Mermnadae prior to Croesus. Far from being a paratactic, associative digression, however, this narrative is very focussed: it gravitates inexorably to Croesus, the goal in whose direction it was first presented. And when the goal is reached (1.26, the beginning of the Croesus *logos* proper), we understand Croesus' position in history better than he does himself. Even though Herodotus himself says that his '*logos* seeks digressions' (4.30.1), very few of his *logoi* are in fact entirely 'digressive'. *Logoi* feed into *logoi*, turning a complex, intricate web of relationships into the comprehensive thread of discourse that is the essence of 'syntaxis'.

Whose *logos*? The *Histories* as 'pointing' (*deixis*)

The syntax of *historiē* is not only a matter of syntaxis, of joining *logoi* into a linear progression, but also of *deixis*, of 'pointing'. *Logos*, speech, as represented in the *Histories* can be oriented in various ways. It can be a communication directly between the speaker-historian and his public, or it can be mediated through the perspective of the characters in the tale; it can be a story (*logos*) itself or part of a story, presented directly or indirectly, and so on.[18] To manage these various possibilities, Herodotus makes innovative use of the system of *deixis* inherent in the Greek language. *Deixis* is the 'pointing function' of language, by which speakers situate themselves or the things they talk about in a 'universe of discourse', according to the parameters time (now–then), place (this–that), and person (me–you/him). As we will see, a key role is reserved here for the demonstrative (deictic) pronouns *houtos* 'that' and *ekeinos* 'that'.[19] These two deictics differ in the degree of proximity to the speaker of the thing pointed at: whereas *houtos* situates something close to the addressee (and so known or visible to him), *ekeinos* designates what is at one further remove: close to a third party. This difference in relative distance is crucial for Herodotus to keep track of the various levels of *logos* that *historiē* involves.

Let us make the important distinction between speech as *action within* a tale and speech as *source for the tale*. In other words, represented speech can either be part of the action represented within a *logos* or it can be the *logos* itself. The former is a concern of storytellers of all kinds, times, and places; the latter is a concern of *historiē* specifically. Herodotus' project of *historiē* may explicitly mark the account of things past as *logos*. Herodotus may pass on the *logos* of others to posterity, thus creating a 'hedge' between his own *logos* and the events recounted. Again, the beginning of the *Histories* is an ideal example:

Περσέων μέν νυν οἱ λόγιοι Φοίνικας αἰτίους φασὶ [*phasi*] γενέσθαι τῆς διαφορῆς.

(1.1.1)

Now the chroniclers of the Persians claim [*phasi*] that it is the Phoenicians who have been responsible for the conflict.

This opens, as we saw, the story of bride-stealing that serves as stepping-stone to Herodotus' own account. That this is not Herodotus' own account is made clear not only by *men nun* as it anticipates *egō de* (see above), but also by the important verb *phasi* 'they say/claim'. This verb governs an infinitive construction that extends far beyond the confines of this first sentence: it comprises the entire *logos*, which thus comes to be dissociated from Herodotus' own voice, or so it seems. Herodotus speaks to us, but he reports on a *phasi*, a complex truth-claim of a third party, which cannot but take the form of a narrative. This external story has been included as an intrusion into Herodotus' account, but is not impervious to intrusions itself. Even though the account of the Persian chroniclers represents a perspective other than that of Herodotus, the voice of the investigator is present throughout. This is clear in the sentence following the previous extract:

τούτους [*toutous*] γὰρ ἀπὸ τῆς Ἐρυθρῆς καλεομένης θαλάσσης ἀπικομένους ἐπὶ τήνδε τὴν θάλασσαν [*tēnde tēn thalassan*] καὶ οἰκήσαντας τοῦτον τὸν χῶρον τὸν καὶ νῦν οἰκέουσι [*touton ton chōron ton kai nūn oikeousi*], αὐτίκα ναυτιλίῃσι μακρῇσι ἐπιθέσθαι . . .

(1.1.1)

These people [i.e., the Phoenicians], they say, after having come from the so-called Red Sea to the sea on our side, and after having settled in that area that they inhabit even now, they immediately engaged in long journeys . . .

The claim is Persian (or is at least presented as Persian), but the perspective is still Greek. That is, the historian puts forward his own perspective as he communicates with his public in his own writing present. This is clear from the use of the deictic (demonstrative) pronouns in the extract. The deictic phrase *tēnde tēn thalassan* ('this sea here') presupposes a deictic centre outside the Persian claim reported: the spatial-geographical orientation of the historian and his Greek public. The designation of the Phoenicians' contemporary homeland involves the temporal adverb *nūn*, which in conveying a discourse-external 'now' represents the historian's writing present in which he communicates with his public: 'our time'. The verb *oikeousi* 'they inhabit' is a finite verb, not an infinitive, and hence not under the 'scope' of the source

99

verb *phasi*; it represents a comment on the part of the historian.[20] A further deictic phrase, *touton ton chōron* ('that land') complements the historian's perspective: the demonstrative pronoun *houtos* conveys that the land in question is known to the listeners, and so is a matter of shared knowledge between them and Herodotus. The same pronoun, we can observe, is used to establish the Phoenicians themselves as protagonists in the story (*toutous*, 'these people'). It signals that even though the story is announced as a Persian *logos*, it is presented from the historian's present perspective. The dialogue, and the real *locus* of *historiē*, is not between Herodotus and the Persians, but between Herodotus and his public.

The Persian chroniclers, then, are the source of the story, not story characters that are represented as saying something. The difference between these possibilities entails two quite distinct types of indirect speech in Herodotus, each with its own deictic orientation. The Persian *logos* itself is an instance of the first type; the second type we encounter when the tale of mutual bride-stealing is well underway:

πέμψαντα τὸν Κόλχον βασιλέα ἐς τὴν Ἑλλάδα κήρυκα αἰτέειν τε δίκας τῆς ἁρπαγῆς καὶ ἀπαιτέειν τὴν θυγατέρα· τοὺς δὲ ὑποκρίνεσθαι ὡς οὐδὲ <u>ἐκεῖνοι</u> [*ekeinoi*] Ἰοῦς τῆς Ἀργείης <u>ἔδοσάν</u> [*edosan*] σφι δίκας τῆς ἁρπαγῆς· <u>οὐδὲ ὦν αὐτοὶ</u> <u>δώσειν ἐκείνοισι</u> [*oude ōn autoi dōsein ekeinoisi*].　　　　　　　　(1.2.3)

The king of the Colchians, they say, sent a messenger to Hellas to demand justice for the abduction and to ask back his daughter. The Greeks, it is held, answered him that *they* had not offered compensation either for the abduction of Io of Argos. <u>So, neither would *they* offer it to *them*</u> [*oude ōn autoi dōsein ekeinoisi*].

In the first sentence the perspective is Herodotus' as he mediates to us the account of the Persians. But this changes in the second sentence (beginning with *tous de hupokrinasthai* 'and they [the Greeks] answered'). We see here another finite verb, *edosan* ('they had given'), but this time there is no comment on the historian's part. The perspective is now internal, as the Greeks in answering the Colchian envoy present their side of the matter. The Greeks' *logos*, indirectly reported in a finite clause with *hōs* 'that', is action within a *logos*, a secondary speech event that comes with its own point of view. Herodotus conveys this shift in perspective with grammatical means, by replacing the pronoun *houtos* with *ekeinos*: the thing pointed at is now at one further remove from the participants in the primary speech event. The richness of the Greek language with its multiple sets of deictic pronouns enables Herodotus to mark the grammatical coding of a complex narrative structure.

The last sentence in the extract is again infinitive. But the construction does not depend on the 'source verb' *phasi*: the perspective of the Greeks is continued, as appears from a further occurrence of *ekeinos*.[21] It presents the conclusion from the previous words as delivered from the point of view of their speakers; accordingly the particle *ōn* (ὦν), too, is operational on the level of the embedded speech. The infinitive sentence blurs the line between speaking and thinking in the representation of an internal point of view: what counts is the motivation or intention for speech represented, not the verbatim repetition of the speech itself.[22]

*

Herodotus' account of the Persian *logos* at the beginning of the *Histories* is a linguistic and narrative *tour de force*. Presented as the stepping-stone that sets the syntactic flow of Herodotus' forward-looking *logos* in motion, it explores complex depths of speech representation and a discourse-internal point of view, putting Greek grammar to new uses. There were no pre-existing models for this. Homer and the epic tradition provided direct speech, with which the singer acts out the words of the past in the present of the performance, but epic is less interested in representing heroes' speech internally, embedded within the discourse as it gives access to the past. Herodotus' successor Thucydides would push the art of representing speech and thought to new heights, but we may wonder what his work would have looked like in this respect without Herodotus as competitor and predecessor. But whereas Herodotus' *deixis* was to be the beginning of a tradition in Greek historiographical narrative, his syntaxis was not. Thucydides abandoned the progressive *logos* as the principle that guides his account, opting instead for a strict division on the basis of the 'real world' entities 'winter and summer'. The result was a separation between *historiē* and its articulation in language that constituted a clear break with Herodotus' project. It made Herodotus' style stand out all the more clearly as a unique phenomenon in the history of Greek narrative.

NOTES

1. On *historiē* in Herodotus, see Bakker (2002) 13–19.
2. Arist. *Rhet.* 1409a29–1409b4. For discussion of this passage, see Bakker (1997) 36–9.
3. See Notopoulos (1949) for a formulation of this idea in terms of an 'oral poetics'.
4. Compare Aristotle's characterisation of the *lexis eiromenē* as devoid of *telos* ('goal', 'end').
5. On ring composition, see van Otterlo (1944).
6. Immerwahr (1966) 49.
7. Immerwahr (1966) 47.

8. The word *suntaxis* denotes the putting together of elements into a composite whole that is geared to the performance of specific tasks: 'order', 'organisation'. Thus the term can denote, for example, the arrangements of soldiers into battle order.

9. This, I believe, is the meaning of *apodexis* in the proem of the *Histories*; see Bakker (2002). On the identity between the narrator and the researcher, see also Munson (2001a) 33.

10. Most clearly at 1.95.1, where the *logos* is presented as 'seeking' (*epidizētai*) Cyrus as the goal that had been set up by the Croesus *logos* that is now completed. Compare 4.30.1. *Logos* is sometimes presented as a road (1.95.1) and narrating as movement (1.5.3: *probēsomai*).

11. See also Lang (1984) 1–17 in an illuminating discussion of Herodotus' style to which the present account is indebted. Of related interest is Munson's notion of the 'prospective sentence' ([2001a] 25–6, 29).

12. In the overall structure of the work, the mentioning of 'cause' (*aitiē*) in the proem points ahead to 5.97.3: the sailing of an Athenian fleet that is called the *archē kakōn* ('beginning of all evil') for Greeks and barbarians alike. Compare Lang (1984) 3; Lateiner (1989) 35.

13. The proem provides an example: 'great and marvellous deeds performed on the one hand (*ta men*) by the Greeks, on the other hand (*ta de*) by the barbarians'.

14. This essential device of discourse cohesion is used by Herodotus to achieve a number of effects that are highly characteristic of his *logos*. See Bakker (1997) 80–85 (for *men* in the flow of Homeric discourse); Bakker (1993) 299–305 (Herodotus).

15. This recapitulative-transitional use of *men (nun)* is extremely common: e.g. 1.21.1; 1.24.8; 1.71.1; 2.4.2; 2.8.2; 2.28.1; 3.1.5, etc.

16. For example Aesch. *Pers.* 412; Soph. *El.* 73, *OC* 96; Eur. *Hipp.* 20.

17. For example 2.123.1; 2.147.1; 7.229.2. On the presence of Herodotus' voice in his work, see also Munson (2001a) 20–44 (especially 24–7), Dewald (2002) 274–7. On Herodotus' reporting on his own activity as researcher, see Marincola (1987).

18. See Pelling in this volume.

19. On *houtos* in epic specifically, and the deixis of narrative, see Bakker (1999).

20. See Bakker (1991).

21. This sentence, in fact, would have been infinitive even without the overarching infinitive construction of the Persian *logos*. See, e.g., 8.61.2, where we have the same structure (finite *hōs*-clause followed by infinitive construction; deictic *ekeinos* signalling speaker's point of view) without the matrix narrative being infinitive itself. Note that *gar* is a common element in cases like this, the infinitive sentence providing the speaker's own explanation for what he had said in the previous speech. See further 2.141.3; 2.162.4; 4.145.2; 9.93.4.

22. The embedded infinitive might be called an early example of 'free indirect speech', a narrative mode in which a character's thought or vision is conveyed through the discourse of the narrator. For introduction to the various kinds of indirect speech, see Coulmas (1984).

7

CHRISTOPHER PELLING

Speech and narrative in the *Histories*

Logos is reason; *logos* is speech. There are of course good reasons why the same word captures what in English are distinct concepts. Internalised 'reasoning' is often figured in a way parallel to external conversation and debate;[1] and if an idea or a projected course of action 'has *logos*', *echei logon*, it is 'reasonable' in that it is capable of being presented in convincing argument.

Yet in Herodotus these two 'senses' of *logos* – or, better, these two English ways of capturing different aspects of the concept – often stand in a problematic relation to one another. How 'reasonable' is a 'speech'? Speakers are struggling to make sense of events, to gauge what is happening – and also (not necessarily the same thing) to gauge what they should wisely say about those events. The text's readers and listeners are doing something similar, constantly measuring a speaker's words against the narrative which the text has given or will go on to give. And there is another reason too not to divorce speech from action, for in an important sense speeches *are* action.[2] They play their part – often initiating, often responsive – in a chain of events; and they also build up a behavioural pattern of *how deliberation works*, often differently in different parts of the world or in different political systems. That is especially important in Herodotus, where the dynamics of *logos* operate in different ways in the autocratic courts of the East and in the diverse political systems of Greece, especially in the fragile alliance of states which confronts the invader.

Were this Thucydides, there would be little difficulty in isolating what is 'a speech'. Thucydides' speeches tend to be formally marked off, and to play their role in a staged, planned, set-piece debate. In Herodotus matters are more complex. Direct speech is very frequent, as we would expect of a writer whose manner so often suggests oral performance (whether or not we should think of this text itself as in any sense 'oral'); just as in Homer, we can sense how a performer or reader could 'dramatise' by allowing a man – or a woman, for Herodotus unlike Thucydides allows women to speak too, often tellingly – a distinctive texture and timbre. Yet often that direct speech comes in modes of language which we would not call quite 'speeches': proclamations, oracles (and often people's responses to oracles), brief *apophthegmata* or jests, simply conversations.[3] A conversation can sometimes develop so that one or both parties deliver a more developed, coherent, articulated 'speech': Solon and Croesus, for instance, or Artabanus and Xerxes at the Hellespont (1.30–3; 7.45–52). Many of the characteristics of formal speeches also typify other sorts of verbal exchanges – how they illustrate the dynamics of a court, with a conversational exchange capturing the imbalance of a power-relationship (Gyges and Candaules, or Xerxes and Masistes, or Cambyses and Croesus: 1.8–9; 9.111; 3.34); how direct speech is used at crucial moments or to highlight crucial themes (the banquet at Orchomenus, or Cyrus in the last chapter of the *Histories*: 9.16, 9.122); how *oratio recta* tends to direct more attention to how people are talking, *oratio obliqua* to the substance of what they say (thus Hecataeus has indirect speech at 5.36 and 125, whereas the rhetorically adept Aristagoras gets direct speech at 5.30–1, 33, 49; at 8.108–9 Eurybiades has indirect, Themistocles direct speech). There are generic affinities too; unsurprisingly, direct speech is often most frequent at times when the texture comes close to tragedy (an extraordinarily large proportion of the tales of Croesus and Atys and of the infant Cyrus are in direct speech[4]), or indeed – once again – to Homeric epic, rich as that too was in quoted speech.[5] In what follows, the examples will in most cases be the longer, more formal, set-piece oral presentations; but no clear line divides these from the many less elaborate cases where characters speak aloud.

The two themes I have already sketched – the dynamics of *logos*, and the reader's comparison of speech and narrative – will be recurrent in what follows. If all speeches were considered, or even if all relevant aspects of a speech were discussed, this chapter would expand to fill a whole book. Such a book, indeed, is still badly needed.[6] Still, even a very selective sample may indicate some of the ironic complexities of Herodotus' depiction of speech.

Solon and Croesus (1.30–3)

Herodotus' speeches range from the very specific – is this strategy wise? – to the vastly universal – is it ever justified to break oaths? It is hopeless to try to subdivide them into the 'moral' and the 'political'. That distinction would not have been real in contemporary Greek thought;[7] it is certainly not real in Herodotean deliberation, as time and again specific political issues are illuminated by and illuminate large concepts: the nature of freedom and tyranny; the tension between loyalty and self-interest; the relation of free choice and divinely imposed necessity.

The first, perhaps the most important, of the speech-makers in the *Histories* has much in common with the wise traveller Herodotus himself, as Solon, renowned for his travel and his wisdom (1.29.2, 30.2), arrives at Croesus' court and imparts some of his wisdom to that listener. The scene is recalled later by verbal echoes, and particularly at those moments when the probing of human existence is at its most intense – Polycrates and his ring, or Artabanus at the Hellespont (3.40–1; 7.46, 49). Nor is it coincidence that this first encounter is between wisdom and power; nor that those who make the power-driven decisions find it so difficult to learn; nor that we begin on the cusp between East and West, in Lydia, the 'eastern' land closest and most familiar to Greece, with customs most similar to the Greek (1.94.1) and with a king fascinated by Greek wisdom and insight; nor that this exchange sits at the more 'universal' end of our spectrum of topics. However we come to understand Croesus' fate, we are encouraged to reflect on what it tells us about all human life.

This is a case where conversation develops into speech. Solon does not arrive with the intention of lecturing Croesus; he answers questions, and his advice is extracted rather than paraded. Wisdom is not conveyed readily. And the conversational dynamic is interesting. The language becomes more intimate as the exchange develops: Solon begins by addressing Croesus as 'O king', the regular mode for a court, but as he dwells on the humanity which both share the address becomes closer also, simply 'Croesus'.[8] But the closeness of language does not go with a closeness of temperament or understanding, and at the end Croesus dismisses Solon as an 'ignoramus' (*amathea*, 1.33) – not just a 'silly fellow', but a word which contrasts with that initial reputation for much-travelled wisdom. This listener finds it difficult to grasp Solon's wisdom, or even to see that wisdom is relevant to the question of human happiness. This first great speech-encounter in the *Histories*, one which introduces so many themes programmatically, is a failure of communication – and that may be programmatic too.[9]

There are other ways, too, in which this communication is skewed: in particular, is Solon sensed as saying all he means? Several themes jostle together in Solon's words: that life is mutable and anyone's fortune may change, upwards as well as downwards – a message for everyone, not just the mighty; or perhaps the mighty are particularly vulnerable, for the divine may be envious of their prosperity and turbulent in bringing them down. But one theme is not made explicit, and this is that Croesus, as one so powerful and so deluded as to his vulnerability, may be particularly likely to *act* in ways that will encompass his own destruction. That indeed is what he goes on to do. Such a theme is not far to seek in the narrative context: Croesus was first introduced as the man 'who began unjust deeds against the Greeks' (1.5.3), and we have seen his indiscriminate aggression against Ionians and Aeolians, 'bringing different grievances against different peoples, bigger ones when he could find any and in some cases trivial ones' (1.26.3). Immediately after Solon's departure the narrative continues (1.34.1): 'After Solon's departure a great righteous indignation (*nemesis*) came from God and struck Croesus, presumably because he thought himself the most prosperous of all mortals.' So far, it is true, Croesus' excessive and over-confident behaviour is a matter of thought rather than deed, but such thoughts all too often precede or accompany dangerously transgressive behaviour as well.[10] One of the most familiar statements of the moral pattern was owed to the historical Solon himself: 'satiety (*koros*) begets hubris, when great prosperity (*olbos*) attends those whose mind is not well-ordered' (*IEG* F 6.3–4). Herodotus makes his Solon echo several other passages in Solon's poems;[11] but not this one, appropriate though the thought might be to this moral case.

Nor is it hard to see why. Croesus is a man of untrammelled power. No one, especially no wise person, will tell a man like this that he is likely to behave badly, and to bring himself as well as others down.[12] Solon treads very tactfully, making generalisations that dwell on the man's bigness rather than his real or potential badness, phrases that gain their purchase by their appreciative recognition of the prosperity of which Croesus is so proud. Indirectness and obliquity are, and have to be, the ways of the court. But that itself points the way that the powerful so seldom get the advice which they need from the wise, for their power ensures that wisdom has to come masked and shrouded. Speech itself is distorted, as the wisest of humans find that they cannot talk straight.

Soclees of Corinth (5.92)

In Greece speakers are usually more direct. At 5.92 the issue is whether the Greek states should interfere with the newly freed Athens, as the Spartan king Cleomenes has asked, and reimpose a tyranny. Soclees urges that they should not: 'if you had experienced tyranny as we have, you would not be urging this upon us . . .' Scholars sense a meta-literary aspect here, as Herodotus' text gives to others the experience of tyranny that – so Soclees claims – leaves so indelible an impression and inescapable a conclusion.[13]

Soclees is said to 'speak freely' (93.2), and that is as a Greek should (though it is true that the other Peloponnesians only make their feelings plain once Soclees has given his lead, 92.1, 93.2). That phrase combines closely with the swearing by the Greek gods (92η.5, 93.1) and the cry – by now a cry of 'every single person' (93.2) – 'not to interfere with a Greek city',[14] a euphemism in this case for 'not to impose a tyranny' – so again the contrast of despotism and freedom is not too far away. The initial Spartan proposal is itself phrased in disquieting ways (91). Cleomenes' argument is parochial: it does glance at the way that the expansionist new Athens has already impinged on Boeotia and Chalcis, but the emphasis is still on the Spartans' wish to punish Athens for its ingratitude towards them. There are some echoes too of the Constitutional Debate in Book 3. This ungrateful *dēmos* has now, claims Cleomenes, 'cocked up its head' (91.2), recalling Darius' claim that evil men in a democracy 'put their heads together' to do harm (3.82.4);[15] this *dēmos* is showing hubris, and Megabyxus at 3.81.2 talked of the inevitable hubris of an undisciplined *dēmos*; this *dēmos* is over-inflated by its success, not unlike the way in which Otanes claimed that a tyrant is led into hubris by his prosperity (3.80.3).[16] That Persian debate led inevitably to Persian tyranny; now Cleomenes sees things similarly, and the echoes give an unsettling hint that Sparta has leanings in the same direction.

Soclees' fine words stem that particular tide: and he does talk straight. For him the lesson of the Corinthians' experience is unambiguous. To talk tyranny is to be un-Greek. And not much here compromises that contrast of free, outspoken Greek rhetoric and the different style of an eastern court. Doubtless, indeed, the episode is allowed so much space because 'it explains something essential about the Greeks'.[17]

Yet there are complications. Soclees, like those Persian grandees, talks only of the *internal* impact of a tyrant, in this case the outrages committed by Cypselus and Periander against their fellow-citizens. Those outrages give a different echo of the Constitutional Debate, validating Otanes' insight on a tyrant's hubris, in particular his jealousy of the 'best men if they survive and live' and his 'violence to women' (3.80.4–5), the points respectively of the Thrasybulus and the Melissa stories here. Yet Cleomenes' point was the *external* threat of Athens to other states, including Corinth itself. If tyranny enfeebles a state, then that might even tell Cleomenes' way: the allies should *want* Athens to be weak. Soclees' rhetoric might seem ill-adjusted to its context,[18] but the point is probably that the Corinthians' experience is so searing that they can only think of the negative aspects of tyranny, and cannot see that these might tell to their own advantage.

Hippias responds to Soclees' speech by predicting 'that the Corinthians would one day long for the Peisistratids, when the time came for them to be pained by the Athenians' (93.1), and he says this as one who has peculiarly close and full knowledge of the oracles. We see something of this 'paining' within the text, where Corinthians and Athenians are several times on edge with one another (8.59, 61, 94–5). It would be hard, too, for a contemporary audience to avoid thought of the outbreak of the Peloponnesian War and a further 'assembling of the allies', when the Corinthians were so outraged by Athenian behaviour that they pressed the Peloponnesian alliance into action, and in particular had to deal with a reluctant Sparta (Thuc. 1.67–87).[19]

The point of Soclees' Thrasybulus and Melissa stories is clear enough:[20] tyranny is bad for a state. The story of Labda, telling how the Bacchiads' henchmen could not bring themselves to kill the baby Cypselus, seems less integrated: yes, a tyrant can seem charming in infancy but can become a monster[21] – but it is the monstrosity rather than the infancy that we should expect to get the space. There may be links with the story of the infant Cyrus, whom again it seemed repugnant to kill (1.109–13), or with other oracles or omens suggesting monstrous futures if a child is born and survives – Cyrus again (1.107–8), Peisistratus (1.59), and, most suggestively of all, Pericles, on one possible interpretation of the surely ambivalent lion-dream at 6.131.2. (In Cypselus' case too the oracle foretells the birth of a 'lion', powerful and ravening.) But there is a further 'infant' in the immediate vicinity of the text which could grow up to be a tyrant: the tyrant city, Athens herself. Soclees' *ainos* is more ambivalent than he knows.

Not that there is a clear moral to be drawn. It would be premature to decide that Soclees was simply wrong, that the infant free state of Athens should have been strangled at birth: the rhetoric of Greek unity is too strong for that.[22] But the richness of the rhetoric suggests reflections that go in different directions. Even when a speaker talks straight, the relation to the narrative, and the relation to extratextual events which the audience will know, must complicate the reader's critique of a speech.

Xerxes, Mardonius, and Artabanus (7.8–11)

No scene shows an uneasy court dynamic more clearly than this, the most elaborate set of speeches of all – and appropriately placed, marking the most momentous decision of the history, for Xerxes has determined to invade Greece. 'Xerxes has determined . . .': the phrasing may seem odd for a debate when he is calling for advice, but the decision has already been taken. 'I have called you here so that I might pass over to you what I have in mind to do' (7.8α.2). 'This is what must be done; but, so that I may not seem to be self-willed, I place the matter before you, bidding anyone of you who wishes to express his opinion' (7.8δ.2). Several phrases in that sentence capture mantras of Greek, especially democratic, debate: 'to express his opinion'; 'place the matter before you', literally 'into the middle', where all around may regard it as equally theirs;[23] 'anyone who wishes', so familiar from Attic decrees.[24] But it is only 'so that I may not *seem* to be self-willed'.

This is already a travesty of debate, at least as Greeks would understand debate.

But it is a travesty with some skilled performers: Mardonius, who knows he has already won, but whose enthusiasm can make the king's decision more attractive (if this is what is meant at 7.10.1, where he has 'smoothed over' the king's words); and Xerxes' uncle Artabanus, who treads more carefully in trying, hopelessly, to deflect him. One cannot be too direct; both Mardonius and Artabanus turn to creating or adopting proverbs. 'Nothing comes of its own accord,' ends Mardonius: 'everything comes to those who try' (7.9γ). It is uncomfortable that he has to resort to such language, as if this were a mere adventure.[25] Artabanus has to be more indirect still.[26] It is good to hear the opposite view, he begins, because it may show up the wisdom of one's own (7.10α.2). 'You see how it is the biggest animals whom God strikes down by lightning . . . the biggest houses and trees which his shafts strike . . .' (7.10ε): once again, as with Solon, it is Xerxes' magnificence rather than his transgressive actions which the cautious adviser knows it is wise to stress. When Artabanus becomes direct, those sharp remarks are reserved for Mardonius (7.10η–θ). One can abuse a fellow-subject; a tyrant is different.

Xerxes' response is one of magnificent fury, and it shows how right Artabanus was to watch his words. It is lucky for him he's Xerxes' uncle; otherwise he would have suffered appropriately for such wild advice (7.11.1). As it is, he will suffer the worst shame, to stay at home and not to play a part. Xerxes owes victory and vengeance to his ancestors, 'driving against these men whom even the Phrygian Pelops, slave of my forefathers, conquered so completely that the men and their land are still to this day called by the name of the man who vanquished it' (7.11.3). *C'est magnifique, mais ce n'est pas la sagesse*: no wonder wisdom is elusive, when such is the response even to one who picked his words so carefully.

How Xerxes speaks sounds perilous too: Persia's realm will be coterminous with Zeus' Heaven, the sun will see no land which is not ours, guilty and non-guilty alike will bear our yoke (7.8γ). But *what* he speaks is not nonsense. His generalisations of 7.11 match those of Artabanus, and they are not crass. Great empires are indeed threatened if they allow the small to defy them, and great kings may be under internal threats if they fail to live up to the expectations generated by a nation's past. Even if the phantom-sequence does go on to articulate a divine necessity, there is still a human necessity too, and Xerxes is trapped by his own nation's history. 'We have never yet been still', he says (7.8α.1). He returns to the theme in his later, more reflective encounter with Artabanus at the Hellespont (7.50.3–4). There is more to this exchange than a crude contrast of a rash king and a cautious sage: there is wisdom in Xerxes' words too.[27]

Mardonius seems less acute, and he is absurdly wrong to think the Greeks will not fight (7.9γ). He tries to use his own experience of Greeks, such as it is – but, then, he reached only Macedonia (7.9α.2). Nor does he use even that experience wisely; after all, this was a man who knew it was wise to impose democracies (6.43.2), and he knew then that freedom has its strengths too. Yet his words of 7.9β invite more thought:

> Yet, so I hear, the Greeks fight their wars in the most ill-counselled way, so unintelligent and stupid are they. Whenever they declare war on one another, they find the fairest and smoothest of places, go there, and fight, so that the victors come off the field with great damage – and, as for the defeated, I say nothing of them, as they are completely destroyed. What they ought to do is this, for they share a single language: they should use heralds and messengers to resolve their differences, and do anything rather than fight about them; and if war turned out to be wholly unavoidable, they should find where each side has the hardest places and make trial of one another there.

'. . . For they share a single language': that looks forward to one of the markers of Greek identity, invoked as the Athenians celebrate the harmony of the Greek triumph (8.144.2, below, p. 113). Mardonius is right to see this as a potential strength of the Greek people; he is wrong to assume that they are incapable of exploiting it. But he is *only just* wrong: the Greek tendency to fragment and fight one another was so nearly catastrophic.[28]

So truth and falsity, insight and rashness come together in these speeches, and the complexities only become clear once the later narrative has offered its perspectives. Speech, even insightful speech, can be delusive; rash and dangerous speech can at least graze a deeper wisdom. Rationality, *logos*, is elusive; and, when the dynamics of a court are the way they are, speeches themselves, *logoi*, get in rationality's way.

Before Salamis (8.57–9)[29]

The contrast between Greek and Persian styles of debate is caught by the two debates before Salamis, where first the Greeks and then the Persians discuss how they should fight. One contribution of the speeches is to illuminate the strategic background.[30] There is force in Themistocles' argument that it is better for the outnumbered Greeks to fight in the narrows where Xerxes cannot deploy his numbers, and to fight in a forward position to defend all the crucial territory.[31] But there is sense in Artemisia's argument too, dissuading Xerxes from fighting on sea at all: at sea the Greeks are as superior to the Persians as men are to women (a delicious irony, of course, in the mouth of the warrior queen[32]); and there is no need to fight a sea-battle at all, for if

Xerxes stays where he is or moves on the Peloponnese the Greeks will have to abandon Salamis anyway. The battle itself is extremely confusing, doubtless expressively so: the climactic moment in the freedom struggle is a matter of tumult and randomness, not a glorious scene of directed heroism; but if we are to make strategic sense of it at all we will find Themistocles' preparatory insights useful. We might, though, remember Artemisia too, and recall that this need never have happened, had her wisdom prevailed.

But it did not, and Themistocles' persuasion did: why? The reasons again have more to do with the rhetorical dynamic of the debate than with the merits of the argument. The regulated nature of the Persian debate – all sitting meekly in order and waiting to be called upon, Xerxes relying on his intermediary Mardonius to report back the contributions (8.67.2) – contrasts with the confusion of the Greek assembly. It is first summoned at 8.49; then interrupted by the news from Athens, so dramatic as to lead some captains to rush headlong to their ships (56) in a recreation of *Iliad* 2. Next Themistocles persuades Eurybiades to reconvene everyone, and this renewed discussion begins with Themistocles' boisterous lobbying (59) and an exchange of insults with Adeimantus of Corinth, a verbal duel which resumes after Themistocles has spoken (59, 61.2). So this is 'freedom' in action, in its most unregulated and roistering form: and the language used to describe it – 'skirmishing' (64.1) – suggests that the bellicosity which should have been spent on the Persians is being spent on one another.

This is a different, less impressive sort of 'speaking freely' than in the case of Soclees; and speech on the Persian side takes a new twist too. For Artemisia *does* speak openly, after (it is true) the initial contributions to the debate had been less outspoken (68.1). This freedom of speech surprises characters in the text too, and her friends expect her to suffer terribly for it and her enemies rejoice (69.1) – more light there on the sly manoeuvrings which typify a court. But their expectations are wrong, as Xerxes is 'delighted by' her advice (69.2, that 'delight' which so often typifies tyrants[33]): this is a calmer figure than the man who so lost his temper with Artabanus. Courts, like Greek states, do not always fit the stereotypes we build of them – even the stereotypes which the narrative has encouraged. But Xerxes still rejects the advice, and for a reason which illuminates tyranny in a different way. He accepts that his men did not fight well at Artemisium, but thinks that this time it will be different, for this time he will be there himself (69.2). He remains as clear of the superiority of one-man directed rule as he was when he talked with Demaratus at 7.103–4; and, here as there, he is not wholly wrong. In the battle his expectations are largely fulfilled (8.86), though this enthusiasm to impress the king does produce some disorder (89.2).

This time, the side where *logos* is distorted is not the Persian. The Greek debate was not merely a shambles in its conduct; it was also one where Themistocles did not speak his mind. The argument which swayed him and Eurybiades too was the one which Mnesiphilus enunciated and Themistocles then 'made out to be his own' (58.2). That had nothing to do with fighting in the narrows; it was rather that, if the Greeks did not fight here, the whole alliance would break up, and all would flee back to their own countries (57.2). But Themistocles evidently cannot say this in public, 'for when the allies were assembled it carried no propriety[34] at all for him to accuse them' (60.1). He has to resort to arguments which are second-best – and it is a further irony that these are the arguments which so capture the nub of the strategic issue, those of fighting in the narrows.

Yet, however wise, these arguments do not carry the day: what decides the issue is the threat that, unless the allies agree to fight, the Athenians will sail away to Italy (62.2). That shows the truth in Themistocles' original fear that fragmentation would be the danger – but only because the Athenians themselves bring the fear so close to realisation. Thus the debate is short-circuited; then a further acrimonious debate (74, cf. 78) is again short-circuited, this time by Sicinnus' message, a different type of speech, a piece of Themistoclean trickery that gains its cogency by the element of truth it contains – and this, once more, points to the real danger that the Greeks will 'run away' (75, cf. 80.2).

So in these crucial debates Greek deliberation is as much a travesty of *logos* as anything we have seen on the Persian side. No one finds it easy to believe that anything is being said straight, even when the speaker is the honest Aristides (81–82.1). This is a different *sort* of travesty, one born of freedom rather than of fear of a master; and if freedom carries the perpetual danger of fragmentation, if the possibility of choosing for oneself means that everyone can go their own way, we have the final paradox that it was the danger of fragmentation that imposed the victorious unity.

The Greek resistance (8.140–4)

Salamis has been won, and Xerxes departs home, leaving Mardonius behind. Alexander of Macedon now arrives to deliver a message to the Athenians, urging them to make terms. His speech is a message within a message within a message: Alexander first tells Xerxes' message to Mardonius, then Mardonius' words to him, then his own message to the Athenians. That is well-judged to make the plea as attractive as such a plea could ever be. He does speak as a concerned friend, commenting independently on the message he has brought.[35] But it also captures the distancing of Persian communications in contrast with the more direct character of Greek debate – the same contrast as we saw before Salamis, when Mardonius reported back the Persian deliberations to a remoter king while the Greeks spoke out for and to themselves.

The Spartans are nervous about what Athens will decide, and mistrust is also suggested by the Athenian delay of their answer until the Spartans can hear it too: they feel they need 'to make clear to the Spartans their own position' (141.2). The language of the Spartans is gruff and graceless, both about Athens and about Alexander;[36] a few echoes remind the sensitive reader of some spots on the Spartans' own record;[37] and, as the Athenians go on to say (144.4), what is now needed is military help once the Persian advance on land comes. That is the note on which the speech and the book ends: 'you' – or 'we'[38] – should move out first to help in Boeotia'. And the Spartans . . . say nothing, and depart.

The Athenians, with their powerful language and high moral tone, clearly carry the day here: it is easy to see this as a sort of counterpart to 7.139, with the leading Athenian contribution to Greece's salvation enunciated in a different way.[39] And *how* they speak is telling too:[40]

> Many and great are the things which prevent us joining in the enslaving of Greece even if we wished: first and most important the images of the gods and the burning and razing of our houses . . . and then what it is to be Greek, sharing one blood and one language, common shrines of the gods and sacrifices and similar ways of life; for Athenians to betray these would not be good. (8.144.2)

Such rhetorical power captures the emotive force of freedom, and the Athenians are given the best freedom tunes – better even than the harsher, more Spartan version which we saw with Demaratus, talking of the Greek 'fear' of law and custom (7.104.4–5).

There are some ironies too, but they need not undermine that force of the freedom rhetoric nor the admiration of Athens: both of those strands are vital if we are to understand why Greece won.

Some of the ironies are extratextual. Contemporary readers or listeners might indeed wonder about Athens' connection with 'freedom', now that this bullying imperial power had in many ways proved Persia's successor as 'the tyrant city'.[41] But the more immediate irony is within the text itself. Within a few chapters not merely will Sparta be exposed as failing to deliver the military aid which the Athenians so badly needed; Athens herself will also be striking a rather different note, threatening the Spartans that they will find an accommodation with the Persians unless Sparta complies. (The threat is only a little oblique at 9.6 and 9.7α.2, and utterly clear by 9.11.1.) Something is being unmasked there, but what? Perhaps it is the fine rhetoric itself of 8.143–4; perhaps the Athenians would indeed have come to terms with Persia.[42] But more probably it is the threat itself that is being exposed as simply a negotiating trick, a way of applying pressure to the Greek allies. After all, trickiness has been Themistocles' diplomatic keynote too; and when the Athenians are not being diplomatic, they are showing a peculiarly, indeed chillingly, clear commitment to liberty. Their men stone to death one Lycides who dared to speak of an accommodation with the invader; their womenfolk finish the job by storming his house and killing his wife and children (9.5).

The beginning of Book 9 tells a story about Sparta too, for those early chapters have an unusual amount of direct speech, as Thebans, Athenians, Argives, and a Tegean all speak: we measure how far each state lives up to its utterances, and to the grand statement of Greek resolve at the end of Book 8. The exception is Sparta. Her representatives say nothing at all until they have already, silently, started to act. This comes when a certain Chileos of Tegea hears from the ephors of the Athenian threats, and points out that there is little point in building the Isthmus Wall if the Athenians betray them: if the Persian fleet controls the sea then 'great street-doors are open to the Peloponnese' (9.9.2). At this, the Spartans finally march out to war. When the other states' envoys repeat their indignation at the 'betrayal', the Spartans simply say that the troops are already on their way (9.11.2). More words, earlier words, from them would have been welcome, and again one can call this a travesty of verbal exchange. But by now they are embarked on deeds. Those are what will eventually count.

It is odd that it takes a Chileos to point out that simple strategic point.[43] One would have expected the Spartans to have realised this already, just as Herodotus' readers have realised it since 7.139.3–4, and been reminded of it by Artemisia at 8.68β (above, pp. 110–11). Possibly the Spartans are over-obsessed with the Isthmus, incapable of thinking in anything other than land-locked terms; or possibly they simply cannot believe that the Athenians would ever really betray Greece. Perhaps, then, they have been *over-persuaded* by the grand rhetoric of 8.143–4, and that is why they now need Chileos to alert them to the danger that the Athenians may indeed defect.

And yet is Chileos *right* about that, given the genuine Athenian commitment to liberty which the text suggests? There are paradoxes everywhere: it is eventually Chileos' misreading of rhetoric, the failure to identify a rhetorical ploy which the more straightforward ephors find unpersuasive, which gets the Spartans to do the right thing.

Pausanias after Plataea (9.76–85)

Pausanias' later history has already been mentioned twice, in an apparently casual way.[44] The swift and allusive nature of those references suggests what we should anyway assume, that the audience knew all about Pausanias' later dalliance with Persian ways – or at least the allegations. In Book 9 he seems to stand for all that is good and Greek, for the moment; but those ironies will be felt.

First comes a beautifully dressed woman from Cos, taken from her homeland to be concubine to a Persian grandee. 'O king of Sparta', she begins (9.76.2): wrongly, for Pausanias is not king, but for a woman so used to Persian ways it was a natural mistake – or perhaps she had just learnt that flattery tends to work with powerful men. She appeals to him to save her as a suppliant, just as he has already helped her by slaying the godless foe: there are hints there of a prayer-form, as if she is addressing him as a god.[45] He responds with graciousness and humanity, recognising a guest-friend relationship with her father, and sends her away to Aegina, the city of her choice (Aegina is oddly recurrent in these chapters). A gorgeously attired woman, coming to a conqueror, who has her wholly in his power. . . . There were other, more tyrannical ways to treat her, but Pausanias' behaviour is exemplary.

Then comes another speaker, Lampon of (again) Aegina. His proposal to maltreat Mardonius' body is immediately stigmatised as 'most impious' (78.1), and Pausanias will have none of it. Such things, he firmly says, befit barbarians rather than Greeks (79.1); Leonidas has been amply avenged. Pausanias may now have the power of an autocrat, and that is clear in the way he dismisses Lampon – be grateful that you go away unscathed (79.2, rather in the style of Xerxes at 7.11.1, above p. 109). But, for the moment, he is using it in much less vindictive a way; just as he will be less vindictive than a Persian might be in sparing the children of a Theban traitor (88). Such torturous cruelty, and to sons as well as culprits, may by the end emerge as a trait which Greeks too may show, in the punishment of Artaÿctes and the stoning of his son before his eyes (9.120.4). But we have not got there yet, and we do not get there with Pausanias.

Soon spoils are heaped upon the whole army, and on Pausanias in particular – 'women [one thinks of the *Iliad*], horses, talents of gold, camels, similarly every other possession' (81.2); the amount of fancy dress in the Persian camp was beyond counting (80.2). For the moment, though, Pausanias seems impervious to its charms. He even puts on a display, ordering the Persians to prepare a meal such as they cooked for Mardonius and then the Spartans to put on a typically Spartan meal. With a laugh, he calls the Greek generals, and points out the difference (82). What, though, is his point? We can distinguish two strands of 'softness' and toughness in the *Histories*. One is 'no wonder we won', no wonder the tough Greeks can overcome such Persian softness: that is the emphasis of Aristagoras, however blandly, at

5.49.3; it has resonance, though unstraightforwardly, in the final chapter of the *Histories* at 9.122. The other is 'what is the point?', why bother to invade a country that is so poor: that is more the theme of the 'warners', people like Sandanis at 1.71.[46] We might expect Pausanias to dwell on the first point; in fact he chooses the second. 'Men[47] of Greece, I have called you here to show you the Persian leader's stupidity: for when he lived like this, he came against us, to rob us of our miserable life.' It is not the line we expect of the Pausanias we have so far seen, but it is a delicious hint of the Pausanias of the future, the person who would indeed find it incomprehensible that anyone would attack Greece for the dubious pleasure of eating a Spartan supper.

Conclusion: Speech and explanation

In his first sentence Herodotus sketches a massive theme, which includes explanation but is not confined to it: 'other things and, in particular, why they fought one another' (*praef.*). In so far as he is concerned with explanation, we have seen ways in which that explanation even goes beyond 'why they fought one another': the text also investigates why the Greeks won, even if it could so easily have gone the other way. Speeches do more than explain events: the differing habits of debate in the Persian and Greek world are an ethnographic interest in themselves. But they do 'explain' as well, not merely in illuminating reasons and motives, but more widely in helping us to locate these great events against patterns of human behaviour in East and West. That is one reason why speeches are particularly frequent and thought-provoking as the text focusses on events and why they happen, and correspondingly absent in those parts which are more concerned with other things (particularly Book 2[48] and the first half of Book 4).

The way this process works, however, has been seen to be a most complex one. Only rarely does a speech set out an actor's motives in a straightforward way; it is much more typical for speakers not to speak straight at all, but to respond to the pressure of their circumstances with deflection, circumlocution, or simple deceit. Those phenomena too can be deeply expressive, and help an audience to understand how decisions are made in a particular political or thought-world; that also illuminates the strengths and weaknesses of those different worlds. But this process requires a constant and energetic readerly involvement in the text, as we criticise a speaker's claims and arguments and measure them against our own understanding of events. In this we are doing no more than any experienced contemporary audience would have done: an Athenian audience in particular would be used to listening to speakers, in assembly or in courts, and criticising their rhetoric in order to get at truth or wisdom; and there are sufficient indications that clever speakers were treated with suspicion as well as acclaim. Nor is this a purely Athenian point, for there were markets and audiences for rhetoric everywhere. Indeed, this demand on the listener is as old as Homeric epic, whether we are comparing Odysseus' 'lying tales' with the truth or in more elaborate cases such as 'Agamemnon's apology' in *Iliad* 19.85–90, when Agamemnon is more charitable about the explanation for his behaviour than most of Homer's listeners or readers would be.

That measuring often suggests 'irony', not – or not only – in the sense of a speaker saying something other than he or she means but in the sense that events themselves can turn out 'ironically': a sequel may fit paradoxically, even if all too explicably, with what precedes. Athens seems to be saying all the right words at the end of Book 8, but then Book 9 follows on in apparently puzzling ways. Soclees' uplifting rhetoric at 5.92 may also look rather different if we remember the later clashes of Corinth and Athens. But a renuancing is not necessarily an undermining; to qualify is not to destroy. Athens *did* deserve credit for what Athenians did and said in 480, and Corinth for what Corinthians did and said c. 504; if Athens later behaved differently, that is because history is complex, and full of such 'ironies'. After reading Herodotus, who should be surprised?

Karl Reinhardt once said that Herodotus' speeches concentrated more on the particularity of events, Thucydides' more on the universal.[49] Yet we have so often seen the way in which Herodotus allows individual moments and decisions to illuminate vast issues of how humans and nations feel and think, learn and teach, inspire and deceive, live and fight and die. Herodotus' speakers rarely leave the particular behind, for that is not in the nature of debate within the press of events; but the reflections they provoke, and sometimes those they utter, have their universal dimension too.[50]

FURTHER READING

As so often, the discussion of Jacoby (1913) was seminal: he treated speeches at cols. 492–6. The thesis of Deffner (1933) on 'The speeches in Herodotus' was alert to the need to relate speech and narrative, but is less useful now than two other more focussed dissertations from the same period, Hellmann (1934) and Bischoff (1932). Following Bischoff's lead, scholars have concentrated more on speeches by 'wise advisers' than on the others: outstanding among those treatments is Lattimore (1939a). Both Hohti (1976) and Lang (1984) usefully catalogue and discuss different types of speeches. Heni (1976) treats 'conversations', acknowledging that his initial distinction of conversations from speeches can only be a rough one. Many articles discuss particular speeches: outstanding are papers by the two Solmsens, (1943),

(1944), and (1974). Waters (1966) discusses 'dramatisation', stressing the way that speeches deepen historical understanding of events. But – unsurprisingly, given the close way in which speeches interact with the rest of the narrative – much of the most valuable comment on speeches is found in the best general treatments, such as (books) Gould (1989) and Lateiner (1989) and (articles) Reinhardt (1940) and Strasburger (1955).

This chapter has had to pass over several speeches of extraordinary importance, especially the Constitutional Debate in Book 3. I discuss this, with bibliography, in Pelling (2002).

NOTES

1. On this cf. especially Gill (1996).
2. As Thucydides realised: thus at 1.22.1 he included both *logoi* and *erga* in 'the things that were done in this war'.
3. For an effort to define what should or should not count as a speech, cf. Jacoby (1913) 492–3; Hohti (1976) 7, 139; Heni (1976) 18–22.
4. Saïd (2002) 130–1, 137, and especially 135 on Croesus; Rieks (1975) especially 34–7; cf. Deffner (1933) 36–7; Gould (1989) 54. Croesus and Atys: twelve direct speech utterances in 1.34–45, totalling some 63 out of 133 lines in the Oxford Classical Text (OCT). Young Cyrus: nineteen direct speech utterances in 1.108–21, totalling some 125 out of 274 OCT lines. In both stories there are also a good number of passages in indirect speech. See also Griffin in this volume.
5. Boedeker (2002) 104, 106.
6. As it was in 1913: Jacoby (1913) 492.
7. Dodds (1973) 45; Macleod (1983) 28–9 (both discussing the *Oresteia*).
8. He reverts to 'O king' at the end, 1.32.9. That is the regular form of address: 1.27.3, 4, 35.3, 36.2, 42.1, 71.2; Croesus duly and expressively adopts it when acknowledging Cyrus as his master, 1.87.3, 88.2, and Cyrus is the next person to address Croesus by name, 1.87.3, 90.1, 3, 155.1. Dickey (1996) 236–7 notes the surprising informality of Solon's 'Croesus', but misses the subtle progression.
9. Dewald (1999) 248–9 observes that this is not even the first failure of communication: the early exchange of abductions and the Candaules story have already shown how delusive speech can be.
10. So much would be common ground between Fisher (1992, e.g. 254, 259, 290 on *Septem*, *Persae*, and *Oresteia*) and Cairns (1996). Compare e.g. Aesch. *Pers.* 807–8, 820–31.
11. Particularly the emphasis on life's uncertainty (e.g. Solon, *IEG* F 13.63–70), the uselessness of wealth in the face of death (F 24.1–10), and the notion of seventy years as man's natural span (F 27): cf. Chiasson (1986); Erbse (1992) 12–13; Harrison (2000) 36–8.
12. So also Cairns (1996) 22; Munson (2001a) 183–5. I elaborate this point in Pelling (2006).
13. Stadter (1992) 782; Moles (2002) 40; cf. Raaflaub (2002a) 186.
14. The phrase is ironically recalled at 8.142.1: see n. 37.

15. On this metaphor see Pelling (2002) 144 n. 66. Eventually other Greek states too join in 'putting the heads together' for liberty: 7.145.2.

16. On such suggestive links of tyranny and democracy here see e.g. Stahl (1983) 218–20; also Pelling (2002) 138–9 n.48 and 142.

17. Lateiner (1989) 39.

18. Compare Forsdyke (2001) 334–5, who suggests that this is a piece of democratic, or democratically influenced, ideology which has been adapted to a different setting (cf. also Forsdyke (1999) especially 367–8, and (2002) 542–5). That need not, I think, follow, though it is doubtless true that anti-tyrant and pro-democratic rhetorical commonplaces frequently blurred into one another.

19. So Strasburger (1955) 12, 18–19 = Marg (1982) 589–90, 599–600; Raaflaub (1987) 223–4 and (2002a) 165; Węcowski (1996) 237–51; Moles (2002) 39–40, and now especially Fowler (2003a), 311–13, 316–17. Perhaps 'irony' (the word favoured also by Węcowski) is too weak a word here, as Fowler says (313): '[o]ne might rather speak of knowingness and resignation than irony; if it is irony, it is the sustained irony of tragedy'.

20. Or at least part of the point: though there are further thought-provoking links with other parts of the text – perhaps with the Glaucus story at 6.86, perhaps with the prominence of other tyrants of Miletus in the wider context of Book 5.

21. Stahl (1983) 214–16.

22. *pace* van der Veen (1996), especially p. 76: 'All through his speech, Soclees is barking up the wrong tree'; p. 84, 'the cynical conclusion presents itself that under these circumstances, tyranny is less of a disaster than freedom because it confines the butchery to one city'. But van der Veen's discussion certainly brings out that the wisdom of Soclees' 'ethical policy' is problematic. Compare Strasburger (1955) 13–15 = Marg (1982) 592–4.

23. Detienne (1995) ch. 5.

24. Rood (1999) 158.

25. Bischoff (1932) 56.

26. Gnomic generalisation tends to recur with Artabanus: there is a lot of it even in 46–52, where the tone is less heated: Bischoff (1932) 57–8, 63–5; Deffner (1933) 89. At a court, that is the register a wise adviser needs to make his own.

27. And, arguably, some parts of Artabanus' advice are less than straightforwardly 'wise': Pelling (1991). Compare the exchange with Demaratus at 7.101–4: there too Xerxes is not stupid in his reasons for believing that the Greeks may fragment; even if he is proved wrong by the sequel, he might easily have been right.

28. It indeed so nearly happens before Salamis: cf. below, and especially Mnesiphilus at 8.57.2, who foresees that if they abandon Salamis the alliance will fragment, and 'Greece will be destroyed by its own ill counsel': 'ill counsel' there echoes Mardonius' 'ill-counselled' here. This way in which Mardonius abuses true insight becomes something of a hallmark: before Plataea he builds a picture of Spartan fearfulness that is not unreasonable given the Spartan behaviour, but is catastrophically erroneous: cf. 9.42, 48 (herald), 58.

29. I discuss this episode more fully in Pelling (1997b). Munson (1988) and Harrison (2002) 568–9 have some very good remarks.

30. Deffner (1933) 51.

31. There are echoes here of both Thermopylae and Artemisium to support Themistocles' argument. The advantages of fighting in the narrows were clear at

7.175–6, applying both to Thermopylae and to Artemisium, and at Thermopylae were realised both in the preliminaries (7.211.2) and even – despite the Persian outflanking – in the heroic battle itself (7.223); then again at Artemisium, though the 'narrows' there were partly created by the Greeks' naval tactics (8.11.1–2, 16). The benefits of defending in a forward position were aired and accepted at 7.172–4, and again at 7.207.

32. On the way in which this queen from Greek Asia Minor challenges and perhaps confirms several stereotypes simultaneously, of gender and of race, cf. especially Munson (1988).

33. Thus with Croesus (1.27.1, etc.), Cyrus (1.156.2), Cambyses (3.32.2, etc.), Darius (3.119.7, etc.), Xerxes earlier at, e.g., 7.28.3, 44, 215; Flory (1978a) 150 and nn. 7–8. Compare 7.105.1 for regal wrath as the *expected* response to outspokenness, and there too this expectation was falsified: Hohti (1974).

34. The Greek word is *kosmos*, 'order', perhaps with a play on the other sorts of 'order' which currently are so lacking in the Greek demeanour. But there is also a contrast with the 'order' which the Greeks show when it comes to the fighting (86): there the roles are reversed, and it is the barbarians who are disordered.

35. F. Solmsen (1974) 103 = (1982) 103.

36. In particular, contrast the brutal dismissiveness about Alexander – 'he is a tyrant, and working with a tyrant' (142.5) – with the firmness but polite concern of the Athenians at 143.3.

37. Especially 142.2, when they call on Athens 'not to interfere rashly ("do anything *neōteron*") in Greece nor accept proposals from the barbarian': at 5.93.2 it was the rest of the Greeks who forced Sparta 'not to interfere ("do anything *neōteron*") with another Greek city' (above p. 107). At that point Sparta was trying to rob Athens of her new-found freedom: that gives an extra perspective to their call now on Athens to live up to their tradition of 'liberating others' (142.3).

38. The reading here is uncertain. Hude follows Wesseling and Valckenaer in emending to 'you', which makes the point utterly clear; Rosén keeps the manuscripts' 'we', probably rightly, but after 144.4 the force would be effectively the same – except for the extra suggestion that it is not just a matter of Spartans 'helping' Athens, but the Athenians are themselves 'helping' the wider cause of the rest of Greece.

39. Kleinknecht (1940); cf. e.g. Strasburger (1955) 2 = (Marg (1982) 576; van der Veen (1996) 103–4.

40. F. Solmsen (1974) 161, 163 = (1982) 100, 102.

41. Moles (2002) 43; Raaflaub (1987) 239–40 and (2002a) 167. That is particularly so if we read 'for your *archē*' in the Spartans' speech at 142.2, with its combination of Homeric echo (for the Trojan War was fought 'for the beginning (*archē*) wrought by Paris', *Il.* 3.100, 6.356) and suggestion of what will come later, when *archē* will mean not merely the 'beginning' that the Athenians gave but the 'rule' which they will go on to derive from the war (cf. 8.3.2, below, n. 44). So Moles (2002) 43, also observing the contact with Croesus' *archē* (beginning/rule) at 1.6.3; Gilula (2003) 85–7; and Rosén.

42. So e.g. Raaflaub (1987) 240. Compare van der Veen (1996) 105–8, stressing rather how swiftly circumstances could change that Athenian resolve.

43. Compare L. Solmsen (1944) 247 = Marg (1982) 656–7; Flower and Marincola (2002) 115 on 9.9.1.

44. 5.32, on the Persian Megabates, 'whose daughter Pausanias son of Cleombrotus, the Spartan – if the story is true – later arranged to marry, when he lusted to become tyrant of Greece'. 8.3.2: 'they' – possibly the Athenians, possibly the allies – later 'took away the leadership from the Spartans on the grounds [or 'pretext'] of Pausanias' hubris'. Flower and Marincola (2002) 12–13 rightly observe that Herodotus keeps a certain distance from those allegations ('if it is true . . . grounds [or 'pretext']').

45. What Pulleyn (1997), especially 17, 27, 33–6, calls the *da-quia-dedisti* formula: e.g. Sappho F 1.5–9; Eur. *IT* 1082–5.

46. Bischoff (1932) 78–81 = Marg (1982) 682–5; Hellmann (1934) 96–7.

47. The locution may be expressive, for they are true 'men', without the effeminacy of the luxurious dinner; if so that may point to the first rather than the second strand. But it is not developed, only hinted at.

48. There are only three speeches in Book 2, those of Amasis at 2.173 and 181 and Proteus at 2.115; cf. Benardete (1969) 53, though he explains it differently – 'What connects all three speeches is Greece'. But that is not really true of 2.173 or 181. It is more relevant that by then Egypt is re-entering the main strand of the narrative, with the Persian conquest.

49. Reinhardt (1960) 173–4 = (Marg (1982) 368. Reinhardt acknowledges that Herodotus too uses particular events to illuminate 'the inner dynamic of the historical process', but still feels that 'what is kernel for Herodotus is shell for Thucydides, and *vice versa*'.

50. Many thanks to Michael Flower, Mathieu de Bakker, Philip Stadter, and especially the editors for their very helpful comments.

8

CAROLYN DEWALD AND RACHEL KITZINGER

Herodotus, Sophocles and the woman who wanted her brother saved

Many different kinds of thematic resonance come into play in the story that both Herodotus and Sophocles use about the woman who wanted to save a brother rather than her husband or son (3.119).[1] Our argument starts with the observation that one of the most important of these resonances, both to Herodotus the historian and to Sophocles the dramatist, lies in the realm of metanarrative. Both Herodotus and Sophocles are skilled in the artful use of *logos* themselves, and they use the story of the woman who wanted her brother saved as a *logos* about the power of *logos*, reflecting on some of the complexities of speech as an act of communication.

A *logos* in Greek can be a word, a story, or an argument; the *logos* or story we have chosen to focus on here is both an anecdote and an argument shared by Herodotus and Sophocles. It seems quite possible that the *logos* of the woman who chose to save her brother rather than a husband or son was brought into play by both Herodotus and Sophocles to depict the tendency of *logos* itself to be manipulated in unusual ways by unusual people, but also to lead to results that subvert the speakers' initial expectations. Herodotus and Sophocles work in different genres, and exploit the possibilities of the anecdote quite differently, but in their different uses of the story, each of them reflects ironically on some of the ambiguities inherent in the intellectual turmoil prevalent in mid-fifth-century Greece about the nature and power of language.

Herodotus' *logos*

In his third book, Herodotus begins the account of Darius' reign, 'And so Darius the son of Hystaspes was made king' (3.88). The extent of Darius' power is the first theme broached; the lands he controls and the political connections represented by his wives provide the bulk of chapter 88: 'Everything was filled with his power.' His satrapies or provinces with all their taxable riches are then described, which flows into a description of the exotic wonders found in the far reaches of the world, in India, Arabia, and Ethiopia, and the improbabilities that Herodotus has heard about the most distant parts of Europe. The whole geographical excursus ends with a remarkable story of the king controlling the irrigation of a large (and imaginary) Asian plateau. Now that this territory has been conquered by the Persians, the inhabitants find that the Persian king controls their water by damming it. In order to get enough water to raise their summer crops, 'going to Persia, they and their wives stand outside the gates of the king and shout and howl, and the king gives an order to release the sluices sending the water to those most in need . . .'. The water is released only after a lot of money, beyond the normal tribute, is paid (3.117). Now the account of the beginning of Darius' reign abruptly resumes, with a story of how his royal power was almost immediately contested by one of his previous co-conspirators: 'But of the seven who had rebelled against the Magus, it happened that one of them, Intaphrenes, committing an act of violence, died immediately after their rebellion' (3.118).

Intaphrenes is part of the Persian historical record, found on Darius' Behistun inscription as Vindafarnah. No rebellion on Vindafarnah's part is referred to in the Behistun inscription; on Darius' official monument Vindafarnah is instead a general for Darius, putting down an insurrection in Babylon.[2] In Herodotus' account, however, Intaphrenes takes offence when he is refused access to Darius, on the pretext (as he thinks, at least) that Darius is sexually engaged with a woman – the one time that the co-conspirators are not to interrupt him, as per prior arrangement (*heudōn meta gunaikos*, 3.84; *gunaiki misgesthai*, 3.118). Darius, sure that a revolt is underway, arrests Intaphrenes and all his male relatives.

At this point one of the most famous anecdotes in the *Histories* begins. Like the people from the plain needing water in the preceding anecdote, Intaphrenes' wife comes to Darius' *thuras*, gates, weeping and wailing. In both passages, a weeping population demands access to resources that one would expect to be rightly theirs rather than the king's (the local water supply, one's male relatives). In the earlier anecdote, the exchange that ensues is a largely commercial one (Darius is the *kapēlos* or shopkeeper, in the judgement of his people, 3.89.3). But the story of Intaphrenes' wife does not simply recapitulate this point. For Intaphrenes' wife participates in a more complex process of exchange than do the landlocked and waterless Asian farmers, because the exchange she undertakes with Darius is a matter of subtle verbal negotiation.[3]

In pity, Darius allows Intaphrenes' wife to choose one male relative to escape the death that he has allotted to the rest. The construction of dubious choices is something of a hallmark of Darius' way of looking at things.

An earlier stage in the Darius story has developed Darius' own pre-royal reputation as a trickster, skilled in setting up and arguing highly debatable positions,[4] but here Intaphrenes' wife gives him back as good as she gets. To his royal astonishment (*thōmasas ton logon*, 3.119), the woman chooses a brother, not her husband or her son – even though, as Darius comments, the brother is more distantly related than the children and less dear than the husband (*allotriōteros toi tōn paidōn kai hēsson kecharismenos tou andros*). In the passage closely echoed by Sophocles, the woman explains that she could get another husband and other children if she discards these, while, with parents no longer living, another brother is an impossibility.

So it appears that Darius is not the only manipulator of language in his kingdom. In effect, Intaphrenes' wife here tacitly declares that she is willing to abandon her husband (subject as he is to Darius' current wrath) and intends to retreat instead, in loyalty to Darius, to her natal family. Darius recognises this as a good move (*eu te dē edoxe tōi Dareiōi eipein hē gunē*), and he rewards her for it. He releases (*apēkē*; cf. *entelletai anoigein tas pulas*, 3.117) not just her brother, as requested, but her eldest son as well.

Superficially, both Darius and Intaphrenes' wife profit by this exchange.[5] But the cleverness of her victorious *logos* rings somewhat hollowly. Viewed in the more long-term trajectory of the *Histories* as a whole, she joins a long string of cynical, compliant courtier-subjects who ultimately corrupt the ability of the Persian king to govern effectively. Both the story of the landlocked plain and the story of Intaphrenes' wife apparently happen at the beginning of Darius' reign, as Herodotus tells it. The concentration of power and resources indicated both on the material level by the story of the landlocked plain and on the human and verbal level by the story of the wife of Intaphrenes creates a docile but manipulative obedience on the part of Darius' subjects and a hubris on the part of the king himself that only the career of Darius' son Xerxes in Greece will fully play out.[6] Seen in this larger light, the cleverness of the wife of Intaphrenes resonates with Otanes' expectations for a monarch, delivered in the Constitutional Debate in which the seven co-conspirators decide on the Persian form of government they will have (3.80): 'he disturbs a country's ancestral customs, coerces women, and kills men without trial'.

Significantly, Herodotus ends the whole *logos* not with a celebration of the woman's cleverness, but with the flat statement: 'now, of the seven, one immediately perished in the way that has been recounted'. The clever *logos* of the wife of Intaphrenes has won her a verbal victory, but a victory that is highly ambiguous because of the seeds of corruption it contains. Darius has invited her to negotiate the most basic familial bonds (just as he invites Indians and Greeks to negotiate the funeral rites they give their parents,

3.38), and she has risen to the challenge. Whether Darius is an important cause of this corruption of language or only one of its many instantiations Herodotus does not make clear, but the systemic problems represented by Intaphrenes' wife go a long way towards explaining the failure of Xerxes' war in Greece.[7]

Sophocles' *logos*

Antigone's use of the argument made by Intaphrenes' wife is more complicated still and occurs in an even darker register (*Ant.* 904–12). The passage has frequently been rejected by scholars of tragedy precisely because it seems to contradict Antigone's earlier justifications for her action and to be jarringly inappropriate to the dramatic context.[8] If, however, we take seriously that Sophocles wanted his audience to recognise Antigone's argument as an importation from Herodotus or some common source, then Sophocles is marking it as a borrowed one, foreign to Antigone's lived experience. She uses the argument in a final attempt to be heard, but in using language which is not her own, she threatens the coherence of the very action for which she is giving her life.

Just after she sings her own funeral lament and before she leaves the stage to die, Antigone tries one final time to explain the action she has taken against the command of Creon, the king: the burial of her dead brother, Polyneices.[9] Antigone, as Polyneices' sister, has performed the burial that her relationship to him demands of her, despite Creon's edict. She has, in the course of the play, tried to explain her action to her sister Ismene; to the chorus of prominent citizens of the city; and to Creon. No one, in her presence, has shown her any understanding, although Haemon, Creon's son and Antigone's betrothed, has tried to convince his father not only of his own support of her action but also the citizen body's. Antigone, however, does not know this; in her eyes, her *logoi* and her action have found no receptive hearing, even, as she fears, from the gods. What she has tried to express – by the mutually authorising power of word and action – has been granted no effect by those who have seen and heard her expression.

What is put into question by Antigone's words not being heard? This deed and the words she uses to explain it are the sole and sufficient expression of her being. Not to be heard is, therefore, not to exist.[10] Antigone is the only surviving member, along with her sister Ismene, of the house of Laius, the ruling house of Thebes for generations. And she is also every woman whose obligation it is by civic and religious custom to bury a dead male relative. But she is as well an unmarried girl who has broken the limit set by her society on her behaviour and a citizen who has defied by her action and her language the edict of the ruler of the city. And she is an agent who has found the moment and the means to bring feeling, thought, language and action into perfect harmony. Sophocles combines the paradigm of a character whose language and action form an integrated whole with the paradigm of a character who transgresses the boundaries created to maintain order. In giving this character no receptive audience, Sophocles poses a question about the definition of right action and the kind of language which gives it authority.

When Antigone delivers her last *logos*, it is her last chance to gain an acknowledgement of the truths her actions embody. At this point Sophocles borrows the argument that Intaphrenes' wife uses to explain her choice to save her brother. Like Intaphrenes' wife, Antigone argues that Polyneices is irreplaceable as her brother, since her parents are not alive to bear another sibling for her. His unique status requires her to act. She has no leeway and can find no compromise, if she is to preserve by her action her identity as the woman with obligations to her family and Polyneices' unique identity as her brother. But the language that Sophocles gives her to express this thought betrays the universal principle on the basis of which she has earlier claimed she has acted.[11] The betrayal happens because, in her desperation to express once again the necessity of her action, she uses words which do not arise from her lived experience.

Antigone borrows, as the counter example to Polyneices, a hypothetical relationship to husband and child who are not hers, and about which she knows nothing, and she says that she would not have defied the city for these relationships. The very inappropriateness of her argument implies, finally, the incompatibility of her position with the ability to find language to persuade others of the value of that position.

The form her argument takes is that of a hypothesis – in logic, a formulation not confirmed by known reality but one that the speaker assumes to be true for the sake of argument. How does the use of an hypothesis, at the last moment of Antigone's expressive existence on stage, push her language beyond its limit? So far, Antigone has, uniquely in the play, embodied the absolute consonance between what she says, feels, thinks and does, so that her actions are perfectly substantiated by her words, and *vice versa*. Here, however, she allows her words to go beyond, no longer to be in touch with, what she feels and has done. She has no knowledge of husband or child. Although we, the audience, know that Haemon supports her actions, she knows nothing of that connection. In her ignorance of what a husband potentially is, and her ignorance of the connection between herself as a mother with a child, she allows herself to say that these relationships would not require of her the same choice.[12]

In Sophocles' vision the power of language to express what we do *not* know, what we have not experienced, what we do not feel, is terrible and painful. Evidence of the danger this *logos* represents can be found in the number of critics who have excised these lines, or who have found them inconsistent with Antigone's character. Sophocles has an acute understanding of the way we can individually embody and express what we know and yet fail to communicate that truth to others. But he also sees that the nature of language itself allows us, uniquely, to lay claim to what we do not know in order to convince, to persuade – in order to win over others to our perspective.

*

In the tradition, Sophocles and Herodotus were friends; Plutarch quotes a fragment of iambic verse: 'When he was fifty-five years old, Sophocles fashioned a song for Herodotus.'[13] It is pleasing to speculate that their friendship was, at least in part, based on a common exploration of the limits of the verbal medium each uses. Their chosen genres, though very different, both confront and grapple with the fluidity and ephemerality of words – the malleability of oral stories and the impermanence of words spoken once on the stage. And in their work each explores the intersection of language and power: Sophocles, appropriately to the medium of drama, in the uneasy and complex relationship between words and actions; Herodotus, as a prose historian, in a more leisured and long-term exploration of the ways *logos* corrupts the exercise of power, both as it is used by those in power and by those serving under them.

FURTHER READING

For the topics and issues discussed in this essay see further Blundell (1989); Cartledge and Greenwood (2002); Cropp (1997); Fisher (2002); Knox (1964); Lane and Lane (1986); Murnaghan (1986); Oudemans and Lardinois (1987); Raaflaub (2002a); Reinhardt (1979); Thomas (2000); and Winnington-Ingram (1980).

NOTES

1. This chapter is collaborative and speculative, in the sense that its two authors did not come together with finished arguments but have set down here some observations generated over a number of years, in conversations about Herodotus and Sophocles. For the broader use of the theme of the woman who wanted her brother saved, see Aarne and Thompson (1961) no. 985 for its appearance in folktale; for its many manifestations in world literature, see Beekes (1986). West

(1999) 129 comments that Herodotus' seems to be 'the oldest extant version of this migratory motif'. For Herodotus' more general connection to the genre of tragedy, see Saïd (2002) and Griffin in this volume; for more on his approach to *logos*, see Gray (2002), Dewald (2002), and Dewald, Griffiths, Luraghi, and Pelling in this volume.

2. *CAH* (2nd edn) IV. 61, 130. For a detailed reconstruction of the different revolts at the beginning of Darius' reign, and Vindafarnah's participation in them, see Balcer (1987) 134–43.

3. Griffiths (2001b) 173 sees the same tacit connection between the two anecdotes (which he calls 'The Watergate Crisis'), but suggests that the linkage is one of which Herodotus remains unaware. Romm in this volume does not think there is an interpretive link; see especially his n. 7.

4. Compare 3.72.4 on Darius' justification for 'necessary lies', and 3.82–97 for the smoothness with which he argues the others into monarchy and then rigs the contest over who should be king; cf. Evans (1991) 60. Like other eastern rulers, he is subject to flattery and manipulation from below: Dewald (2003) 35 n. 33.

5. The pathos of the wife's position is undeniable as well as her cleverness. It is safe to say that Intaphrenes' wife is no Antigone, but rather a survivor, in her political astuteness.

6. Pelling in this volume extensively develops the Herodotean theme. Some of its other resonances in Sophocles, and in particular in the character of Creon in *Antigone*, are well developed by West (1999).

7. See, for instance, the scene with Xerxes' advisers (8.68–9); the others are not thinking about the wisdom of Artemisia's advice, but rather what will happen to her because she has given it. Compare 7.235–6 and 8.90. Herodotus' hypothetical speculations about what Xerxes would have done if he had been in danger at sea, going back to Asia (8.118–19), may be read as a wry comment on the management of the war by his most trusted councillors. He did indeed seat Persian grandees at the oars of the ship of state.

8. See Neuberg (1990) *passim*, for a concise summary of the arguments used to excise the passage and an argument based on thematic considerations for its retention.

9. Creon has considered Polyneices a traitor for bringing an army to attack his native city after he had been expelled by his brother, Eteocles. The brothers meet in the battle and kill each other, and Creon takes over the rule of Thebes. His first edict as king attempts to heal the wound created by the strife between the two brothers; he 'expels' Polyneices again, this time by throwing out his corpse, and forbids his burial on pain of death.

10. As she has expressed to Ismene when her sister promises to keep Antigone's act secret (86–7: 'No, shout it out. You will be a far greater enemy in your silence, if you do not tell everyone of these acts'). Public recognition of what she has done is a necessary component of what her act means.

11. For a well-reasoned argument that she is not denying the universal principle of her earlier arguments, see Foley (2001) 177. Foley concludes that Antigone 'would not have challenged the state for a set of relations that are hypothetical to a virgin' (178). Foley's very interesting discussion of this passage concludes that Antigone's moral stance is determined by the very particular familial and social circumstance she is in and cannot be universalised.

12. She borrows the *logos* of Intaphrenes' wife to express the uniqueness of her brother to her and her understanding of the extremity of her action in defiance of the city's law. These things she knows. But the language she uses, in a final attempt to communicate to others, contains things which she cannot know the truth of; thus it is a language which is not her own.

13. Plut. *Moralia* 785b = *IEG* II, 166; for discussion of its authenticity, see West (1999) 112–13.

9

ALAN GRIFFITHS

Stories and storytelling in the *Histories*

Any reader who approaches Herodotus' great book with the conventional assumptions of what a modern, Western, post-Thucydidean narrative history is or ought to be – that is, expecting a generally austere concentration on political and military affairs, perhaps citing the texts of treaties, adducing inscriptional evidence, and so on – is likely to be disconcerted, if also delighted, by the way the text unfolds itself. One does not immediately see what is coming. The prospectus-paragraph sets out the project clearly enough. Two parallel clauses, the second of which reinforces, varies and amplifies the first, declare the author's aim as being 'to prevent the memory of human actions being obliterated by the passage of time, and to ensure that great and wonderful achievements, whether carried out by Greeks or by foreigners, are not denied their proper celebration'. It goes on immediately to define a more precise focus: 'to investigate why they (the Greeks and foreigners) went to war with each other' (*praef.*).

And indeed by the beginning of chapter 6 (say, in our terms, a couple of pages), Herodotus fingers the man who he is 'personally convinced' set the long series of hostilities in motion: Croesus the king of Lydia. Croesus was the first ruler to levy tribute from the Greek settlements on the west coast of Asia Minor; he was also, we go on to discover in the course of the first book, the man who made the fateful mistake of attempting an eastward expansion of his kingdom and suffered a disastrous defeat at the hands of the Persians, thus bringing Greeks and Persians face to face for the first time and setting the scene for the wars that would follow.

But before attention settles on Croesus, and immediately after the short prologue, we are treated to a series of thumbnail sketches of events from much earlier history in which (we are supposed to believe) alternative eastern accounts of the origin of the enmity are presented. The Persian version starts as follows (1.1):

Persian scholars say that the Phoenicians were responsible for the conflict. Arriving in the Mediterranean as immigrants from the 'Red Sea', and making their home in the country where they still live, they set straight to work in the business of long-haul trading in Egyptian and Assyrian commodities. One of the ports at which they touched was Argos, at that time indisputably the chief city of what we now call Greece. Putting in, then, at this place Argos, they set out their wares; and on the fifth or sixth day after their arrival, when they were almost out of stock, down to the beach came a crowd of women which included the king's daughter. Her name, they say – and the Greeks concur in this – was Io, and her father Inachus. As these women clustered around the stern of the ship, each buying what looked the most attractive articles, suddenly the Phoenicians exchanged a signal and rushed forward to grab them. Most got away safely, but Io was among a group who were seized. The Phoenicians bundled them into the hold and took off for Egypt.

And that, according to the Persians – but not the Greeks – is how Io ended up in Egypt, and that was the first act of aggression.

From generality we are instantly plunged into specificity: a moment in what even Herodotus would have called ancient history (but which we might call myth, or legend). And here we find immediately displayed some of the characteristic stigmata of the Herodotean story: a talent for vivid realisation in almost cinematographic detail ('clustered around the stern of the ship'); clever touches of pseudo-precision ('fifth or sixth day');[1] the rationalisation of mythical stories into real-world, natural events; fussy authorial nudges; and claimed sources ('Persian scholars say'; 'the Greeks concur in this'; 'according to the Persians – but not the Greeks').

I draw attention to this very first micro-narrative not simply because it is the first of so many but because Herodotus might almost have written it as a programmatic sample of the wares he was himself about to offer to his readers. Implicitly it seems to say: this is what I have for sale; this is what you should expect if you choose to continue. You are going to have to get used along the way to constant sharp-focussed diversions of this sort. Will you buy the product? Will you allow yourself to be seduced and carried off to Egypt?

The prospective purchaser then notes how this eccentric version of the Io myth is followed by three similar accounts of the legends of Medea, Europa and Helen, all radically recast; how then the Croesus narrative line has hardly begun before Herodotus reverts to a flashback about his ancestor Gyges (ch. 8); and finally, how the story of the poet Arion is told at ch. 24 without even a token semblance of proper motivation: 'It was to Periander' – who has himself, we may observe, entered the story rather obliquely – 'that the

Corinthians, backed up by the Lesbians, say a most amazing event happened: the carrying ashore at Tainaron on a dolphin's back of Arion of Methymna.' An event which he proceeds to recount in detail. And this is how the *Histories*, or better *Inquiry*, continues through to the end, even if the side-glances thin out somewhat once we reach the second half of the work. Clearly, Herodotus is the kind of writer who conceives of historical narrative as a discourse which needs constant variation and enlivening by means of vivid digressions – as he himself asserts (4.30: 'right from the beginning my text has been on the look-out for additional material').

Reconstructing the past is a necessarily complex business in which the more facets that can be induced to refract the light, the better. Some attempt must be made to reproduce in the text not just political and military events but the full bandwidth of human activity. His declared intention to probe the history of 'small cities as well as great' (1.5) demonstrates his belief that explanatory significance may be found at the microscopic level as well as the macro. A goal-driven, unilinear narrative of event and causation, he feels, lacks flavour. Simply to shove a leg of lamb into the oven is not enough: to make a properly enjoyable dish it must first be spiked with garlic, rosemary and anchovy fillets, well seasoned and anointed with olive oil.

Another metaphor – text as stream – may help to illustrate how I propose to delimit the subject of 'storytelling' in this chapter. In his dialogue 'The Orator', Cicero characterises Herodotus' prose as 'flowing like a calm river without rocks or rapids': *sine ullis salebris quasi sedatus amnis fluit* (*Orat.* 39). But though he may be free of rough waters, that doesn't mean a bland and undifferentiated evenness. There are plenty of creeks and ox-bows off to the side of the main stream, and plenty of places where the current temporarily pools and pauses. Let us distinguish these two kinds of opportunities for subsidiary narrative. If for our purposes we define a story as an embedded, discrete episodic unit[2] – 'pericope', in the jargon of New Testament study – it may be either a thickened, concentrated and closely-focussed detail of the main current ('pool') or a lateral diversion, backwards or forwards in narrative time ('creek'). Some examples will make this clearer:

- **Pools in the stream.** Here I exclude, as non-narrative, digressions of a factual kind, like those on the supposed impossibility of breeding mules in Elis (4.30), or the biological excursus on animal population size (3.108–9).
  - Scenes with memorable dialogue or visual effects. The author homes in, as if with a zoom lens, to provide vivid human interest in what had so far been a relatively neutral, unmarked account of events unfolding along the natural time-line of his history. So, for instance, two reports about

envoys requesting help from the Spartans: the Samian exiles who, driven to distraction by the obstinate laconicism of their hosts, finally abandon their eloquent rhetoric, hold up a sack, point to it, and say 'Bag needs flour' (3.46); and King Cleomenes' young daughter Gorgo shrewdly advising her father to send Aristagoras packing (5.51; compare 7.239). Sometimes this kind of foregrounding, with direct exchange of speech, may extend for several pages: think of the upbringing of King Cyrus of Persia (1.107–22), and note there how the author steps back from the drama to reclaim his narrative as the story approaches its devastating conclusion in ch. 119, before the lively dialogue-style resumes.[3] A few notable examples from the multitude: Aristodicus remonstrates with Apollo (1.159); the unmasking of the Earless Impostor by the daughter of Otanes, with its lively exchange of letters and its tense climax (3.68–9); how the Persian Bagaeus encompassed the downfall of Oroetes (3.127–8); Euelthon's exasperated response to the nagging of Pheretime of Cyrene (4.162); and the terrible tale of Xerxes' passion for his brother Masistes' wife – and then Masistes' daughter (9.108–13).

– Incidents in which, although there is no temporal dislocation, a tale seems to be told for its own sake, arbitrarily placed where it is either because Herodotus was determined to put it *somewhere*, or because he needed to fill out a slot which would otherwise have been embarrassingly empty. Take, for example, the account of the poet Arion, hung precariously on the chronological hook of the reign of the Corinthian dictator Periander (1.24); or the little moral tale of the delegation from Elis, judges of the Olympic games, visiting Egypt (!) and receiving some chastening advice on how their competition could be run more fairly (2.160). In the latter case it is surely clear that Herodotus knew nothing at all about the Pharaoh Psammis, and used this story – which could have gone anywhere – to create a sense of individual identity. Perhaps he thought of the Sicilian victor *Psaumis*, celebrated by Pindar in the fourth and fifth Olympian Odes.

• Creeks off to the side
  – Creeks looping backwards ('analeptic' material in Genette's narratological terminology). This type is ubiquitous, for when a new character crops up in the narrative it is natural for the author to supply relevant background information. Thus when Croesus is looking for Greek allies we get a resumé of recent events at Athens (1.59–64) and Sparta (65–8), each survey itself rich with subsidiary incident. The introduction of the Athenian aristocratic clan of the Alcmaeonidae at 6.115 triggers, after a short delay, an account of their previous history, culminating in the comic diptych of Alcmaeon emerging from Croesus' gold-vault

and Hippocleides dancing away his marriage to Agariste (6.125, 126–30). Sometimes such flashbacks occur at a further remove, as exemplary tales (*ainoi*) in speeches delivered by Herodotus' characters (see below, p. 135, on Soclees and Leotychidas).

– Creeks looping forwards ('proleptic'). Less common is the detail which jumps ahead in time; perhaps because if done too obtrusively an author risks seeming to arrogate to himself the function of the prophet, or the inspired poet, or Apollo himself, 'who knew what was, what is, and is to be'. In spite of his deep interest in oracles, Herodotus himself projects a more modest persona than that of the omniscient time-lord. But note the little clutch of fast-forwards associated with the battle of Thermopylae: how the lucky Ameinocles later found grief (7.190); how the traitor Ephialtes eventually came to a bad end (7.213–14); what was to happen to the Spartiates who failed to die, for various reasons, along with their three hundred comrades (7.229–32); and the fate that lay in store for the Theban Leontiadas' son Eurymachus (7.233).

Of course, even if he had wanted to provide a straightforward history of the Persian Wars together with the minimum amount of antecedent material necessary to their understanding, Herodotus would have found the data hard to control. Multi-threaded historical development cannot, by definition, be unrolled in a single narrative line, and events which take place in parallel must somehow be handled in series. What is so impressive about Herodotus is the way he turns this difficulty to advantage, cunningly building up his composite picture by choosing a single fundamental line (East v. West), and subordinating the other strands which he will need to introduce; the latter are then cut up and spliced into the main thread at carefully chosen points (e.g. the Athens and Sparta 'digression' in Book 1, already mentioned). As Felix Jacoby observed, 'It is hardly an exaggeration to say that Herodotus' entire art of organising his material consists in how and at what points he is able to incorporate digressions.'[4]

It is important to be clear, then, that the old view of Herodotus as a 'naïve' composer, and the consequent and condescending dismissal of his intricate construction as 'rambling', is no more helpful than was the ascription of Hesiod's compositional quirks to something called 'archaic thought', or the allegation in the heyday of positivist psychiatry that Tibullus' exquisitely-architectured dreamy style was due to the poet's 'defective secondary brain function'.[5] The knots and burrs in the growth of Herodotus' narrative grain are not defects, but intrinsic to the attraction of the timber's polished surface; they reflect his belief in the complex interaction between factors at the macro and the micro level (1.5).

Homer the dominant model

Herodotus' predecessors in prose-writing – geographers, mythographers and proto-historians – seem not to have constructed multi-threaded texts like this. So where did he get the idea from? From the model whose influence suffuses his work at every level: the Homeric poems. The recently-discovered verse inscription in praise of his birthplace, Halicarnassus, is right not only to regard him as one of the city's chief glories, but also to encapsulate him neatly as 'the prose Homer'.[6] In the first four ethnically-orientated books he casts himself in the role of an Odysseus who 'saw the cities of many peoples and got to know their mentality' (*Od.* 1.3); then he shifts imperceptibly into the mode of the *Iliad* poet, recounting the events and celebrating the heroes of a great conflict. His own expressed desire in the proem that great deeds should not be denied their *kleos*, glory, clearly recalls one of the central preoccupations of the *Iliad*. That great poem functioned as the ground bass underlying all Greek cultural expression up to and far beyond Herodotus' own day, and it is the authoritative familiarity of Homer that makes this style both attractive to Herodotus and acceptable to his audience. Homer is regularly appealed to in the *Histories* (e.g. 4.29), and many Homeric features reappear. Most obviously, there is the predominantly Ionic dialect, which enables the historian to generate verbal echoes of epic language, or even cite phrases (e.g. *ou gar ameinon*, 'For such is not the better course', used by Darius to close his speeches at 3.71 and 3.82, recalling Agamemnon at *Il.* 1.217; *epi gēraos oudōi*, 'on death's doorstep', 3.14). To this one may easily add: the overall structure, based on generous expansion of a simple plot-core by the addition of supplementary material; the use of ring-composition which eases the incorporation of digressive material by allowing a graceful exit from and re-entrance into the main narrative flow; characters who perform the role of 'the wise adviser', or 'warner'; and persuasive speeches which draw on earlier history for their argument.[7]

The last item deserves to be particularly highlighted. Many important subsidiary anecdotes in Herodotus are distanced from direct authorial responsibility by being assigned to actors within his story. Often they are embedded in contexts of debate – that is, they are 'paradigmatic', they recommend a course of action appealing positively or negatively to exemplary past events. Take, for example, the speech which the Corinthian Soclees is made to make to the Spartans on the issue of tyranny (dictatorship) at 5.92, offering dark – but entertaining – vignettes of how life in his home city had been conducted under the rule of Cypselus and Periander; or the one which is put into the mouth of the Spartan king Leotychidas (6.86), the cautionary tale he tells to the Athenians about his countryman Glaucus, who once tried to cheat his way out of a contract. This narrative tactic has a venerable Iliadic pedigree. Phoenix urges Achilles to return to the battle by citing the example of Meleager; Achilles in turn tries to persuade Priam to take food in spite of his grief by pointing to the story of Niobe (*Il.* 9.543–605; 24.602–17). More generally, Diomedes recounts Bellerophon's life-story to Glaucus (*Il.* 6.155–95), and room is made for all kinds of fascinating antiquarian material ('how we used to use chariots in battle in the old days') by assigning them to the greybeard Nestor. The Pylian commander recalls, for example, his victory over the Arcadian champion Ereuthalion, who fought not with bow or spear but a huge bronze mace (*Il.* 7.136–56); and one can see this motif of 'the unusual weapon' echoed by Herodotus in his description of Sophanes of Decelea, who ensured that he would hold his ground at the battle of Plataea by fixing himself in place with an iron anchor (9.74).

Many other aspects of epic influence in the way stories are told could be mentioned, such as the glancing affective focus on minor figures who fall in battle, but one passage deserves particular attention. The famous tale of how Cleisthenes the sixth-century ruler of Sicyon sought the most eligible bachelor in Greece as husband for his daughter Agariste is a highlight of Book 6 (126–30). It is conceived in terms of epic style and behaviour throughout, from the catalogue of arriving suitors to the feasting and competitions which follow; it corresponds closely to accounts of the marriage of Helen in 'mythological' sources. Many phrases even fall easily into quasi-epic rhythm. It is a nice question whether this patterning has emerged merely as a result of the shaping of the story by Herodotus and the storytellers who lie behind him (perhaps drawing on a poetic source), or because, as Oswyn Murray has argued, the proceedings were actually orchestrated by the monarch himself so as to conform to heroic best practice; life imitating art.[8] Either way, the centrality of the epic presentation of life to Greek literature, not least Herodotus, is clear.

Where the stories come from: oral tradition

If Homeric poetry (in the broadest sense, including the so-called 'cyclic' epics) was one of the strong determinants of narrative *form*, what about content? Since Herodotus is the main, and often unique, source for many events of Greek history in the archaic and early classical period – and sometimes even for Near Eastern history – scholars have naturally been very keen to try and track down his likely sources of information, and then to assess its value.[9] But the historian is not very forthcoming about his informants, and even where he is, we may choose to disbelieve him. At the very outset, he claims to have access to the accounts of Persian *logioi*, 'chroniclers', but we may suspect an ironic usage which his audience would have been well able to recognise as such (as if Persians would have their own variant accounts of Greek legends!). Throughout the work he is eager to cite *generalised* sources ('the Samians say . . .'), and especially to record alleged disagreements ('the Spartans say . . . but the people of Chios . . . say') and concurrences. This habit led Detlev Fehling to point to inconsistencies and improbabilities in the way Herodotus cited 'sources',[10] but though he may well have been both economical with the truth and a skilled embellisher of it, there can be no question of wholesale invention *e nihilo*.[11]

Herodotus did not need to invent, because oral tradition supplied him with a vast, if undigested, mass of traditions about the past.[12] This has long been recognised in principle, but historians have usually been too hasty in attempting to identify these oral sources in terms of political ideology and *parti pris*.[13] What kind of axe was this or that informant busily grinding? Is the account of Agariste's wedding a pro- or anti-Alcmaeonid story?[14] What developments is this or that Delphic oracle attempting to justify, or cover up? When carried out with subtlety such exercises can be very revealing, as in the case of Walter Burkert's brilliant dissection of the different strata of prejudice which are layered into Demaratus' mother's improbable tale of the involvement of the courtyard god Astrabacus in his begetting (6.67–9); or Simon Hornblower's identification of the symbolic role of the territory of Atarneus in the story of the terrible revenge of Hermotimos (8.104–6).[15] But most often all we can be sure of is that most of his source-material *was*, somehow, orally transmitted.

This emerges not so much from his own statements ('the priests told me . . .'), as from the nature of the stories themselves, which bear all the tell-tale signs of narratives which have passed from mouth to ear to mouth again. Wolf Aly showed how many of the typical features of the early modern European folktale, or of *The Thousand Nights and a Night*, can be paralleled in the story-motifs and, more importantly, the organic structures of Herodotean pericopes.[16] One need only compare the elaborate tale of Rhampsinitus and the Thief (2.121) with *Der Meisterdieb*, collected by the Grimm brothers in south Germany in the early nineteenth century.[17] Of course many traditions preserved in Herodotus' text have, or once had, some kind of historical basis, but they have been so thoroughly processed by generations of intermediaries that the specificities of historical contingency have often been eroded away in favour of the generic features which guarantee a story a successful reception. Heroes become more perfectly heroic and villains more villainous still; the rough edges of messy actuality are smoothed into streamlined form. Stories possess, and continue to develop, their own autonomous dynamic.

The point can perhaps be most easily demonstrated by considering how many tales told by Herodotus fall into a series of overlapping, genetically-related sets. This is an obvious feature of the folktale, where we immediately recognise themes like 'The eventual triumph of the disregarded youngest brother' or 'The princess who escapes marriage to the monster at the last minute', or of the more sophisticated but equally traditional yarns spun by Boccaccio; it is also typical of the dirty joke (one of the last genres of oral literature to survive and flourish), where one can often watch the process of evolution in action, as new variants are spawned by word of mouth or across the Internet.[18] And so in Herodotus we find two stories about a queen called Nitocris who doubled as a hydraulic engineer (1.186, a Babylonian story; 2.100, another in Egypt: Herodotus himself notices the coincidence of names). I have already mentioned the theme of The Wise Adviser, which constitutes a familiar set. One might also cite a 'Holocaust' set, in which wicked foreigners burn their enemies alive: 2.111, the Pharaoh called 'Pharaoh', and 2.107, Sesostris' brother (heightened here, because of the double involvement of relatives – first the brother who tries to kill the returning king along with his family, second the wife who advises laying the bodies of two of their children over the flames so that the rest can escape). At 4.164 the perpetrator, Arcesilaus, is a Cyrenean, but more usually the idea is toned down when Greeks are involved: thus Polycrates only threatens immolation (3.45), and Periander burns not the women of Corinth themselves, but only their festive finery (5.92). Or again: many stories re-present the theme of The Awful Dilemma, in which an agonizing choice, like that of Agamemnon at Aulis, is forced upon the protagonist. Sesostris' wife, who chose to sacrifice two of her six children to save the rest of the family, belongs here (and this makes the point that of course a story may belong to more than one set); so do the wife of Intaphernes, ranking brother over sons and husband (3.119); Arion, ordered to kill himself if he wants burial, or jump overboard and drown (1.24); the thief in the Rhampsinitus story, who is urged by his own brother to kill him for the sake of the family (2.121); and Gyges the faithful servant of Candaules, who must either kill his king or die himself (1.11). Or yet again: stories about *messages* form a further group – tattooed on a slave's scalp (5.35), concealed in a dead hare (1.123), scratched on the wood of a writing tablet under an innocent coating of smooth wax (7.239), hidden under arrow feathers (8.128), coded as an apparently meaningless *acte gratuit* to baffle the messenger (5.92, the prodigal wheat-wasting), or culminating in a deliberately puzzling threat (6.37). Gifts, too, may function as implied messages.[19] Other sets which have already received attention include those of the King's Parade and the Philosophical Pharaoh;[20] more detailed research, and a synthetic overview, are needed.

Finally under this heading we may consider two particular classes of tale. First, stories are hooked into Herodotus' narrative as appendages not only to people and dynasties, but also *objects*;[21] and this is a widespread feature of popular storytelling. Physical marvels (*thōmata*) or monuments act as a kind of validatory aide-memoire – history frozen in stone or bronze. Indeed, that is often why they were erected in the first place; but the traditions that become attached to them are often not the ones originally intended. Among many examples of mass being converted into energy in this way: one of the minor pyramids at Giza is supposed to have been built by the daughter of the Pharaoh Cheops; he had forced her into a brothel as a money-making scheme, but on her own account she persuaded each of her clients to stump up a block of stone for her memorial (2.126). The statues of 'Cleobis' and 'Biton' at Delphi come with a story (1.31), and so do those of 'Arion' the dolphin-rider at Tainaron (1.24) and of the Persian horseman associated with the dirty trick of Oebares (3.85–8). Peculiarities invite just-so stories. The kneeling statues on Aegina once stood upright, before they were assaulted and fell to their supplicatory posture (5.86); and the missing hands of the attendant statues clustered around the supposed figure of Mycerinus' daughter were explained, says Herodotus, as replicating the real-life mutilation of the girl's treacherous servants (2.131). In both of the last two cases the author distances himself from the versions he gives, but he gives them all the same. He knows how to have his cake and eat it too.

Second, fables. Since Herodotus knows about Aesop 'the storyteller', *logopoios* (2.134), and is fascinated by animal behaviour (cats, camels, winged snakes, gold-digging ants), it may seem surprising that there is only a single explicit fable in the book, the one told by Cyrus to the Ionians and Aeolians at 1.141. In fact the patterns characteristic of fable permeate Herodotean narrative, which has a similarly moralistic thrust; and many individual pericopes show a clear relationship to particular fables. Compare the scene of Cyrus confronting the emissaries of Artembares at the very end of the work (9.122) with the following animal tales, all to be found in Perry's excellent Loeb edition:[22] Babrius 24, 61, 85, 93, 100, 128, 142 and (especially) 108. Herodotus' Arion story only really makes sense if the poet's farewell performance is a deliberate strategy to bring about his rescue, as it is at No. 97 in Perry's Appendix (p. 440, The Kid and the Wolf). And if Maeandrius' proposal to introduce *isonomia* at 3.142 recalls Perry No. 348, the wolf's proposal for 'equal shares',[23] the very next chapter, in which Maeandrius lures his rivals into his stronghold (and then falls ill), echoes the scheme of The Sick Lion.[24]

A complete assemblage of the intricate network of oral narratives which lies behind and beyond the text would obviously tell us a great deal about the fears and fascinations of fifth-century Greeks – but what does it tell us about Herodotus as a historian? It does not of course mean the dissolution of all 'history' into a mere minestrone of popular motifs; people *did* lure their enemies into buildings, lock them in, and incinerate them, and they continue to do so. Such stories may be true. But a proper recognition of their status as constantly recurring allegations in orally-transmitted rumour highlights the need for caution on the part of those who would assert their historicity.

How the stories are re-shaped and placed

If Herodotus had done no more than preserve the multifarious traditions about the past that were current in his day, he would still have performed a valuable service for future historians. In fact he is much more than a hunter-gatherer: with his generally Homeric ideal in mind, he subjects the raw material he has collected to a thoughtful process of selection, adaptation and disposition.

We have already seen that in a 'normal' telling of the Arion story, the request to be allowed to sing one last aria was probably motivated by the poet's wish to appeal for help to his patron god Apollo (as did Croesus on the pyre in the supposed 'Lydian' version, 1.87). Why then has Herodotus edited out the god, so that the dolphin suddenly surfaces as if by chance? Because it is one of his self-imposed rules – analogous to Homer's censoring out of the traditional epic elements of magic, monstrosity and invulnerability from the *Iliad* – that he will not himself be responsible for claims of divine intervention in the human world of the historical, as opposed, roughly, to what we would call the legendary period.[25] (His characters and his sources are not, of course, bound by the same constraints – compare the 'Lydian version' just mentioned.) We can see a similar principle at work if we examine the story of Gyges, chief of the security staff in the palace of King Candaules of Lydia (1.8–12). Here everything is real-world and rational, in accordance with Herodotus' practice – simple human foolishness leads to murder and the overthrow of an entire dynasty. Yet in this case we are lucky to have a quite different account in another author, for Plato tells the tale in Book 2 of the *Republic* (359c–360b). Now, instead of a bodyguard, the hero is a shepherd, a mere nobody at the opposite end of the power spectrum from the king; yet with the assistance of a magic ring discovered in an ancient burial, which confers upon him the power of invisibility, he is able to enter the palace unseen, seduce the queen, kill the king, and win power for himself. This is the naïve fantasy world of the folktale, and it is surely Plato's version which circulated in the wild and needed some inventive tidying-up before it was presentable enough to appear as Herodotean history.

We can perhaps detect the same stripping away of the supernatural in the tale of the birth of Cypselus at 5.92. First time round, the assassins sent to do away with the fateful baby are caught out by their sentimental feelings and withdraw; but once they have steeled themselves to the task, they return to Labda's house determined not to make the same mistake twice. Yet – even though they must know the infant is somewhere on the premises – their search of the house produces no results. Why? 'Cypselus' was etymologised by the Greeks from *kupselē*, a chest or storage-box – hence, supposedly, his dedication of the great chest at Olympia, described by Pausanias (5.17–19). Yet how could the murderers have failed to open every chest in the house in their search for the baby? But *kupselē* is also the Greek for a kind of terracotta bee-hive; and since innumerable tales of ancient hero-figures describe their miraculous preservation from exposure or untimely death by helpful animals,[26] it looks as though Georges Roux may have been right to argue that in the pre-Herodotean version the mother, in an extremity of desperation, placed her child where no one would think of looking for it – the bee-hive in the garden.[27]

Almost as important as the re-casting of his source-material is the way Herodotus distributes it throughout the *Inquiry* so that it may exert maximum effect. Here we should remember that whether or not we can recover (more or less) the smaller recitation-units from which the nine Hellenistic books were made up,[28] book-boundaries at all events should also have been *logos*-boundaries; and so we may note how he likes to start and end a performance with a striking story like that of Psammetichus' search for the *Ursprache* (2.2), or the blind slaves of Scythia (4.2–4), or the awesome exploit of the Persian general Zopyrus (3.150–60). Furthermore, we may note how he has composed the stories of Gyges and the wife of Candaules (1.8) and Xerxes and the wife of his brother Masistes (9.108–13) so that they form a responding pair, with many correspondences of phrasing ('Fell in love with his own (!) / Masistes' wife'; 'Since he was doomed to come to a bad end'; 'Master, what is this you are telling me to do?'; 'As time went on'; 'When she found out what he had done, she didn't cry out /didn't get angry'; 'But since he couldn't talk her out of it'). The twin tales are then placed at the extreme ends of his work, to form a kind of ring-composition, a structure which some have thought can be detected in the overall scheme of the *Iliad*, as well as in its subsidiary narratives.[29] His idea is presumably to suggest that oriental monarchies are incapable of learning from their mistakes, and are doomed to repeat their history – except that the message here seems to be that what initially occurs as bedroom farce is recapitulated as gruesome tragedy.

With this example in mind, we may be sure that he paid great attention to setting out his stall to best advantage. The Arion story was referred to above (pp. 131–2) as being apparently 'arbitrarily placed'; yet however thin the reason given for its introduction, we may speculate that it was important to Herodotus to introduce a tale about divine justice at the earliest possible moment, in order to put down a programmatic marker for the course of the whole *Inquiry*. If that is so, and bearing in mind the symmetrical disposition of the two stories about oriental wives, it may be that the tale of Euenius the prophet, which holds up the action just before the final battle of Mycale (9.92–6), was intended to act as a matching element at the end of the work; it too concerns divine correction of human injustice.[30] Placing is not just done for effect, placing helps to *determine* effect.

*

All historiography – even when we are following, or being led along, a main narrative line – is ultimately storytelling, the construction of a text targeted at engaging and persuading real or imaginary, present or future, listeners or readers (who include, of course, the author him- or herself in internalised receptive rather than actively suasive mode). But Herodotus sparkles with so many facets, with what the Greeks called *poikilia*, that he is a special case. The total effect is kaleidoscopic; it is not so much the individual fragments as the patterns they form in combination which are so satisfying. Recurring *Leitmotive* mean that, as one story recalls another, the book becomes more than the sum of its parts and complex, resonating harmonics are set up. Once we realise how this intricate ensemble works, we can even ask seemingly impossible questions which go beyond the text, like (3.42): Did the fisherman who brought his prize catch as a present for Polycrates enjoy the dinner to which the grateful tyrant invited him? Herodotus doesn't tell us, but a reading of the parallel story of the feast to which Astyages invited Harpagus (1.118–19) allows us to deduce the ending of the unfinished example from the complete one. The fateful baby Cyrus was supposed to have been lost and gone forever, and so was the ring which was found in the fish's belly. The second king will have been no more pleased than the first to find that what he had tried to throw away turned out to be a boomerang. No, it can not have been a happy meal.[31]

FURTHER READING

O. Murray's 1987 essay 'Herodotus and Oral History', reviewing the sources question in the light of research by Vansina and Finnegan into communal memory in Africa, is now more accessibly reprinted, with minor additions (Murray 2001a). Gray (2002) 291–317 provides a rich selection of examples with thoughtful analysis. Kazazis (1978) shows how a limited stock of strategies can be creatively re-shuffled to produce elaborate realisations at the level of the individual tale. Two useful studies of story-sets (of the kind I have suggested, above p. 138, we need more of), are Flory (1978b) and Stern (1991).

Finally, there are many lessons, both comparative and contrastive, to be learnt from other Near Eastern narrative texts. The historical books of the Bible (for which see Alter [1981]) suggest many tangents to Herodotus' work, and both Hornblower (2003) and I myself (Griffiths [1987]) have found parallels in the Joseph saga. It is worth singling out the tale of the Assyrian vizier Ahiqar, a story which has a rich medieval tradition (see Conybeare et al. [1898]; cf. Charles [1913]), and is proved by an Aramaic papyrus to go back in some form to Herodotus' own time (Cowley [1923]); it gives some idea of the character of the international Eastern Mediterranean tradition which Herodotus both drew on and contributed to.

NOTES

1. What Peter Wiseman has dubbed 'spurious *akribeia*': Wiseman (1983) 21.
2. That is, I shall not deal here with more complex concatenations like the accounts of the careers of Croesus, Polycrates or Miltiades.
3. Use of the word 'drama' is not entirely casual, for the narratives of Croesus, Atys and Adrastus (1.34–45) and Periander and Lycophron (3.50–53) show strong influence from Attic tragedy; see Griffin in this volume. These extended scenes have sometimes been called 'novellae' – stories which are told in such detail that they temporarily hold centre-stage in their own right (compare too the long account of Rhampsinitus and the Thief, 2.121).
4. Jacoby, *RE* col. 380: 'Man kann wohl ohne Übertreibung sagen: Herodots ganze Kunst, seinen Stoff zu disponieren, besteht in der Art, wie und wo er Exkurse anbringen kann.' Compare Griffin in this volume, n. 29.
5. 'Tibull ist ein Ideenflüchtiger, und als solcher gehört er zu den Menschen mit mangelhafter zerebraler Sekundär-Funktion' (van Wageningen [1913] 355, categorising him according to the system of Otto Gross).
6. See Lloyd-Jones (1999); verse 43 runs *Hērodoton ton pezon en historiaisin Homēron*.
7. For more on Herodotus and Homer see Marincola in this volume; for speeches see also Pelling.
8. Murray (1993) 212–13: 'everything that is known of the life style of the aristocracy suggests that it is true'.
9. For a sensitive and circumspect treatment of this question see Hornblower (2002), concluding with a comparison with Thucydides: 'Herodotus' cheerful march across the intellectual disciplines takes him across a wider territory and his footprints are that much harder to trace.'
10. Fehling (1989).
11. Even if Penguin's first, wartime edition of Herodotus (Harmondsworth 1941) did appear in the series 'Fiction'.

12. What I have elsewhere (Griffiths [2001a]) called the 'hintertext'. On oral tradition in Herodotus see Luraghi in this volume.
13. Thus for a reductionist like Oost (1972) Periander's bonfire of the vanities (5.92) is a transformed folk memory of Corinthian sumptuary legislation.
14. See Thomas (1989) 266–7; Griffiths (2001b) 167–8.
15. Burkert (1965); Hornblower (2003).
16. Aly (1921/1969).
17. Fehling (1972) has argued that where there are striking similarities between ancient and modern *Märchen* this is to be explained as the result of reintroduction into popular tradition of stories known from books. This possibility can and should not be completely excluded, but it will not begin to account for the deep and pervasive nature of the cross-correspondences, which while remaining impressive show just the kind of mutations – those enabling a folktale to continue functioning in a Christian culture, for example – that one would expect after a period of many centuries of oral transmission.
18. Only the successful mutations survive. Compare the hero of Saki's short story *The Seventh Pullet* (Saki [1914]), who finds to his surprise that his boastful but wholly invented anecdote is actually winning acceptance: 'Unconsciously all sorts of little details and improvements began to suggest themselves.'
19. Gould (1989) 57; all three of his examples are ominous (4.131; 3.21; 4.162).
20. Griffiths (2001b) and Christ (1994), respectively.
21. See Dewald (1993).
22. Perry (1965).
23. So Detienne and Svenbro (1989) 150–2.
24. Babrius 103, cf. 95, 97; Phaedrus 4.2, Appendix 389.
25. For the divine in Herodotus see Scullion in this volume.
26. See Binder (1964).
27. Roux (1963). Compare Theocritus 7.78–82, Comatas hidden from the wicked king in a box and fed by the bees on honeycomb. More demystification at Hdt. 1.110 (cf. 122): Cyrus was not suckled in the wild by a bitch, but brought up by a woman whose name means 'Bitch' in Persian.
28. An attempt was made by Cagnazzi (1975).
29. For an extreme statement of the case see Whitman (1958), especially the final chart.
30. See further Griffiths (1999).
31. This bit of reconstructive surgery poses a further question: *why* did Herodotus choose not to finish the story? Partly because here the focus is firmly on Polycrates, while in Book 1 Astyages and Harpagus were equally interesting characters; but also because Herodotus normally draws back from ascribing to Greeks, even Greek tyrants, the full gamut of cruel behaviour which orientals are allowed to indulge in. Note also that here Polycrates delivered the original invitation in good faith and with the best of intentions, not as a deceptive lure. So once more the point about sets – not just that they exist, but that it's the *use* of them which is important – applies.

IO

CAROLYN DEWALD

Humour and danger in Herodotus

As Alan Griffiths has commented, 'humour is altogether a funny business'.[1] What one culture finds funny, another might well find appalling; humour in every culture, however, blends a tacit recognition of conventional, expected standards of behaviour and narrative logic, coupled with a transient, unexpected (and sometimes illicit) pleasure at their momentary transgression.[2] It is safe to say that Herodotus, the father of history, knows how to tell a good story, and his stories frequently strike the suggestible reader as funny. I will make several claims here: first, that humour is one aspect of Herodotus' text that makes credible his assertion that the *logoi* he tells are not his own invention; moreover, that the humour of the *Histories* is tied closely to the theme of transgressive violence and danger. Finally, the recurring and various connections between humour and danger in Herodotus point to one of the most fundamental assumptions of historiography: the importance but also the difficulty of ascertaining what is real in *to anthrōpinon*, the realm of the human.

The first extant history of the Western world begins magisterially enough, with some sonorous and even mildly portentous opening clauses (*praef.*):

– This (*hēde*) is the display/publication of the investigation of Herodotus of Halicarnassus (or, of Thurii, as Aristotle's text had it);
– both so that things happening in the human sphere (literally: from human beings) should not become worn away/faded in time;
– and so that great and marvellous deeds, some displayed by Greeks and others by foreigners, should not become unrenowned;
– both in other respects and in the cause for which they went to war with one another.

From this august beginning, it is fair to say, things slide rapidly and comically downhill, or at least down genre.[3] The narrative proper opens soberly enough, purporting to report the account of some Persian *logioi* or learned men, whose first *logos* or story of East/West enmities is a rationalised version of some Greek myths. They explain the origins of Greco–barbarian hostilities (including the great Persian Wars of 481–479 that provide the climax of the *Histories*) by starting with Io, a long-ago Greek princess from Argos, who went down to the port one day on a shopping expedition and was abducted by the Phoenician traders whose wares she was examining. Herodotus tells the account of the Persian savants that follows in indirect discourse. According to the learned Persians, the Phoenician abduction of Io set off an arms race of sorts. Jason the famous Argonaut, happening to be in Colchis on other business, abducts Medea, a Colchian princess, repaying the easterners tit for tat for the abduction of Io. Still according to the Persian *logioi*, some Greeks then abduct Europa from Tyre in Phoenicia in the Levant, which gives Alexander the Trojan the idea that he can get himself a Greek wife by abducting Helen, a Spartan princess without having to pay for her – the others had gotten away with it, after all. This, say the Persians, is where things really degenerated, since the Greeks took the abduction of Helen seriously and began a war to get her back, when any sensible man would know women aren't abducted who don't want to be abducted.[4]

Herodotus himself, reporting the whole sequence as something the Persians have told him, wisely avoids more extended authorial comment here, and concludes only by saying that this was the Persian version of the commencement of East–West hostilities – but that the Phoenicians, on the whole agreeing with the Persians, have one correction to add: Io wasn't exactly *abducted* by the Phoenicians. It turns out she had been sleeping with the ship's captain, got pregnant, and didn't want her parents to find out (*aideomenē tous tokeas*). So the Phoenicians took her away with them, to enable her to avoid the difficulties she would have encountered had she stayed in Argos – just being helpful (1.1–5).

As Aristophanes in *Acharnians* saw, this account contains elements of slapstick comedy.[5] But its opéra bouffe quality serves several more serious historiographic ends as well. The women in the account are drawn from Argos in the northern Peloponnese, Colchis on the east coast of the Black Sea (part of the territory Herodotus considers in his treatment of Scythia in Book 4), Phoenicia in the northern Levant, and Sparta in the southern Peloponnese. In the Persian *logos* and more generally in Greek myth, Io is taken to Egypt after a *periplous* of her own around the eastern Mediterranean, Medea goes to Corinth, Athens, and eventually Media, Europa to Crete, and Helen to Troy. So all four women in their origins and their endpoints map out many of the major areas of the Mediterranean world that the *Histories* as a narrative intends to cover – their brief stories serve as a sort of Gilbert-and-Sullivan overture, hinting at the geographical scope of what is to come.

Moreover, any Greek listening to Herodotus deliver this proem would have realised that these are not just random women; they are deflated myths. Io, the girl who became a cow in traditional Greek myth, is assimilated to Isis, the Egyptian goddess mother (a process only alluded to in Herodotus, 2.41); Medea later gives her name to the Medes (this according to Herodotus himself is what the Medes say, 7.62); Europa has all of Europe, the largest continent, named after her (4.45; Herodotus comments that he has no idea why), while the name of Helen, the fourth and final abducted woman in the sequence had at least before Herodotus been developed as a pun on the aorist infinitive *helein*, the destructiveness of war.[6] In some respects this bumptious beginning of the first history is a meditation on the process of exogamy itself. The women in the story have become over the centuries mythic figures that iconically represent not their natal origins but the areas of the world to which they are taken: Egypt, the Persian empire, Europe, and the contested area of the Hellespont, the flashpoint of the very East–West divide the *Histories* will take as its task to consider. In (so to speak) flattening old mythic and poetic versions of heroine abduction in this way, Herodotus is perhaps poking mild fun at the rationalising procedures of his great predecessor, Hecataeus, but he is also making a kind of point about mythic meaning that Hecataeus might have made. One has to watch out for these stories from the past – they need to be massively reworked if they are to be at all connected to ordinary human reality.

In any case, by starting the first history with the Persian and Phoenician variant versions of deflated, rationalised, and tendentious myth, Herodotus the narrator is also suggesting that *all* of the *logoi* or accounts out of which he will construct his huge narrative of a century and more of Greco–Persian enmity are liable to be self-interested, since the point of the Persian version of the abduction sequence he has just recounted is to lay blame for the beginning of East–West enmity not on the Persians, the aggressors in the actual Persian Wars with which the *Histories* will end, but on the Greeks, back in the mythic times before the Trojan War. This point becomes even clearer when the Phoenicians agree with the Persians in all details – except of course those that impugn the good faith of Phoenicians.[7] Herodotus concludes the proem as a whole by shrugging and saying he won't judge whether any of it was true or not. As narrator, *he* intends at this point to go on to the man who he knows (here he uses the verb *oida*) first committed violence against the Greeks of Asia – Croesus the Lydian, in the mid-sixth century BCE.[8]

So it is arguably complicated, subtle, historiographically sophisticated comedy, but comedy nonetheless, that launches the narrative genre that Herodotus invented. The humour does not end with the playful proem; it also pervades the whole of the *Histories* that follows. The larger question that needs to be considered is two-pronged: how does this humorous strain manifest itself, and what historiographical purposes does it serve?

Humour in Herodotus is not an entirely unstudied subject. Various aspects of it have been addressed, hostilely by the imperial literary critic Plutarch, germanically if obliquely by Wolf Aly in his exhaustive 1921 study of folk motifs in Herodotus, philologically by Enoch Powell in a learned 1937 article on Herodotean puns, and thematically, by Donald Lateiner and Stewart Flory in the late 1970s and by Alan Griffiths in 1995.[9] Most of these studies have considered humour in the *Histories* either as a commentary on the hubris of the powerful, revealed by misplaced laughter of people inside the account, or instead as an aspect of Herodotus' own quirky psychology – the great French Budé editor Legrand remarks on Herodotus' indulgence of (or at least willingness to be entertained by) others' 'habilité, même associée avec l'indélicatesse'.[10]

Herodotus' humour is seen as needing explanation, because this is one aspect of his narrative art that his *epigonoi*, in particular his first and greatest successor, Thucydides, conspicuously did not adopt.[11] This has in part to do with the fact that Herodotus, and Herodotus alone, presents his *Histories* as a composite account, constructed out of oral reports from the past. As narrator he frequently emphasises that his narrative has been fashioned, even stitched together, out of hundreds of oral *logoi* that he has gathered from all over the Mediterranean basin.[12] Herodotus' refusal to own the content of his history's narrative as his own work truly makes him the *pater historiae* that Cicero calls him (*De legibus* 1.1.5). Herodotus has collected and arranged together hundreds of little narratives told by others, to become in his hands a huge road-map of the known sixth- and fifth-century world, within which he can then trace the sixth-century rise of the Persian empire and its astonishing fifth-century check in Greece. Repeatedly he insists that the stories themselves are not his own invention, but rather accounts he has received from many different informants, Greek and barbarian. He has investigated them as best he can for accuracy, against a variety of extant empirical data – but as the *logoi* of the Persians and Phoenicians that begin the *Histories* show, Herodotus believes that the *logoi* are only as trustworthy as the informants who have delivered them – informants very likely themselves to be self-interested in shaping their accounts.

Seen from this angle, the jokes, the puns, and the two structural varieties of humour we shall shortly consider are worth noting, since they too implicitly testify to the validity of Herodotus' claim that his *logoi are* genuine reports from the past and the distant reaches of the present, and that he really *is* their appreciative but also empirically-minded recorder and investigator. It is a reasonable supposition that Herodotus was able to collect many such stories in the mid-fifth century BCE – that is, that they were still around to be collected – because their wit had left them in oral circulation for three or four generations. The quality of the humour often suggests the nature of the biases, animosities, and rivalries of the various governing classes that had told and retold them, until they could be saved from extinction – from becoming *exitēla*, as the proem says – by the workings of Herodotus' stylus in about 440 BCE.

Some of the humour seems to be distinctively marked by city or *ethnos*, as emerges from the apparent consistency of some subsets of national anecdote.[13] Spartans in Herodotus, for instance, tend to exhibit a dry verbal wit that expresses itself (of course) laconically. Amompharetus, the Spartan commander in charge of the so-called Pitanate company at the battle of Plataea, refuses to obey a command to beat a strategic retreat. He picks up a giant boulder and drops it at the feet of Pausanias, his commander-in-chief, saying 'this is my vote against fleeing the strangers' (9.55). (In Greek he has delivered himself of a pun; his *psēphos* (pebble) is a large rock and Amompharetus says that he has used it to 'vote' [*psēphizesthai*].)[14] Cleomenes, the eccentric but gifted sixth-century Spartan king, seems to have left a string of witticisms behind him. When he is foiled in his attempt to take hostages from Aegina by an Aeginetan named Crius, or Ram, he is reported to have replied: 'Right now, Mr. Ram, bronze up your horns, since you're about to get in big trouble' (6.50).[15] One of the best Spartan stories, though, concerns a complicated sixth-century rivalry between Sparta and Samos, then ruled by the famous tyrant Polycrates. Some exiled Samians go to Sparta for help in attacking Polycrates; there they make a long speech about the urgency of their need. The Lacedaemonian response to this first audience, however, is to critique its long-windedness. I quote Herodotus here (3.46):

> they replied to this first speech that they had forgotten the parts spoken earlier and didn't understand the later ones. The Samians, making a second attempt, now said nothing at all except, bringing a bag with them, 'the bag needs grain'. The Lacedaemonians replied that the word 'bag' was superfluous – but then they decided to help them anyway.[16]

So much for Spartans. The Egyptians, as Alan Lloyd's commentary notes,[17] seem to specialise in ribald and somewhat exaggerated stories, like that of the forced prostitution of the pharaoh Rhampsinitus' daughter. Rhampsinitus wants to know who has been stealing from his treasury; to catch the thief, he requires his own daughter to become a prostitute, asking each of her clients as payment that he tell her about his cleverest dastardly deed (*ho ti dē en tōi biōi ergastai autōi sophōtaton kai anosiōtaton*, 2.121ε.2). His brilliant plan misfires, however, since the real thief has brought a spare arm and hand with him to the bedroom (a long story, this – it might well be his brother's)[18] – anyway, he leaves this spare arm behind in the girl's clutches, when she tries to hold him, after he tells her that he has been stealing from the treasury.[19] The pharaoh, overcome with the thief's obvious intelligence, makes him his son-in-law.

Some of the most extravagant Egyptian stories concern the mid-sixth-century upstart pharaoh Amasis.[20] While Amasis is still a commoner, he decides to throw his lot in with the group revolting from King Apries and is then faced with a scolding harangue from his royal master, delivered by an underling. 'Amasis, for he happened to be on horseback, lifting himself in the saddle, farted, and ordered him to take *that* back to Apries' (2.162.3). When Amasis himself becomes king, he is not treated with the respect he feels the office of pharaoh deserves – especially by his previous rowdy comrades-in-arms (2.172–3). And so (2.172.3–5):

> He had thousands of possessions, and among them was a gold footbath, in which Amasis and all his dinner guests on each occasion used to wash their feet. Chopping up this footbath, he had a statue of a god made from it, and he set it up in just the right place in the city, where the Egyptians coming along would treat it with great reverence. When he learned what they were doing, Amasis called them together and made a speech. He revealed that the statue had been made out of the footbath in which they had previously vomited and urinated and washed their feet, but which they now greatly venerated. At this point, he said that very similar things had happened to him and this footbath. For if earlier he had been a commoner, nevertheless now he was their king, and he ordered them to honour and respect him too.

Finally, Athenian political humour represents yet a third distinctive kind. It is quite pointed, politically partisan, and tends to show eminent members of famous and powerful political families misbehaving themselves, or behaving in a way that punctures their pretensions – the kind of thing that Plutarch singles out for special disapprobation in the *De malignitate* more than five centuries later. Many of the most pointed anecdotes are directed against the Alcmaeonidae, the noble family from which the great fifth-century general Pericles was descended, on his mother's side.[21] In 6.125 there occurs a story about the sixth-century founder of the family, Alcmaeon himself. Invited by Croesus, the tyrant of Lydia, to take as much gold from Croesus' treasury as he could carry, Alcmaeon

> planned and achieved the following operation: putting on a huge tunic and leaving in it a deep fold, he found the biggest possible boots and put them on and entered the treasury, when they led him there. Falling on the heap of gold dust, first he packed next to his shins as much of the gold as his boots

would carry, and next he filled his tunic full of gold and, sprinkling the hair of his head with gold dust and taking more into his mouth, he left the treasury dragging his boots with difficulty, resembling anything except a human being – his mouth was crammed to bursting and he was bulging in every direction. Croesus, looking at him, was struck with laughter, and he gave him all this and, in addition, at least as much more. That is how this family grew hugely rich, and this same Alcmaeon, keeping a four-in-hand, took the prize at Olympia. (6.125)

Alcmaeon's son Megacles collected stories around him as well. In the mid-sixth century Megacles became the famous tyrant-hater, the enemy of the Peisistratids, but Herodotus traces this hatred back to a scabrous Athenian story, one that is not by twenty-first-century standards very funny, but would have probably counted as political humour in the world of fifth-century Athens. Herodotus reports that originally Megacles plotted to have his daughter marry the tyrant Peisistratus, presumably in order to have grandchildren who were tyrants (1.61). When he discovered, however, that the tyrant had outwitted him by making love to his daughter 'not in the usual way' (*ou kata nomon*), Megacles then became reconciled to Peisistratus' enemies and Peisistratus went into exile for the second time, according to Herodotus.[22]

An Athenian political story that does strike us as amusing, indeed as one of the most classic anecdotes in Herodotus, also concerns the Alcmaeonids and especially Megacles, Pericles' great-grandfather. Herodotus, tracing the rise of the Alcmaeonid family fortunes, tells how Megacles won the hand of the daughter of the famous tyrant Cleisthenes of Sicyon in the early sixth century. Cleisthenes was ambitious for his daughter and wanted her husband to be the best man in Greece (*Hellēnōn hapantōn exeurōn ton ariston*), and to that end threw a year-long house party for Agariste's numerous aristocratic suitors (6.126–31). Generally agreed to be the best of all of them was an Athenian, Hippocleides son of Tisander, for his manliness (*andragathiēn*), but also because he was related to the Cypselid family of Corinth (he was probably a Philaid himself). The day for the marriage came, and Cleisthenes threw a feast at which the bridegroom would be announced. I will let Herodotus take over here (6.129):

As the drinking went on, Hippocleides, outstripping the others, then ordered the flute player to play, and he began to dance. Now Hippocleides danced in a way that he himself liked a lot, but Cleisthenes, looking on, was getting annoyed at the whole business. After a bit Hippocleides ordered a table to be brought in and, when the table arrived, he first danced some Spartan steps, then some Attic ones, and, thirdly, standing on his head on the table, he waved his legs about. After the first and second dances, Cleisthenes hated the thought that Hippocleides would be his son-in-law, because of his dancing and general shamelessness. He restrained himself, however, so as not to scold. But when he saw Hippocleides waving his legs about, he was unable to contain himself. 'O son of Tisander', he said, 'you have danced away your marriage.' But Hippocleides, replying, said, 'No problem for Hippocleides (*ou phrontis Hippokleidēi*).' And from this comes the proverb.

So Megacles the Alcmaeonid got the girl, Herodotus goes on to add, and Agariste had a granddaughter, another Agariste, who gave birth to Pericles, after dreaming she gave birth to a lion.

It is quite likely that clusters of oral accounts like these, some of them marked by a distinctive regional or ethnic brand of humour, remained in circulation and thus available to Herodotus as much as a century later, precisely because they were funny and were passed down to him with their humour intact, possibly in the context of clusters of similar stories. In one sense, it is oblique testimony to Herodotus' integrity as an ethnographer that he so often reports the point of the anecdote, even when its larger purpose within his ongoing narrative is a serious historical one. In the case of all the Alcmaeonid stories, the context suggests that in play are probably a thinly-veiled allusion to the pretensions of Pericles' crypto-tyrannical position as the *primus inter pares* in Athens at the height of Athens' fifth-century democracy and the resentments this gave rise to in Athenian political circles.[23]

What has been argued so far? As the abduction stories at the opening of the *Histories* show, Herodotus is aware that oral anecdote is likely to be self-interested, but sometimes it contains the best (or the only) information he has about the complicated sets of developments, both eastern and western, that led to the sixth-century rise of the Persian empire and its early-fifth-century check in Greece. In terms of suggestively regional brands of humour, I have considered ten anecdotes in all – the proem and nine *logoi* drawn from Sparta, Egypt, and Athens, to show something of the flavour of these bits of material that Herodotus has saved from their originally highly charged local contexts, and also to show how humour can suggest a variety of different interpretive positions on the part of the author himself without making them explicit.

But more can be said that gets us more explicitly into the announced topic of this chapter, humour and danger. Looking structurally at the ten *logoi* we have already considered, we find that they fall into two basic groups: (a) those in which an individual inside the account focalises the humour, either saying something funny or setting up a deliberately humorous situation; or (b) those in which the humour is created, as it were, from the outside – by the narrator, Herodotus himself or his informant, looking at the doings of all the actors in the story from a distance.

Although I did not foresee it when I first outlined this chapter, all three of the ethnic clusterings considered above contain both kinds of focalisation. In the Spartan stories, the story of Cleomenes and Crius the Aeginetan 'ram' and the story of the Samians and Lacedaemonians with their sack of grain are of the first type, where an individual or group inside the account focalises the humour, while the story of Amompharetus and his boulder is largely of the second type. Amompharetus' mild pun deflates a Homeric conceit by depicting the giant rock, not hurled by the hero but dropped, as a huge voting pebble. Amompharetus, however, is not laughing; he is very angry. The real humour in the scene is set up by the narrator and involves the collision of Amompharetus' Ajax-like indignation and the complexity of what his harassed commander is trying to achieve at Plataea.[24] Of the Egyptian stories, Amasis the upstart pharaoh is the comic director of both his anecdotes: *he* produces both the fart and the royal footbath/statue as commentary; the joke is his joke. The story of Rhampsinitus' daughter and the temple thief, on the other hand, is of the second type, where the principal humour lies in the story as a whole, as the narrator presents it. Finally, in the Athenian stories, Hippocleides waving his legs about is the focaliser of his story – Herodotus even comments that a proverb arose from Hippocleides' drunkenly insouciant retort to his powerful almost-father-in-law – while the point of the two Alcmaeonid stories about Alcmaeon's expandable tunic and Megacles' humiliation at Peisistratus' treatment of his daughter comes not from an internal focalisation, but from the way the narrator himself has set up the account, looking on from the outside.

These two differently focalised types of *logos*, though they share a flavour of narrative ebullience that is distinctively Herodotean in tone, go in two very different directions in terms of the other narrative elements out of which Herodotus has created his monumental work. Both of them, however, are connected to the notion of danger.

The stories in which an individual inside the narrative focalises the humour are perhaps best understood if we go back to Freud's treatment of wit within a joke that someone delivers. Freud talks of some jokes as condensations that contain within them judgement: the individual setting up the joke makes a metaphorical or metonymic condensation of the action or person he or she wishes to criticise – and the humour in it, funny because of the condensation, is often highly critical, even aggressive.[25] Amasis' fart sent back to his royal master, Hippocleides' vulgar display of his nether limbs on the last day of a year-long genteel house party given by a tyrant, the Lacedaemonians topping the Samian show-and-tell about the sack with a verbal riposte of their own (they imply that even their notoriously slow Laconian wits have gotten the fact that the imperative 'give!' is the whole point of the fancy Samian speech): all of these comments are aimed at and meant to criticise someone. Such jokes, whether made verbally or in the medium of body language, support and embellish another very strong narrative thread in Herodotus' account: the prevalence of valiant trickster figures, often marginal underdogs themselves, who regard those with power over them with a jaundiced but cunning eye. Tricksters inside the narrative of Herodotus often exploit and thus expose to the reader of the *Histories* the political machinations that lie beneath a seemingly innocuous surface.[26] The best of them act themselves as postmodern commentators about the seductiveness of symbolic structures: Amasis lecturing the Egyptian nobility on the mutability and extreme deceptiveness of appearances – their holy statue has recently been a footbath/vomitorium/pisspot – is also asking them to adopt a Derridean scepticism about meaning itself. Yes, the Egyptians have misread the origins of the golden religious statue, but they are also misreading him, Amasis, if they do not accept the profound mutability of things: he really now is Pharaoh, to the extent that that term means anything at all, just as the erstwhile footbath is really now a statue of divinity. Meaning, Amasis believes, is largely contextual.[27]

Many of the tricksters in Herodotus manipulate objects as successfully as they manipulate language, and many of these manipulations are not particularly funny – or, the humour in them shades into a very bitter irony, since it is often connected to violence and death. Nitocris, a princess in Egypt, wants to avenge her brother's death at the hands of his political enemies, so she sets up an underground dining chamber. Claiming she wishes to forgive and forget, she stages an elaborate banquet in it, during which all her enemies are drowned inside the chamber, by a river to which she has built a secret channel (2.100). Alexander, the prince of Macedon, seeing that the Persian grandees visiting his royal father are getting drunker by the minute and have started to paw the noble Macedonian women who have been forced to entertain them, substitutes clean-shaven Macedonian men for the outraged women, who then use daggers to kill the Persians at their banquet (5.20). But the bitter trick is turned at the end against Alexander. Herodotus adds that a Persian investigator is sent to see why so many of his noble countrymen have disappeared in Macedon, and Alexander must at the end marry his own sister to Bubares the investigator, to buy his silence (5.21).[28]

I will mention only one more story of this kind, about tricksters and their machinations. It is one of the most violent but oddly satisfying in the *Histories*; it shows quite clearly, however, how thin the line is between the humour of the ordinary trickster figure and a deadly serious violence that occasionally emerges, with complex reverberations, in the text. At the end of the battle of Salamis, Xerxes must send his children back to Persia, and he entrusts them not only to Artemisia but also to one of his most powerful eunuchs, Hermotimus. At this point Herodotus interrupts his account of the great battle and its aftermath to indulge in a long parenthesis (8.105–6). Hermotimus the eunuch, Herodotus says, took the greatest vengeance when he was wronged of anyone in Herodotus' knowledge (*megistē tisis ēdē adikēthenti egeneto pantōn tōn hēmeis idmen*). He had been kidnapped as a young Greek boy by enemies and sold to Panionius, a Greek slave trader, who had castrated and sold him east into slavery. Happening to become part of the royal bureaucracy and rising to be Xerxes' most valuable eunuch, Hermotimus encounters his erstwhile captor while on the king's business in Atarneus in Mysia. He tells Panionius that without his good offices – meaning the castration – he, Hermotimus, would never have risen as far as he did. Because one good turn deserves another, Hermotimus persuades Panionius to relocate with all his family to Atarneus. Once Panionius and his family are in Hermotimus' power, Hermotimus forces Panionius to castrate all four of his sons, and then the sons to castrate their father (8.106), and he gives them a bitter, improving speech in the bargain. Herodotus, calling this the greatest vengeance ever achieved, narrates it at the point in the larger story when Xerxes' *own* bastard children are being hurried back eastward to Ephesus by the trickster queen Artemisia – and by his trusted eunuch Hermotimus. The ironies here, obviously, are multiple (what a babysitter for his children! and what then does Hermotimus' story say about Xerxes' judgement as the head of an empire, or understanding of foreigners in important positions?), but Herodotus leaves us to tease them out.[29] In the immediate context he does allow himself the following piece of sarcasm, however. Xerxes has asked for Artemisia's advice on whether to stay on in Greece, or to retreat back to Persia himself, but Herodotus observes: 'I don't think that he would have stayed, even if all men and all women had advised him to remain – he was that terrified' (8.103).

So the set of anecdotes we have been considering so far – those in which a character inside the account, trickster-like, controls the joke – reveals a first, Freudian way in which humour is connected to danger in Herodotus. Over and over, with varying degrees of the comedic involved, enterprising individuals inside the *Histories* exploit appearances. Everyone – women and slaves, grandees and commoners – aggressively seeks to manipulate the surface appearance of reality in order to achieve ends of their own. Often, especially if they are underdogs, they are brilliantly successful, and we enjoy watching the discomfiture of the powerful that results. But the meaning is applicable to everyone, even to us, as Herodotus' readers. *Our* wonderful golden religious statue too may turn out to have a most peculiar past, and we are better readers and actors in the present, more like Herodotus' own trickster figures ourselves, if we recognise this – but we have to accept the lived realities of the present as well. We are back at one of the themes of the Solon/Croesus story. The consequences of not reading wisely both past and present can be very dire, as the anecdote about Hermotimus and Panionius shows. Appearances, especially when allied with duplicitous language, are sometimes dangerously misleading, especially to those in power smugly convinced of their own invincibility.

The second group of anecdotes, consisting of those in which the narrative control of the humour is maintained by the narrator himself, is harder to think about. Since they are not jokes delivered by someone inside the account, they are not properly instances of Freud's definition of wit, the joke proper. In terms of theories of the comic (itself a somewhat funny concept), they respond rather to Bergson's little treatise on laughter, since they generally are constructed around a narrated instance of what Bergson calls a 'raideur mécanique' or mechanical rigidity suddenly being disrupted.[30] Most of the anecdotes of the second type considered above fit this description well. Megacles' discomfiture at the hands of Peisistratus comes because Megacles has not, as it were, been able to think outside the dynastic box – marriage in his mind leads to children (1.61). And the vulgarity of the topic (and of my sentence) makes a larger point in Herodotus' narrative: Herodotus does not like tyranny, and Peisistratus' tyranny is metaphorically doing to the Athenian citizen body what he has overtly done to Megacles' daughter. The Athenians themselves, so to speak, may be the final butt of Herodotus' brief anecdote, as well as the longer story about the establishment of Peisistratus' tyranny, in which the story of Megacles' daughter plays an important part.

Raideur mécanique comes into the other anecdotes of this second type too. The story of Alcmaeon and his expandable tunic hinges on the obsessive entrepreneurial vulgarity of the Athenian nobleman, which Croesus the royal Lydian finds funny – but as Flory and Lateiner have shown us, Croesus himself is only able to laugh because of his own rigidity of thinking, imagining that his royal position and vast wealth will always exempt him from the kinds of greedy obsessiveness that Alcmaeon exhibits. The story of Amompharetus and his huge voting pebble is droll, but it also points to a Spartan rigidity and parochialism that comes dangerously close to losing the battle of Plataea; Amompharetus himself dies in the battle. Very often, as in the story of Alcmaeon or Amompharetus, or the abduction sequence that begins the whole *Histories*, the humour comes not from the *raideur mécanique* of one actor alone, but from the way that everyone inside the account is trapped in habitual structures of expectation that prohibit them from seeing the realities of their situation that Herodotus as narrator eventually discloses to the rest of us. Like the trickster motif discussed above, this is one of the most basic of Herodotus' narrative ploys, and I would like to list a few of its instantiations, just to explore the pervasiveness of its appearance in the *Histories*.

First, kings and other powerful people, of the sort that Lateiner and Flory have found to indulge in the habit of inappropriate laughter. After the initial story of Croesus, the *Histories* as a whole are structured around the reigns of four Persian monarchs: Cyrus, Cambyses, Darius, and Xerxes; it is over the course of these four reigns that Herodotus traces the rise and fall of Persian imperial arms against Greece. All four kings are talented and initially successful individuals – even the madman Cambyses conquers Egypt! – but all four of them are presented as undone by the kinds of automatic thinking that the humorous anecdotes in Herodotus disclose. The royal narratives are not always funny themselves, even though they are constructed on the same principle as the externally focalised funny stories. Cyrus, the founder of the Persian empire, ends his life decapitated and his head is stuffed by Queen Tomyris in a bag filled with blood because, Herodotus says, he simply cannot imagine he will not be successful against the barbarian Massagetae (1.214). Cambyses, Cyrus' son and successor, has a dream that his throne is taken by his brother Smerdis, so Cambyses has his brother killed – only to discover that a Mede, also named Smerdis, has usurped his royal powers while he is away conquering Egypt (3.64–5). Darius, the most successful Persian monarch of them all, is repeatedly undone by the misrepresentations of enterprising underlings. The most egregious example comes in Book 3, where Darius' wife Atossa persuades him to mount an invasion of Greece. He takes her argument at face value, but does not understand that she has been taught, *didachtheisa*, by a Greek physician, Democedes, who wants the excuse of a scouting expedition sent to Greece with himself in charge as a means of escaping home to Croton (3.134–6). Finally, and most disastrously, King Xerxes, Darius' son, mounts a massive invasion of Greece, compelled by his own need to live up to family traditions, and by the flattery of his ambitious cousin, Mardonius. Additionally, his habitual assumptions about the vast extent of his own power effectively blind him to the possibility of failure.[31] All four of these kings, like Croesus before them, think their power entitles them to success in all their undertakings; all of them are disappointed in their expectations. And they are not alone; restriction of space prevents the exploration of the same kinds of blindness on the part of other people with power – tyrants, Greek kings, political and military leaders.[32] The theme is not humorous *per se*, but the humorous versions of this motif highlight and give point to its thematic pervasiveness in this largest geopolitical and historical realm as well.[33]

It is not just kings and other people in power who come to grief because of the automatism of their assumptions, their *raideur mécanique*. Very often the humour of a Herodotean narrative has to do with a larger incommensurability between *two* competing sets of assumptions, so that we, the readers, see the different expectations in comic, or not so comic, collision. Sometimes an ethnic mutual incomprehension is in play. The Scythians in Book 4 want the Ionian tyrants guarding the bridge for King Darius to break the bridge and strand Darius in Scythia, where the Scythians will pick him off and in consequence set the Ionians free. The Ionians guarding the bridge are all for the scheme until one of their number, Histiaeus, reminds them that they are not just Ionians but Ionian tyrants, and they owe their positions to the favour of their Persian masters (4.137).[34] So then on the one hand they say to the Scythians, 'yes, we are convinced', but on the other in secret they work furiously to secure Darius' safe return. The Scythians are scornful when they find out what has happened, saying that Ionians make pathetic men (*kakistous te kai anandrotatous*), but excellent slaves (*philodespota kai adrēsta*, 4.142). The Scythians, however, noble savages that they are, have not understood that they are dealing not with 'Ionians', but with Ionian tyrants – a very different matter.

There are many other stories of this type, in which the humour, egregious in the examples first cited, is so subtle and pervasive that, as in the trickster stories, it shades at the end into a kind of bitter irony.[35] (In some respects, Plutarch is a better reader of this aspect of the *Histories* than many of Herodotus' modern commentators.) Men misunderstand women – I think of the two kings Candaules and Xerxes whose wives destroy them, at the beginning and end of the *Histories*, because they have not taken the trouble to see their wives as serious political players. Underlings misinterpret the interests of those more powerful than they are: two Paeonian brothers from the northwest corner of the Aegean get their sister up as a version of the Rumpelstiltskin-story wonder woman, who can spin and carry water and care for a horse all at the same time (5.12). Their hope is to trap Darius into making them satraps of a tyranny centred on the Strymon river, governed by themselves. However, Darius, when he sees the girl's incredible industry, has the whole Paeonian *ethnos* captured and shipped off to Asia Minor, to Phrygia – so much for her brothers' grandiose dreams of tyranny. In a comic version, they foreshadow the much darker replay of this theme in the account of the Ionian revolt that follows.

The larger point to be made here is this: in the numerous stories in the *Histories* about the incommensurability of various human expectations,

Herodotus repeatedly shows the actors in events moving blindly into disaster because, trapped by the rigidity of their own beliefs and expectations, they cannot adjust to the actual circumstances that confront them. This is a crucial point of the humorous abduction sequence that begins the *Histories'* proem and began this chapter. As we have already seen, Herodotus constructs the account to focus on the fact that the abducted women become mythic and variously eponymous figureheads of the countries to which they are taken. It is because of historical events outside her control that Io, the Greek girl from Argos, becomes an important Egyptian goddess. Medea, the girl from Georgia, gives her name to the people among whom she finally settles, the Medes. Europa, the Phoenician, has Europe named after her, and well-travelled Helen the Spartan (from a Sparta that is in Herodotus' day both provincial and laconic) is responsible at the end for East–West enmity and the long stories to which that enmity has given rise, both Homer's and Herodotus'. When we consider the nature of humour itself, the fact that this is a theme, and a pretty funny one as Herodotus develops it, also directs our attention to a fundamental historiographical question: how do we as ordinary human beings, without loquacious muses speaking in our ear, or much luck in deciphering various signs of meaning sent by the gods, decide what reality is? Even if we do learn by *historiē* to select data that are both real and significant, how do we learn to use them in order to tell a historical story – a story that is not the product of our assumptions, our preconditioned rigidities? In short, how do we learn to see clearly the real dangers that confront us, in the bewildering plethora of appearances and *logoi* that constitute the fabric of our daily lives? How do we learn to narrate their reality to others?

To this question Herodotus does not supply an easy or direct answer. But one is suggested obliquely, at the end of the abduction sequence (1.5):

> This now is what the Persians and Phoenicians say. But I am not going to declare about these things that they happened in this way or otherwise, but will go on to the man I know first committed unjust deeds against the Greeks. Indicating him, I will proceed to the rest of the story, going through small and large human settlements alike. For those that were earlier big have mostly become small, while those big in my time were earlier small. Knowing that human happiness never remains long in the same place, I will record both alike.

In other words: Herodotus' expressed interest here is not in deciding the meaning of history. He has data from the past – some of it, like the rationalised mythic *logoi* he has just recounted, data of very dubious historicity. But rather than choose among his data, he will grid it all for us to look at, both the apparently significant and the apparently insignificant.[36] We look at what we have available, and understand what we can of it.

We have known for a while now that when people inside the *Histories* laugh, it is almost always a mistake – a sign that, in the Kiplingesque words of the wall plaque, 'if you can keep your head while all about you are losing theirs – you haven't understood the seriousness of the situation'. But Herodotus' own authorial laughter, so disliked by Plutarch, is of a qualitatively different sort. In both the accounts where the joke is focalised through a character in the account, and the accounts where it is more diffusely the preserve of the narrator himself, the humour arises out of Herodotus' own acute perception of the lack of fit between ordinary human perception and the world that human beings live in and try to shape; certainly none of the enterprising figures of the abduction sequence that begins the *Histories* intend to establish an all-but-unbridgeable cultural divide between East and West, or to be bringing on the fifth-century Persian Wars. By laughing, and helping us too to laugh, Herodotus teaches us to think historically, because he exposes us to the dangers of the arbitrary constructedness of the *logoi* we tell ourselves about the world and its realities. In fact, when he tells us he does laugh, in 4.36, it is at people like those who think they understand the pattern, and draw maps of the world as perfectly round 'as if by a compass, and making Asia the equivalent of Europe' (*hōs apo tornou, kai tēn Asiēn tēi Eurōpēi poieuntōn isēn*).

We cannot tell where happiness will fall next, very often we cannot control the simplest things about reality, because we so profoundly and so often misunderstand the rudiments of its translation into narrative. Big is always in the process of becoming small, and small big. But if, like the tricksters, we learn to move attentively with the slipperiness of the world, honouring the realities that the available data do give us, at least, like Amasis, we can then lecture our friends on where their shiny gold statues have been before we started worshipping them – and also learn to see the incommensurability that separates what we think we know from the realities that underlie and subvert our assumptions, all the time. This is a large part of what it means to begin to think historically, and Herodotus showed the rest of us how to begin to do it.[37]

FURTHER READING

For the modern bibliography on humour in Herodotus, see n. 9 below. As Freudenberg (1993) 56–9 remarks, very little survives of ancient rhetorical, ethical, and poetic theories of humour, especially from before the first century BCE. Demetrius of Phaleron, Theophrastus, Eratosthenes, and Aristophanes of Byzantium all wrote substantial treatises on poetic humour we no longer possess; Aristotle's section on comedy in the *Poetics* is missing; if Fulgentius is to be believed, Tacitus either wrote a joke book or had one compiled from his witticisms (Plass [1988] frontispiece).

For extant ancient theories of what is amusing, Grant (1924) is still a basic collection of evidence. Halliwell (1991) clarifies basic Greek categories of humour; the Greek vocabulary for laughter is discussed by Lopez Eire (2000). Plato in the *Philebus*, Aristotle in the *Nicomachean Ethics*, and Cicero in the *De oratore*, *Orator*, and *De officiis* consider the topic of humour and the amusing, although often in terms of their utility for the orator in winning a case; brief passages are excerpted in Morreall (1987), along with thoughts on the same subject by later Western philosophers.

For an extensive bibliography of articles and books on both modern and ancient humour, see Milanezi (2000) 591–623; the whole volume (in French, edited by M.-L. Desclos) is quite helpful. For a good short list of useful work on ancient humour and modern theory, see Branham (1989) 221 n.17. Meredith (1956), Freud (1963, 1966), Bergson (1940), and Bakhtin (1968) remain authorities often cited for various theoretical approaches to humour, and especially its connections to dangerous transgression and aggression. Other studies on humour in literature I found helpful include Gurewitch (1975), Galligan (1984), and Purdie (1993), whose introductory chapter and notes give further bibliography. Booth (1974) remains essential in locating humour in the larger context of irony, stable and unstable; Pelling (2000) 122–63 usefully and entertainingly discusses humour in the context of historical interpretation.

NOTES

1. Griffiths (1995) 32.
2. Griffiths (1995) 32 n.7 cites the famous example of Colin Turnbull's Ik: 'Men would watch a child with eager anticipation as it crawled toward the fire, then burst into gay and happy laughter as it plunged a skinny hand into the coals'; cf. David (1989) 23 n.71. See also Purdie (1993) 176: '. . . there is a systematic connection between the cultural variation that can be found in dominant modes of identity formation, constructions of "proper" language – in every sense of that phrase – and modes of joking'. (And cf. further Douglas [1975] 94–114. . . . But there is also something to be said for W. C. Field's observation: 'I know what makes [people] laugh, but trying to get your hands on the why of it is like trying to pick an eel out of a tub of water' (Levine [1969] 2).)
3. Despite the indignant protests of the great Herodotus scholar Felix Jacoby (1913) 484, as noted by Griffin, above, p. 134.
4. Plutarch's sarcastic comments in the *De malignitate* on this passage are relevant (*Mor.* 856E–857B); as throughout this treatise, it is not clear whether he does not

appreciate Herodotus' humour or irony, does not find them funny, or is making an extended sortie of his own by pretended indignation.

5. Aristoph. *Acharn.* 523–9.

6. Aesch. *Agam.* 687–8.

7. Taken altogether, the proem of Herodotus makes the point that we need an impartial and informed *histor*, or investigator – in short a Herodotus – as narrator, to decode how to read such accounts from the past: see Connor (1993), Bakker (2002), and Fowler in this volume. For the general point that oral narrative is self-interested, see Luraghi in this volume.

8. These observations, of course, do not exhaust the interpretive force of Herodotus' proem; see also the chapters of Bakker, Fowler, Friedman, Griffin, Griffiths, and Luraghi in this volume.

9. See the bibliography, below; for Plutarch, see Pearson and Sandbach (1965). Lateiner (1977) and Flory (1978a) both study instances of good humour expressed by characters in the *Histories*, Flory emphasising the connection of pleasure and laughter with instability of fortune and consequent unhappiness, Lateiner emphasising mistaken judgement and, very often, hubris on the part of the one who laughs. Griffiths (1995) considers various aspects of Herodotus' humour as a narrator: its delivery is often dry, and even deadpan; it involves a strong sense of the ridiculous, and the puncturing/deflating of pretensions of various sorts; it can involve a throwaway climax to an episode; and also for reasons of narrative appropriateness (*to prepon*) it is mostly very subtle indeed.

10. Legrand (1966) 125. He is thinking particularly of Herodotus' delight at tricksters and their 'bons tours'.

11. Darbo-Peschanski (2000) 210 notes that history, in one sense, begins with the laughter of Hecataeus (*FGrHist* 1 F 1a), but in Thucydides' hands (and thereafter, except for two instances of laughter in Polybius) it is transfigured into a 'critique rationnelle' instead.

12. See Fowler, Griffiths, and Luraghi in this volume, and Luraghi (2001b).

13. See Murray (2001a) 25–34 and (2001b) 317 for the larger project of remaining alert to the presence of different and differently distinctive oral traditions in Herodotus, a project of which these observations form a small and tentative part.

14. Amompharetus' humour is sarcastic, not genial; cf. Tritle, this volume, who is more focussed on the military implications of the anecdote. David (1989) 2–4 well observes, however, that humour itself was a deadly serious business in Sparta; 'Laughter' was a divinity, with a sanctuary and cult of its own, and laughter served several crucial functions in various forms of social control in the Spartan state. For other Herodotean puns ('the same word or . . . the same series of sounds twice in the same context with different senses or implications'), see Powell (1939). In Herodotus, laconic humour delivered when under enemy attack also figures in the witticism of Dieneces, who was happy to fight in the shade created by the mass of Persian arrows at Thermopylae (7.226).

15. Alan Griffiths points out to me that sacrificial victims have their horns gilded, adding a sinister undertone to the overt threat, that Crius will need additional defensive armour. David (1989) nn. 5, 25, and 75 mark later collections of Spartan apophthegms; Xenophon, Sosibius, and Plutarch were influential here.

16. Spartans, at least in Herodotus, tend to be suspicious of foreign entanglement; cf. the humour of the failed interviews of Aristagoras the Milesian with Cleomenes (5.50–51); such stories prepare for the alacrity with which the Spartans abandon Ionia to the Athenians after the war (9.106).

17. Lloyd (1975–88) I.103–4, II.175–6, 213–15.

18. Some other under-the-radar aspects of Herodotus' humour contained in this story are referred to by Griffiths (1995) 36, including the use of the deadpan 'throwaway line'. One of my favourites occurs in 2.121β.2, where the thief's brother, caught in the trap set for them in the pyramid, orders his brother to kill him as quickly as possible and cut off his head, so as to avoid detection. The story blandly continues, 'he thought this was good advice and, persuaded to do these things and fitting back the stone, he went away . . .'. One sees why the mother in the story, on hearing what happened, was very, very annoyed.

19. See Lloyd (1975–88) III.53–4 and Griffiths (2001a) 75–6, and above, p. 137, for enduring aspects of this story, resurfacing as it does more than two millennia later in the Grimm brothers' *Der Meisterdieb*, as well as in versions from Africa, Tibet and Scotland.

20. Lloyd (1975–88) III.212–13 thinks a Greek element enters into the Amasis stories, although they retain an Egyptian folk base. He notes for 2.172–3 that Egyptians do not wash the feet before meals or set up cult statues in a public place.

21. For Plutarch's criticism of Herodotus' treatment of the Alcmaeonids, see *Her. Mal.* 16, 27 = *Mor.* 858C, 862C–863B). Herodotus includes dubious anecdotes about Miltiades and the Peisistratids as well (1.59; 6.39, 103, 132–5), although these latter are treated relatively kindly, considering their traditional role in sixth-century Athenian politics; see further Dewald (2002) 37, 45–8. For a general discussion of aggressive joking as a part of ancient partisan politics (although in a Roman context), see Plass (1988) and below, nn. 22, 25.

22. See the biting political humour that Halliwell (1991) 283 places under the category of 'consequential laughter' – 'marked by, first, its direction towards some definite result other than autonomous pleasure (e.g. causing embarrassment or shame, signalling hostility, damaging a reputation, contributing to the defeat of an opponent, delivering public chastisement) . . . secondly, its deployment of . . . ridiculing tones, from mild derision to the vitriolic or outrageously offensive . . .'. In the *De malignitate* (16, 27 = *Mor.* 858C, 863B), Plutarch twice mocks Herodotus' use of this story.

23. One certainly might see all of these anecdotes as linked to an anti-Alcmaeonid bias, since Megacles as Agariste's successful suitor profited from Hippocleides' cheerful and inebriated exhibitionism. See, however, Fowler (2003a) for the suggestion that it is a democratic snub to would-be aristocrats. Powell (1937) 104 sees a pun based on the verb *exogkein*, 'to bulge, to puff out', expressly linking the story of Alcmaeon in the treasury to his son Megacles as Agariste's suitor a chapter later (6.125.4, 126.3 – these are the only two uses of the verb in Herodotus).

24. It does not deprive the scene of intense seriousness; Amompharetus dies at Plataea, and is later honoured by the Spartans (9.71, 85).

25. Freud (1963) 41, 102ff. Freud is thinking of laughter principally in terms of the release of inhibitions on the part of the (laughing) audience of the joke. See Levine (1969) 2–20, 128–35 for accounts of experimental psychoanalytic

studies of Freud's treatment of the aggressive, tendentious joke. (Again, a culture's sense of the appropriate response to a joke can change within a generation; one has some sympathy for the population of New Haven clinically studied in the 1960s for their sense of humour.) Halliwell (1991) usefully separates two ancient Greek ways of regarding laughter, the playful and the consequential; Freud's jokes would fall in the category of 'consequential laughter', *spoudaia* rather than merely *geloia*, good-humoured fun. See above, n. 22.

26. Lateiner (1987) and Dewald (1993) consider the communicative power of objects and other non-verbal signals in Herodotus in this context.

27. This suggests an implicitly conservative aspect of humour – 'carnival', the ritualised grotesque, exists in part as a safety valve, to palliate, and thus to reinforce the status quo, when the 'normal' situation reasserts itself. For the connection with M. Bakhtin's theories, see Emerson (2002) and, with specific reference to ancient comedy, Edwards (2002). David (1989) develops the notion of humour as a mode of reinforcement of current power relationships in the Spartan state.

28. It is commonly assumed that this story was invented after the fact by the Macedonian royal house, to cover up the extent of their sixth-century complicity in Persian imperial affairs: *CAH* (2nd edn) IV.495–6.

29. For the first Persian king described as father, cf. 3.89. See Hornblower (2003) for the relevance of puns on names in the Hermotimus story; I agree with him that the beard-growing priestess of Pedasa is symbolically suggestive in this context. Compare also the other instances of treachery that cluster around Atarneus (1.160; 6.4, 6.29). The connection between humour and horror in Herodotus is suggested in the concluding lines of the verse that graces the front of the volume honouring George Forrest in which Hornblower's article appears: 'Put them on now, dear reader, / Your best pair of spectacles: / Look what can be done with / Hermotimos' testicles!'

30. Bergson (1940) 8 = (1956) 67.

31. Konstan (1987) points out the Persian predilection for gathering together large amounts of accumulated resources, and for viewing them in heaps. For the Persian interest in control of resources, cf. the episodes that begin the description of Darius' reign, discussed in the chapters of Romm and Dewald and Kitzinger in this volume.

32. Fisher (2002) 217–24.

33. See Immerwahr (1966) 306-26; Gould (1989) 63-85.

34. The ironies implicit in Histiaeus' speech are not lost on the reader of Books 5 and 6 (see for instance 5.35–6, 5.106–7; 6.1–5, 6.28–30).

35. Might the bitterness colouring many of Herodotus' accounts, as well as his general pessimism concerning the possibility of human understanding, be an intellectual legacy stemming ultimately from the Ionian defeat in the 490s, but also from their contemporary relationship to Athenian imperialism? See Murray (2000a) 32–3. For the instability of irony, and the difficulty of locating it definitively as *geloion* or *spoudaion* (to use Halliwell's terms), see the last two chapters of Booth (1974).

36. See van der Veen (1996) for further elaborations on this theme.

37. I thank D. Boedeker, A. Griffiths, D. Lateiner, and R. Munson for help on this chapter.

11

RACHEL FRIEDMAN

Location and dislocation in Herodotus

The *Histories* begins with Herodotus' retelling of the Persian account of the origin of the enmity between the Greeks and the barbarians.[1] He traces it back to the abductions of the four mythical women Io, Europa, Medea, and Helen. It is, in particular, according to the Persians, because of the Greek decision to retrieve Helen and thereby put an end to a pattern of reciprocal abduction whereby one woman is replaced by another, that a situation of permanent enmity was created (1.4.4):

> The Persians say that while they, from Asia, did not make a big deal about the abduction of their women, the Greeks gathered a great army because of a woman from Lacedaemon, and then invaded Asia and destroyed the power of Priam. From that time on, the Persians have regarded the Greek people as their enemy. They think of Asia and the non-Greek peoples living there as their own, but regard Europe and the Greek people as utterly separate from themselves.[2]

In this account of the beginning of the conflict, the culmination of the series of abductions and the physical marker of the enmity is the emergence of a fixed difference between Asia, inhabited by the Persians and other barbarians, and Europe, inhabited by the Greeks. Herodotus seems to stress not only the fixity, at least in the minds of the Persians, of this division between the continents but also, and perhaps more importantly, the created nature of this division. This separation between the continents did not always exist but was created by a process of historical differentiation.[3] At the beginning of the prologue Herodotus speaks merely of the difference (*diaphorē*) between the Greeks and the Persians, but by the end of the narrative of the abductions, this difference has grown into a deep schism marked by an emphatic, though imagined, geographical boundary.[4]

After he supplements the Persian account with an alternative Phoenician version of the abduction of Io, Herodotus says that he won't comment on the veracity of the stories he has told, but will move immediately to Croesus the man whom 'he *knows*' first wronged the Greeks. Carolyn Dewald speaks of this as Herodotus' first narrative move in the *Histories* and describes it as the 'creation of an initial binary division between two different voices.' She distinguishes the non-partisan voice of the narrator from the partisan voice of his informants.[5] Of particular interest to me here is the way in which Herodotus chooses to enter his narrative and distinguish his voice from that of others. As is frequently noted, the language of his first statement of authorial method is the language of travel: Once he identifies the man who first wronged the Greeks, he will 'go forward [*probēsomai*] in his account, going through [*epexiōn*] the small and large cities of men alike' (1.5.3). With this sentence, evocative of the opening of the ancient travel tale *par excellence*, the *Odyssey*, where the poet asks the Muse to sing of the man who 'wandered much . . . and saw the cities of many men and knew their minds' (*Od.* 1.1–3), Herodotus introduces his authorial persona as that of a traveller. If the Persian and Phoenician sources locate the beginning of the conflict between the Greeks and barbarians in the moment when each people became firmly anchored in their own land, Herodotus, in representing himself as a traveller, adopts a confrontational stance towards the territorial affiliations that he has just evoked. As narrator and interpreter of the conflict, Herodotus must be free of the boundaries that restrict and define his subjects. He must cultivate a kind of relationship to place that enables him to traverse boundaries freely. In contrast to his subjects' firm attachments to their own lands, Herodotus' perspective will be a deterritorialised one.[6]

In explaining the type of travel he will undertake, Herodotus says that he will go through the big and small cities of men 'alike' or 'equally,' (*homoiōs*). This *homoiōs* establishes a parity between different places that is an important comment on the nature of Herodotus' relationship to place. His approach to the places he visits will be inclusive. He will pay attention to small and large cities alike, equally, without the partiality of their inhabitants. Because he knows that human happiness never stays in the same place, he has committed himself, as its student and observer, to follow its migrant ways. The prologue ends with the repetition of 'alike' (*homoiōs*) as its last word (1.5.4), emphatically reasserting the equanimity that will characterise the perspective which Herodotus the traveller must have in relation to the many places he will visit. Herodotus' lack of attachment to one particular place is also reflected in the ancient biographical tradition about him which records that he was born in Halicarnassus in Asia Minor, but was twice exiled from there and then eventually participated in the panhellenic colonisation of Thurii in southern Italy.[7] In the tradition he exists always somehow between these two places, Halicarnassus, the place of his birth, and Thurii, the place of his death, without being firmly attached to either of them. The *Histories* begins with a famous textual problem that reflects this tension. All of our manuscripts begin 'This is the display of the research of Herodotus of Halicarnassus', but it is clear that there was a variant reading in antiquity which identified Herodotus not as a Halicarnassian, but as a Thurian.[8]

In representing himself in the *Histories* as a traveller who is able to see the big picture, Herodotus not only creates an important distinction between his perspective and that of his subjects, but also creates some interesting analogies between himself and some of the figures who populate his work. His comments in the prologue, in particular, anticipate the famous story that he tells a little later in Book 1 (29–33), of Solon the Athenian sage.[9] When Solon visits Croesus in Sardis, and Croesus (convinced that he himself will take the honour) asks Solon who is the happiest (*olbiōtatos*) man alive, Solon surprises him by saying that he cannot call a man happy until he has seen that he has ended his life well, because 'it is necessary to look at the end of everything . . . to see how it will turn out, because there are many to whom the god has granted prosperity, only to utterly destroy them later on' (1.32.9). Solon, like Herodotus, or, maybe we should say, Herodotus, like Solon, is capable of a certain ability to see human affairs in the broadest of possible contexts. It is an ability that is linked, for both of them, with their experience of travel. When Solon arrives at the court of Croesus, Croesus welcomes him by saying 'we have often heard about you in Sardis: you are famous for your learning (*sophiē*) and your travels (*planē*). We hear that you love knowledge (*philosopheōn*) and have journeyed far and wide, to see the world (*theōriēs heineken*)' (1.30.2). This passage, in its linking of travel (*planē*) and wisdom (*sophiē*), has often rightly been seen as a crucial one for the clues that it offers us into Herodotus' understanding of the role of travel in his construction of his own authorial persona. Of particular interest is Croesus' use here of the word *theōriē*, the word that gives us the English 'theory' and 'theorise,' to describe Solon's 'seeing' of the world.[10] Whatever type of universal wisdom, or, we might say, theoretical knowledge, both Solon and Herodotus might have, is inextricably linked with their own placelessness and engagement with *theōriē*. As the anthropologist James Clifford observes: 'Theory is a product of displacement, comparison, a certain distance. To theorise, one leaves home.'[11]

Solon, then, can be seen as a figure who performs a metanarrative function in his echoing of these crucial aspects of Herodotus' own authorial persona. In fact the *Histories* are filled with a number of travelling theorists who help us better learn to understand Herodotus' own conception of his groundbreaking project and his role within it. Keeping Solon in mind and staying focussed on the question of Herodotus' relationship to place, I'd like here to look briefly at two such figures whose stories should, I think, problematise, or expose a tension in, Herodotus' representation of himself as a traveller. In particular, these stories, when placed in their appropriate metanarrative context, complicate our understanding of the productive side of Herodotus' placelessness, and force us to think about Herodotus not just in terms of *theōriē*, a productive and creative engagement with the foreign, but also with a profound sense of *nostalgia*, in its Greek sense, which means 'longing for return home' (*nostos*). Our understanding, then, of the way in which Herodotus represents to us his own role in the *Histories* must take into account not just what we might call the explicit *theoric* impulse but also this subtler sense of nostalgia. The *Histories*, at the same time as it represents itself as putting forth a type of wisdom that is directly connected to its author's ability to see beyond attachment to a particular place, must also be seen as expressing a sense of loss or longing for place that also tells us something crucial about the vision of its creator.

I turn, then, to the stories of Arion (1.23–4), a poet, and Democedes (3.125, 129–137), a doctor. While these figures might initially seem unrelated to each other and less obviously related to Herodotus than someone like Solon, both poet and doctor belong to a class of professionals in antiquity called *dēmiourgoi*, literally those who 'work for the people.' Common to all *dēmiourgoi*, a category that also includes the seer and the craftsman, is the professional itinerancy that required them to travel around from place to place to practise their craft in the service of the greater community. When Odysseus is forced to beg from the suitors in his own house and Antinoös reproaches Eumaeus for bringing in another beggar, Eumaeus reminds him that those foreigners who are habitually invited in are not beggars, but *dēmiourgoi* accorded a special status by the work that they perform for the people (*Od.* 17. 382–6):

> For who is ever going to approach, on his own, a stranger from abroad and invite him in, unless he happens to be one of the *dēmiourgoi*, either a seer (*mantis*), or a healer (*iētēra*), or skilled workman (*tektōn*), or an inspired bard (*aoidos*) who gives delight with his song? For these are the men who are invited all over the vast earth.

All of these figures possess a specialised knowledge that is inextricably linked with their outsider status, their ability to serve the community as a whole with their own placelessness. While other scholars have proposed individual members of the class of *dēmiourgos* in attempts to contextualise Herodotus and his professional identity, these efforts have largely been at odds with each other and have failed to consider the category of *dēmiourgos* as a whole. Gregory Nagy, for example, has suggested that the archaic *aoidos* provides us with the best model for understanding Herodotus and his project. Though the *aoidos* communicates through poetry and Herodotus through prose, both situate themselves in a privileged position from which they convey a moral message to those in their audience capable of understanding it.[12] Rosalind Thomas sees another one of the *dēmiourgoi*, namely the physician/scientist, as the best model for understanding Herodotus' own conception of himself and his professional role.[13] She locates Herodotus within fifth-century traditions of rationalism and says that Herodotus' particular wisdom is derived from the ability of the scientist to see and think cross-culturally. While Nagy and Thomas place Herodotus in two very different contexts and cultural milieux, the figure of the *dēmiourgos* provides us with a more synthetic model for understanding Herodotus' self-presentation in his narrative, one that accommodates both Herodotus the *aoidos* in prose and Herodotus the 'scientist,' emblematised both in the tradition and in Thomas' discussion of fifth-century science by the physician.

In both the stories of Arion and Democedes, Herodotus highlights the paradigmatic nature of these *dēmiourgoi* and their practice of their skill (*technē*). He makes it clear that Arion is not just any poet, but that there is something exemplary about his relationship to his craft. 'He is second to *no other* lyre player in his time' (1.23), 'he is the world's *best aoidos*' (1.24.5), and 'he was the *first* one to compose and name the dithyramb and produce it in Corinth' (1.23). Though it is a brief and economically told narrative, the story's importance is further highlighted by its position early in Book 1, and by its prominence as one of the first 'digressive' stories, embedded but only loosely connected to the account of Croesus' father's siege of Miletus. Herodotus' account of Democedes, is, like his account of Arion, filled with superlatives which suggest that there is something paradigmatic about his skill: He was 'the best practitioner of medicine in his time' (3.25.1), he is able to cure Darius when none of the Egyptian doctors are (3.129), and it was because of him that the people of Croton, his hometown, first earned the reputation for being skilled physicians (3.131). This story, too, occupies a prominent position in the narrative because it is the story that Herodotus tells to trace the original cause of the first Persian campaign against Greece. Both of these stories, by their emphasis on the paradigmatic nature of the *dēmiourgos'* practice of his craft and by their prominent placement in the narrative, thematise the complexities of the interconnectedness between the *dēmiourgos'* practice of his *technē* and his relationship to place.

When he first names Arion, Herodotus calls him Arion of Methymna, identifying Arion with his birthplace in Lesbos. But the story quickly comes to associate him also with Corinth, a place where, Herodotus tells us, he spent a good deal of time in the court of Periander the tyrant. Though it is not stated explicitly, the logic of the narrative assumes that what brought him to Corinth was his craft, and that he is functioning in Periander's court as a poet. This impression is strengthened when we remember that Herodotus specifies that it was at Corinth that Arion invented and produced the dithyramb for the first time. The story that Herodotus tells thus draws our attention to Arion's placement between his birthplace of Lesbos on the one hand and his workplace of Corinth on the other, and the story is framed by references to his two homes in the form of statements by inhabitants of both places attesting to the truth value of the story.[14] Like Herodotus, Arion cannot be firmly located in space, but exists somehow in between these two places.

Herodotus introduces the story of Arion as about the great wonder that happened to Periander, and the wonder turns out to be the way in which Arion made it back to Corinth after a trip to Italy. The story, then, is the story of a *nostos*, a return journey, though it also thematises the connections between Arion's performance of his craft and a more linear movement through space. Herodotus moves in one sentence (1.24.1) from the fact that Arion spent much time at the court of Periander in Corinth, to his desire to sail to Italy, to the fact that he made a lot of money there, and to his desire to go back to Corinth. At the same time that he accounts for Arion's trip to Italy as a work-related one, and tells us that Arion made a lot of money while there, Herodotus frames this account of the itinerant poet with references to Corinth as both the starting and ending point of his journey. The story highlights the connections between Arion's journey and the performance of his skill, while also insisting on a journey of circular return and not just an unfinished, linear or centrifugal pattern of itinerancy. It is one of the ironies of the story that when he is ready to go back to Corinth, he hires a boat of Corinthian sailors because, Herodotus says, he trusted no one more than them. These are, however, the very sailors who endanger his life. One wonders here if we are meant to make something of the fact that Arion has somehow mistakenly put his trust in the people of a place not truly his own. He is, after all, as Herodotus has made clear to us, a performer in Corinth, a poet at the court of Periander, and not a native son.

When he is out at sea on his way back to Corinth, Arion is threatened by the sailors, who give him the impossible choice of killing himself on board so that he can have a proper burial, or of throwing himself into the sea. Before jumping overboard, Arion begs for the chance to perform in front of the sailors. They grant him his request, and we then get an incredible image of Arion, all decked out in his performance gear, performing his song on a ship sailing in the middle of the sea between Sicily and Greece. It is a perfectly encapsulated image, I suggest, of the intersection of his *technē* and his itinerancy. Herodotus tells us *four* times (1.24.4–6) that Arion was wearing his equipment (*skeuē*) that clearly identifies him as a bard and thus places particular emphasis on the role Arion was performing. In depicting him singing his song on a ship moving in the middle of the sea, detached completely from any fixed place, he also gives us the perfect image of the poet who moves from place to place to perform his craft. Herodotus specifies that the song he is performing is the *orthios nomos*. It's hard not to read this as a play on the more usual meaning of *nomos* in the *Histories*, namely, 'law' or 'custom'. The poet is presented as autonomous, alone with his song/*nomos* in the middle of the sea; because he is not bound to one particular place, his song is also his *nomos*. The image of Arion performing his song in the middle of the sea can be seen as an expression of the power of the poet and his song in the face of danger, but also as pointing to the great vulnerability of the itinerant poet. The narrative might seem to suggest, culminating as it does with Arion's dedication of an offering to the god Poseidon, that Arion performs his song so as to summon the dolphins, or some other form of divine assistance.[15] Herodotus does not specify this, though, and we are left instead with an image of the poet alone with his song, requiring divine assistance to rescue him from a life-threatening situation occasioned by his itinerancy. It is a powerful snapshot of the despair of placelessness itself and of the connection between this despair and the poet's performance of his craft.

This snapshot image is not a fully developed one, but if we turn to the story of Democedes, we see that what is, in the story of Arion, just a hint of a tension between the itinerancy of the *dēmiourgos* and his desire for a more centripetal relationship to space, becomes, with Democedes, a profound longing for home that leads the *dēmiourgos* to disavow his knowledge of his craft because he is afraid that to acknowledge his expertise will keep him from home forever. The story that Herodotus tells about him highlights both the incredible skill of a particular *dēmiourgos* and the grief that this skill causes him because it puts him in danger of being permanently displaced from his home. It is remarkable not only for the vivid picture of longing for home that it creates, but also because of the prominence that Herodotus gives it by naming it as the original cause of a first Persian campaign against Greece.

Democedes had been serving in the court of Polycrates in Samos. When Polycrates was killed by the Persian satrap Oroetes, all of his followers were packed up and sent to Susa as slaves. While Democedes is languishing in prison there, Darius hurts his ankle, and all of the Egyptian doctors in his court fail to heal him. Someone in Darius' court had heard of Democedes and makes his skill known to Darius. Remarkably, Democedes denies being a doctor when he is brought in to examine Darius because he is terrified that if he admits it, he will be deprived of Greece forever (3.130.1). He equates the practice of his *technē* with a permanent loss of home. Darius is not convinced by Democedes' disavowal, and under torture, Democedes concedes that though he himself is not a doctor, he has spent time with one so that he has some rudimentary knowledge of medicine. Once he cures Darius, Democedes is rewarded lavishly and receives every possible financial remuneration. Herodotus tells us that he has everything, except for a return home (3.132.1). The successful practice of his skill actually prevents him from having the one thing that he wants, which is here identified with a return to Greece. Finally, when the queen Atossa develops a growth on her breast, Democedes takes advantage of this opportunity as a means to achieving his *nostos*. He agrees to cure her, but only if she grant him his one request. She agrees, and at Democedes' suggestion, she urges Darius to make an attack on Greece and to send Democedes with the expedition as a guide. This is how Democedes finally makes it back to Croton, and remarkably, this is the story that Herodotus tells to account for Darius' first expedition against Greece.

Significantly, unlike the story of Arion where a desire for *nostos* seems to emerge directly as a consequence of his professional itinerary, the nostalgia that seizes Democedes is not represented simply as a byproduct of the performance of his *technē*. Herodotus is at great pains to show us that it was not to practise medicine that Democedes originally left home in Croton, but that he left under emotional duress after a fight with his father (3.131.1). Once he has been forced to leave home, he does then sustain himself through the itinerant practice of medicine, first in Aegina, then at Athens, and finally in Samos, but Herodotus says that he did this despite the fact that he had none of his equipment with him (*askeuēs*), emphasising once again that the journey from home was not intended as a professional one. This centrifugal journey of professional itinerancy which led to his enslavement in Susa and forced service as physician to Darius is thus embedded in the larger story of his departure from home under emotional duress and his subsequent profound longing for return. It is at the point of intersection between these two journeys that Democedes becomes convinced that the only way to achieve his *nostos* is by renouncing his *technē*, but we are first forced to think about his circular journey of *nostos*, and about the profound nostalgia that drives it, on its own terms and not just as a byproduct of his professional itinerancy. While the story of Arion should cause us to think about the longing for place as emerging as a direct and obvious secondary consequence of the professional itinerancy of the *dēmiourgos*, the story of Democedes forces us to confront this sense of dislocation and resultant nostalgia more directly and to see it as independently generated. The *dēmiourgos* is, from the beginning, inherently marked by the experience of nostalgia.

This fundamental association between a primary experience of dislocation and the possession of a certain type of theoretical wisdom can be shown to be true even for Solon, the paradigmatic travelling wise man with whom I began. We've seen how important the concept of *theōriē* is in Herodotus' account of Solon's travels. Significantly though, even in this narrative, the connection between Solon's wandering and his wisdom is made more complicated by the presence of other factors contributing to his absence from Athens. In introducing the story of Solon's travels and fateful meeting with Croesus in Sardis, Herodotus says that Solon left Athens for ten years after he made the laws for two reasons: he sailed, Herodotus tells us, for the professed reason (*prophasis*) of *theōriē*, but really so that he would not be forced to abolish any of his laws (1.29.1). Solon's desire for *theōriē* is represented as secondary to his desire to leave so as to preserve lawfulness in Athens. The ordering of these reasons is made clear also after Herodotus explains that the Athenians had sworn to use the laws for ten years without abolishing them and then says that it was for this reason, and *also* for *theōriē*, that Solon left Athens (1.30.1). While he establishes important links between Solon's *theōriē* and his related professional roles of sage and lawmaker – it is because of his experience as a traveller that he is wise and able to make laws – Herodotus, in prioritising Solon's function in Athens in his account of his travels and naming his desire for *theōriē* only secondarily, forces us to understand that it is not just Solon's engagement with the foreign that makes him wise, but that there is also something essentially important about his intentionally positioning himself in a relationship of displacement from his homeland. For him to remain home in Athens would be destructive of Athens itself, the very community he is trying to serve, and would render him unable to fulfil his professional role there. The dislocated perspective, the stance towards place that I might call nostalgic, emerges here not just as a *consequence* of *theōriē*, but also and more importantly as an actively chosen component of Solon's political functioning in his community. This nostalgic stance needs then, to be understood on its own terms. If my suggestions about the model of the *dēmiourgos* and the metanarrative significance of the stories of Arion and Democedes are to be pursued, then we have to wonder now why this nostalgia is something that Herodotus wants us to understand about his authorial persona.

We first have to recognise that the dislocated stance of the narrator is one that is reflected repeatedly, on multiple levels, throughout the *Histories*. The *Histories* is populated not only with many exiles and wanderers like those considered here, but also with many communities that are displaced by the arrival of the Persians, either because the Persians actually forcibly dislocate them or because they decide to abandon their territory prophylactically in anticipation of the Persian arrival.[16] The stories that Herodotus tells of communal displacement must be understood to provide a larger context within which to see stories of personal nostalgia. Among the communities that choose to leave their land are the Athenians themselves who twice abandon Athens during the war. Remarkably, when the Corinthian Adeimantus taunts Themistocles, the Athenian general, for being cityless (*apolis*) after the second evacuation of Athens, Themistocles replies that the Athenians have a city (*polis*) and a land (*gē*) as long as they have two hundred manned ships (8.61). This is a radical reformulation of what it means to be an Athenian and to have an Athenian homeland, and Herodotus makes it clear that such a decision to leave and reconstitute one's sense of home comes at a great cost. There is no more poignant story, in this regard, than that of the Phocaeans in Book 1. When the threat of capture by Harpagus is imminent, because they cannot bear the thought of enslavement they decide to abandon their city and prepare to sail to Corsica. Once they have left the city but before leaving for Corsica, they decide to stop off in Phocaea and kill the Persian guard there. This unexpected return to their homeland, though, proves to be too much for some of the Phocaeans (1.165):

> While they were setting sail for Corsica, they first sailed back to Phocaea and killed the Persian guard there. . . . Afterwards, once they had done this, they cursed strongly anyone from their expedition who should stay behind. In addition to this, they sunk a bar of iron into the sea and swore that they would not return to Phocaea before this bar resurfaced. But when they were setting out for Corsica, longing (*pothos*) and pity for their city and all the familiar places of their land overtook more than half of the Phocaeans on the expedition and they became false to their oaths and sailed back to Phocaea.

The nostalgia of Democedes, the placelessness of Arion, the attachment of Solon to Athens, must all be understood in this larger context within which the shape of the world and its boundaries were shifting in a disorienting and potentially troubling way.

In the context of all of this movement, it is clear that the Persian Wars marked a 'decisive moment in the way that Greeks conceived of their identity'.[17] It was in the face of the barbarian enemy and Other that the Greeks were able to form a more developed sense than they had in the past of their common Greekness, of a notion of some sort of panhellenic, as opposed to what Jonathan Hall calls 'intrahellenic' identity.[18] Herodotus' role in this process, as the narrator of the events surrounding the war, was clearly a central one, and one way we traditionally have of thinking about Herodotus' engagement in *theōriē* is that it is precisely this openness to the encounter with the Other that enables him to constitute a type of panhellenic identity that transcends local attachments and identifications. Thus it even becomes possible for him to put in the mouths of the Athenians, in Book 8, their famous and often quoted definition of such a thing as 'Greekness,' or 'Hellenicity' (*to Hellenikon*): 'We are one in blood and one in language, we share common cult places and sacrifices and the same habits and customs' (8.144).

Herodotus' placement of this remark in the mouths of the Athenians, however, is ironic, given the fact that the *Histories* was composed at a time when the Peloponnesian War, which pitted Athens and Sparta against each other and dissolved any notion of panhellenic unity, had already erupted.[19] This irony is heightened by the fact that the Athenians offer this definition just at a moment when they are trying to convince the Spartans that they would not betray them by forming an alliance with the barbarian. Significantly, the one thing conspicuously absent from the Athenian definition of 'Greekness' is land. There is no mention of common territory. Whatever idea of a panhellenic 'Greece' can be seen as emerging in the *Histories* is emerging, paradoxically, in a territorially fragmented and decentred way. Prior to the fifth century, when ethnicity in Greece was defined locally, intrahellenically as opposed to panhellenically, the key criteria that defined an ethnic group were the *connection with a specific territory* and a common myth of descent. In the fifth century, by contrast, a definition of Greek ethnicity based solely on cultural criteria developed.[20] While the elision of any mention of a common territory in the Athenian definition is therefore an understandable one given its contemporary context, it seems nonetheless striking in a work that looks deeply into the past and appears, beginning with the stories of the abducted women in the prologue, so acutely sensitive to the central role that the connection to natal place plays in the constitution of both individual and communal identity.

Perhaps we should see Herodotus – who wrote *of* a moment in which it was possible to imagine a panhellenic identity but *at* a moment in which the possibility was proving to be an untenable one – as placing himself in this position of longing and nostalgia so as to create for the Greeks a sense of what had been lost. The lack of a shared territory in the Athenian definition provides a concrete symbol for this loss. One way to think, then, about the historian's longing for place is as his longing for a territorialised Greece, for a panhellenic Greece made more durable by its groundedness in space, for the idea, we might say, of a Greek homeland. It is a lost homeland, though, an idea that can be articulated only through its absence. If Herodotus is the deterritorialised narrator of the prologue, with a perspective broader than that of his subjects – each locked in their own continent and their own vision – then he must also be seen as longing for a sense of homeland, for an idea of Greece that can be concretised in space and thus reified, though he presents himself as a witness to the impossibility of the idea.[21]

FURTHER READING

The best place to begin thinking further about Herodotus' dislocated stance is with the *Odyssey*. While Odysseus, poet and wanderer, is announced at the opening of the poem as the one who 'learned the minds of men' on his travels, his wanderings are, throughout, marked by a profound nostalgia. Two modern works that are acutely sensitive to this tension in the *Odyssey* and to the fundamental link between the poet and a sense of dislocation and nostalgia are Walcott's *Omeros* (1990) and his stage version of the *Odyssey* (1993). Dougherty (2001), who also makes use of Walcott, offers a very interesting and relevant examination of Odysseus' linked roles as traveller, craftsman, and poet. Hartog (2001) also focusses on Odysseus the traveller, but uses him as a starting point from which to consider the figure of the traveller more broadly in antiquity, paying particular attention to the role that he played in shaping Greek ideas about their concepts of self and Other. Martin (1992), in an article that focusses, as I do here, on the persona of the author, looks not at Homer, but at Hesiod, and considers the interpretive significance of the fact that he represents himself as an immigrant and outsider. My understanding, more generally, of Herodotus' authorial persona and of the usefulness of narratology in making sense of the *Histories*, has been most influenced by the work of Dewald (1987 and 2002). For the idea that Herodotus uses figures in the *Histories* to represent himself in the text and to flesh out his authorial persona, see Bischoff (1932), Lattimore (1939a), Redfield (1985) and Christ (1994).

NOTES

1. This essay is an outgrowth of my dissertation (Friedman 1997). In it I explore many of the points made here more fully and unpack more thoroughly the web of associations surrounding the ideas of location and dislocation in the *Histories*. I am currently working on a reformulation of the ideas developed there.
2. Compare also the Persian claim at the end of the *Histories* (9.116.3) that the territory of Asia is theirs.
3. On the ways in which Herodotus repeatedly rejects overly schematic geographical boundaries and divisions, see Munson (2001a) 84–6 and Thomas (2000) 98–100.
4. Long (1987) 49.
5. Dewald (2002) 271.

6. Compare Dewald (2002) 267–8 on Herodotus as a 'professional outsider' and Munson (2001a) 272.

7. Our primary source for this is the *Suda* (s.v. *Herodotus* and *Thourioi*), a lexicon from the tenth century CE.

8. See Munson (2001a) 267–72 and in this volume.

9. On Herodotus' self-referential use of Solon, see Redfield (1985) and Shapiro (1996).

10. Compare Dougherty (2001) 4: 'In its use here, *theoria* designates the process of traveling to see something to sightsee, but we can see how its later meaning of "speculate" or "think about" evolves through this connection between the processes of traveling and looking and that of intellectual effort.'

11. Cited by Dougherty (2001) 4.

12. Nagy (1987) and (1990) 215–338.

13. Thomas (2000) and in this volume.

14. Herodotus introduces his story (1.23) by saying that 'Periander was tyrant in Corinth. The Corinthians say, and the Lesbians agree with them, that a great wonder happened to him in his lifetime', and he concludes the story (1.24.8) by saying that 'this is what the Corinthians and the Lesbians say'.

15. Gray (2001) 13–14. See also Griffiths in this volume, pp. 139–40.

16. See Friedman (1997) 105–48.

17. This formulation is Hall's (2002) 175, where he also reviews other articulations of this widely accepted idea

18. Intrahellenic identity is the subject of Hall (1997).

19. On the dating of the composition of the *Histories* and the importance of reading Herodotus' account of the Persian Wars in light of the Peloponnesian Wars, see Fornara (1971a).

20. Hall (1997) 25.

21. For their very useful comments on a talk related to this paper, I would like to thank my colleagues Robert Brown, Rachel Kitzinger, Bert Lott, Mitch Miller, and Barbara Olsen, as well as fellow participants and audience members at the conference on 'The Greek Historians in an Age of Ambiguity and Uncertainty' held at the Center for the Ancient Mediterranean at Columbia University in December 2002. Special thanks are also due to Carolyn Dewald for the generosity with which she has shared her ideas and offered assistance of various kinds.

12

JAMES ROMM

Herodotus and the natural world

Strepsiades: But you haven't taught me anything about thunder.
Socrates: What? Haven't you heard my theory – that the Clouds,
Dense when filled with water, make thunder when they clash
together?
Strepsiades: Can you really believe *that*?
(Aristophanes, *Clouds* 382–5)

Lear: First let me talk with this philosopher.
What is the cause of thunder?
(Shakespeare, *King Lear*)

Herodotus set his story of the wars between Asia and Europe on the greatest of all possible stages, that of the entire earth. He understood, in a way that few Greeks of his day probably did, that the Persian empire was a national entity of unprecedented geographic scope and that the outcome of its wars against Greece had huge significance not just for human societies but for the earth as a whole. Thus his descriptions of distant lands, and even his biological and geographical inquiries, though often labelled 'digressions' by modern scholars and thus sidelined from the main narrative, are in fact very much a part of his artistic plan for his work. Persia was the first state in history that could plausibly assert the goal of making all lands *one* land, such that the sun would never shine on anything beyond its borders (7.8γ); indeed it succeeded, on two occasions, in uniting the continents of Europe and Asia by bridging the waters that stood between them – making all lands one in a geographic if not a political sense. This was world war in the truest sense: war threatening to change the world, including the world of nature.

Herodotus as naturalist

To put Herodotus' work in its proper context, it should be said that most Greek literature and art of his day had surprisingly little interest in the natural world, preferring to focus on themes connected to the *polis*, a walled space from which wild nature was largely excluded. It has often been observed, for example, that Greek vase painting, an art which developed to full maturity during Herodotus' lifetime, portrays human and divine figures in fine detail but ignores almost totally the landscapes in which their actions are set. By contrast the Near Eastern and Egyptian civilisations of the same period often focussed on animal and plant life in their artwork, and indeed, in the few instances where we find Greek artists interested in themes from nature, they seem mostly to be imitating eastern models rather than observing the world around them. Only towards the end of the classical period, the time of Aristotle and Theophrastus, did the Greeks develop a serious scientific and, to some extent, artistic interest in the world of nature as opposed to the political and social realm. Significantly, Aristotle begins one of his biological works, the *De partibus animalium*, by trying to convince his readers that the study of animals, though ordinarily scorned by educated people, was in fact useful and important.

Before Herodotus' time, the natural world interested the Greeks primarily at a macroscopic level, which meant that the study of the earth, the heavens, and physical matter were their primary pursuits. Geography, climatology, astronomy and an abstract kind of cosmology were already well advanced among Ionian thinkers when Herodotus came on the scene. Hecataeus of Miletus, who appears on several occasions as a character in the *Histories* and who is generally thought to be Herodotus' most influential forerunner, produced a treatise sometime before 500 BCE tracing an outline of the known world and describing its many tribes and nations (some of whom were so primitive as to be closer to the natural than the human realm, in Greek terms).[1] Others besides Hecataeus had similarly investigated world geography, as we know from Herodotus' polemic at 4.36 against 'the many who draw circuits of the earth' by tracing a perfect circle. Elsewhere in the *Histories* we find Herodotus disputing the geographic theories of 'the Ionians' (2.17) who had divided Asia from Libya using the boundary of the river Nile, and of 'certain Greeks wishing to appear illustrious in wisdom' (2.20) who had proposed various explanations for the summer flooding of the Nile. Geography and cartography, it seems, were the topics that interested him most among those debated by Greek thinkers in the decades before he wrote. (It is also likely that, as has recently been suggested by Rosalind Thomas,[2] issues in medicine, then emerging in writings and debates by his contemporaries, especially intrigued him, though his comments on such issues are not explicitly framed as adversarial positions, as are his geographic theories.)

By contrast Herodotus took little interest in the Ionian tradition of cosmology and physical science, the theories of Thales, Anaximander, Anaximenes, Heraclitus and other so-called Presocratic philosophers. Thales alone receives mention in the *Histories*, and only then because he happened to be (or was rumoured to be) involved personally in two of the events Herodotus relates; he appears as a historical figure, that is, rather than as an intellectual forerunner. This is noteworthy given the prominence of Thales and his successors in the Ionian intellectual tradition to which Herodotus was undoubtedly exposed. In their theorising about the natural world, these thinkers had moved into a realm of speculation and abstraction which was alien to Herodotus' cast of mind. Mistrustful of intangibles and non-empirical arguments, Herodotus clung firmly wherever possible to the evidence of his own eyes, a resource he labels *opsis*, or, failing that, the reports of those who had seen for themselves, *akoē*. For lack of such evidence, even the great river Ocean, though attested by poets and geographers alike, was rejected by Herodotus as belonging to the *aphanes*, the invisible realm, beyond the reach of *opsis* and *akoē* both (2.23).[3] The celestial and sub-atomic theories of the Presocratics lay even further beyond the reach of empirical investigation and therefore outside the scope of the *Histories*. Where Herodotus does speculate about the heavens, he shows a surprising naïveté, as in his assertion that the sun is blown by storms from one region of the sky to another (2.24) or might leave the sky entirely in the middle of the day (7.37).

Where terrestrial matters are concerned, however, Herodotus' scientific curiosity and powers of observation are remarkably keen, unequalled by those of any extant Greek writer before Aristotle. What is more, he exercised these faculties wherever he went in the world, and his travels covered an immense diversity of landscapes, climates, and environments. Consider, for example, the following passage, in which Herodotus argues in support of a theory, gleaned from a brotherhood of priests in Memphis, that the land of Egypt had been formed from Nile silt (2.5, 12):

> For it's clear to anyone who sees firsthand and who has understanding, even if he has not been told in advance, that Egypt – I mean the land to which the Greeks now voyage [i.e., the Delta] – is new-made land and the gift of the river; and I know this is true also of the region south of Lake Moeris for an additional three days' sail, even though the priests said nothing to me about this tract. For the quality of Egypt is such that, if you sail as far as a day's journey off the coast and drop a plumb-line into the sea, you will bring up silt from the bottom and find the depth to be only eleven fathoms. This evidence shows how far out the soil is carried by the river's flow. . . . Therefore I trust the priests in what they tell me about Egypt, and what is more I am confident for my own part that they are right, for I have seen that Egypt sticks out into the sea, compared with the land around it; I have seen sea-shells discovered in the mountains; I have seen salty extrusions that corrode even the pyramids; and I've noted that the mountains south of Memphis are the only ones in Egypt

containing sand, and that Egypt, unlike the countries of Arabia and Libya that border it, has a blackish and clod-filled soil, as though it were formed from mud and silt carried down by the river. Libyan soil is redder and sandier, as I have observed, while that of Arabia and Syria is more clayey and almost rocky.

This remarkable litany of evidence culminates in a comparison of soil types from three different regions of North Africa and the Near East – not the sort of information noted or retained by the average tourist. We must assume that Herodotus took careful notes during his travels on all aspects of the natural world, so as to permit him to make such comparisons and to draw deductions from them. And in cases where he could collect no data himself, he eagerly questioned those who might shed some light on questions of physical geography: at 2.19, for example, he mentions a series of (fruitless) inquiries he made among the priests in Egypt as to why the Nile floods in summer and why, alone among rivers, it creates no breezes.

When he moves beyond earth science and gives an account of foreign flora and fauna, Herodotus reveals both his strengths and weaknesses as a proto-biologist, a century before Aristotle and Theophrastus made the study of nature a recognisable scientific pursuit. Describing such Egyptian creatures as the crocodile (2.67) and ibis bird (2.76) for his Greek audience, for instance, Herodotus resisted what must have been a strong inclination to sensationalise. His descriptions clearly come from first-hand observations that, if not always correct or verifiable, are also not fictionalised in any way (as were the descriptions of Indian wildlife by Ctesias of Cnidus, some three decades later). Yet between these two passages come two other, less responsible pieces of animal lore for which Herodotus has been much criticised. First, the hippopotamus (2.71) is said to have a horse's mane and tail and to neigh like a horse, indicating that Herodotus has merely conjured up the image of a 'river-horse' based on its Greek name and nothing else. Shortly thereafter we come to the infamous 'flying snakes' of Buto (2.75). Herodotus reports that, while on an expedition to investigate a local legend, he was shown heaps of bones near a place called Buto, on the border of Arabia. The priests had told him that winged snakes flying in from Arabia were slaughtered annually by flocks of ibis birds at just such a spot. Though he does not explicitly identify these bones with the slaughtered serpents, he does describe the flying snakes as though he had seen them himself – 'They have membranes instead of wings, very much like the wings of bats' (2.76) – and on another occasion (3.109) asserts with some confidence that such snakes are numerous in Arabia. Just what it was Herodotus was shown has been the source of much speculation,[4] but his subsequent credulity regarding the existence of flying snakes shows that the tall tale, though reinforced by only ambiguous physical evidence, had had a powerful influence on him.

Much the same combination of shrewd observation and willing embrace of fable emerges from a curious passage in which Herodotus examines the reproductive patterns of lions, hares, and harmful snakes (including the above-mentioned winged serpents). The point Herodotus wishes to demonstrate is clearly stated at the outset of this discussion (3.108):

> It seems that the divine mind, which plans wisely (as by all indications it does), has arranged that creatures which are timid and make easy prey are also very prolific in the bearing of young, so that they are not preyed upon to the point of extinction; while fierce and menacing creatures bear few young.

The disproportion in populations of predators and their prey is astutely noted, but Herodotus goes on to adduce three utterly spurious accounts of animal reproduction in order to explain it. The female hare, he says, is so fecund that, alone of all species, it can conceive a new brood of young while already pregnant (3.108): 'In its womb you can find the furry foetuses beside the ones still hairless, or the embryos already developing beside the ones just starting.' The modern reader longs to know what made Herodotus so certain of such arcane information; had he performed a dissection, or witnessed one? If so he misinterpreted what he saw based on what he expected to see, just as he seems to have done in the case of Buto's snake skeletons. He then goes on to recount tales explaining why two predator species, lions and vipers, do not become very numerous: in both cases the young destroy the mother's womb as they exit from it, the lion cub by scratching with its razor-sharp claws, the viper by gnawing right through the belly. Hence the females of both species give birth only once, and the lioness, moreover, to only one cub – a pattern which, had Herodotus thought it through, would have meant the sure extinction of all lions within a few generations. But in fact he does not work out the logical implications of his claim, nor seek empirical confirmation (which he would not have found). Instead he allows his larger notions about the natural world, and its governance by 'the forethought of the divine,' to guide his selection and presentation of material, drawn in this case from the world of hearsay and legend rather than from observation of nature itself.

The natural world and the divine

The 'forethought of the divine', *tou theiou hē pronoiē*, is a large notion indeed, especially when it is applied to such minutiae as the reproductive patterns of rabbits and snakes. The passage discussed above forms one of Herodotus' most important statements both about the natural world and about divinity, and so raises the question of the interaction or over-lap between these two realms. Throughout his work, beginning with the speeches of Solon to Croesus in Book 1, Herodotus is intensely interested in the moral framework established in human life by 'the divine', *to theion*, or 'the god', *ho theos*. We learn from Solon at 1.32 that this 'divine' is a jealous or grudge-bearing power which causes trouble for humankind, a lesson which is repeated by Amasis at 3.40 in his letter to the tyrant Polycrates; we learn also that 'the god' causes a particular kind of trouble by destroying happy and prosperous men, which again is a point reconfirmed by Amasis in his letter. The idea that this same 'divine' exercises forethought, however, or that it can be described as 'wise' (*sophē*), is new information, stated here for the first time in the *Histories*, as is the idea that *to theion* exercises dominion over the natural world as well as the human.

Or is Herodotus' depiction of the providence shown by *to theion* in nature really any different from the jealousy Solon and Amasis attribute to it in human life? Consider the speech of Artabanus to Xerxes at the beginning of Book 7, which, although it refers to 'the god' rather than 'the divine', otherwise echoes the attempts of Solon and Amasis to describe the universal moral framework in which all human action must be situated. At a crucial point in his speech, the point at which Artabanus begins this moral analysis, he introduces an exemplum drawn from the natural world (7.10ε):

> Do you see how the god hurls his lightnings at the more powerful beasts and stops their proud displays, while the smaller creatures bother him not at all? Do you see how his bolts fall without fail on the biggest houses and trees? Thus does the god diminish all things outsized.

The idea of large animals getting struck by divine lightnings carries little conviction as an actual natural phenomenon, but in terms of the imagery pattern of the *Histories*, it perfectly blends the two descriptions of *to theion* given earlier in the text: Solon's jealous power which overthrows the wealthy and fortunate, and Herodotus' benevolent balancing mechanism which keeps dangerous species from overwhelming the earth. In the latter case, after all, it is the lion's sharp claws which cause the rending of the mother's womb, and similarly the viper's fangs which enable it to gnaw through its mother's belly; the very weapons which render these species so potent also diminish their populations and hence their dominion over other species. In the case of vipers, moreover, this diminution is said to be the result of a *tisis*, a retribution, in that the baby snake takes vengeance on the mother for her earlier crime of having bitten through the father's neck at the moment of insemination – as though a miniature *Oresteia* were played out in the snake world with each new generation of young. If such retribution is seen as part of an impersonal natural order, it appears benign and systematic, an aspect of the wise forethought of the divine; if, on the other hand, it is attributed to a sentient power that experiences the human emotions of envy, spite and anger, it appears ominous and threatening, like the god of Artabanus hurling thunderbolts at powerful animals while sparing weak ones. Herodotus' text seems to encompass both characterisations.

In other ways, too, Herodotus' thinking about the natural world seems to merge a systematic or even scientific approach, in which natural phenomena are explained by regularly occurring forces and processes, with a more myth-based and religious mode of thought which sees the will of an anthropomorphic divinity behind such phenomena. Let us take as an example his varying ideas about topography, the configuration of lands and waters that defines the surface of the earth. In an important anecdote related in Book 1, a group of Cnidians, threatened with invasion by land, attempt to alter this configuration by digging a canal through the isthmus that connects their peninsula to the mainland. The workers engaged on the project, however, are deterred by shards of rock that keep flying into their eyes. The oracle at Delphi is consulted about the problem and the Cnidians are told (1.174): 'Do not fortify the Isthmus; stop your digging / Zeus would have made an island there, had he wished.' The Olympian gods, in this case, are seen as the creators and defenders of the earth's topography, and as angry avengers of those who would alter it. But in Book 2, as we have already seen, Herodotus asserts in his own voice that the land of Egypt was created out of depositions of silt that filled in a great gulf of sea over the course of many millennia. In the latter case, sea is turned into land on a regular, even daily, basis, whereas in the former the attempt to turn land into sea – by the cutting of a canal – incurs violent divine retribution. And whereas Zeus is named in the Cnidian story as the deity presiding over the arrangement of lands and waters, in the Egyptian *logos* we see only the actions of a river which is described as being not only huge but 'productive' (*ergatikou*), a word which seems to imply that it contains within itself the creative forces shaping the earth's surface (2.11).

One cannot easily explain such a mixture of views by assigning them variously to different periods in Herodotus' intellectual development and composition of the *Histories*, or by claiming that one belongs to Herodotus himself while another is reported or attributed. Rather, it seems likely that Herodotus was influenced by both the scientific and religious strains of thought prevalent in the archaic Greek world, finding elements of each to be useful in explaining natural phenomena even where they appear, to us moderns at least, irreconcilable. Moreover in the few cases where his inquiry presses him to make a choice between religious and scientific explanations, Herodotus seems unwilling to choose. Discussing, for example, the origin of the Peneus river gorge – a chasm which, by allowing egress of waters trapped within a ring of mountains, transformed Thessaly from an inland lake into a plain – Herodotus equivocates (7.129):

> The Thessalians themselves claim that it was Poseidon who created the gorge through which the Peneus flows, and they speak reasonably. For if someone supposes that Poseidon causes earthquakes and that chasms created by earthquake are the work of this god, then, seeing this one, he would say Poseidon had caused it. For the opening between the mountains, as it seems to me, is indeed the result of an earthquake.

While clearly sympathetic to the religious explanation offered by the Thessalians, Herodotus also holds himself notably aloof from it, asserting only in conditional and hypothetical form the idea that Poseidon himself is the cause of earthquakes.[5] For his own part he is willing to say that the gorge was caused by an earthquake, but no more. His reticence is the more surprising in that he had earlier (6.98) espoused the view that an earthquake at Delos served as an omen of coming misfortunes for Greece, and, moreover, was foretold by an oracle in which a god (presumably Apollo) had claimed responsibility for the quake. Perhaps one could claim that Herodotus believes in the divine origin of some earthquakes, i.e. those which foretell future disasters, but not of others, but that would be to give a complexity to his views which borders on inconsistency.

Much the same kind of complexity can be observed in Herodotus' various views of storms, a phenomenon that looms large in his narrative of Xerxes' attack on Greece. In two episodes separated by only a few days of historical time, the Persian fleet of 480 BCE suffered grave losses due to storms at sea, greatly reducing their capacity to harm the Greeks. In the first case Herodotus reports a story told by the Athenians that they had invoked Boreas, the god of the North Wind, who had raised the storm in response to their prayers. Herodotus, however, remains noncommittal (7.189): 'I cannot say whether it was Boreas who fell upon the barbarian ships riding at anchor.' When the same storm suddenly abates, Herodotus again maintains a studied ambivalence regarding the possible explanations (7.191): 'At long last the Magi priests stopped the wind after three days, by offering sacrifices and shouting incantations, as well as by sacrificing to Thetis and the Nereids; or else it was otherwise and the wind stopped by itself, as it is wont to do.' The second storm, however, which comes accompanied by thunder and puts the Persians into a panic, as well as sinking a large number of ships, prompts a very different sort of comment from Herodotus (8.13): 'Everything was being done by the god to render the Persian fleet an even match for the Greek one, and not much more numerous.' Is it the violence of the second storm, with its thunderbolts neatly bearing out Artabanus' moralisms about the spiteful wrath of 'the god', that causes Herodotus to assert his pious belief in divine agency, whereas he had held that view at arm's length just a few chapters before? Or does he have an easier time espousing divine control of nature when a nameless, formless deity is involved, 'the god', as opposed to an anthropomorphised Boreas or Thetis? Or does he, as an author known for his shifting and ironic stance toward his material,[6] actively seek to include within his text a range of views on such questions, as if to demonstrate that no certainty is possible?

Human dominion over nature

The question of divine control over the natural world looms particularly large in the case of yet another ship-shattering storm, the tempest which destroyed the first set of bridges built by King Xerxes across the Hellespont (7.34). Herodotus says almost nothing about this tempest except that it was huge. But its destructive effects goad Xerxes into perhaps his most memorable act in the *Histories*: he orders his servants to lash the waters of the Hellespont and even (according to some of Herodotus' sources) throw fetters into them, while uttering the following threats and insults (7.35):

> 'You bitter water! Your master (*despotēs*) punishes you thus, because you wronged him when he did no wrong to you. King Xerxes will cross you, whether you will it or not. Indeed it's right that no one of all humankind makes sacrifice to you, since you are a muddy and a salty river.'

With these words, which Herodotus singles out among all Persian utterances as being 'reckless and barbaric', Xerxes orders his bridge engineers beheaded, and appoints a new team, who succeed where their predecessors had failed. The new Hellespont bridge stands firm, for the time being at least (for later another storm will wash it away too), and the Persians march across into Europe to begin their massive assault on the Greeks.

Were we in a tragic drama rather than Herodotean historical narrative, we would know exactly how to read this scene: as a struggle between untameable nature and a hubristic hero determined to impose his will upon it. We would also sense instinctively, according to the retributive patterns that dominate the tragic universe, that this attempt to control a force of nature condemns the hero to an untimely doom. Indeed Xerxes' bridging of the Hellespont had been set into exactly this pattern by the tragedian Aeschylus some decades before Herodotus wrote. In the *Persians*, Aeschylus summoned up the mantic figure of Darius, Xerxes' dead father, from the underworld to denounce the bridge project as an offence against the gods themselves:

> My son did this unthinkingly, with a young man's brashness,
> He who thought he could restrain the holy Hellespont with shackles,
> Like a slave, and Bosporus the stream of god.
> He reshaped the straits, throwing hammer-forged bonds around it,
> Making a great path for his great army.
> Though a mortal, he thought he could master the gods – foully planned! –
> And master Poseidon.   (*Persians* 744–50, my translation)

It was this act of hubris, Darius implies, that caused the tragic universe to turn against Xerxes and engineer his downfall, the destruction of his vast invasion forces. Indeed Aeschylus underscores this retributive pattern in a grim passage which describes the doom of many of those forces: while retreating across the frozen Strymon they broke through the ice and drowned, thus paying the penalty, in their inability to 'bridge' a river, for Xerxes' determination to bridge the Hellespont. Nature, which in tragedy is closely linked to the divine, defeats and punishes any human attempt to control it.

Herodotus almost certainly knew Aeschylus' play, and it is often supposed that he followed Aeschylus' view of the bridging of the Hellespont in his own treatment, casting Xerxes as a tragic hero who incurs doom by challenging the forces of nature. This is a reasonable assumption, and the fact that in the *Histories* the Persian defeat is partly attributed to two later sea-storms, one of which Herodotus claims was sent by 'the god' to diminish the Persian fleet, seems to bear it out nicely. But none of the narrative patterns informing the *Histories* work out as neatly or as consistently as they do in other genres, and the retributive pattern of tragedy is a case in point. We have already seen above that Herodotus takes a variety of positions on a question that would be unproblematic for a tragedian, namely whether natural forces are caused by, or protected by, the gods; hence he refuses to endorse popular conceptions of his time which saw divine agency behind the first of the two great sea-storms. We can now examine the related question of whether he regards human control of nature as an act of hubris or an offence against the gods, and once again, we will find that the answer is not simple or uniform across the vast expanse of the *Histories*.

This question is especially pressing to Herodotus' readers, moreover, in that the human quest to control or harness nature forms a clear and inescapable parallel to the drive toward empire that is a central concern of the *Histories*. In fact, imperial ambitions, as depicted in the text, often rely upon or require a control of the earth, and in particular of rivers and straits, in order to progress, since waters must be crossed if borders are to expand. The first invasion mounted by an expansive power in the *Histories*, Lydia's attack on Persia in Book 1, makes use of an engineering scheme (according to a legend discredited by Herodotus but nevertheless retold at length, 1.75) in order to rechannel the flow of the river Halys; thereafter the Persian empire erects bridges over the Araxes (1.205), Bosporus (4.88–9), Danube (4.89, 97) and Hellespont (7.33–7) in its invasions of Europe under three successive kings. Even more striking is the episode in which Cyrus, founder and guiding spirit of the Persian empire, angrily divides the river Gyndes into 360 feeble streams, to punish it for having drowned one of his horses: as he marches toward Babylon and his first great military campaign, Cyrus here demonstrates his dominion over the realm by forcing even an intractable river to submit to his will (1.189–90). This episode stands out in even greater relief if we take it as a forerunner to Xerxes' later punishment of the Hellespont, as seems inevitable given the numerous times Cyrus, as well as Cambyses and Darius, are recalled by the text as models, both positive and negative, for Xerxes' expansionism (e.g. 7.7α, 7.10γ, 7.11, 7.18).

The ability to tame rivers also figures prominently in another passage, less often discussed in this context, in which Herodotus explores the imperial character of the Achaemenid Persian state. At 3.117, a chapter only loosely connected to what precedes,[7] Herodotus describes a plain in central Asia ringed round by mountains on all sides; five rivers flow out of five passes between these mountains and irrigate the surrounding lands in all directions. But the Persian king (not named here), according to Herodotus, has constructed dams to retain these rivers and deprive the local tribes of vital water supplies. Each tribe sends delegations to the Persian capital to bewail their distress before the royal palace, and the king orders each dam in turn to be opened for a time, rewarding those whose wails attest to the greatest privations. 'And, as I know myself from report, the king gets a great deal of money for opening the dams, in addition to his regular yearly tribute', Herodotus says by way of conclusion, implying that not just wails but bribes are required of the petitioners. The passage creates a vivid image of imperial domination, achieved not by military means in this case but by an engineering scheme that allows human beings to control the natural world. The Persians, in their quest to subjugate the peoples of Asia, must also subdue its rivers, creating a vast sea out of what was once a mountain-ringed plain (the precise inverse, interestingly enough, of the transformation wrought at Thessaly by an earthquake).

Does such control over nature constitute an abuse of power in Herodotus' view, and is the entire Persian empire therefore tainted by it? The tone of the passage in which the central Asian reservoir is described reveals nothing about the author's view of it, unless perhaps we detect a certain approbation in his final note about the 'great deal of money' it produces. Moreover when we look elsewhere in the *Histories* at other engineering projects of similar scale, we find cases in which Herodotus clearly admires human efforts to rechannel rivers and thus turn land into water, or vice versa. The long history of Egyptian civilisation, starting with Min around 3000 BCE, is marked by manipulation of the river Nile: Min himself built the city of Memphis on land he created by damming the Nile (2.99), and after him Sesostris diverted the river into numerous irrigation ditches, giving inland towns access to fresh drinking water (2.108). Most impressive of all, in Herodotus' eyes, are the ducts and tunnels that created Lake Moeris, a body of water more than 400 miles in circumference, where once was parched desert (2.149). Such grand-scale reshapings of the earth's topography elicit wonder and amazement, not disapproval, from Herodotus, and he often implies, as in the case of the works of Min and Sesostris, that the people of Egypt have materially benefited from them. In the case of Lake Moeris, a final note informs us that the harvesting of fish swimming in and out of the lake pays a handsome annual sum to the Egyptian treasury (echoing the mercenary conclusion to the description of the Persian reservoir system). Competing in Herodotus' mind with a sense of the inviolability of nature, in other words, is an esteem for human technological progress, especially when it achieves monumental changes in the landscape or in the quality of civilised life. *Sophiē*, a kind of cleverness often associated with problem-solving and therefore with technology, stands out in his text as a mark of cultural advancement; the Scythians of the Black Sea region, who lack this quality, do not win his admiration (4.46), while the Phoenicians, who possess it, clearly do (7.23). Nitocris, a Babylonian queen singled out for her intelligence (1.185), rechannelled the Euphrates river to create maeanders and excavated a basin for a huge lake, all for the sake of protecting her city from attack.

Even when an aggressor nation forces a river out of its channel to expedite an invasion, as the Lydians do at the river Halys – forcing the ambitions of empire to supersede the sanctity of the terrestrial landscape – Herodotus pauses to admire the ingenuity with which the task might be achieved: no less worthy a sage than Thales of Miletus is credited with the solution to the problem, according to a story Herodotus disbelieves but, again, retells with keen interest. Similarly Mandrocles, who was not only Greek but Samian (that is, from a polity Herodotus clearly admired for its artisanship and works of engineering, as he shows at 3.60), is named as the architect of Darius' bridge across the Bosporus, in a passage that practically celebrates his achievement. Mandrocles, Herodotus tells us, commissioned a painting showing the bridging of the strait and the crossing by Darius' army, and dedicated this picture in the Heraion at Samos. Attached was a four-line epigram which Herodotus quotes (4.88):

> Mandrocles gave this to Hera as a memorial of his bridge,
>   After he spanned the fishy straits of Bosporus;
> He thereby won a crown for himself and glory for Samos,
>   Having accomplished the will of the Great King, Darius.

Nothing here suggests that Mandrocles, or Herodotus, thought of the Bosporus bridge as an offence to the gods; indeed the implication is quite the reverse.

Such instances where engineering works are held up for admiration, even when they cause a reshaping of the earth's topography, direct us toward a more complex reading of Xerxes' struggle at the Hellespont to dominate the rebellious forces of wind and water. Certainly the tragic model of humankind's relationship to the natural world, based on the idea that hubris incurs divine retribution, is present here, as it is at other points in the *Histories*. But present as well is Herodotus' more progressive or *sophiē*-reverencing impulse. The method by which the successful bridges were built is recounted in fond detail, including in particular the design of the enormous cables holding them together, said by Herodotus to possess not only size but 'beauty' (*kallonē*, 7.36). It was these same cables, according to Aeschylus' tragic portrait of the same episode, that imprisoned the 'holy' Hellespont and thus incurred the wrath of the gods. To Herodotus they are symbolic of an immense human achievement, and they too, like Mandrocles' portrait of the Bosporus bridge, are dedicated in the temples of the gods at the end of the narrative (9.121).[8]

From the start of their imperial history, that is from Cyrus' attack on Babylon and his concomitant splitting of the Gyndes, the Persians have used technology to control the natural world and to extend their dominion; empire and technology, for Herodotus, are both extensions of the Persian, and indeed the human, will to power. But whereas empire relies on force to achieve its aims, technology relies on the cleverness of the human intellect, and this gives it an entirely different moral dimension. Complexities arise when the two kinds of effort are conjoined, as they are at the Hellespont, where a massive bridge-building project paves the way for a massive military incursion. But even here, Herodotus is unwilling to take Aeschylus' line and to cast the bridge as an offence against the gods, or even to suppress his admiration for the *sophiē* that made possible such monumental changes to the earth.

NOTES

1. See Fowler (2000a) for a complete collection of Hecataeus' fragments.
2. See Thomas (2000) especially ch. 2, and in this volume.
3. I have elsewhere discussed Ocean and related issues of distant geography at more length; see Romm (1989). See Luraghi in this volume for *opsis*, *akoē*, and *gnōmē*.
4. See the summary of relevant theories in Lloyd (1975–88) II. 326–7.
5. My interpretation of this passage is at odds with one recently advanced by Harrison (2000) 95–7, as I have discussed more fully in Romm (2002). For more on Herodotus and religion see Scullion in this volume.
6. On the topic of Herodotus as ironic narrator, see especially Dewald (1987), (2002), and her chapter in this volume.
7. I take issue here with the discussion of Gould (1989) 106–8 (cf. Dewald and Kitzinger in this volume), who sees a connection between this passage and the event which *follows* it in the text, Darius' execution of Intaphrenes (3.118). This connection, I believe, is accidental and does not bear the thematic weight Gould gives it. The last line of the Aces *logos* concerns the tribute, *phoros*, produced by the dam, and thus links it to the chain of *phoros*-based *logoi* which Herodotus began back at 3.88. With his standard topic-closing comment at the end of 3.117, 'that's how these things are (*tauta men de exei houtō*)', Herodotus puts an endpoint to this discussion of *phoroi* and resumes his previous narrative, concerning the fate of the seven conspirators against the Magi.
8. My reading here is at odds with the prevailing view of Herodotus' relationship to Aeschylus' *Persae*, which emphasises the harmony between the two Hellespont crossings rather than the dissonances. See in particular Lateiner (1985) 88–90 and (1989) 128–9, Asheri (1988a) xlvi; cf. also Griffin in this volume on the differences between Herodotus and Aeschylus.

13

SCOTT SCULLION

Herodotus and Greek religion

The *Histories* contains a great deal of information about specific elements of Greek religion, from sacrificial practice to oracles delivered at Delphi, but questions about the general role of religion in the work and about Herodotus' own religious attitudes suggest themselves to every reader and are the natural focus of a brief account. What distinguishes Herodotus' treatment of religion from that of other writers? Is there an overarching religious theme in the *Histories*? Can we construct a Herodotean theology? Difficulty in answering these questions is caused by the contrast between Herodotus' largely uncritical handling of religious material and his few critical or sceptical statements of general import. Most scholars focus on the former and neglect or explain away the latter; others, notably Burkert, stress the scepticism without adequately reconciling it with the usual, uncritical treatment.[1] I attempt such a reconciliation here, primarily on the basis of Herodotus' ambivalent attitude to custom and convention (*nomos*).

Herodotus and the poets (Homer, Solon, Aeschylus) on religion

If there is anything in the increasingly popular view that Herodotus was a self-conscious heir of Homer,[2] the exclusion of the gods from the programmatic preface (and indeed the first twelve chapters) of the *Histories* is marked. The proem of the *Iliad* (1.1–7) establishes the fulfilment of Zeus's plan as the trajectory of events and Apollo's anger at Agamemnon as their proximate cause. Why does Herodotus, widely regarded as a model of piety, not do something similar? The answer, it has been suggested, is that 'quite simply, he felt no need in the proem to mention the presence of the gods',[3] but this seems rather to protect an assumption of ours than to account for a choice of his. Why should a Greek writer represented as deeply committed to a religious explanation of events also be held to regard a statement of that commitment in his preface as superfluous?

The absence of the gods from the preface seems less surprising when one observes that what is generally reckoned a key religious premise of Herodotus' narrative of the war has no real basis in the text. As in Aeschylus' *Persians* so in Herodotus, the standard interpretation holds, Xerxes' 'yoking' of the Hellespont is a sacrilegious transgression of the natural boundary between Europe and Asia and of itself brings divine wrath upon him.[4] It is clear that Aeschylus was thinking in these terms, but not at all clear that Herodotus was.[5] Careful consideration of this issue brings out distinctively Herodotean approaches and attitudes widely operative in the *Histories* and illustrates the complexities involved in interpreting religious elements with due attention to their context and their role in the work as a whole.

Herodotus represents Xerxes' behaviour at the Hellespont as arrogant, but he appears to have no objection to the bridging of the Hellespont as such. It has been convincingly argued that Herodotus regards the division of the 'one earth' (4.45) into separate continents as a dubious convention, and that it would in any case be surprising if a Greek from Asia Minor were to insist on a distinction between Europe and Asia entailing Persian domination of the latter.[6] There are moreover many indications in the *Histories* that Herodotus regarded crossings of water-boundaries as crucial strategic and narrative junctures, but beyond that rather as intriguing tests of human ingenuity than violations of cosmic law. He was clearly fascinated by the bridging of the Hellespont, and it is difficult to see his detailed description of that feat of engineering as an indictment of religious crime (7.36). The rivers crossed and diverted, canals, and tunnel in the *Histories* are not problematised on religious grounds and are sometimes lovingly described.[7] The key analogy is Darius' bridge over the Bosporus for his invasion of Scythia, which differs from Xerxes' only by linking Asia to Europe at a different point. If bridging the continents is a religious offence, why does the 'wise adviser' Artabanus fail to say so either to Darius or to Xerxes, and in fact warn Xerxes only of the vulnerability of bridges from a strategic point of view, citing not the Bosporus but the Ister bridge of Darius (7.10β.1-γ.2)? Herodotus tells us that Mandrocles of Samos, who built the Bosporus bridge, dedicated a painting of it with an inscription in the temple of Hera (4.88), and there is no suggestion that this was anything other than an appropriate memorial of a great accomplishment.

It has been suggested that 'Herodotus has oracular testimony to argue against interfering with nature'.[8] The Cnidians, digging to turn their peninsula into an island fastness against the Persians, are told by the Pythia that 'Zeus would have made it an island had he wished' (1.174). It is, however, a mistake to universalise without further ado such *ad hoc* oracular statements, this one offering sententious camouflage for the Medising of the oracle itself or of the Cnidian faction that consulted it. Interference with nature can indeed be implicitly endorsed, as in the oracle ordering the citizens of Acanthus to institute hero-cult for the Persian Artachaees, supervisor of the construction of Xerxes' canal through Athos (7.117), and perhaps also in that telling the pharaoh Necho to cease work on the Nile–Red Sea canal on the grounds that he was doing the barbarian's work for him, that is anticipating Darius' eventual completion of it (2.158).

Xerxes' bridging of the Hellespont is then 'fateful' in the loose sense – his Rubicon – but not a sacrilege. When he has the Hellespont lashed, shackled and reviled, however, Herodotus does emphatically disapprove (7.35), later raising the possibility that Xerxes repented of it and implying that he ought to have done so (7.54.3). In denouncing Xerxes, Themistocles refers back to the lashing (8.109.3, below, p. 203), itself reminiscent of Pheros' angry spear-cast into the Nile (2.111.2); the adjective *atasthalos*, 'reckless' links these three passages, and together with Cyrus' angry punishment of the Gyndes River (1.189.1–190.1) they constitute a distinctive *topos* in the *Histories*. It is evidently a *topos* of despotic arrogance rather than of a recondite species of sacrilege, the language of which is absent. Artabanus, warning Xerxes against the invasion of Greece, says that 'the god allows no one but himself to think haughtily', *phroneein mega* (7.10ε); Herodotus attributes the decision to dig the Athos canal to Xerxes' 'haughtiness', *megalophrosunē* (7.24), and interprets an omen as indicating that Xerxes will invade Greece 'with the greatest pride and grandiosity', *megaloprepestata*, but depart it running for his life (7.57.1). Xerxes' behaviour at the Hellespont seems to signify as a manifestation of his haughtiness rather than as a technical offence.

This is a distinction of fundamental importance. The *Histories* is replete with acts of sacrilege, most commonly violations of sanctuaries, that meet with divine retribution, but it is almost exclusively such narrowly 'religious' offences that explicitly do so.[9] Wrongdoing such as despotic arrogance and aggression that drives the general course of events is by contrast elusive of religious definition and divine sanction. This distinction corresponds to the contrast between Herodotus' interest in ritual and his wariness of theology.[10] Xerxes' haughtiness and defeat are not commensurable with such crimes and punishments as Poseidon's drowning of Persians who had violated his sanctuary (8.129) or the gods' punishment of the Trojans (2.120.5) for Paris' violation of guest-friendship (2.114.3, 115.6). In Xerxes' case there is only a generic divinity and no explicit retribution.[11]

'The god', Artabanus tells Xerxes, using the noun four times, does not allow haughty thinking, resents what is or makes itself superior, and checks or destroys it (7.10ε); just before saying this, Artabanus has stressed the role of chance (*tuchē*) in human affairs (7.108.2). This pairing of chance with the resentment of a generic divinity clearly harks back to that of 'the god' or 'the divine' (*to theion*) with chance (*tuchē* or *symphorē*) in Solon's advice to the same effect to Croesus (1.32, 34.1). These two scenes are the set-pieces in which a general, presumably authorial, view of the human condition is most fully developed. Chance and the divine are close congeners – Herodotus regularly speaks of 'divine chance', *theiē tuchē*[12] – and require the same response from prudent men: Solon's principle of 'looking to the end' (1.32.9), familiar also to Artabanus (7.51.3). 'The god' is hardly more personalised than 'chance', as the absence of proper name or of any trace of anthropomorphism and the interchangeability of 'the god' with the neuter abstract 'the divine' all indicate. 'The god' is cognate with chance in that he is in effect chance rationalised or moralised. That 'the good fortune of men does not abide' (1.5.4) is in itself a function of chance, but change of fortune that can be understood as humiliation of the superior is attributed to 'the god' or 'the divine'. Citing a derivation of *theoi*, 'gods', from *tithēmi*, 'to set/establish', Herodotus says that the Pelasgians addressed only 'gods' in general, and called them by that name 'because they had set all things and their distribution in order' (2.52.1). It is just such a generalised ordering function that 'the god' of the set-pieces performs.[13] Herodotus describes balance in the natural world as a result of 'the providence of the divine' (*tou theiou hē pronoiē*), which is 'wise' (3.108.2); this personification of an abstraction – the attribution of a humanly comprehensible programme to an impersonal 'divine' – is parallel to, and makes a good gloss on, Herodotus' talk of 'the god'.

There are thus two basic models: on the one hand sacrilegious behaviour inevitably punished by the relevant god, on the other superiority exposed to the caprice of chance and the counteraction of an abstract divinity. It is the latter model, better suited to uncertainty and complexity, that is relevant to the general significance of the Persian Wars. Focussing on the punishment of Persian sacrilege tends to obscure key symmetries in Herodotus' design. It is clearly important, for example, that the idea of getting the troops to Greece by bridging the Hellespont comes from a Greek, Onomacritus, oracle-monger of the Peisistratids (7.6.4); Xerxes' adoption of it is marked as such by verbal repetition (7.8β.1, cf. 7.10β.1). So similarly Xerxes' overreaching desire to make the Persian empire coextensive with 'the aether of Zeus' (7.8γ.1–2) corresponds to Greek overreaching and Aristagoras' claim that those who support the Ionian revolt and capture Susa will 'challenge Zeus in wealth' (5.49.7). This 'fools' the Athenians (5.97.1, 2), who despatch the twenty ships that are 'the beginning of evils for Greeks and barbarians' (5.97.3). This is Herodotus' clearest statement of the genesis of the war, and here too Greeks share responsibility for it. One is reminded of the opening chapters of the *Histories*, with their mythical model of a cycle of aggression between Europe and Asia that thrives on mutual recrimination but cannot be traced objectively to an ultimate cause.

Beyond the narrow realm of sacrilege there is nothing automatic or straightforward about the operation of 'divinity'. The difference is at its most patent when Herodotus tells us that he cannot say what punishment was inflicted on the Athenians for the sacrilege of murdering Darius' heralds 'except that the country and city were devastated, but I do not consider that to have happened for this reason' (7.133.2). The destruction of Athens eludes the simple calculus of sacrilege and punishment; it could only be accounted for on a different conceptual plane, where things are not so simple, and neither here nor elsewhere does Herodotus in fact attribute it to a determinate cause.

'Great resentment from divinity (*ek theou nemesis*) seized on Croesus, one supposes (*hōs eikasai*) for thinking himself the most blessed of men' (1.34.1). Such a relatively clear statement – importantly qualified by *hōs eikasai* and the vague *ek theou* – might seem to establish a conceptual model of general applicability. It refers only to his son's death, however, and Croesus' status *vis-à-vis* the divine is in fact shifting and unstable, resisting final assessment as his story, fading from the *Histories*, resists closure. From this point of view too he is, in Pelling's words, 'a figure who is hard to place'.[14] There is no clear model here adequate to the complexities of the Persian Wars, and statements of this sort are in any case rare indeed.

Who or what is the Herodotean 'divine'? 'The god(s)' and 'the divine' are the terms in which general propositions about divinity are expressed, but they are not mere shorthand for 'Zeus' or 'the Greek gods'. If from one point of view 'the divinity' is moralised chance, it figures in Xerxes' decision-making as equivalent to Persian 'custom' (*nomos*). He says that in proposing to attack Athens he is following a traditional Persian *nomos*, the continual waging of war, and goes on to say that 'the divinity (*theos*) guides (*agei*) us in this way' (7.8α.1). Equation of *theos* with *nomos* should not cause surprise. Thought of *nomos* prompted Herodotus to quote (3.38.4) the first phrase of a passage of Pindar whose continuation is illuminating: 'Nomos king of all, of mortals and immortals, guides (*agei*), justifying great violence with its sovereign hand' (F 169a.1–4, cf. F 215a.2–3). Demaratus speaks of *nomos* as *despotēs*, 'lord' of the Spartans (7.104.4), and Powell rightly classifies the sense of *despotēs* here under the rubric 'of a god'. Xerxes aspires to rule every land under 'the aether of Zeus', and Herodotus elsewhere notes that the Persians 'call the whole circle of the sky Zeus' (1.131.2); there is surely a connection with the god on the tomb of Darius, depicted within a winged disc in the sky and called in the inscriptions Ahura Mazda, who bestows the earth upon Darius to reduce to order and rule over.[15] Xerxes' prayer, while facing the sun (7.54.2), to 'the gods who have Persia in their power' (7.53.2) points to the same conclusion; his equated *nomos* and *theos* are distinctively Persian.

It is this apotheosis of the Persian *nomos* of imperial expansion that through dreams drives Xerxes and Artabanus to accept an attack on Athens as 'what must happen' (7.17.2). This conclusion takes the urgency out of the question whether the dreams are deceptive.[16] The divinity's motivation, conceived as that of an existent Persian god, is bafflingly opaque, both on the view that he is simply ordering and on the view that he is deceiving both king and 'wise adviser' into undertaking a doomed invasion. Zeus's immediate motivation and long-term intention in sending Agamemnon a false dream in *Iliad* 2 are clearly spelled out, as are the intentions of deceiving divinities elsewhere in the *Histories* (1.159; 2.120.5, 139.2). Herodotus' concern here, however, is to represent the fateful trajectory of *nomos*, and he takes no trouble to make the outcome of the dreams comprehensible as the intentional programme of a personalised Persian god.

The abstract idiom in which Herodotus couches higher-level operations of the divine calls for explanation.[17] That the abstraction is deliberate and distinctive there ought to be no doubt. In the case of the Persians it might be taken for tentative generalisation of the foreign, but Herodotus clearly has a concept of trans-cultural divinity (4.119.3), and 'the god' he puts in the mouth of Artabanus finds an exact parallel in his representation of Solon. In his own poetry the historical Solon refers straightforwardly to Zeus and other gods,[18] but the Herodotean character speaks only of 'the divinity' and 'the divine'. Indeed, though the mother of Cleobis and Biton naturally speaks of Hera as 'the goddess' (1.31.4), Herodotus makes Solon as narrator attribute what happened at Hera's temple to 'the god' (1.31.3),[19] which suggests that the idiom corresponds to a concept of a divinity 'behind' the usual gods. So too Herodotus as narrator never connects divine activity of general significance to the course of the war with Zeus or any other named Greek god, in this case in sharp contrast to Aeschylus.[20] This difference in idiom between Herodotus and the poets corresponds to a distinction of narrative register in the *Histories* themselves. In the set-pieces Solon and Artabanus use Herodotus' own idiom, but when reporting oracles or violations of sanctuary or retailing stories or events Herodotus often allows the routine language of Greek polytheism to emerge. Thus, among numberless possible examples, Croesus refers to Zeus in both technical (1.44.2) and general (1.207.1) contexts, and the Athenians tell the Spartans that out of reverence for Zeus they will not betray Greece (9.7.2).

It is in fact the case that in his own narrative voice Herodotus almost never names a Greek god. His regular use of the idiom identifying Zeus or 'the god' with the sky, that is the weather, or the sun and his lists of the gods worshipped by foreigners obviously do not count.[21] The genuine exceptions are only three. The first is Herodotus' argument that Heracles the god is primary and taken over from the Egyptians, Heracles the hero a late derivative of the god (2.43–5). He concludes this startling reversal of Greek tradition with a wish for benevolence from the gods and heroes (2.45.3). This passage may be paired with his later comment 'I suppose, if one may make suppositions about divine matters' that Demeter kept the Persians who had burnt her sanctuary at Eleusis out of that at Plataea (9.65.2). So straightforward an application of the sacrilege model needs no excuse, and the easiest explanation is that both here and in the controversial case of Heracles Herodotus is marking and excusing speculation about a named divinity undertaken on his own narrative initiative. There is finally the 'anger of Talthybius' (7.134–7), which Herodotus emphatically counts a 'divine matter' (7.137.1–2). This tale, pretty clearly invented by Athenians to whitewash their killing of Spartan heralds in 430 BCE, is not only very tendentious in itself but also tendentiously narrated by Herodotus.[22] It seems then that a strong political rather than religious motive prompted him to endorse this story and the essential role played in it by the Spartan patron of heralds. By my reckoning Herodotus nowhere else chooses to speak *in propria persona* of named Greek gods, and, subjective as such reckoning inevitably is, there is at any rate a reticence here that needs explaining. We must turn for an explanation to Herodotus' theories on theology and the history of Greek religion.

Herodotus as religious theorist

Careful study of Herodotus' statements about the history of human knowledge of the divine is fundamental to an understanding of his theology. He famously claims that 'the names of almost all the gods came to Greece from Egypt' (2.50.1). There is an unresolved debate about what he means by 'names' here, some maintaining that the Greek word can only mean the actual vocable, others that he must be using it as roughly equivalent to 'designation': designations of distinct divine personalities, but designations that vary linguistically between cultures.[23] Herodotus is manifestly aware that nations identify the same gods by different vocables,[24] and it is difficult to believe that a Greek who writes 'the Egyptians call Zeus *Amoun*' (2.42.5, cf. 2.79) considers 'Zeus' an Egyptian name. It seems likelier that he is using *onoma* in an unparalleled but comprehensible sense. It is in any case clear that Herodotus is a diffusionist; despite what we know to have been pronounced differences between Greek gods and the Egyptian gods with whom they were identified, Herodotus concluded that the Greeks had taken theirs over from the Pelasgians, who had in turn taken most of theirs over from the Egyptians.

It is often claimed that Herodotus regarded what was diffused in this way as knowledge of cross-cultural universals, indeed of a single set of existent divinities.[25] Diffusionism and polytheistic universalism, however, are not an entirely natural pair. Herodotus is given to *post hoc propter hoc* reasoning about the diffusion of human 'inventions', from festivals and processions (2.58) to circumcision (2.104.2–4),[26] but the notion that human knowledge of an existent pantheon can only have spread by diffusion, that it is derived from privileged, culturally-specific revelations of the divine in the distant past, is nonetheless surprising. Herodotus' diffusionist view would be easier to understand if he regarded his cross-cultural cast of divine characters as itself a product of human invention. There are good grounds for concluding that this was in fact his view.[27] Various elements in Herodotus' treatment of the gods, susceptible severally to more or less plausible explanations on other grounds, can be coherently accounted for on this hypothesis.

Immediately after he tells us that the names of most of the gods came to the Greeks from Egypt, a few from the Pelasgians, and that of Poseidon from Libya, Herodotus sums up by saying 'these and other things the Greeks have adopted as customs (*nenomikasi*) from the Egyptians' (2.51.1). The language of *nomos*, connected with the gods also by Xerxes, is telling.[28] When he says that it is the customary attitude of all men that one's own customs are the best (3.38.1–2) Herodotus has contrasting customs in view, but the diffused, and so shared, divine 'names' here are no less clearly presented as *nomos*. This is reinforced by the account of the process of transmission from Egyptians to Pelasgians that follows. The oracle at Dodona instructs the Pelasgians to 'use' the divine names that have 'arrived' from Egypt instead of sacrificing simply to 'the gods' (2.52); what is apparently represented here is the adoption of a custom, a change in form of address, rather than a revelation of divine personality. This in turn is confirmed by the sequel, where it emerges that much or all of what constitutes for us and constituted for the Greeks the essential personality of the various gods was, on what Herodotus explicitly calls his own view, invented 'yesterday or the day before' by the poets Hesiod and Homer (2.53, cf. 2.23). We are surely obliged to conclude that for Herodotus the names handed on by the Egyptians, whether he thought of them as vocables or 'designations', were at any rate little more than names. This has the advantage of resolving the paradox of the identification of Greek and Egyptian gods of different character: the Egyptian gods were diffused to the Greeks as mere names, to which the Greeks subsequently attached characteristics of their own invention.

One might of course argue that Herodotus' list of what the poets created – the gods' provenance, genealogy, appearance, epithets, privileges (*timai*), and competences (*technai*) (2.53.1–2) – leaves a remainder we might identify as their essential, existent personalities, but it is difficult to see what this remainder might consist of, unless a sort of disembodied ethos. It looks rather as if we have to do here with a diffusionist model that provides very considerable scope indeed for cultural variation. Herodotus' fondness for stories of wholesale cultural transformation effected by alteration of customs or environment is a measure of the ample scope for variation he allows.[29] Cross-cultural diffusion too can produce startling results, the outstanding example for Herodotus being the garbled transmission of Heracles, Dionysus, and Pan from Egypt to Greece. The wholly divine nature and the great antiquity – 15,000 and more years – of these Egyptian gods were radically misunderstood by the Greeks, who gave them each a mortal parent and placed their births between 800 and 1,600 years before Herodotus' day (2.43–4, 145–6). Herodotus is clear that the Greeks mistook the time when they first heard about these gods as the time of their birth, and the obvious implication is that much of the Greek lore about them is falsehood based on faulty diffusion – diffusion, we may add, of the divine lore of a people, the Egyptians, that (to anticipate a little) knows no more about the divine than any other. One wonders what drew Herodotus to a model that, to say the least, is difficult to reconcile with standard Greek assumptions about the nature and antiquity of the gods. Various passages in the *Histories* provide a tolerably clear answer to this question.

In the introduction to his account of Egypt, Herodotus says: 'The divine elements in such reports as I have heard, except for their names alone, I am not keen to retail, being of the opinion that all men have equal knowledge about these things' (2.3.2). He reemphasises this programme later in the same book, speaking of 'divine matters, which I specially avoid dealing with' (2.65.2). These passages are of cardinal importance to interpretation of the *Histories*, as Burkert has seen.[30] It is sometimes suggested that they refer primarily to a series of explicit suppressions of details of Egyptian religion,[31] but what Herodotus says is at a level of generality disproportionate to the justification of such pious omissions (which anyway require none), and coheres conceptually with his much later comment about the sanctuary of Demeter (9.65.2, above). It is evidently detailed presentation or analysis of theology that he will avoid. The idiom of 'equal knowledge' clearly signifies 'equally little'; where genuine knowledge is possible, disparities in knowledge are inevitable.[32] Herodotus thus aligns himself with the intellectual tradition of scepticism about the gods going back to Xenophanes, and here as elsewhere manifests an affinity with the thought of his older contemporary, the sophist Protagoras, in particular.[33] In the famous first sentence of *On the Gods* Protagoras says: 'Concerning the gods I am unable to know that they exist, or that they do not exist, or what they are like in appearance' (*VS* 80 B 4). Burkert notes that when Herodotus attributes 'what [the gods] are like in appearance' (2.53.1) to Hesiod and Homer his words are a close parallel to Protagoras' phrase.[34] Herodotus also shares his interest in custom/convention (*nomos*) with Protagoras. As Herodotus appears to hold that religion is a matter of diffused 'names' and national conventions, so Plato attributes to Protagoras, for whom 'man is the measure of all things' (*VS* 80 B 1), the view that 'whatever things seem just and right to each city are so for it, as long as it makes them a matter of custom/convention'.[35] This is precisely equivalent to Herodotus' claim, mentioned above, that all peoples prefer their own customs, which he illustrates by the story of Darius' fruitless attempt to induce Greeks and Indians to adopt one another's funerary practices (3.38).

Many aspects of Herodotus' treatment of the divine fall into place on this view. His discussion of custom supports his inference that Cambyses 'was mad in a big way' on the ground that only a madman would mock 'holy and conventional things', *hiroisi te kai nomaioisi* (3.38.1). The mockery Herodotus has primarily in mind is Cambyses' killing of the Apis bull (3.27–30.1, 33, 64.3). He gives no sign of accepting the premise that the bull done to death is a god, and one naturally assumes that he would reject this as he rejects or doubts other epiphanies.[36] Thus mockery even of unsound custom argues madness. There is a point of fundamental importance to be made here. Whatever Herodotus may have made of the conventions of Greek religion, we must not expect him to speak of them in a spirit of mockery. If the customs of foreigners are to be treated with respect, so surely are those of one's own culture. Herodotus' criticisms of Greek theology and practice are correspondingly indirect or diplomatic; it is no accident that he places most of them within his discussions of Egyptian and other foreign religions.

The fact that Herodotus' treatment of religion is overwhelmingly respectful in tone – much of it, of course, neutral reportage of beliefs and practices – should therefore occasion no surprise. After all, even a more aggressive sceptic such as Xenophanes was capable of seeing what was 'beneficial' (*chrēston*) in ordinary piety and regarding it as 'fitting' (*chrē*) 'to have a proper mindfulness of the gods' (*VS* 21 B 1.13, 23–4). A famous 'contradiction' in Xenophanes testifies rather to the 'negative capability' of operating simultaneously with the different kinds of truth in philosophical and in conventional religion: 'There is one god, greatest among gods and men, not at all resembling mortals in body or mind' (*VS* 21 B 23). As Heraclitus puts it, 'The one thing, the alone wise, is unwilling and is willing to be called by the name "Zeus"' (*VS* 22 B 32). Herodotus' theological stance is very much that of Protagoras and his predecessors. Apart from the exceptions noted above, every 'statement of belief' in Herodotus has to do with 'the divine' or 'the god(s)' (or the validity of oracles) rather than with named Greek divinities.[37] Heraclitus' divine unity that may be spoken of as Zeus or as 'the lord (*anax*) to whom belongs the oracle at Delphi' (*VS* 22 B 93) is an essence 'behind' the conventional gods; so too the Herodotean divinity, which, as we have seen, can stand behind Apollo or even Hera.

It is sometimes claimed that Herodotus' sceptical attitude is no more than the manifestation of an 'uncertainty principle' basic to Greek religion.[38] There is however an essential difference – obvious, for example, to Aristophanes – between the scepticism, studied terminological abstraction, and consciousness of convention in Herodotus and the sophists and such uncertainty internal to piety as is expressed, for example, in Aeschylus' 'Zeus, whoever he is, if it pleases him to be called by this name, by this name I address him'.[39]

Perhaps we might adapt Heraclitus' phrase (*VS* 22 B 32, above) and say that Herodotus, like many of the philosophers and sophists, is both uncomfortable and comfortable with Greek polytheism as a matter of *nomos*, but is really only comfortable with 'the divine' conceptually. With his occasional talk of 'the gods', however, he resists being pressed on the issue of the unity of the divine. Greek anthropomorphism of the gods is a different matter. He says that the Persians not only do not use statues, temples, and altars, but 'accuse those who do so of being fools, I suppose because they have not established the convention (*ouk . . . enomisan*), as the Greeks have, that the gods are of human form' (1.131.1). Burkert suggests that this is roundabout criticism of the Homeric conception of the gods and the Greek sacrificial practice suited to it.[40] Criticism by indirection is certainly a technique known to Herodotus, who leaves it to the Scythians to reproach the Greeks for 'inventing a god who induces men to go mad' (4.79.3) and to call the Ionians the most cowardly of free men and most master-loving of slaves (4.142). Burkert's interpretation of 1.131.1 ought to be accepted. It coheres with Herodotus' clearly depreciatory 'yesterday or the day before' of the inventions of Homer and Hesiod,[41] and perhaps with other passages as well. His evident discomfort with sex in temples, even as a matter of foreign *nomos*, and, more obviously, his doubt or rejection of epiphanies and of human descent from or contact with gods might be taken as resistance to association of corporeality with the divine, a deliberate distancing of immortal from mortal. Saying that it was the Athenians who, 'next to the gods', repelled the Persians (7.139.5), he omits the heroes Athenians themselves name alongside the gods (8.109.3, 143.2).[42] Herodotus' divinity is real and active but remote, intelligible primarily as a set of principles governing the universe. The positive propositions he clearly accepts are that it tends to balance extremes and check excess, and that, like Heraclitus' lord of Delphi, it 'gives signs' of what is to come.[43]

We must, however, revert to and refine the necessary qualifications of these propositions. Herodotus is happy with *post hoc propter hoc* inferences when perpetrators of sacrilege suffer, and is content to speak of such things within the terms of Greek *nomos*. Convention, after all, need not be seriously misleading in every respect, and the divinity 'behind' the gods can operate 'through' conventionally sacral media. In less cut-and-dried cases of excess, such as those of cruelty or arrogance, Herodotus is less confident. The closest we get to a final judgement on Xerxes and the divine is doubly distanced from his narrative voice; it is embedded in a speech of Themistocles, and the speech is explicitly a deception (8.110.1). In the debate over whether to go to the Hellespont to block Xerxes' retreat, Themistocles urges inactivity on the Greeks as a way of ingratiating himself with the Persians, and does so by appealing to a passive, deterministic theology, arguing that the Greeks should content themselves with the victory granted them by the gods (8.109.3):[44]

> For it is not we who have accomplished these things, but the gods and heroes, who begrudged a single man the rule of Asia and Europe, an impious and reckless man who confounded sacred and private things, burning and overthrowing the images of the gods, who scourged and fettered even the sea.

A vigorous denunciation, no doubt, but in its narrative register and its context hardly a ringing close to a general theme of crime and punishment. It might be claimed that Herodotus has registered and contextualised his final judgement inattentively, but it is hard to believe he was as naïve a writer as all that. He left the divine out of the programme in the preface, refused, in the face of Athenian sacrilege, to attribute the destruction of Athens to a definite cause, and here delivers in a deliberately ironic context a tempting but uncertain judgement on the failure of the Persian invasion. He may indeed be consciously embedding this judgement in Greek *nomos* as he embedded Xerxes' dreams in Persian. On the level of generality and complexity of the war, criteria of *nomos* are not straightforwardly applicable, the operations of the divine are not transparent, and so conclusions are necessarily tentative.

We have been preoccupied with Herodotus' religious views, but we must not lose sight of the fact – we must indeed, to interpret his theology aright, be conscious of the fact – that he is primarily a teller of tales. Many improving stories are also entertaining stories, and Herodotus the putative 'evangelist'[45] is often merely Herodotus the narrator of tales. The story of Artaÿctes and the frying fish brought back to life by the hero Protesilaus is a good example (9.120). Herodotus explicitly attributes it to the people of the Chersonese, and there is no reason to conclude that he 'believes' it, nor to worry about whether he does or does not; it is a lively tale and promotes a *nomos*, respect for sanctuaries, dear to his heart. Hundreds of stories that found their way into the *Histories* commended themselves to Herodotus on one or both of these grounds. This one, however, is almost the last of them, and ends in a darker key. The Athenians reject Artaÿctes' offer of restitution for his violation of Protesilaus' sanctuary, and, at the point where Xerxes' bridge had reached Europe, nail him to a board and stone his son to death in front of him. Traditionally seen as concluding recompense for the Persian crimes that began with Xerxes' impiety on the opposite shore, the episode is now persuasively read as ambivalent.[46] Human cruelty overshadows divine sanction for sacrilege, and the wrong on the Asian shore confronts on the European not its righting but another wrong. The final act in Herodotus' book (like the hero Protesilaus) points back beyond Xerxes to the mythical cycle of aggression at its beginning. The story of Artaÿctes' sacrilege is tidily closed, but the wider perspective on the war Herodotus opens through it produces no analogous closure. Final judgement of the rights and wrongs of the war turns on questions of the ultimate purposes of the divine to which Herodotus has no confident answers.

FURTHER READING

The view of Herodotus' attitude to religion taken here is closest to that of Burkert; both his articles are highly recommended to those able to read German, but Burkert (1990) is more accessible and broader in scope. Recent scholarship in English offers two very different views, which can only be roughly sketched here: Herodotus as comfortably in the mainstream of uncomplicated, popular belief, and Herodotus as a rationalist who keeps his residue of belief distinct from his analysis of historical causation. Lateiner's book (1989) is the classic example of the latter approach. He surely exaggerates Herodotus' rationalism, but rightly insists on the distinction between what Herodotus says or endorses and what he merely retails. This is not a straightforward distinction, but the other view relies heavily on the assumption that Herodotus accepts most of what he relates, and gives less weight to the few but centrally important passages where he states a theoretical position. The attempt to do full justice to the latter produces the pious sceptic of Burkert's and the present account rather than the pious believer of the traditional and still dominant view, well represented recently in Mikalson's valuable brief sketch (2002) and Harrison's monograph (2000). Even those who are not persuaded by these scholars that Herodotus would endorse the premises of most of the religious matter he narrates will profit by their analysis of the matter itself, the *Histories* being on any view a major source for the study of Greek religion. Harrison's intelligent but highly tendentious book is fairly comprehensive, and with its very full (if often very snide) references to other work is now the best place to begin following up particular issues. In his article (1994) Gould takes the same sort of traditional line as Harrison and Mikalson, but, as even more impressively in his fine book (1989), evinces a livelier sense of the *Histories* as literature. Fisher (2002) has much of relevance to religion; he relates the religious elements to other aspects of the Herodotean worldview proportionally and sensibly.

NOTES

1. Contrast, e.g., the brief and gingerly discussion of the problematic passages in the second book and elsewhere by Mikalson (2002) 196–7 with the close concentration on them in Burkert (1985), (1990).
2. As there surely is: see Marincola in this volume.
3. Harrison (2000) 33.
4. The most elaborate treatment is Lateiner (1989) 126–35; cf. e.g. Harrison (2000) 81 n. 48, 98, 238–9; Mikalson (2002) 194. Immerwahr (1954) especially 18–30, in a neglected but valuable discussion, is more cautious, contrasting the 'systematic theology' of Aeschylus (29) with Herodotus' 'complex of human motivations and superhuman forces, a complex which is not intelligible to him under a simple theological scheme' (30).
5. Aesch. *Pers.* 65–72, 130–2, 186–96, 721–6, 736, 742–5. James Romm and I have come independently to much the same conclusion on this issue; see his contribution to this volume.
6. Thomas (2000) 75–101, who however accepts the traditional view of the crossing of the Hellespont (99–100). On 'one earth' the relevant passages are 2.16–17, 4.42–5. The Persian claim to dominate Asia is presented as merely their claim: 1.4.4, 9.116.3.
7. Rivers crossed and diverted: 1.75 (Croesus at the Halys), 1.185–186.1 (Nitocris transforms the Euphrates), 1.191 (Cyrus diverts it), 1.205–9 (Cyrus at the Araxes), 4.83–9, 118 (Darius' bridge over the Bosporus), 6.43.4 (Mardonius crosses the Hellespont with ships in 492), 7.130 (Xerxes imagines damming Tempe: no condemnatory language). Canals: 2.158 (to Red Sea, begun by Necho, finished by Darius), 7.22–4, 117 (Xerxes' through Athos). Tunnel: 3.60 (through Samian mountain, among 'the greatest achievements of all Greeks').
8. Lateiner (1989) 129.
9. Examples at the end of the paragraph; cf. e.g. 9.120 (Protesilaus). Contrast Harrison (2000) 107–10, whose examples of retribution for non-religious offences are few and, because the retribution he assumes is generally not explicit in the text, unpersuasive.
10. See Burkert (1990), especially 3–5; Gould (1994) 98–106.

11. Herodotus describes the violation and burning of specific sanctuaries by the Persians (e.g. 8.32.2–33, 53.2–54), but even in these cases he nowhere speaks *in propria persona* of corresponding divine retribution, though Themistocles (8.109.3) and the Athenians (8.143.2) express confidence that the gods opposed Xerxes on this ground; more on this issue at the end of the chapter.

12. Close congeners: this is particularly clear of *to theion* at 1.32.1 and *symphorē* at 1.32.4. *Theiē tuchē*: 1.126.6, 3.139.3, 4.8.3, 5.92γ.3.

13. On 2.52.1 and Herodotus' view of the divine see Dewald (1998) xxxvi.

14. Pelling (1997b) 5.

15. See e.g. Root (1979) for the depictions, Kent (1953) DNa 1–38 for the inscription on Darius' tomb.

16. For the view that they are not deceptive see e.g. Saïd (2002) 144; *contra*, e.g. Harrison (2000) 136–7 with further references in n. 52, Boedeker (2002) 103, Fisher (2002) 223. Immerwahr (1954) 33–7 is still worth reading on the dreams.

17. There is a similar abstraction in his language of fate, of 'what must be' or 'was bound to be': see Immerwahr (1954) 33 and the excellent discussion of Gould (1989) 71–8: 'the narrative impulse itself, the impulse towards "closure" and the sense of an ending, is retrojected to become "explanation"' (78).

18. Zeus: *IEG* FF 4.1; 13.17, 25, 75; 31.1.

19. There is a close parallel at 6.82.2, where the omen Cleomenes takes from the statue of Hera indicates that he has done what 'the god' wished; cf. Harrison (2000) 174–5. Note also 1.87, where Croesus calls on Apollo for help (87.1) and blames him as 'god of the Greeks' for his misfortune (87.3), but concludes in the Herodotean idiom: *alla tauta daimoni kou philon ēn houtō genesthai*, 'but it was somehow pleasing to the divinity that these things happen in this way' (87.4). In all these cases, there is a marked contrast between underlying narrative and narrator's exposition.

20. Zeus at *Pers.* 532–4, 739–40, 762–4, 827–8, 915–17.

21. 2.13.3, 24.2; 3.124.1, 117.4; 4.79.2. Awareness of this idiom resolves the apparent paradox at 4.94.4 worried about by Harrison (2000) 218–19. Lists of foreign gods: Persian, 1.131.2–3; Ethiopian, 2.29.7; Egyptian, 2.42; Scythian, 4.59; Thracian, 5.7.

22. See Macan (1895) II.98–100, especially his conclusions, 100. Herodotus' explanation accounts for only two of what Thucydides (2.67) tells us were in fact six deaths, and his phrase *apethanon hupo Athēnaiōn*, 'died at the hands of the Athenians' (7.137.3), is both an obvious euphemism and postponed until the end of the story. Most importantly, it can hardly have been the Spartans, as Herodotus claims (7.137.1), who looked back fifty years for a reason to blame themselves for the Athenian assassination of their heralds. One might compare the politically loaded story of the miraculously halted Persian advance on Delphi (8.35–9), which stands in contradiction with 9.42.3 and is an obvious invention exculpatory of the oracle's dealings with the Persians. This is too good (and too improving) a story not to relate (see the concluding paragraph of this chapter), but Herodotus does not explicitly endorse it.

23. The classic statement of the first view is Lattimore (1939b), of the second Linforth (1926) especially 18–19, (1940). Harrison (2000) 251–64 has recently favoured the first, but Burkert (1985) 125–31 makes a good case for the second (despite basing a central argument (130) on a mistranslation of a phrase at

4.45.2). Those favouring the second view generally have in mind a fairly developed divine 'personality'; I give below my reasons for preferring the minimalist notion of 'designation'.

24. For example, 1.131.3; 2.42, 46.3, 59.2, 137.5, 144.2, 156.5; 4.59.2, 180.2.

25. See e.g. Linforth (1926) especially 25, Rudhardt (1992), Harrison (2000) 208–14 with qualifications 214–22.

26. See Lloyd (1975–88) I.147–9.

27. This is the conclusion of Burkert (1990) 26–7.

28. On Herodotus' use of *nomos*-language in the sense of non-binding custom see Heinimann (1945) 78–83; Burkert (1990) 22–4; Thomas (2000) 83–6, 102–34.

29. The Lydians are turned into 'women', 1.155, 157. Cyrus' inducement of the Persians to opt for the soft life (1.125–6) and his disapproval of their moving to a soft land that will breed soft men (9.122.3–4) are not easily reconciled, and one suspects that Herodotus has incorporated two stories of a favourite type without being attentive to historical plausibility. Compare 2.35.2 on Egyptian ways and customs as the opposite of those of other men.

30. Burkert (1985) 131, (1990) 24–9.

31. See most recently Harrison (2000) 182–9, with further bibliography at 183 n. 4.

32. On the sense of the phrase cf. Burkert (1990) 24.

33. Xenophanes *VS* 21 B 11, 14–16, 34; cf. e.g. Heraclitus 22 B 78, Alcmaeon 24 B 1, Parmenides 28 B 1.30. On Herodotus and the sophists with special reference to religion see Burkert (1985), (1990); in general Nestle (1942) 503–14, Dihle (1962a), Lloyd (1975–88) I.156–70. When Herodotus says that Cambyses had the disease 'some call the "sacred"' (3.33) he is aligning himself with the view reflected in the first chapter of the Hippocratic treatise *On the Sacred Disease*; see Thomas (2000) 34, and, for the many other parallels she finds between Herodotus and the Hippocratics, her second chapter and the index s.v. 'Hippocratic Corpus', and her contribution in this volume.

34. Burkert (1985) 131. I take it that 'the gods' Protagoras has in mind are Herodotus' Homeric-Hesiodic gods, the normative Greek pantheon, rather than 'divinities' or 'divinity' of any kind; if this is not right, his scepticism goes beyond that of Herodotus.

35. *VS* 80 A 21a.25–6; cf. Xenophanes 21 B 34.4: 'seeming is spread over all things'.

36. 1.182.1, cf. 1.60; 2.91.3, 142.3; 4.5.1; 5.86; cf. 6.105.

37. 1.210.1, 4.205, 6.27, 6.98.1, 8.77, 8.96.2, 9.100.2.

38. Gould (1994) 94; Harrison (2000) 191.

39. *Ag.* 160–2, which Harrison (2000) 191 quotes as exegesis of Herodotus' attitude. Such pious uncertainty is in fact seldom expressed; see Pulleyn (1997) 101–8, who places *Ag.* 160–2 and similar passages in the right sort of context.

40. Burkert (1990) 20–1; the obvious parallels here are Xenophanes *VS* 21 B 11–12 (cf. 10), 14–16.

41. The coherence of these passages weighs heavily against the venturesome claim of Harrison (2000) 192 that their invention by Homer and Hesiod 'seems in no way to devalue those traditional sets of attributes' of the gods.

42. Sex in temples: 1.199 (Babylon and Cyprus), 2.64 (Egypt), 9.116.3 (Artaÿctes); epiphanies: see n. 36; descent from gods: 4.5.1 (Targitaus), 2.142–3 (Hecataeus); contact with gods: 2.122–3 (Rhampsinitus). At 2.45.3 (cited above) Herodotus

is excusing his views about Heracles as god and as hero and therefore mentions heroes alongside gods.

43. Balance extremes: 3.108–9 (nature), 4.119.3, 8.13 (but contrast 8.66). Check excess: 4.205 (Pheretime), 6.72.1 (Leotychidas), 6.84.3 (Cleomenes). These categories, which share the language of *tisis*, 'recompense' (3.109.2, 6.72.1, 6.84.3), are related. *Tisis* is a vivid term, but, as its application to the habitual behaviour of snakes (3.109.2) indicates, it is a process that can be conceived very abstractly, as a structural mechanism of the cosmos rather than an *ad hoc* intervention by a personified being; Anaximander, *VS* 12 B 1 uses it in the same sense (cf. Romm, above, p. 183). Gives signs: 6.27 (Chios), 6.98 (Delos earthquake), 8.77, 8.96 (oracles), 9.100 (rumour of Plataea at Mycale).

44. The passivity stands out sharply against Themistocles' (sincere) statement earlier in the book that 'even the god is unwilling to aid human judgement in the case of those who do not make proper plans' (8.60γ).

45. See Harrison (2000) 116, 243 (citing the Artaÿctes story).

46. The contrast with Pausanias' restraint after Plataea (9.78-9, cf. 7.238) is marked. For the ambivalent reading of the Artaÿctes story see Boedeker (1988); Pelling (1997b) 8; further bibliography in Flower and Marincola (2002) 302-3.

14

LAWRENCE TRITLE

Warfare in Herodotus

Towards the beginning of the fifth century BCE the Ionian philosopher Heraclitus observed that 'war is the father of all things' (*VS* 22 B 53); perhaps he was influenced by the contemporary turmoil in Ionia, as the burdens of Persian rule increasingly pressed down the eastern Greeks. As John Gould remarks, however, Heraclitus' statement reveals a central truth that in the early twenty-first century we also acknowledge. Like Heraclitus and after him Herodotus, we too see war as 'the ultimate expression and at the same time the ultimate theatre for the "display" of "great and astonishing achievements", a theatre where success and failure are visible to all and awesome in their consequences'.[1] It was Herodotus' goal that these 'great and astonishing achievements' should not be forgotten, as he notes in the preface to his *Histories*. Yet while he recognised the heroism of men in battle, he was also an acute and critical observer of the horror of war and of its ironies – including the bitter irony that some conflicts were necessary, while others were not.[2]

Herodotus and the experience of war

Exiled from his native Halicarnassus as young man, Herodotus probably had a personal experience with war that was brief yet violently formative. As a member of an elite family, he would have acquired experience in arms as a basic element in his education. For someone bright and inquisitive, such training would have been enough: Greek military tactics were not complex and the most important thing, as the poet Tyrtaeus stressed, was keeping 'the shield wall tight' (*IEG* F 11.31–4) – presumably saying this because it did not always happen. But if Herodotus participated in the overthrow of the tyrant Lygdamis of Halicarnassus, as the biographical tradition states, here he would have received his 'baptism of fire'.[3]

An inscription from Herodotus' native Halicarnassus, published only in 1999, refers to him as the 'pedestrian' or prose Homer, and underlines the

Homeric flavour that infuses his *Histories*, particularly in its battle accounts –
he writes in the shadow of Achilles and Hector, Greeks and Trojans.[4] Alongside the Homeric narrative tradition was the rich cultural background of
sixth- and fifth-century Ionian thought – in natural philosophy and medicine,
especially – and these too influenced Herodotus in recounting the Persian
Wars.[5]

Herodotus' personal acquaintance with war allowed him to appreciate
the stories that were told him as he travelled through Greece, talking with
those survivors of the war wherever he could find them, as John Myres
notes, 'in the taverns, on the quay side'.[6] Yet his informants would have
been the once young men who received the orders and did the fighting, not
the commanders who made the decisions.[7] These veterans' understanding of
what they experienced would not always have been consistent or coherent,
since the 'Clausewitzian fog of battle' creates an instant obstacle to any writer
who would disentangle what happens on the battlefield. This is a problem
even today in an age of modern communications, when combatants can
converse relatively easily and respond to a change of orders. In a time when
signals consisted of blasts on a horn or shouts, neither always heard, and
when troop movements were often beyond anyone's control, it was far more
difficult to discover what might have happened.

As Henry Immerwahr noted, military action provides the spiritual centre
of Herodotus' *Histories*. When Immerwahr wrote in 1966, 'military history'
was largely seen as a matter of 'drums and trumpets', focussing on biogra-
phies of great generals, studies of strategy and tactics, and related arcana. In
this highly formal context, Herodotus was despised for his credulity about
numbers and seeming incoherence of strategy and tactics, and his account
fared poorly; Immerwahr himself referred to Herodotus as a 'non-military'
historian.[8] The arrival of John Keegan's *The Face of Battle* (1976), however,
revolutionised the study of war, as it argued for the investigation of battle
as a reality fought by soldiers on the ground. Although Keegan preferred
Thucydides to Herodotus as the paradigm for the 'new' military history, it is
clear that Herodotus has much to say about how soldiers fought, the range
of their experiences from heroism to cowardice, and their ability to cope
with the terror of the battlefield.[9]

Herodotus and the 'face of battle'

Napoleon once observed that an army lived on its stomach. Herodotus
clearly understood this axiom of war, as a close reading of his account
of the Persian king Xerxes' descent on Greece in 480 BCE shows. When
Xerxes decided to 'punish' the Greeks he gave orders that a canal be built

through the Athos peninsula, thereby enabling his fleet to avoid the dangerous voyage around the peninsula. Herodotus describes the digging of the canal, the preparation of the cables and bridges that were used to construct it (7.22, 23–5), as well as a road built in Thrace (7.115.3) that the local people still regarded with awe in Herodotus' day.[10] The abilities of the engineering corps of the Persian army were exceeded perhaps only by those of its quartermaster corps, as the Persians additionally established supply depots for the army along the route of the march into Greece (e.g. 7.25). This was necessary as Xerxes brought an army of nearly two million, if Herodotus is to be believed (7.184.4), but the problems of providing food and water for so many in ancient times (or modern!) makes this number highly unlikely. Numbers in antiquity are notoriously difficult. In 1930 F. Maurice, a British army officer, suggested that Herodotus confused Persian terms for chiliarchy and myriarchy (one thousand and ten thousand respectively) and so multiplied all figures by ten.[11] Some scholars have accepted this, and the revised calculation, of something like 210,000 for the Persian army, is a more likely, and possible, figure.[12] Again, however, the unreliability of numbers must be stressed, as also the literary, and especially Homeric, influences that might have prompted Herodotus to compile such numbers in the first place.

The Persian ability to supply an army in the field dwarfed that of the Greeks. This is evident in Herodotus' treatment of Greek military operations in the campaign leading up to the battle of Plataea in 479 BCE. In confronting the Persian force of Mardonius then occupying Boeotia and dominating the region, the Greeks fielded the largest army they had ever assembled. The numbers are controversial, but it appears that there were something like 38,700 Greeks assembled in and around Plataea, not counting light-armed troops and non-combatants such as baggage handlers.[13] This is a great many mouths to feed at any time and Herodotus relates how provisions were brought through the mountains from Attica to supply the men in the field (9.25, 51). Attacks on an enemy's supply and communications lines are critical to the actions of any army: they create disruption, and, if the enemy's food rations are captured, he is starved and one's own forces are fed. In the days preceding the final action at Plataea, the Persians enjoyed success in this respect; the entire Greek army was endangered as the crucial supply lines could not be protected against repeated strikes by Persian cavalry. Providing the stuffs of war and deciding where to fight were fundamentals of war that Herodotus understood.

This does not mean that he thought war a good thing. In a famous passage, Herodotus attributes to the Persian general Mardonius a damning critique of the Greek practice of war (7.9β.1):

> Furthermore, I hear that the Greeks are accustomed to stirring up war in the most ill-advised way through their foolishness and stupidity. When they declare war on one another they find the best and flattest piece of land and go there and fight. The result is that the victors depart with heavy losses; about the losers I can't begin to say – they're utterly destroyed.[14]

Mardonius, so Herodotus claimed, went on to say that the Greeks would be better off, since they spoke the same language, to make use of diplomacy since anything was preferable to war. This remark matches an earlier statement in which Herodotus attributes to the Lydian king Croesus the irony and tragedy of war: in peacetime sons bury their fathers but in war fathers bury their sons (1.87).

In other passages Herodotus also criticises the Greeks of his own day for their factional warfare and their inability to co-exist and work together as they had against the Persians (8.3.2).[15] So while he was impressed by the many great achievements of Greeks and non-Greeks on the battlefield and desirous of preserving the memory of what they had done, Herodotus also realised that war was itself in some sense by definition a *mega thōma* (*praef.*), a brutal affair, full of strange and violent happenings.[16]

In writing his account of Greeks and Persians at war, Herodotus did not spare the sensibilities of his audiences in relating the horrors of war. He tells how at Marathon some soldiers suffered traumatic amputations (6.114) while others went blind (6.117), and how after a brutal battle men practised further brutalities on the defenceless. The unnamed marine from Troezen, captured by the Persians in the first fight at Artemisium, became a human sacrifice (7.180); the body of the Spartan king Leonidas was mutilated in death, his head impaled on a spear for all to see (7.238); the Persian cavalry commander, Masistius, was unseated, repeatedly struck by blows to the body, and finally stabbed through the eye (9.22).[17] Such details bring to life the often savage nature of hoplite battle as lines become confused, rage an element in the fighting, and any object a lethal weapon. Not just spears and swords, but when these break – as they will – helmets, shields, and even rocks are used to kill in the madness that is close combat.

Discussion of the battles in Herodotus has often been dominated by issues of topography, attempting to identify and fix the places mentioned in the course of telling of these great battles. In an article published in 1964 but written over forty years earlier, the Oxford scholar N. Whatley pointed to the problems of not only identifying the places named by Herodotus, but also (and what is arguably more important) the absence of information about how deeply the Greek formations were lined up – not to mention the stationing of the light-armed troops and attendants who would also have been present.[18]

These would have included Spartan helots, who both attended to the Spartan warriors and were armed and fought at Plataea as well as Thermopylae.[19] Discussion (arguments really) over the topography of Herodotus' battles will likely remain inconclusive, and for that reason will be little touched on here. Of greater interest for today's reader is the experience of battle in classical Greece, and that is now our focus.

Herodotus' wars

The subject of war, particularly the nature of the Persian war machine that took the Persians into western Asia (Book 1), Egypt (Book 2), and the steppe country of Russia (Darius' great invasion, Book 4) dominates the early (Odyssean) part of the *Histories*.[20] In all of these Herodotus provides significant information relating to the practice and conduct of war, and not only by the Persians but also the Lydians and Scythians. He knows, for example, that the Lydians used pipes and harps on the march, and that they practised 'scorched-earth' tactics (1.17). He tells how the Scythians nearly defeated Darius' invasion of 522 BCE with their favoured tactics of feigned withdrawal and scorched-earth, followed by deadly and unrelenting cavalry raids by day and night (4.120, 122, 123, 125–28.3). On the Persian side, Herodotus reports on logistical preparations for war (4.83, 97–8), siege warfare (4.200), and, in a cultural note, Persian attitudes regarding manliness and courage (1.136, 4.84).

The conquest of Lydia by Cyrus the Great brought the Greeks of Asia into the Persian orbit and they now paid Cyrus the tribute formerly due their Lydian overlords. Relations between Persians and Greeks were generally not cordial, and in 499 BCE a revolt among the Ionian states erupted, weakly supported by Athens and Eretria. From nearby Halicarnassus, Herodotus was in a position to have learned from his elders of the initial Ionian success in taking Sardis, from which the Persians ruled, followed by the disastrous battle of Lade (494 BCE) where the allied Ionian fleet succumbed to treachery and petty rivalries and broke before the Persians (6.11–16). Before the battle, however, the Persian army and fleet was already advancing on Miletus, the focus of Ionian resistance, and Herodotus shows a fair understanding of how an army and navy cooperated in an advance by land and sea (6.6). His later (Iliadic) account of the great Persian Wars of 490–479 BCE had by then been well prepared.[21]

In 1966 Immerwahr observed that the battles occupy centre stage in the *Histories*.[22] It is my contention that these battles are described very individually rather than as 'set pieces'; very likely they were constructed out of accounts told to Herodotus by the veterans themselves, or by others who reported what actual combatants had told them. Rosalind Thomas points to the 'floating gap' or 'hourglass effect' of oral tradition in which the recent past, that is, the past that falls within living memory, is remembered simply because it is recent.[23] Through such eyewitnesses as he could find, Herodotus conveyed what people remembered as having happened; in part, he wrote his findings up into a narrative so that their various memories should not simply become *exitēla*, faded away, through the workings of time (*praef.*). Frail memories, limits imposed by the fog of war, the possible influence of various oral narrative styles or literary models – all these posed various difficulties for Herodotus which opened the door to later generations of critics (e.g. Ephorus, Plutarch, not to mention the moderns) to claim they knew better than he did what happened on the battlefields of the Persian Wars. Nonetheless, Thermopylae takes place in a narrow pass, Marathon and Plataea are fought in plains, while Salamis is a naval battle; all are very distinctive, highly idiosyncratic accounts and worth taking seriously as such.

Marathon (6.96–120)

Following their capture and destruction of Eretria (490 BCE), the Persians with a fleet of 600 ships landed at Marathon. While the battle that ensued was but the introduction to the invasion of Xerxes, it would be rewritten by the Athenians later in the fifth century BCE as their own 'finest hour' and as justification for their hegemony over Greece.[24] And they had a point. Except for the help of a thousand men of Plataea, the Athenians fought the Persians alone at Marathon, and though outnumbered perhaps two or three to one, they attacked and routed the invading Persian army.

The credit for this incredible victory surely belonged to Miltiades, whose past military experience included service with the Persians (4.137). Miltiades devised a strategy that gave the edge to the much more heavily armed Athenians – the advance at a run, with a lengthened line. Information such as this Herodotus could have acquired from eyewitnesses who would have remembered such notable manoeuvres and tactics as they had performed them.

But these witnesses remembered too the ferocity and chaos of the fighting. The experience of the Athenian Epizelus illustrates this with utter clarity. Epizelus watched the man next to him cut down; his last sight – as he told everyone to the end of his days who would listen – was an enemy soldier so tall that his beard draped over Epizelus' shield, after which Epizelus became instantly blind (6.117). This passage has puzzled commentators, some of whom ignore it, while others have misunderstood it.[25] What happened to Epizelus, however, has been experienced by other soldiers too in the modern era – hysterical blindness, in which the mind intervenes to protect the body from the horror confronting it.[26] Perhaps no other evidence attesting ancient warfare gives clearer indication of the terror of battle than this, and Herodotus' inclusion of it in his narrative reveals something about his efforts to relate great and amazing things that happened in battle, but things that are true as well.

Epizelus lived to tell his story, unlike Cynegirus, the brother of the poet Aeschylus, who died, Herodotus tells, while attempting to grab hold of a Persian ship that was trying to get away (6.114). While there is clear Homeric inspiration in the description of this scene, there seems no reason to doubt its essential truth.[27] The traumatic amputation Cynegirus suffered might not have killed him immediately (that would have come a little later, from loss of blood), and he might have been able to tell another what happened, or others might well have seen it.

Thermopylae (7.201–38)

In late summer 480 BCE the massive invasion of Greece planned by Xerxes to avenge his father Darius' failure at Marathon began to draw closer, drinking rivers dry, according to Herodotus (7.109, 119, 127). As the Persians advanced southward, an initial Greek defensive position at the Vale of Tempe proved untenable and the Greeks fell back into central Greece. Herodotus notes the withdrawal of both land and sea forces at this time, showing again that he recognised the mutual dependence of naval and land forces on each other for support. Greek triremes especially were fragile craft and required secure harbours or beaches so that the crews could come ashore, cook hot meals, rest, and in other ways prepare for battle. Intent upon denying the Persians entry into central Greece, the Greeks established new blocking positions at Thermopylae and Artemisium. While Artemisium, the initial sea battle, has been all but forgotten, the land battle, Thermopylae, has gone down in legend in the same way as Roland at Roncesvalles and the defence of the Alamo.

A three-day standoff between a small Greek force of some 7,000 men, commanded by the Spartan king Leonidas, and the great Persian army ensued. Inconclusive naval manoeuvring by both sides occurred at nearby Artemisium, as the Persians organised their massive numbers for an attack, in the hope or expectation that the Greeks, awed, would simply run away. For two days the Persians attempted to push through the narrow pass only to find that the Greeks, fighting in relays of fresh troops, presented an impassable front that chewed up the hordes of attacking Persians – even Xerxes' famous 'Immortals' (7.211).

Thanks to the treachery of a local Greek, Ephialtes of Malis, the elite Persian Immortals took a path through the mountains and flanked the Greek position, turning up in Leonidas' rear. When Leonidas realised that his position was untenable, he ordered away most of the Greeks, some of whom were already slipping off while others were clearly unenthusiastic about fighting on. What followed then has surprised some scholars: Leonidas attacked. He advanced out of the narrow confines of the pass he had been defending and charged into the massed Persian force opposite him, also forming for an attack. Why? Leonidas attacked because that was his only option. The elite of the Persian army would soon threaten his rear, while in his front there were Persian cavalry units that could ride down the retreating Greeks he had sent away, tired men who had fought hard for several days and were certainly burdened by wounded comrades. Leonidas could perhaps anticipate that the Persians, upon seeing the Spartans advance against them, would not be eager to face them again, and that this would buy him time to cover the retreating Greeks.[28] In any event, the final action at Thermopylae was fiercely contested and in the end the Spartans and Thespians fought to the last man.[29]

Two brothers of Xerxes were killed and Leonidas himself was mortally wounded. A brutal fight for his body swept back and forth before the Spartans and their allies were finally able to pick up Leonidas and retreat to what would be their last stand. Fact or fiction? Is Herodotus so imitating Homer here that he has created a fictional scene, or is he rather emulating Homer, but telling what really happened? The latter seems likeliest, as in the nature of battle in classical Greece, kings and generals shared the dangers of those they led and there seems no reason to doubt that Herodotus learned of the Homeric but very real death of Leonidas and the fight for his body. During the Vietnam War, correspondent Michael Herr tells of young Marines charging into battle imitating John Wayne at Iwo Jima; in Marine veteran Gustav Hasford's *The Short-Timer*, another says, 'I'm gonna hate this movie'.[30] Leonidas and his Spartans (and other Greeks too) knew of the fights over the body of Patroclus and other heroes from the *Iliad* and this to a certain extent shaped their expectations for themselves in battle. In the struggle over the body of Leonidas we have, then, an example of art and life coming together so that the result is a narrative with a Homeric flavour, but also a Herodotean instance of the real 'face of battle'.

Salamis (8.71–100)

Leonidas' sacrifice at Thermopylae bought time for the Greeks to organise defences farther south. As the Persian army and fleet advanced, the Athenians abandoned their city torched by the Persians. The allied Greek fleet, numbering some 380 ships, including 180 Athenian ships, assembled around Salamis island opposite Athens and debated strategy. Many argued for further withdrawal southward to the Peloponnese, where the narrow isthmus was being fortified for a final stand against the Persians. The Athenian Themistocles, however, would not abandon Athens. He refused to allow the Greeks to withdraw and used every ounce of argument and guile to persuade the Greeks to stand and fight. Quite possibly he tricked the already confident Xerxes to launch an attack into a prepared trap – the narrow waters around Salamis – where the Persian fleet's great numbers would actually work against them. The result was the incredible victory of Salamis and the salvation of Greece.

Reconstructing Salamis may have been Herodotus' greatest challenge, since he had to discern the sequence of events involving thousands of men and hundreds of ships, all of it obscured by the (literally) fluid and hard-to-see conditions under which naval warfare occurs. Immerwahr claims that Salamis is almost barren of substantive details. This he suggests is explained by Herodotus' focus on Greek disunity (possibly as a warning to his own time?) and by the Greeks' own lack of enthusiasm for battle; Aeschylus' *Persians* may also have led Herodotus to look for something different to say about what happened at Salamis.[31] Some of these considerations may be seen in the opening action of the battle. Herodotus refers to the Greek fleet 'backing water' or retreating, until (a) the Athenian Ameinias sent his ship into the attack, or (b) the Aeginetan ship bringing the cult statues of the Aeacidae started the action, or (c) a feminine apparition shouted out, 'Fools, when will you stop retreating?', which put some backbone into the Greeks, who then attacked (8.84).

The Athenian and Aeginetan versions testify to the mutual rivalry and dislike the two communities shared; all three versions point to the chaos of battle, the fog of war, and Herodotus' inability (through no fault of his own) to learn what the Greek plan of attack was. The retreat followed by a Greek attack does provide one clue, as does the reported flight of the Corinthian squadron.[32] What might have happened is that the Greeks feigned a cowardly withdrawal and flight by backing water, to simulate treason, in order to draw on the gullible Persians. The Persians expected such conduct, as the Ionian Greeks had done exactly this at the disastrous battle of Lade (494 BCE).

But was Herodotus skimpy in his treatment of Salamis? Herodotus notes the desertion of a Tenian ship from the Persians shortly before the battle (which won for them inclusion on the Delphic victory tripod), the names of Samians who remained loyal to Xerxes and were rewarded for their services to him, the names of those Greeks honoured for conspicuous gallantry (Polycritus of Aegina, Eumenes and Ameinias of Athens), and the action at Psyttaleia carried out by Aristides.[33] Prior to the battle the Persians had landed a force of men on the small island of Psyttaleia to set up a base from which they might aid their friends. As the battle raged, the Athenian Aristides carried out an amphibious landing on Psyttaleia with a force of hoplites, slaughtering the Persians and retaking the island (8.95). The verb Herodotus uses, *kataphoneein*, means not simply slaughter but to spill blood murderously; this bloody footnote closes Herodotus' account of Salamis.

All of these anecdotes taken together suggest that a substantial body of oral tradition preserved the heroics of named individuals. But the way that the pledge of the introductory statement of the *Histories*, that it will memorialise heroic deeds, is fulfilled here shows that Herodotus intended to remember not just famous individuals but the actions of the anonymous as well. These include the crew of a Samothracian trireme that disabled an Athenian ship only to be rammed by an Aeginetan, which the Samothracians then boarded, killing the Aeginetans and taking over their ship (8.90). As in the confused opening of the battle of Salamis, it was difficult to know who they were individually, but their bravery and skill were no less deserving of recording.

Plataea (9.10–89)

His fleet destroyed or demoralised, Xerxes returned home. He left a large army to winter in Greece, under the command of his cousin Mardonius. Mardonius established a base of operations in central Greece where those Greeks in 'occupied territory' were obliged to join him, though their enthusiasm varied considerably. The Greek coalition moved to meet this threat, and by late summer of 479, an army of nearly 40,000 men had assembled south of Plataea under the command of the Spartan Pausanias. Here the two armies faced off, each testing the other with feints and surprise movements, each attempting to force the other into a false move that would spell disaster.

Plataea, the victory of the 'Dorian spear' according to Aeschylus (*Pers.* 816–17), was fought over a rolling countryside amid places that might have been known to Herodotus' auditors and readers but mean little to us today. It was a battle with a cast of thousands, which makes reconstruction even more difficult, as the critical depth of ranks was not preserved. It was also a battle which the Greek commanders may have planned, but the rank and file fought and won. Try as historians might to make sense of the final day, it remains clear that the action was fluid and often resulted from the reactions of those immediately caught up in the fighting who, if given a plan, were forced to abandon it and act as events dictated.

A Greek army the size of that at Plataea had never before taken the field, and the Greeks quickly discovered the problems of supplying such a large force. The Persians, operating from a shortened base of supply, had much greater freedom of action. Mardonius seized on this advantage and with his superior cavalry disrupted Greek supply lines, fouling their primary source of water, and forcing the Greek command onto the defensive. It was in one of these actions that the Persian cavalry commander Masistius was killed and a 'heroic' battle raged over his body (9.22). This account has been variously queried, some thinking it Homeric imitation, others arguing that it is an Athenian invention to make themselves look good.[34] Yet the anonymity of the passage testifies to the possibility at least of authenticity. Fighting is chaos. Herodotus' informants did not know who it was that killed Masistius, only that he was killed.[35] This again bears the mark of the fog of war in which soldiers fight knowing only what is happening around them, and afterwards are able to provide only the basics and not much in the way of details.[36]

The same confusion underlies the night movement attempted by Pausanias, which actually provoked the final Persian assault on the Greeks. This reordering of the line was disrupted, so Herodotus tells, by one of his own captains, Amompharetus, who refused to run from the 'strangers'. Reluctant to abandon his stubborn subordinate, Pausanias spent much of the night arguing with him. This story has been treated sceptically. An Athenian messenger, sent to find out what was delaying the Spartans, watched Amompharetus pick up a rock and throw it down at Pausanias' feet, saying this was his vote against retreating (9.55.2).

This has been dismissed as Athenian invention because only the Athenians 'voted' with pebbles or rocks. But this misses the point. All Amompharetus was doing was demonstrating that he was a rock, and once in position he would not budge.[37] Why he took this stance cannot now be known, as he died in the battle and could not afterwards explain himself. Some modern commentators argue that Herodotus' account distorts what really happened, that Amompharetus' company was actually the rearguard of the whole Spartan army, making a deliberate movement.[38] Perhaps so. But Spartan officers exercised a good deal of independence and modern ideas of a 'chain of command' do not exactly apply. The refusal of Aristocles and Hipponoidas to carry out King Agis' orders at the battle of Mantinea (418 BCE) and Clearchus' refusal to follow Spartan authorities' instructions in the northern Aegean (c. 404/403 BCE) support Herodotus' picture of a Spartan officer acting independently, defiantly challenging orders.[39]

Herodotus knew a good deal about the Spartans at Plataea, as he provides extensive information on those Spartans nominated for prizes of valour; among them was the obstinate Amompharetus. He also displayed some critical judgement, saying that in his view Aristodamus, the survivor of Thermopylae, most deserved the prize of valour. Herodotus tells how the Spartans believed that Aristodamus had rushed 'forward with the fury of a madman in his desire to be killed before his comrades' eyes' (9.71). Yet like Herodotus we need to keep in mind that Aristodamus had stood in the line with the rest of the Spartans until the battle began. He waited, that is, under the barrage of arrows until the sacrifices had been made, the paean sung, the commands given. One can imagine him standing there watching and thinking, not of the imminent battle, but rather of the haunting memory of his friends killed the previous year. When the fight finally began, he may have rushed forward, not as Herodotus says the Spartans believed, to retrieve his lost honour, but rather out of a sense of guilt at having survived.[40] This, however, his fellow Spartans would not have acknowledged. Rather, they preferred to believe that he fought like a madman that he might die and atone for his 'sin' of not dying at Thermopylae with the other 298 Spartans and his king (7.231, 9.71).[41] It is not difficult to see the underlying jealously that pervaded the warrior culture of Sparta, as Herodotus indeed notes.

Herodotus and writing on war

Herodotus' account is rich in the exploits of individuals such as Amompharetus and Aristodamus as well as those of unsung heroes such as the Athenians who killed Masistius. Most of the time he seems able to recognise the inter-state rivalries that plagued Greece, like that between Athens and Corinth, and to see through petty jealousies like those of the competing Spartan claims for the prize of valour at Plataea. In the end, he includes, in his explanation of the incredible victory won by the Greeks, both the insights of a Persian prince and the self-serving comments of an Athenian general. At Thermopylae, Herodotus paints a vivid picture of Persian officers treating their men like slaves, and resorting to whips to push them into battle (7.223.3). As the Persians afterwards seek to understand men (and here it seems fair to include all the Greeks who fought the Persians) who would fight to certain death, Xerxes' cousin Tritantaechmes observes that, terrifyingly enough, it is for olive wreaths and fame, not wealth, that the Greeks hold contests among themselves. It is difficult to imagine a starker contrast between the two sides, as Herodotus drives home his explanation of the victory of the Greeks, fighting in the cause of freedom to defend their homes against an imperialistic war of expansion (8.26). But perhaps Themistocles has the ironic final word, explaining duplicitously to the other Greeks why they should let Xerxes flee unharmed back to Asia (8.109): 'These things we did not accomplish, but rather the gods and heroes, who refused to have a single man ruling both Asia and Europe.'

FURTHER READING

For further discussion on military issues, readers might consult the recent works of de Souza (2003) and van Wees (2000). Older but still useful are Hanson (1989) and (1991). A vast encyclopedia of Greek military practices is to be found in Pritchett (1971–91). Valuable overview discussions of the wars are to be found in the essays of O. Murray, N.G.L. Hammond, and J.P. Barron in *CAH* (2nd edn) IV. 461–622.

While Herodotus' account is basic for the Persian Wars, Aeschylus' *Persians*, written only seven years after the defeat of Xerxes' great expedition, remains a valuable text; Hall's (1996) text of the play, accompanied by introduction and commentary, is helpful though some views, e.g. the image of the Persians in the drama, are not as certain as Hall argues. Similarly Bowen (1992) provides a helpful introduction to Plutarch's *On the Malice of Herodotus*, a work that also challenges some of the statements Herodotus made about Greek support for the Persians.

For those interested in the topography and topographical debate see especially Pritchett (1995) and (1965–85), Vols. I and V. Burn (1977) also offers a valuable review of discussions and finds.

Finally, for treatment of battlefield trauma see Shay (1994) and Edelstein and Edelstein (1945) I.235–7, which refers to several cases of traumatic wounds and a case of hysterical blindness, like that of Epizelus at Marathon.

NOTES

1. Gould (1989) 60–1.
2. Discussion in Munson (2001a) 211–17, (2001b) 41–3, mostly beyond the scope of this essay.
3. *Suda*, s.v. *Herodotos*. Momigliano (1966) 120 notes the constant presence of war in Greek life.
4. Boedeker (2003) 29–30.
5. Thomas (2000) 4–16; Marincola (2001) 37. See, in this volume, Fowler, Romm, Thomas and Marincola.
6. Myres (1953) 212.
7. Burn (1984) 5.
8. Immerwahr (1966) 238–9.
9. As pointed out by Kiesling (2003) 88–93.
10. See Scullion and Romm in this volume on Herodotus' interest in *sophiē*.
11. Maurice (1930) 226; cf. Hignett (1963) 351, Lazenby (1993) 91. See Lateiner (1989) 32–3 for Herodotean numbers.
12. For example, Green (1996) 58–9.
13. Burn (1984) 524, provides the figure, accepted by Green (1996) 249–50.
14. Waldemar Heckel (University of Calgary) and I have debated the lethality of hoplite battle. Herodotus' words here argue that it was indeed deadly. One reason for thinking so is that he was writing in the 440s and 430s BCE, i.e., after the

events of the 'First' Peloponnesian War in which there were the sort of costly battles he mentions here through the voice of Mardonius. Among these was the battle of Coronea (447/446 BCE) in which the Athenian general Tolmides was killed along with many Athenians. Note also the fight on Sphacteria island (424 BCE) where out of a Spartan force of 420 men only 292 survived – i.e., 31 percent were killed in action, an extremely high death rate by any standard at any time. Compare Holladay (1982) 97, for an opposite conclusion, though Sphacteria is omitted from the list of battles cited.

15. See further Flower and Marincola (2002) 3.

16. Again note the sentiment in the preface to his *Histories*.

17. At Plataea Mardonius was killed with a rock by the Spartan Aeimnestus (9.63, the detail of the rock provided by Plut. *Arist.* 19.1). The name of the killer is variously reported: see Flower and Marincola (2002) 220 for discussion.

18. Whatley (1964) 124. Flower and Marincola (2002) 23 note also that Herodotus did not intend to give precise details of the topography and did not expect his auditors and readers to go exploring battlefields with his text in hand.

19. Hunt (1998) 31–41.

20. For the Odyssean and Iliadic elements to the *Histories* see Marincola (2001) 27 and in this volume.

21. On the Persians in Herodotus see Flower in this volume.

22. Immerwahr (1966) 238.

23. Thomas (2001) 198.

24. Immerwahr (1966) 248.

25. Compare Grundy (1901) and Lazenby (1993) 80.

26. Tritle (2000) 159–60.

27. Flower (1998) 375 argues effectively for the Homeric touches, but I see no reason to doubt the account. Would not Aeschylus have tried to find out what happened to his brother?

28. The tactic by which a strong attack covers a withdrawal is not unusual. During the Second World War, the German army did this so commonly that allied troops knew that a furious German attack announced the withdrawal of the main elements opposite them (as noted by Hollywood director John Huston in his 1944 US Army documentary 'The Battle of San Pietro'). Some scholars (e.g. Flower [1998] 368) have claimed the Thebans were forced to fight by Leonidas, but I think this unlikely. He had more than enough to worry about in facing the Persians. To allow quislings in his own ranks defies belief.

29. See Flower (1998) 365–79 for an alternative account of the end at Thermopylae. He suggests that the historian Ephorus' account of a night attack on Xerxes' camp by Leonidas – leading to the final destruction of the Greek forces there – provides as plausible a version as that given by Herodotus. Flower questions how Herodotus might have learned of the last stand of the Spartans. Some of the Thebans lived and, though taken prisoner and not proud of this, could have told what happened. Additionally, Herodotus relates a conversation between the Greek Thersander and a Persian notable at Plataea before the big battle (9.16). Conversations such as these might have provided informants for what also happened (or again what people remembered hearing happened) at Thermopylae.

30. Herr (1978) 209; Hasford (1979) 4 (Hasford's novel later appeared as *Full Metal Jacket*; Herr collaborated in the making of both that film and *Apocalypse Now*).

31. Immerwahr (1966) 280–1, but see below. On Aeschylus and Herodotus see Pelling (1997a) 2.
32. The Corinthian flight is something Herodotus heard from Athenian sources (at a time when Athens and Corinth were bitter enemies) but did not believe, as he states that all the rest of the Greeks knew better (8.94.4).
33. Hdt. 8.82, 84, 92–3.
34. Respectively Boedeker (2003) 21; Flower and Marincola (2002) 29.
35. Boedeker (2003) 21. I would concede that Homer might have been behind and inspired the detail that Masistes was stabbed in the eye. On the other hand, it could be expected that an elite Persian officer would be well armoured and thus hard to kill. The blow to the face is not necessarily pure luck. At Agincourt English archers killed immobilised and wounded French knights by thrusting knives through the slits of visors, just as was done to Masistes.
36. See Keegan (1976) 103.
37. See also Flower and Marincola (2002) 205.
38. For example, Burn (1984) 531–2; Green (1996) 263–5.
39. Thuc. 5.72.1; Xen. *Anab.* 2.6.2-6.
40. Tritle (2000) 76–7. The post-Plataea Spartan traditions preserved by Herodotus show that the Spartans indeed numbered Aristodamus among those considered for honours. Their discussion shows that while they may have appreciated his courage, they placed a higher premium on the courage of men fighting to live.
41. Boedeker (2003) 26 does not include Pantites, the other possible survivor of Thermopylae, said to have hanged himself, not able to bear the shame (so the Spartans thought) but more likely the guilt of having survived. This too surely drove Aristodamus.

15

SARA FORSDYKE

Herodotus, political history and political thought

> The Ethiopians have customs which are different from all other men,
> especially concerning their rulers. For they choose as king the person among
> the citizens who is biggest and strongest.
>
> (3.20.2)

Observations about the political practices of Greeks and non-Greeks such as the one in the epigraph above were once taken as indicative of Herodotus' interest in the odd or unusual features of societies, rather than the systematic analysis of politics. According to this view, Herodotus was a naïve storyteller who had no deep of understanding of (or interest in) politics. The prime example of Herodotus' alleged lack of understanding of politics is his statement that the Athenian statesman Cleisthenes was imitating his grandfather Cleisthenes, tyrant of Sicyon, when he enacted the tribal reforms which were central to the founding of the democracy at Athens (5.67.1). Rather than recording the details of Cleisthenes' groundbreaking reforms as modern historians might wish, Herodotus mentions only the creation of new tribal divisions and 'digresses' on a similar change in tribal names made by Cleisthenes' grandfather, tyrant of Sicyon. Victor Ehrenburg, commenting on this passage in 1950, states emphatically that Herodotus 'had no discriminating knowledge of political and constitutional issues'.[1]

The last twenty years, however, have witnessed a reversal of this negative view of Herodotus' political understanding. Herodotus is now seen as deeply embedded in the intellectual milieu of the late fifth century, and consequently well-versed in the political debates of his time. Furthermore, Herodotus is now considered not simply a teller of tales about the marvellous, but rather a skilled narrator who, through careful construction of thematic and verbal patterns, expressed views on some of the most pressing political issues of his day. Finally, rather than being seen as inadequately discriminating in his accounts of political history when compared to the contemporary Athenian historian and shrewd political analyst, Thucydides, Herodotus is now credited with a much broader conception, and hence by current standards, much more satisfying view of politics than Thucydides. The breadth of Herodotus' account, moreover, makes him a much more valuable source not simply for the historical development of the Greek communities but also for the values, beliefs and ideologies of his fifth-century audience.

This new view of Herodotus' political understanding is a product of several new scholarly approaches both in classical studies generally and in Herodotean studies in particular. In the first part of this chapter, I briefly describe the new approaches which have affected the evaluation of politics in the *Histories*. In the second part, I demonstrate, using a few selective examples, the impact of these new approaches on our understanding of the political nature of Herodotus' *Histories*.

New approaches to politics and Herodotus' *Histories*

Most fundamental among the new approaches to politics in the ancient world has been a revision in the view of what constitutes politics and hence what the proper subject of political history is. Rather than viewing politics as comprised of the military history and constitutional development of various states, scholars (following trends in other academic disciplines) have begun to view politics as implicated in the totality of social practices and norms.[2] Thus sexual practices, attitudes towards women, religious beliefs, burial rituals and other areas of social life are now considered integral to understanding the dynamics of power (politics) in societies. On this account of politics, Herodotus' interest (itself tied to wider interest among natural scientists, physicians, and a group of intellectuals known as 'sophists') in examining the *nomoi* (customs) of the various Greek and non-Greek communities is now seen as tightly connected to his concern with the political culture and history of the communities he discusses, rather than a separate element that needs to be explained.[3]

Alongside this broader definition of politics is a new emphasis on the synchronic analysis of the beliefs, norms, and ideologies of ancient societies, rather than the diachronic narration of political and military events.[4] In the context of this development, Herodotus' *Histories* have taken on a new importance. In the first place, following the publication of François Hartog's landmark study, scholars have recognised that Herodotus' accounts of foreign cultures (e.g., Persians, Egyptians, Scythians) are formulated according to Greek cultural categories and Greek self-perception, and thus are an important source for identifying the ways that the Greeks defined themselves and articulated their norms and values.[5] Among the key features of Greek self-definition, as we shall see, were political freedom, respect for law, and the principle of open debate in the decision-making process. Recent scholarship has shown, moreover, that Herodotus not only articulates Greek cultural categories and norms through his portraits of foreign cultures, but also subjects them to critical examination. It was through this critical examination of Greek understandings of Self and Other that Herodotus contributed to the political thought and debate of his time.[6]

Related to the new interest in the ethnographical portions of the *Histories* is an interest in Herodotus' narrative of the past as a product of the Greeks' representation of themselves in relation to the world about them. Borrowing from developments in the study of social memory, scholars have recognised that the versions of the past preserved in Herodotus' narrative reflect what various groups in Greek society (e.g. families and communities such as *poleis*) actively chose to remember, and therefore are not a systematic or inert record of past events. Indeed studies of social memory, particularly in oral societies such as fifth-century Greece, have shown that a group's memory of the past is largely determined by contemporary needs of the group. Important among group needs are the justification of the social and political order, and the validation of social and political norms.[7] As groups change over time, moreover, their version of the past changes: elements incompatible with a group's self-presentation, values and norms are de-emphasised or removed, and other elements are emphasised or even invented.[8] Finally, different groups within a society may preserve different versions of the past, and may use the past in different ways in order to promote their particular interests within society.

These insights into the nature of social memory have provided many new perspectives on Herodotus' *Histories*. First of all, scholars now recognise that Herodotean narratives often reveal more about the ideological needs of Herodotus' later fifth-century oral informants than about the archaic and early classical past.[9] Scholarly interest therefore has refocussed on the competing ideologies and self-presentations inherent in the stories about the past told by various groups within Greek society. For example, Herodotus' accounts of Spartan and Athenian history in the archaic period are now taken as important sources for the way that these rival *poleis* used the past to articulate distinctive identities and justify their claims to power within the Greek world in the second half of the fifth century. Moreover, these accounts are also analysed for what they can tell us of internal ideological struggles within particular Greek *poleis*, since it is now recognised that Herodotus made use not only of elite family traditions for this history, but also official *polis* and popular traditions.[10]

The scholarly trends discussed so far treat Herodotus' narratives as reflections of the versions of the past told by his informants. Yet Herodotus himself, of course, played an active role in the shaping of the stories that he presents. Several further scholarly developments have increased our understanding of the ways that Herodotus fashioned his narrative in order to give his own particular perspective on the past and hence express his political views. Most generally, the arguments made by Hayden White regarding the literary aspects of historical prose have renewed interest in the ways that Herodotus uses literary techniques to create certain effects in his audience.[11] Since Herodotus performed his *Histories* orally, this scholarly trend has resulted in a new emphasis on the ways that he made use of the narrative techniques of oral storytellers in order to lend meaning to his narratives.

Among the narrative techniques most used by Herodotus is his tendency to emphasise connections between different historical events through narrative patterning, that is, the repetition of key terms, the use of common themes, and the emphasis on similar sequences of events. It is through the examination of such narrative patterns that scholars have been able to understand the way in which Herodotus gave political meaning to his narratives and expressed his political views.[12] At the most sophisticated end of the literary analysis of Herodotus' *Histories*, scholars have used the analytical framework offered by narratology in order to understand how Herodotus uses different types of narrative – most importantly statements in his own voice (metanarrative), but also including disruption of the 'natural' chronological and geographical sequence of events (narrative disjunction) – in order to express his views about the meaning of historical events.[13]

It is in part through the study of Herodotus' narrative techniques that new insights have been gained regarding the ways that Herodotus gives political meaning to his text. These insights, in turn, have led to the realisation of how similar Herodotus' political themes, concepts and language are to those of other intellectuals of his time. Most important among these thinkers are Thucydides, the medical writers and the 'sophists'.[14] With regard to Thucydides in particular, scholars have noted strong parallels between Thucydides' representation and analysis of political affairs at the time of the Peloponnesian War and Herodotus' account of the earlier history of the Greek *poleis*.[15] These parallels show that Herodotus was well versed in contemporary political debate as well as theory. Many have argued, moreover, that Herodotus' use of concepts, themes and the language of contemporary political debate invite his audience to compare the past with the present, and thus to consider his *Histories* not simply as an antiquarian inquiry into the distant past, but as an active lesson for the political realities of his own day.[16] Although Herodotus never explicitly claims a didactic aim for his narrative as does Thucydides, these scholars argue that the *Histories*, like other forms of ancient literature including tragedy and epic, offered the Greeks of

Herodotus' time an opportunity to think through the (political) problems of their own day through the contemplation of the past.

It is this last feature of Herodotus' *Histories* on which I will concentrate in this essay, namely the ways that Herodotus makes use of the past to encourage his audience to think through contemporary political realities. Despite this focus on the way that Herodotus (and his fifth-century oral sources) refashioned the past to engage in political debate about the present, I turn briefly at the end of the essay to an example of the way that Herodotus' narrative preserves historically accurate information about the political history of archaic and early classical Greece. This last example will demonstrate that the complaints of an earlier generation of scholars that Herodotus ignored or misunderstood the earlier political history of Greece are based on an anachronistic conception of politics.

Political history, political thought and the meaning of Herodotus' *Histories*

At its most fundamental level, Herodotus' *Histories* is about the expansion of Persian power until it came into conflict with a coalition of the mainland Greeks, headed by Athens and Sparta. Herodotus seeks to explain how Persia came to confront the Greeks, and why the Greeks won. As we shall see, Herodotus' explanations of these two phenomena borrow from contemporary Greek thought on the nature of imperialism, the value of political freedom, and the relation between geography, climate, and culture (including political culture). These areas of Greek thought were of utmost importance to the Greeks of the late fifth century – a time when Athens had subjected much of the Greek world, when Athens and Sparta engaged in rivalry over power which brought the whole Greek and much of the non-Greek world into conflict, and finally when Greek contact with non-Greek cultures was raising new questions about the relation between nature and culture. I will argue that Herodotus engages critically with these areas of contemporary Greek political thought and debate in his presentation of the causes and course of the Persian Wars. I begin with Herodotus' analysis of Persian expansion, and then turn to his explanation of the Greek victory.

Herodotus explains Persian expansion by two principles both of which derive from late fifth-century debate about Athenian imperialism. The first reason for Persian expansion according to Herodotus is the inevitable need of states to expand or be absorbed by another expanding power. Herodotus articulates this principle on several occasions in his *Histories*, most strikingly in the context of the Persian King Xerxes' decision to invade Greece. Meeting with a group of noble Persians, Xerxes says (7.11.2):

> I know well that if we remain at peace (*hēsuchiēn axomen*), they [the Greeks] will not. And indeed they will invade our land, if we are to judge by what they have already undertaken, namely the burning of Sardis and the invasion of Asia. It is not possible for either of us to retreat and withdraw, but it lies before us to act or to suffer. Either the Greeks or the Persians must do these things.[17]

As Kurt Raaflaub has noted, this reason for Persian expansion echoes arguments made by several characters in Thucydides' history, and presumably reflects contemporary debate about the growth of Athenian power.[18] In the debate at Sparta which led to the Spartan decision to declare war on Athens, for example, the Corinthians rebuke the Spartans for their failure to check the growth of Athenian power, and demand immediate action before the Athenians subject all of Greece (Thuc. 1.68–71).[19] In this speech, the Athenians are characterised as continually active in pursuit of increasing their empire.[20] Thucydides' language is significant (1.70):

> When they defeat their enemies, they seek more conquests, and when they are defeated, they hardly fall back at all . . . They toil at these dangerous and difficult tasks all of their lives, and they hardly enjoy what they have because of their continual pursuit of more. They consider nothing else a holiday than to do what is necessary and they consider idle rest (*hēsuchian*) no less a misfortune than toilsome leisure. One might say, in sum, that they were born neither to be at rest themselves (*echein hēsuchian*), nor to allow others to rest.[21]

The parallelism between Athenian and Persian imperial expansion is even more marked in the manner that Herodotus has Xerxes cite the exploits of his ancestors as the motivation for further expansion of Persian power over Greece. As Raaflaub has again pointed out, the Athenians of Herodotus' generation used the example of their ancestors' exploits in the Persian Wars as a reason for the maintenance and extension of Athenian power, just as Herodotus' Xerxes does (7.8α.1):[22]

> Persian men, I will not criticise the following custom, but I will accept it and make use of it. For I have learned from my elders that we [the Persians] have never yet kept quiet since we took over power from the Medes. . . . Since I took up the throne, I have been thinking about how I might not be less than my predecessors in honour and how I might not add less power to the Persian empire.

With this passage we may compare Pericles' exhortation of the Athenians to follow the example of their ancestors not only to preserve Athenian power, but to hand it down to their descendants greater than it was when they inherited it (2.36.1–3):

> Our ancestors are worthy of praise, especially your fathers, who [at the time of the Persian Wars] handed down to us in addition to that which they inherited, the empire which we now possess, having acquired it through considerable toil. And those of us who are in middle age have augmented our city most of all and made it the most self-sufficient city both in war and peace.[23]

The fact that Herodotus puts similar words in the mouth of a despotic barbarian king could not but have encouraged Herodotus' late fifth-century audience to view negatively, or at least question, contemporary Athenian arguments in justification of their imperial expansion. Indeed, just as Pelling has drawn attention to the parallel between the Persian Artabanus in Herodotus and the Spartan Archidamus in Thucydides, so the words of the Persian Xerxes in Herodotus parallel the words of Pericles in Thucydides.[24] Through his portrait of Xerxes, Herodotus draws a tacit parallel between Athens under Pericles and Persia under Xerxes that suggests the injustice and dangers of Athenian imperialism.

To cite one further example, one might note that both Xerxes and Pericles make grand, indeed by Greek standards, hubristic, claims for the future extent of their state's power. Xerxes, for example, boasts that (7.8γ.1–3):

> If we conquer these men [the Athenians] and those who inhabit the land of Phrygian Pelops [the Spartans] then the Persian land will share boundaries with Zeus' sky. For the sun will not look upon any land bordering ours, but I will make all lands one when I pass through Europe . . . and thus I will enslave both those who are to blame [the Athenians] and those who are without blame [the Peloponnesians].

Similarly, Pericles says of Athenian power (2.41.4):

> We have supplied clear indications of our power for the men of our time, and we will be marvelled at in the future . . . We have made every sea and every land susceptible to our power as a result of our daring, and everywhere we have left unseen monuments both of vengeance against enemies and aid to friends.[25]

By echoing and sharpening contemporary Athenian rhetoric – note especially Xerxes' boast that he will make his empire border on Zeus' own kingdom – Herodotus points to the hubris and dangers of Athenian expansion.

Besides the theme of the imperial imperative, Herodotus uses a second principle of Greek thought which not only explains how the Persians expanded to such an extent that they ultimately confronted the Greeks, but also is a key factor in Herodotus' explanation of the Greek victory over the Persians. This second explanatory principle, which also appears in contemporary medical literature, is the notion that infertile lands with extreme climates give rise to tough and warlike people who are easily able to conquer 'soft' people who live in more hospitable lands.[26] In contemporary Greek thought, non-Greek eastern lands, such as those ruled by the Persians, were considered soft and luxurious, and thus easily conquered. By contrast, the Greeks prided themselves on their warlike toughness, a characteristic they attributed to their residence in a relatively infertile land. This ideological construction is evident in contemporary literature, such as tragedy, as well as in Herodotus' portrait of the barbarian hordes that make up Xerxes' army, who are easily felled by the Greeks.[27] On one level, therefore, Herodotus explains early Persian expansion as a product of their confrontation with soft eastern cultures. Similarly, the defeat of Xerxes' army by the Greeks in the Persian Wars is attributed to the hardness of Greek culture in relation to the 'softened' Persian culture of this time.[28]

In this aspect of his explanation of the Greek victory over the Persians, it is likely that Herodotus echoes contemporary uses of the Persian Wars and the non-Greek Other in the articulation of both panhellenic Greek identity and the collective identities of individual *poleis*. Yet Herodotus' narrative is not simply a passive reflection of contemporary Greek ideologies; rather, Herodotus makes active use of these cultural constructions in order to raise questions about Greek self-perception and particularly to give a warning about the potential consequences of the Greek victory over the Persians and their eastern allies. For, just as Persia had once been a hard culture which was able to dominate its soft eastern neighbors, and thus become rich and powerful, so the Greeks (particularly the Athenians) had become rich and powerful as a consequence of their victory over the Persians. Herodotus demonstrates the Persian trajectory from hard to soft culture, as a result of their control over the resources of their softer subjects, and thus explains their descent from conqueror to conquered.[29] Furthermore, he points to the hardness of Greek culture at the time of the Persian Wars in implicit contrast to his own day, suggesting that the Greeks themselves, and particularly the Athenians, might become soft and thus easy prey to harder cultures in the future.[30]

The idea that the Greeks, and particularly the Athenians, might follow the same pattern of rise and fall as the Persians is evident not only in the parallels between Persian and Athenian imperialism pointed out already, but also most prominently in the ending of the *Histories*, where Herodotus recalls the earlier poverty and toughness of the Persians and contrasts it to the luxury of the Persians of the time of the Persian Wars.[31] Similarly, Herodotus recalls the poverty and toughness of the Greeks at the time of the Persian Wars, and implicitly contrasts it with the Greeks of his own day. As a number of scholars have noted, the ending of Herodotus' *Histories* – once thought to be an indication of the incompleteness of the work – is carefully constructed to evoke this among other key themes of the *Histories*.[32] In the final vignette of the *Histories*, Herodotus tells the story of how the first great Persian king, Cyrus, was once advised to migrate from the small and infertile land of Persia to the better land of their neighbours. Cyrus responded negatively to the suggestion, saying that migration would result in the Persians becoming subjects rather than rulers: 'Soft lands usually produce soft peoples; for it is not at all the case that the same land begets both marvellous crops and good fighters' (9.122).

Besides evoking the key explanatory principle for Persian expansion, this final anecdote allows Herodotus to contrast the Persians of Cyrus' day with those of the Persian Wars, and at the same time implicitly contrast the Greeks of the time of the Persian Wars with those of his own time. For only a few chapters before this final vignette, Herodotus has the Spartan king Pausanias comment on the luxuriousness of the Persian king Xerxes' lifestyle in contrast to that of the Greeks (9.82).[33] Yet it was well known to Herodotus' Greek audience that, following the Greek victory, Pausanias adopted the luxurious ways of the Persians, and was deprived of the command partly for this reason (Thuc. 1.130). Herodotus' use of the anecdote about Pausanias' ridicule of Persian wealth, therefore, serves as an ironic symbol of the corruption of Greece by eastern wealth and luxury.

Similarly, Herodotus' accounts of the activities of several Athenian leaders following the Persian Wars point to the corrupting effect of the growth of Athenian power and wealth in the post-Persian-Wars period. Immediately following the Greek victory, for example, the Athenians inflict a brutal punishment on a Persian named Artaÿctes and his son, crucifying the former and stoning to death the latter (9.116–21). Such treatment evokes Greek conceptions of oriental despotism, and suggests that Athens is the successor of Persia in the brutal use of power.[34] Moreover, as many have noted, Herodotus' representation of the Athenian general Themistocles in the final part of the *Histories* is a particularly powerful symbol of Athenian greed and abuse of power in the post-Persian Wars period. Themistocles' extortion of money from the Andrians in the post-war period evokes Athenian imperial policy in the later fifth century. Indeed Derow has labelled Themistocles' dialogue with the Andrians (8.111) the 'Andrian Dialogue', thus drawing attention to the parallels with the so-called 'Melian Dialogue' of Thucydides, in which the Athenians famously used the argument of Might to compel the Melians to submit to their power.[35]

If we now turn from Herodotus' explanation of Persian expansion to his account of why the Greeks won, we find a third key element of fifth-century Greek political thought, namely the relation between political freedom and military strength.[36] Several passages in Herodotus suggest that the Greeks attributed their victory over the Persians in part to their free and open political system. Most famously, the dialogue between the exiled Spartan king Demaratus and the Persian king Xerxes (7.101–4) sets up this interpretative frame for the Greek victory. Xerxes' incredulous question – 'How could a thousand, or even ten or fifty thousand [Greeks] resist my army, indeed especially if they are all equally free and not ruled by one man?' (7.103.3) – illustrates by contrast to the Greek victory that ensues, the validity of Greek belief in the military value of political freedom. The same interpretation of the Greek victory is expressed in parallel ways in Aeschylus' *Persians*. I have argued elsewhere that the idea of a connection between political freedom and military strength probably arose following the Greek victory as a way of articulating Greek identity and maintaining panhellenic unity in the aftermath of the Persian Wars.[37]

The contrast between Persian despotism and Greek freedom played a role not simply on the panhellenic level but also on the inter-*polis* level, as various Greek city states asserted their political identities *vis-à-vis* other *poleis* through the representation of their role in fighting the Persian foe. The Athenians in particular made use of the Persian Wars to validate their democratic political system in contrast to the Spartan oligarchy. Herodotus, moreover, echoes this aspect of Athenian democratic ideology in his most explicit articulation of the value of political freedom (5.78):[38]

It is clear that democracy (*isēgoriē*)[39] is an excellent thing not just in one aspect but in every way. For the Athenians, when ruled by tyrants, were not better than any of their neighbours in war, but when they got rid of the tyrants, they became first by far. This shows, therefore, that when they were held down [by the tyrant], they were cowardly, on the grounds that they were working for a master, but when they had been liberated, each man was eager to work for himself.

In these aspects of his narrative, Herodotus appears to be deeply versed in Greek and, in particular, Athenian political ideologies. Yet as recent commentators point out, Herodotus does not simply echo the ideological construction of the value of political freedom, but subjects it to critical evaluation in a manner not dissimilar to Thucydides and other critics of democratic rule.[40]

The double-sidedness of Herodotus' evaluation of political freedom is perhaps best illustrated in his representation of the 'debate' between Xerxes and his advisers which led to the decision to invade Greece (7.8–11). On the one hand, Herodotus' narrative points to the lack of truly free and open debate in Persia; on the other hand, however, Herodotus' account also simultaneously suggests that democratic debate in such *poleis* as Athens may suffer from the same dangerous tendencies as occur in the Persian debate.

Herodotus highlights the lack of open debate in Persia in several ways. First, although Xerxes states that he wants to put the matter up for open debate (*to pragma eis meson*, 7.8δ.2), he grows angry when his uncle Artabanus voices objections to his plan. Moreover, Xerxes only stops short of physically punishing Artabanus because he is a relative. The speech of Mardonius in favour of Xerxes' plan, furthermore, is full of subservient flattery and patent falsehoods. Herodotus makes clear the superficiality and falseness of Mardonius' speech not just by his comment that Mardonius made Xerxes' plan *seem* plausible (*epileēnas*, 7.10.1), but also by Mardonius' hyperbolic flattery of Xerxes at the beginning of the speech: 'Master, not only are you alone the best of the Persians who lived before, but you are also the best of the Persians of the future' (7.9.1). Finally, Mardonius' claim that 'we [the Persians] are the best in war' is not only fully countered by the evidence of the previous Persian campaign against Greece presented by Artabanus, but is full of dramatic irony for Herodotus' Greek audience who of course knew the disastrous outcome of Xerxes' own campaign.[41]

Despite this seeming vindication of the Greek value of open debate, however, Herodotus echoes some of the criticisms of the Athenian democracy when he suggests that Xerxes succumbs to the persuasive, yet false arguments of Mardonius. Indeed Artabanus criticises Mardonius for his foolish words about the Greeks, and suggests that Mardonius is intentionally falsely representing (*diaballein*) the Greeks in order to make Xerxes more eager for the campaign (7.10η.1). Artabanus' criticism evokes the arguments made by elite critics of the Athenian democracy, who argued that clever speakers in the assembly use flattery, falsehood and appeals to the selfish desires of the Athenian masses to goad the Athenians into policy decisions which ultimately harm them.[42] In fact, Herodotus himself draws attention to the parallel between Xerxes' susceptibility to flattery and falsehood and the Athenian democracy's similar tendency in his representation of the Milesian Aristagoras' embassy to Sparta and Athens in quest of allies for the Ionian revolt in 499. Herodotus chooses to describe Aristagoras' visit to Sparta and Athens at length, and emphasises that Aristagoras' deceptive arguments had no hold at Sparta, but were accepted by the Athenians who were eager for the wealth that might come from an Asian campaign: 'It seems that it is easier to deceive (*diaballein*) the masses than one man, since [Aristagoras] was not able to deceive the Spartan Cleomenes, but he was successful in his deception of 30,000 Athenians' (5.97.2). As Rood has noted, the parallels with the Athenians' decision to invade Sicily, as represented by Thucydides, are clear, and Herodotus too appears to be critiquing the propensity of the Athenian democracy to make bad policy decisions because of their ignorance and personal greed.[43]

Ironically, however, one aspect of Mardonius' speech does appear to be insightful, and that is his remark that since the Greeks belong to the same race, they ought to resolve their differences through diplomacy, not open warfare (7.9β.2). As many have noted, Mardonius' critique of Greek quarrelsomeness alludes to the great conflict between the Greek states that culminated in the Peloponnesian War, and echoes comments that Herodotus makes in his own voice about the dire consequences of internal Greek feuding. In reference to the Athenian decision to put aside their claim to the leadership in the interests of Greek unity in the face of the Persian Wars, for instance, Herodotus comments (8.3.1):

> When the allies objected [to Athenian leadership], the Athenians yielded for they thought it better that Greece survive, and they knew that if they argued about the leadership, then Greece would perish. And they were right, since conflict among people of the same race (*stasis emphulos*) is a greater evil than a united war effort in as much as war is worse than peace.[44]

Although Herodotus does not say so explicitly, implicitly he criticises contemporary Athenians through reference to their noble action in the past. As Thucydides' character, the Spartan ephor Sthenelaidas, says bluntly (1.86.1): 'To the extent that the Athenians were good men at that time [the Persian Wars], they are worthy of double the blame if they are bad men now, since they have become bad after being good.'

Ideology and history

The analysis so far has focussed on the ways that Herodotus and his oral sources made use of the past in order to engage in debate about contemporary political conditions. This treatment may suggest that the *Histories* is of little use in understanding the actual political history of the past, especially the remoter archaic past. Yet this is hardly the case, since Herodotus preserves a good deal of useful information about archaic Greek political history.[45] Indeed, it is precisely by identifying the ways that later oral traditions adapted the past to their own (political) purposes, that we can best appreciate what the *Histories* can tell us about the earlier past. Perhaps the best example of how Herodotus' narrative both adapts and preserves the past is his portraits of archaic Greek tyrants.[46] On one level, Herodotus' representations of tyrants exemplify the negative features of one-man rule as sketched in the Constitutional Debate (3.80). On this reading, Herodotus' tyrants are recognisable as products of fifth-century Greek political thought and ideology.[47] Yet it has also been observed that there is some individuation in Herodotus' portraits of Greek tyrants, and Herodotus' view of them is not unequivocally negative.[48]

Two explanations have been offered for the specificity of Herodotus' portraits of individual Greek tyrants and the ambiguity of his overall presentation of tyranny. First, Herodotus' stories about Greek tyrants are not only designed to reinforce certain political lessons, such as the value of political freedom; rather, stories about tyrants serve a variety of ethical, moral and philosophical purposes both in Herodotus' narrative and presumably for the societies in which they were orally transmitted.[49] The story of the Samian tyrant Polycrates, for example, details many of the tyrant's great accomplishments, in part in order to demonstrate the historical/philosophical lesson that prosperity never abides in one place for long.[50] The second explanation for the ambiguity of Herodotus' portraits of tyranny is that while traditions about the past are largely shaped by the contemporary needs of the society which transmits them, not all features of the past are lost in this reshaping.[51] An excellent example of this principle can be found in Herodotus' account of how the Athenian tyrant Peisistratus rose to power.

Famously, Herodotus describes how Peisistratus seized power for a second time by dressing up a tall woman as Athena and pretending that the goddess Athena herself was escorting him back from exile into power in Athens (1.60). Herodotus (and his oral sources) retell this story as an example of how tyrants deceive the citizens in order to seize power. For a long time, modern historians accepted this explanation of the episode in archaic Athenian history. In 1987 Robert Connor argued, by contrast, that Herodotus' explanation of the event was a product of fifth-century beliefs, and did not adequately explain the meaning of the episode in terms of archaic political conditions.[52] Borrowing from models of social drama developed by anthropologists, Connor argued that Peisistratus did not dress up the woman as Athena in order to deceive the Athenians, but rather enacted a social ritual by which the Athenians articulated in symbolic terms their acceptance of Peisistratus as leader. This explanation makes much more sense of the episode, since we know that the Athenians of the archaic period did not revile tyranny as did their fifth-century descendants, and therefore had no need to be deceived into accepting Peisistratus.[53] In this narrative, therefore, we see an example of how Herodotus and his oral sources preserve a feature of archaic politics, but reinterpret it to make sense in terms of their own political values and conditions.

The gap between archaic Greek political conditions and those of Herodotus' fifth-century Greeks may serve as a paradigm for the gap between modern historians of an earlier generation who castigated Herodotus for not recording details of Greek constitutional history, and those of the present time, who credit him with a broad and deep understanding of ancient politics. The former scholars expect to find detailed discussion of the institutions of government and are disappointed that Herodotus does not, for example, describe the institutional arrangements of Cleisthenes' democratic reforms. Current historians, however, recognise that ancient politics cannot be understood solely from the institutionalist perspective of the modern state. Rather, Cleisthenes' actions in changing the names of the tribal divisions of the Athenian community, as highlighted by Herodotus, must be recognised as the key to understanding the meaning of the reforms for late sixth- and fifth-century Athenians. Politics itself meant something different to fifth-century Athenians than it does to us. It is in the climate of this new understanding of ancient politics that future breakthroughs regarding the political content and meaning of Herodotus' *Histories* will be made.

FURTHER READING

For Herodotus' contribution to our understanding of Greek political history, see the essays of Osborne, Forsdyke and Harrison in Bakker, de Jong and van Wees (2002) 497–578. For an overview of Herodotus' contribution to ancient political thought, see Winton (2000). For more detailed studies, see Raaflaub (2002a) and Thomas (2000).

For Herodotus' relation to the Athenian democracy and Athenian democratic thought and ideology, see Moles (2002), Saxonhouse (1996), and Forsdyke (2001). On Herodotus and Athenian imperialism, see Balot (2001) ch. 4.

For an insightful and lively account of Greek political identity as constructed in Greek art and literature (especially Herodotus' *Histories*), see Cartledge (2002). For a more detailed treatment, see Hall (2002).

NOTES

1. Ehrenberg (1950) 535–6. Compare Strasburger (1955) 585: 'It does not matter to [Herodotus] in the least to evaluate the constitutional technicalities of

democratisation besides the human–ethical factors' (my translation). Despite these comments, Strasburger concludes his article thus: 'Overall one feels that Herodotus reflected much more deeply on the political problems of his own time than he allows to appear' (602, my translation), and indeed, Strasburger's article marks a turning point in the appreciation of Herodotus as a political thinker, as Raaflaub (1987) 221 n.1 observes.

2. This scholarly turn is of course a product of developments in other academic disciplines, especially anthropology, political theory and sociology. For an overview of these developments, see Burke (1992).

3. For examples of this new wider interest in Herodotus' descriptions of *nomoi* as connected to his political interests, see Thomas in this volume; also Thomas (2000) 102–34 and Munson (2001a) *passim*. For a summary of earlier attempts to reconcile the ethnographical and historical portions of the *Histories*, see Marincola (2001) 22–3.

4. For this trend in ancient history in general, see, for example, Ober (1989a), (1989b), and Boegehold and Scafuro (1994).

5. Hartog (1988/1991).

6. See especially Pelling (1997b), Munson (2001a), Cartledge (1995) and (2002) 36–77, and below.

7. Recent important studies of social memory and oral tradition include: Vansina (1985), Fentress and Wickham (1992), Le Goff (1977/1992), and Assman (1992). For applications of these ideas in ancient Greece and Rome, see Thomas (1989), Gehrke and Möller (1996), Alcock (2002), and the following three notes.

8. Compare the phrase 'creative remembering' used by Giangiulio (2001) 117.

9. It has long been recognised that Herodotus gathered his information primarily from oral informants: Jacoby (1913) 413, Thomas (1989) 4. See Fowler (2001) and Luraghi (this volume) for recent discussion.

10. Thomas (1989) is fundamental, though Murray (2001a) took early steps towards the differentiation of various types of oral tradition in the *Histories*. For recent discussion, see essays of Fowler, Luraghi, Thomas, and Murray in Luraghi (2001c). See also the chapters of Luraghi, Stadter and Dewald in this volume.

11. White (1973), (1987).

12. The bibliography on narrative patterns in Herodotus is extensive. Immerwahr (1966) is fundamental. See recently Lateiner (1989), Dillery (1996) and Dewald (2003).

13. Dewald (1987), (2002); Munson (2001a); de Jong (2002); and Luraghi (this volume).

14. See especially Thomas (2000) and in this volume, and Raaflaub (2002a).

15. Raaflaub (1987) and (2002b), Pelling (1991), Rood (1999).

16. Strasburger (1955), Fornara (1971a), Raaflaub (1987), Stadter (1992), Derow (1995), Moles (1996) and (2002).

17. See also, for example, Herodotus' presentation of the reason for the Lydian king Croesus' decision to attack Persia: 'The growth of the Persian empire . . . set Croesus to thinking how he might destroy the growing power of Persia before the Persians became mighty' (1.46.1).

18. Raaflaub (1987) 227–8 and (2002b).

19. According to Thucydides, the Spartans declare war due to their fear of the growth of Athenian power (1.23.6; 1.88.1; 1.118.2).

20. For a similar characterisation of the Athenians as 'daring, aggressive and brave' in Herodotus' *Histories*, see Flower and Marincola (2002) 14.

21. Compare Pericles at Thuc. 2.62: 'Consider our freedom. If we take it back, then we will preserve and recover it, but if we yield to others, then even what we have achieved will be lost. And don't be less than your ancestors who through their toil, and not through inheritance, both acquired and preserved our empire to be handed down to you.' And a little later (2.63.2): 'It is no longer possible to give up the empire . . . For your empire is like a tyranny. While it may seem to have been unjust to take it, it certainly is dangerous to let it go.'

22. See Raaflaub (2002b).

23. For the importance of the idea of extending Athenian power in Athenian civic ideology, compare the fourth-century ephebic oath where young men swear to leave behind their fatherland greater than it was when they inherited it (Tod (1985) 204).

24. Pelling (1991). Rood (1999) 152–9 demonstrates the parallels between Herodotus' Mardonius and Artabanus at Xerxes' court and Thucydides' Alcibiades and Nicias in the Athenian assembly.

25. Compare Pericles' words at Thuc. 2.62: 'Of the two parts which make up the world – the land and the sea – you are masters of the latter, both the part that you now control and any further part you might wish. There is no one who can prevent you from sailing wherever you like, not the Persian king nor any other race that currently exists.'

26. Hipp. *Airs, Waters, Places* 12, 16, 23–4. On Herodotus and the medical writers, see Thomas (2000), especially 102–34, and this volume.

27. For tragedy, see Hall (1989). For this contrast in Herodotus, see Hartog (1988) and Forsdyke (2001). For this contrast in Aristotle, see Cartledge (2002) 54–6. As Pelling (1997b) points out, however, the Persians themselves (as opposed to their subjects) fight bravely. On Persian bravery, see Flower and Marincola (2002) 15, 312.

28. Raaflaub (1987) 244–6, and Thomas in this volume. Flower and Marincola (2002) 312, however, express doubts about this interpretation.

29. Of course the Persian empire was still powerful in Herodotus' own day (and beyond), so Herodotus' choice of the Persian defeat in 479 as the ending point for his narrative constructs a false sense of Persian decline.

30. Compare Stadter (1992), Moles (1996), Raaflaub (1987) and (2002b).

31. The theme of rise and fall of states and individuals is a key one, expressed explicitly by Herodotus in his programmatic statement at 1.5.3–4 and thematically in such short stories as Croesus' encounter with Solon (1.30–33).

32. On the ending of the *Histories*, see most recently, Derow (1995), Pelling (1997b), Dewald (1997), and Flower and Marincola (2002).

33. This contrast is most famously evoked in the conversation between the exiled Spartan king Demaratus and Xerxes (especially 7.102.1).

34. Boedeker (1988), Derow (1995), and Pelling (1997b).

35. Derow (1995) 42, also noted by Strasburger (1955). Both Derow and Balot (2001) 99–135 lay emphasis on Herodotus' portrait of the Athenian Alcmaeon emerging from Croesus' treasury with his cheeks stuffed full of gold as a symbol both of Greek inheritance of Eastern wealth and luxury and more particularly of Athenian greed (cf. Dewald in this volume). Compare also Herodotus'

mention of Miltiades' Parian campaign, where the Athenians are enticed by the promise of gold (6.136), and the parallel with the arguments made by Aristagoras to the Athenians in 499 (5.97.1), which were unsuccessful at Sparta (5.49.8).

36. For a full analysis of this element of Greek thought in Herodotus' *Histories* and in Athenian democratic ideology, see Forsdyke (2001). Compare Gray (1997); Cartledge (2002) 77, 112–13.

37. Forsdyke (2001). For a detailed treatment of the formation of Greek identity, see Hall (2002).

38. Although Herodotus articulates this principle in his own voice in this passage, parallels with other expressions of Athenian democratic ideology in Greek literature show that Herodotus is echoing here Athenian modes of validating their political system: see Forsdyke (2001).

39. For the term *isēgoriē* as a reference to democracy, see Cartledge (2002) 112. On this and other circumlocutions for democracy in Herodotus, see Forsdyke (2001) 333 n.13.

40. See Raaflaub (1987), Derow (1995), Pelling (1997b), Dewald (1997).

41. On this debate, see also Pelling in this volume.

42. Raaflaub (1987) 229. See especially the arguments of Cleon and Diodotus in the Mytilenean debate (Thuc. 3.42), as pointed out by Raaflaub, as well as Thucydides' representation of the Athenian decision to invade Sicily (6.8–26), and Aristophanes' representation of Athenian decision-making, especially in the *Knights*. See also Plato's *Gorgias* for the comparison of democratic politicians to pastrycooks. For a complete discussion of critics of democratic rule, see Ober (1998).

43. Rood (1999). On greed and Athenian imperialism, see Balot (2001) chs. 4–5. Pelling (1997b) 2–3 points out that Herodotus represents Themistocles as utilising deception to get the Greeks to fight the Persians at Salamis, and thus casts further doubt on the Greek value of open debate.

44. See also 6.98.2, where Herodotus comments on the extreme suffering of the Greeks as a result of both the Persian Wars and conflict among the Greeks themselves (the Peloponnesian War).

45. See Osborne (2002), Forsdyke (2002), and Harrison (2002).

46. The bibliography on tyranny in Herodotus is extensive: see Dewald (2003) for a recent summary of previous scholarship.

47. Lateiner (1989) 163–86.

48. Waters (1971), Gray (1996), Dewald (2003).

49. This is also true for Herodotus' portraits of oriental monarchs, which according to Dewald (2003) are more prominently shaped according to the construction of tyranny in Greek ideology.

50. This theme most famously shapes the story of the Lydian King Croesus' encounter with the Athenian statesman Solon (1.30–33). Yet in the case of Croesus, several scholars have argued that the story is formed in part as an illustration of the principle of democratic equality (Kurke [1999] 148–50, Wohl [2002] 232–3). For Herodotus as a theorist of democratic equality, see also Saxonhouse (1996). For Herodotus and modern political theory, see Thompson (1996).

51. Vansina (1985), Appadurai (1981). See Forsdyke (1999) for an example of how one of Herodotus' narratives reveals traces of its original political context in the archaic period.
52. Connor (1987).
53. See Sinos (1994), Bassi (1998), Blok (2000), and Forsdyke (2005) 112–18 for further discussion of this episode in terms of the role of civic ritual in creating political legitimacy among archaic Greek leaders.

16

PHILIP STADTER

Herodotus and the cities of mainland Greece

> This much I know: if everyone in the world were to bring his own evils along
> to market to barter them with his neighbours, a glimpse of his neighbours'
> evils would make him happy to take back home those he had brought. The
> Argives didn't act more shamefully than others.
>
> (Hdt. 7.152)

Herodotus no doubt violated the expectations of his Spartan, Athenian, Theban, and Corinthian audiences. Reading his written text, they discovered that when he promised to 'travel through both small and large "cities of men"' (1.5.3), he would have much to say about Lydia, Egypt, Persia, Scythia, and Libya, but not give their own cities a major part until Book 5, half-way through the *Histories*, and even then in a curiously fragmented and disjointed manner. Only with the sequence of grand battles against the Persians (7.131–9.113) do the Greek cities come to centre stage.

The structure of Herodotus' written history – and no doubt the topics of many of his oral performances – shifted the perspective of his audience from their own civic world and inter-city rivalries to a much broader view in space and time. Herodotus, after all, was in several ways an outsider. Born in Halicarnassus, a tributary state first of Persia, then of Athens, into a mixed Carian-Greek family,[1] he left his city as an exile and travelled extensively in both Greek and non-Greek lands, until he settled in the new Athenian-sponsored but panhellenic city of Thurii on the heel of Italy.[2] A marginal figure, half Greek, half barbarian, he could view the events of mainland Greece with a curious but detached eye. As he composed his history c. 445–428 BCE, Greece was convulsed by the rivalry, and finally the open war, of Sparta and Athens. This contemporary conflict furnished a sharp contrast to the united effort which had driven off the invader in 480–479, but a keen observer could see the roots of the later clash even in that heroic moment.

The perspective of an outsider frames Herodotus' first significant passage on Greek history (1.56–68). Sparta and Athens enter the narrative because Croesus of Lydia needed Greek allies in the 540s for his war against Persia.[3] The next major segment of Greek pre-Persian Wars history, 5.39–96, is introduced ostensibly for the same reason, when Aristagoras of Miletus sought aid in 499 from the same two cities for the revolt he was raising in Ionia.[4] In

Herodotus' narrative Sparta and Athens are the strongest cities of Greece and the bravest and most effective defenders against Persia; other mainland cities appear chiefly as they become involved with them, or refuse to participate in the Persian Wars. Of the two, Sparta's power was the better established, based on its early domination of the Peloponnese (1.68.6). Athens, long held down by the Peisistratid tyranny, only became a leading power, as shown by its defeat of Chalcis, after the establishment of the democracy c. 508 (5.77–8). From that time on, the *Histories* presents Greek affairs as centred on the efforts of the two cities to defend their own interests and extend their control. Fortunately for Greece, Sparta's and Athens' interests coincided – but just barely – during the Persian invasion.

The role of the historian-inquirer, the *histor*, was to sort through stories and traditions about the past, and when possible to make some sort of evaluation. Although Herodotus' stated purpose is to assign praise, he is not afraid to blame as well, beginning from his prefatory statement that Croesus was the 'first to wrong the Greeks' (1.5). In one sense his work is an encomium of the Greek struggle for freedom, yet he does not see history in black and white. At the point when the Argives decide not to join the Greek cause, he offers a parable, 'the market of evils', which is quoted in the epigraph of this article. Each city, like each individual, has acted badly at some point, and the historian reveals both good and bad actions in his narrative.

Herodotus' account is far too complex to summarise, nor is this the place to review the individual histories of the Greek cities. Close examination of a limited number of anecdotes and their relations with other parts of the *Histories* will illuminate what this 'outside observer' thought of the actions of the Greek cities both before and during the Persian Wars, and in his own day. Herodotus' preface tells us what to look for: great deeds, responsibility or guilt (*aitiē*), and the instability of human affairs.

Sparta

The Spartan dual kingship distinguished Sparta from the rest of the Greek *poleis*, and assimilated it more to Lydia or Persia. As with these countries, in speaking of Sparta Herodotus focusses on the actions and quarrels of the kings, to the almost complete exclusion of other internal politics. In an ethnographic digression unique to his accounts of the Greek cities, Herodotus highlights the kings' extraordinary privileges, including their special burial rites and their right to wage war against whatever land they wished (6.56). For us the precise truth of the latter assertion is less important than what it says about Herodotus' representation of Sparta. The Spartan kings, like the Persian, have absolute power to wage war, although unlike the Persian kings, they might be opposed by their co-king, as Cleomenes was in Attica (5.75), or put on trial after their return, as happened to Cleomenes after his Argive campaign (6.82.1). A king's position, though exalted, was never secure: Cleomenes challenged Demaratus' legitimacy, and drove him from the throne; he himself had to flee Sparta when his tricks were discovered; Leotychidas went into exile after being accused of accepting bribes (6.72).

Several Spartan scenes illuminate themes of dominance and defeat, of bravery and isolation, and of poverty and the longing for wealth. Sparta first appears at 1.65–8: after Lycurgus' constitutional changes have established good government, the Spartans immediately decide to conquer Arcadia, chains in hand. Their marching out with fetters to enslave presents a model of imperialism; that they end up fettered themselves proves the inscrutability of divine communication, the instability of human prosperity, and the eventual defeat of the conqueror.

Fetters reappear at significant moments in the *Histories*. Croesus, who thought to conquer Cyrus, is defeated and ends up in fetters on a funeral pyre (1.86.2). The fetters establish a parallel between Sparta's confidence in its new prosperity and eagerness to conquer other nations and Croesus' confidence in his wealth and desire to attack the Persians preemptively, 'to stop their power as it was growing' (1.46). Later the Spartans imitate Croesus in wanting to forestall the dangers of Athens' rapid growth under the democracy by reinstalling Hippias as tyrant (5.91.1–2). Significantly, Thucydides assigns the same reason to Sparta's decision to go to war in 432.[5] The Spartan fetters resonate also with the fetters which Xerxes throws into the Hellespont, believing he was enslaving the sea – an analogy for his bridging of the Hellespont and attempt to enslave Greece (7.35.1, cf. 8.109.3).

Fetters are a symbol of domination and enslavement; in each of these cases they are also associated with misunderstanding the relation of man and god, and eventual defeat.[6] Herodotus introduces Sparta as a city which wishes to dominate and does. The first attempt at enslavement of Tegea failed, but later, after bringing the bones of Orestes to Sparta, they defeat the Tegeans. The secret is a new kind of 'fetter'. Led by an oracle, the Spartan Lichas discovers at a smithy in Arcadia the bones of Orestes, 'where blow answers blow, and grief is piled on grief' (1.67). Fetters are made in smithies, and bring grief: the bones of Orestes will provide the new, gentler bonds which defeat Tegea, and bring most of the Peloponnese under their control (1.68).

Sparta, confident in its good government and prosperity, acts as an imperial power to dominate others. Several times Sparta attempts to project its power in Libya, Italy, and Sicily, and across the Aegean to Asia, without success.[7] Its focus thus remains in mainland Greece, especially during the extremely aggressive reign of Cleomenes, who invaded Athens twice (5.64–5, 74–5),[8] took hostages from Aegina, and destroyed the military might of Argos.

Regarding the attacks on Athens, Herodotus expects his audience to have the contemporary history of Sparta's invasions of Attica in mind. Cleomenes' failed second invasion of Attica, he notes, was the fourth Dorian invasion of Attica, two for the good of the Athenian people, two for harm (5.76.1). This list of invasions stimulates his audience to extend it into their own time, remembering that Sparta had promised to invade Attica c. 465 (Thuc. 1.101.2), invaded in 446 (Thuc. 1.114.2), and finally began regular annual invasions in 431.[9]

Cleomenes finally killed himself by slicing himself into mincemeat. The explanations of the Greeks and Spartans for so horrendous an end indicate violation of custom (*nomos*), those of the Athenians and Argives tie Cleomenes' military aggression to divine transgression (6.75.3–84).[10] Cleomenes is a madman: like Cambyses (3.38.1), he violates human and divine law. As king of Sparta, he personifies the imperialist side of Sparta, its urge to dominate both within the Peloponnese, including Argos and Aegina, and beyond, with its invasions of Athens.

Yet Sparta shows, alongside the desire to dominate, and hand in hand with its extraordinary bravery, a fundamental isolation, a drawing in upon itself. The battle of Thermopylae represents the acme of Spartan bravery and self-sacrifice, especially after they learn of their encirclement (7.223–5). Leonidas consciously chose death, knowing that only by the death of a king could Sparta be saved and win glory (7.220). The Spartan sacrifice established the model for Greek resistance. Yet the Spartans died in splendid isolation from the main body of Greeks. Their fate resembles that which Herodotus earlier had envisioned if the Athenians had not resisted the Persians: 'the Spartans would have been abandoned, and under those circumstances would have died bravely, after performing great deeds' (7.139).[11] This passage highlights Sparta's independence of action, and its cost. The wall across the Isthmus, on which they and the Peloponnesians they led placed such reliance, would be useless. The Persian fleet would circumvent the Isthmian wall as surely as Xerxes' men had bypassed the wall Leonidas defended at the pass.[12]

Herodotus offers a sceptical reading for the Peloponnesians' frantic effort to fortify the Isthmus, behind which the Peloponnesian army and most of the Greek navy wished to hide,[13] and shows its effect on Athens. The Athenians were disappointed after Thermopylae at learning that 'the Peloponnesians were constructing a wall across the Isthmus, because what mattered to them was the survival of the Peloponnese, and therefore they were defending it and letting the rest go' (8.40.2). In winter 480/479, after the battle of Salamis, the

Spartans refused to aid Athens, Herodotus reports, because 'they had built the wall at the Isthmus and thought they no longer needed the Athenians' (9.8.2). Sparta does not fight for Greece, but first for itself, then for the Peloponnese which it controls. Only when struck with fear that the wall might not suffice do they march to the aid of Athens (9.9–10). As Herodotus tells it, the battle of Plataea, a resounding achievement of Spartan courage, was fought not to save Greece – and certainly not to save Athens – but to keep Athens on the Peloponnesian side. The rock by which Amompharetus signaled at Plataea his refusal to move from his position (9.55.2) represents both the courageous solidity in standing and fighting and the pigheaded foolishness of the Spartan isolationist position. After the victories of Plataea and Mycale, King Leotychidas will withdraw most of the Greek fleet from Ionia, and leave the Aegean to the Athenians (9.114). His action foreshadows Sparta's renunciation of a role in Ionia and is of a piece with its earlier isolationism and trust in infantry warfare. The Athenians will gladly expand to fill the vacuum of power.

The Spartans are austere but feel the allure of riches, and often succumb. Cleomenes twice was sorely tempted (3.148; 5.51), and the Spartan commanders Eurybiades and Leotychidas took bribes (8.4–5; 6.72). Even Glaucus, reputedly the most honest of the Spartans, tried to keep money deposited with him (6.86). Herodotus' contemporary audience knew that Pausanias had not been satisfied with the enormous wealth he gained as victor at Plataea – 'the most glorious of any victory known to us' (9.64.1) – but that he later tried to ally himself with the Persians.[14] The very detail of the description of the royal table which Pausanias had set after Plataea to mock the Persians ironically highlights the Spartan fascination with luxury.

Herodotus admires unreservedly the heroic aspect of Spartan *nomos*, that customary law which the exiled king Demaratus told Xerxes was the Spartans' master. The Spartans are brave, he said, and 'as a group they are the bravest of men. For while they are free, they are not completely free. Over them *nomos* rules as a despot, which they fear even more than your troops do you. . . . It exhorts them to remain in their battle position, and to conquer or die' (7.104). Leonidas at Thermopylae proved the truth of his words. In two anecdotes occurring after Plataea, the victor Pausanias observes other Spartan *nomoi*: he spares a captive Greek woman who had been a Persian concubine (9.76), and he refuses to mistreat Mardonius' corpse as Xerxes had Leonidas' (9.78). Noble actions, except that there is again an ironic subtext for the reader, for Pausanias later was accused of killing a young free woman of Byzantium whom he had summoned to his bed.[15] Earlier Herodotus had alluded to the hubris which alienated Pausanias from the Ionians (8.3.2, cf. Thuc. 1.95.1). Incidents like Cleomenes' sacrileges and

Pausanias' hubris remind the audience that not all Spartans follow the noble *nomos* described by Demaratus.

In Herodotus' narrative, then, the Spartans were exceptionally brave, but given to dominate others with their army whenever they could, and to withdraw into the Peloponnese when they couldn't. Major decisions were in the hands of the twin monarchs, and their struggle to acquire or maintain power dominated the internal politics of the city. Spartan claims to lead Greece were self-interested, and challenged by the rise of Athens. While Spartans were proud of their subjection to *nomos* and their poor and tough way of life, leaders often eagerly grasped at wealth and luxury when offered the opportunity.

Athens

When we turn to Croesus' and Aristagoras' other focus of attention, Athens, we discover that Herodotus' narrative centres on three major features: the Athenians' heroic decision to abandon their city and fight from their ships; democracy as a source of strength for the Athenians; and the relation of Athenian freedom to their imperialism. Herodotus' Athenians thus share some moral features with the Spartans – notably bravery and a desire for power, but their character, shaped by democracy and the willingness to take risks, is quite different.

Herodotus is amazed that the Athenians, though they were forced to abandon their city, continued to fight the invaders with their fleet. Their aggressive bravery is dramatised in the dialogue of Adeimantus and Themistocles before Salamis (8.61) and elicits Herodotus' extraordinary statement (7.139):

> whoever should claim that the Athenians were saviours of Greece would accurately state the truth . . . . Once they chose for Greece to remain free, they were the ones who roused all the rest of Greece . . . and with the help of the gods, pushed back the king.

While the Peloponnesians hoped to hide behind the Isthmus wall, the Athenians, by their willingness to fight despite the destruction of their city, kept themselves and the other Greeks free. Themistocles' strategy of taking to the ships proved the Athenians' absolute commitment to freedom, as Leonidas' heroic stand at Thermopylae had done for Sparta. Like their daring charge against the Persians at Marathon (6.112.3), it demonstrates their democratic dedication to freedom. The Athenians renew their commitment the following winter, when Alexander of Macedon appeals to them to join Persia. In their reply to the Spartans who feared they would accept, they insist, 'as long as just one Athenian survives, we will never make an agreement with Xerxes'

(8.144). Nevertheless, they had to see Attica occupied a second time. It is a measure, not of the Athenians' resolve, but of their abandonment by Sparta, that in spring 479, frustrated by Spartan delays, they threaten to join the invader (9.11).[16]

Sparta was led by its two kings; Athens found its strength in citizen equality. In Croesus' day the tyrant Peisistratus had held the city in subjection (1.59–64). His son Hippias was expelled in 510, and soon after Cleisthenes established the democracy. This new system allowed the Athenians to resist Cleomenes' attempt to reimpose tyranny in Athens, and then to defeat in one day the Boeotians and Chalcidians (5.72, 77). Herodotus does not explain how the new system actually functioned, but he marvels at its success: 'Once they were freed, each man eagerly achieved something for himself' (5.78). Themistocles offers a special example of the individual energy released by democratic freedom. He brilliantly devised the defence at Salamis, and equally successfully schemed to gain wealth for himself and favour with the Persian king.

Athenian freedom and dynamism, in Herodotus' view, expressed themselves in the Athenians' resistance to the Persians at Marathon and Salamis, but also lay behind their later push to win empire. The victory over Chalcis was the first step toward empire; typically, it was a response to pressure from Sparta and its allies. Athens' foolhardy decision to join the Ionian revolt similarly was stimulated by Spartan and Persian support of Hippias' return (5.91, 96). Before the battle of Marathon Miltiades set the choice starkly: Athens could submit, or win and 'become the first city of Greece' (6.109.3). Herodotus couples the courage to resist with the ambition to rule. The Athenians restrained their desire for preeminence for the duration of the war (famously at Artemisium, 8.3, and at Plataea, 9.27), but when opportunity offered, they struck out on their own. Profiting from the hubris of Pausanias, they 'snatched hegemony from the Lacedaemonians' (8.3.2). To Herodotus' audience Athens' domination of the cities of the Aegean was a reality founded on the power of its fleet, exaction of tribute, and ruthless suppression of revolts. Herodotus intimates these developments when he shows Themistocles using the Greek fleet to extort money immediately after Salamis, though not at this point for Athens alone (8.111).[17] The Athenians' patronage of the Ionians in the conference at Samos (9.109) would quickly lead to an Athenian empire. Herodotus knew that Athens would follow Croesus' precedent in subjecting the Greeks to pay tribute (1.6, cf. 1.27). That tribute, he notes, was being paid 'down to my day' (6.42) – to Athens.[18]

As the wily Themistocles balances the stolid Pausanias, two Athenian noble families, the Alcmaeonids and the Philaids, seem to be counterparts to the two Spartan royal families, and like them offer anecdotes which help define the city. Alcmaeon son of Megacles used his ingenuity to enrich his family with the gold of Croesus, and was not ashamed to look ridiculous doing so (6.125). His family, the Alcmaeonids, produced another Megacles, a sometime associate and later enemy of Peisistratus, Cleisthenes, the founder of the democracy, and finally Pericles (6.131). The difference of Alcmaeon's opportunism from Solon's thoughtful calm in the presence of Croesus' gold is striking. Solon, though an Athenian, seems more a type of Herodotus himself.[19] Pericles appears not the heir of Solon, but of a much more practical man. The other nobleman is Miltiades, who fled his tyranny in the Chersonese first to Lemnos, which he seized for the Athenians, then to Athens, just in time to become a hero at Marathon. Buoyed by his success, he attempted to extort 100 talents from Paros, but failed and died in disgrace (6.133–6). His son Cimon was an outstanding commander and a rival of Pericles. These Athenians, like Themistocles, are characterised as doers, able to deal with diverse situations, and this partially explains their willingness to accept Spartan leadership during the Persian Wars, if it would permit them to drive the enemy from Attica. Their dynamism laid the groundwork for Athens' empire in the Aegean.

The Athenians proclaim Herodotus' most noble statement of Greek unity, recalling to the Spartans 'our Greekness – one blood, one language, with shared temples to the gods and religious rites, and a shared way of life' (8.144.2). This vision was utopian: such unity had not and would not exist. Herodotus is well aware of the irony of the Athenians' enthusiasm, which only a few months later would fade as the Spartans refused to send help.[20] Athens' resolution may have been short-lived, but the truth it expressed was real. The speeches capture both the nobility and ephemerality of the panhellenic idea. Other moments of nobility are also tinged with irony. The fateful decision to help the Ionian revolt (5.97) is motivated by ignorance of Persian strength, but also a desire to rescue Miletus, which had been settled from Athens. Herodotus smiles at the folly of the crowd's decision, which Cleomenes had managed to avoid. The same support for their Ionian kin reappears in 479, when the question of protecting Ionia comes up (9.106). The Peloponnesians offered to resettle the Ionians in mainland Greece, an action fraught with pain for both Ionia and Greece. The Athenians chose to ally themselves with the Ionians, a decision combining foolhardiness, concern for their kin, and political ambition. Unlike the Spartans, the Athenians did not wish to withdraw behind an Isthmus wall, but to reach out across the Aegean. Herodotus' audience would perceive the irony of the Athenian support and the Ionians' pledge 'to remain in the alliance and never revolt' (9.106). They knew that the alliance would become an empire, revolts would be put down ruthlessly, and the dream of Greek unity would become a struggle for domination.

Other cities: Argos, Thebes, Aegina, and Corinth

The other mainland cities Herodotus presents in the shadow of the two leaders, as they were in his day, when the Greek cities were forced to choose sides between the two rivals. Though many others are mentioned (twenty-one are listed at Salamis, twenty-four at Plataea),[21] Herodotus is chiefly interested in Argos, Thebes, Aegina, and Corinth, which had famous pasts, and whose actions during the Persian Wars and at the outset of the Peloponnesian War created the possibility of an irony seldom explicitly stated.

The portrait of Argos thrusts to the fore the problem of Spartan aggression in the Peloponnese. Argos was an ancient city fallen on hard times: Herodotus recalls its legendary history (1.1, 5.61) and the strong tyrant Pheidon (6.127), but also its defeat by Sparta at Thyrea c. 545 (1.82). Cleomenes of Sparta destroyed Argive military strength early in the fifth century (6.76–82). When the Greek league asked that Argos join the fight against the Persian invaders (7.148–52), the Argives insisted on two things: a treaty with Sparta – Herodotus explains, 'they feared they would find themselves under Spartan control forever . . . if they met another disaster at the hands of the Persians' – and a return to their legendary role in Peloponnesian affairs. Herodotus knows other versions which made Argos an active Persian ally, but his chief point is that Sparta's aggression against Argos has soured any possibility of Argos joining the Greek alliance. As the Argives state succinctly, 'they preferred to be ruled by the Persians rather than submit to the Spartans' (7.149).[22]

Thebes exemplifies a city whose leaders willingly support the Persians. Though an ancient Greek city, home of Laius and Oedipus (5.58–61), its position directly on the invasion march and their hostility to the newly victorious Athenian democracy combine to make them oppose the Greek alliance.[23] Again, a dynamic state's assertion of power over a neighbour explains a split in the common Greek cause, though Herodotus is not explicit. When Xerxes asked for earth and water, the Thebans complied (7.132). Herodotus asserts that 300 Thebans were present at Thermopylae against their will, and rushed forward to surrender to the Persians (7.233). This appears to be an anti-Theban legend, reported by Herodotus to set up an antithesis between Spartan bravery and Theban acquiescence to superior power. From this point on, the Thebans are unremittingly hostile to the alliance. Before Salamis, they urge the Persians to burn Plataea and Thespiae (8.50). When Mardonius reenters Boeotia in spring 479, the Thebans urge him to make his base at Thebes, treacherously suggesting that bribes will be more effective than warfare in defeating the Greeks (9.2). When Mardonius establishes himself at Thebes, they honour the Persians with banquets (9.15–16), and offer advice before the battle of Plataea (9.31, 38, 40). In the battle they fight eagerly, without holding back, against the Athenians and at the last moment cut down 600 Megarians and Phleiasians (9.67, 69). When the Thebans after a siege finally surrender their leaders to the Greeks, Pausanias has them executed at once (9.86–8). Herodotus' portrait of the Thebans, 'enthusiastic Medisers' (9.40), is thus uniformly negative. In part this presentation suggests how much the Athenians might have hurt the Greeks if they too had gone over to the Persians, whether to preserve their land from destruction or to assume the hegemony with Persian support. Other themes are less certain, but should include the general revulsion of the Athenians and Peloponnesians toward the Thebans' behaviour, irony at the Peloponnesians' alliance with Thebes in 432,[24] and not least criticism of the Thebans' treacherous attack on Plataea, which triggered the Peloponnesian War. Herodotus reminds his audience of this attack when he identifies the Theban leader at Thermopylae, Leontiadas, as father of Eurymachus, the leader of the band of Thebans killed by the Plataeans after he had captured their city.[25]

Herodotus' account of Aegina portrays a state which might have accepted Persian rule, but under Spartan and Athenian pressure chose to join the Greeks and fought heroically at Salamis. The path was tortuous, but is exemplary for how Herodotus saw hostility among the Greek cities as yielding to a short-lived unity, and even being required for Greek success. The ancient and wealthy sea-power[26] already held a grudge against Athens when, in response to a Theban appeal for their aid against the new democracy, they raided the Attic coast (5.79–81). When they also promised earth and water to Darius, the Athenians complained to Cleomenes, who after fighting with his colleague Demaratus took hostages from Aegina and deposited them in Athens. From this, and Athens' later refusal to restore the hostages, arose a war which divided Aegina and led to a major naval battle, which Athens won (6.87–94). Herodotus does not take clear sides, finding injustice in both camps.[27] However, whereas the wars of Sparta and Argos had incapacitated the latter, Aegina and Athens grew stronger. The Aeginetan threat persuaded the Athenians to accept Themistocles' advice to use their windfall discovery of the Laurion silver mine to build 200 new triremes, ships which were first used in the war with Persia. Herodotus underlines the paradox: 'the outbreak of this war saved Greece by forcing the Athenians to become seamen' (7.144). Without the hostility of Aegina, Herodotus asserts, the Athenians would never have attempted the control of the sea. The war with Aegina, like the defeat of Chalcis, also gave the young democracy the self-confidence from which sprang not only the victory over Persia but the fifth-century Athenian empire. As the Persians advanced, Aegina and Athens, like other cities, agreed to set aside their quarrel (7.145), and at Salamis we find Polycritus, son of one of the Aeginetan hostages who had caused so much trouble, joking ironically with the Athenian commander, Themistocles (8.92) and winning the prize for bravery.[28] But the moment of camaraderie would soon pass: in mid-century war broke out once more, the Athenians besieged Aegina and subjected it to tribute, and at the beginning of the Peloponnesian War, banished them and resettled the island (6.91.1, cf. Thuc. 2.27). Their ties with Sparta now made them untrustworthy. For Herodotus and his audience, Greek unity belonged to an almost inconceivable past.

Corinth, like Aegina, had to negotiate a path between Sparta and Athens, but was always fully committed to the Greek cause and is represented in all the major battles. Stories of its sixth-century tyrants, Cypselus and Periander, allow Herodotus to explore themes of political and personal power more often associated with the despots of Persia. Thus although in the Arion story Periander plays the role of a wise judge (1.23–4), in two other stories he is the complete tyrant, who kills his wife, makes his son an outcast, and sends Corcyraean children to Persia to be eunuchs (3.48–53), while slaughtering the best men of Corinth and insulting their wives (5.92η).[29] These stories echo those of the mad violence of Cambyses, or the vicious whims of Darius and Xerxes.[30] However, they also insist on the attractiveness of tyranny, despite its evils: 'it is better to be envied than pitied', Periander tells his son (3.52.5). Tyranny can be attractive not only to the tyrant, but also to those who permit it to grow, as Soclees' story of Cypselus demonstrates. The Bacchiads of Corinth cannot bring themselves to kill the young Cypselus, nor, Soclees suggests, can Sparta resist installing Hippias as tyrant in Athens (5.92). Corinth has had the experience of tyranny, knows its dangers, and perhaps for this reason staunchly resists the Persians. Yet Corinth's experience demonstrates that despotism is not confined to Persia: Greeks also lust after it when they can.[31]

A firm ally of Sparta, Corinth can nevertheless contest Sparta's attempt to dominate Athens, refusing to invade Attica with Cleomenes, and opposing the restoration of Hippias (5.75, 92). For a time relations with Athens were good, such that Corinth lent twenty ships to Athens to use against Aegina (6.89). Herodotus expected his audience to find this surprising, noting that the cities 'were especially friendly in those days' (6.89). Trouble would come, as Hippias prophesied (5.93). The allusion certainly is to the mid-fifth-century warfare between the two cities, culminating in Corinth's participation in the Peloponnesian invasion of Attica in 431. In Herodotus' narrative, their hostility emerges into the open at the time of the battle of

Salamis. In council, Adeimantus, the Corinthian commander harshly opposes Themistocles' plan to fight in the straits, and the two exchange insults (8.59–61). Herodotus seems to report an Athenian version of the battle, in which Adeimantus and the Corinthians fled at the first encounter, only to show Athenian hostility, for he notes that the Corinthians claimed to be among the first to fight, 'and the rest of Greece supports them' (8.94). Whatever the Athenians said, the Corinthians did not abandon the Greek cause. Like the other Peloponnesians, they hoped to find safety behind the Isthmian wall, but 5,000 marched to Plataea (9.28). At Mycale the Corinthians fought by the side of the Athenians, and took the second prize for bravery (9.105). After its experience of tyranny, Corinth rejected Sparta's attempt to impose a tyrant on Athens, but joined Sparta in its opposition to Persian rule.

*

The *Histories* shows each city to be noble in some cases, self-serving in others. The parable of 'the market of evils' with which Herodotus defended his role as *histor* is borne out. In the great crisis of the Persian invasion, Athens and Sparta led the cities of Greece to victory, but their exceptional nobility and courage was born in a stew of ambitions for domination, petty arguments, and rash action. The struggles of Argos, Aegina, and Corinth to play their own part enrich the canvas with themes of defeat, injustice, and tyranny. Only Thebes comes across as wholly unworthy of its legendary past.

Herodotus' focus on Sparta and Athens as the two preeminent powers in Greece made his *Histories* immediate to his audience. As has been seen, he ties past events to his own time frequently throughout his work. In particular, he connects prominent men from several cities with their sons active c. 430, mentioning Pericles and Archidamus, the Athenian and Spartan leaders of the war, as well as the Corinthian Adeimantus and the Theban Eurymachus.[32] These obvious references to the time of composition encourage us to consider how the text might have been understood, recalling always how audience perspectives would have varied, both from city to city, and within the cities.

The evils for Greece which began under Darius, Herodotus insists, continued under Xerxes and Artaxerxes beyond his own stopping point of 479, and came not only from the Persians, but 'from the wars of the leading states (of Greece) for domination' (6.98). The double question of freedom and domination, so fundamental to the *Histories*, was central not only to the struggle against Persia, but also to Herodotus' own day, when Sparta and Athens were locked in a new war, in which the Peloponnesians claimed to be 'freeing Greece', and the Athenians asserted that they would 'never yield' to Spartan rule (Thuc. 2.8.4, 1.140.1).

Recently scholars, rejecting the view that Herodotus was pro-Athenian, have noted that at the end of his work Athens takes on the role which Persia held in Ionia, and that it was on the road to enslave the cities of its league, as Sparta and its allies proclaimed in justification for the Peloponnesian War (Thuc. 2.8.4).[33] This reading must be balanced against Herodotus' presentation of Sparta. In the *Histories*, Sparta's power is based on its domination of the Peloponnese, which was established early and confirmed by Cleomenes' near-destruction of Argos. Cleomenes crossed every sort of boundary, physical, religious, and moral. Sparta, which relied on its peerless army to interfere in other states, notably Athens and Aegina, is similar to eastern kings in responding with aggression to the growth of a rival, in violating boundaries, the proper treatment of gods, and customary law (especially seen in the 'madness' of Cleomenes), and in waging war at the whim of a monarch (3.80). Sparta itself is well-governed, and rejects tyrants, but is eager to instal a tyrant at Athens to protect its own interests, and its greatest commander, Pausanias, later attempted to establish himself as a tyrant in Greece. Thus Sparta emerges with its own evils, parallel to those of Athens. The idea of Sparta fighting for the freedom of Greece in 431 is distinctly ironic to one who has absorbed Herodotus' accounts of the Greek cities.

The *Histories* demonstrates, on the other hand, that Greece was able to defeat the Persians only when Sparta and Athens, the two leading powers, realised that each needed the other. Only by fighting side by side could either one preserve its freedom. The praise of Athens at 7.139 counters the Spartan propaganda that it alone saved Greece from the Persians, and would again save it in 431 from the Athenians. The parable of 'the market of evils' (7.152) holds true especially for the two leading cities: neither state would want to take up the evils of the other; neither could say that it was better. Herodotus seems to have found in his inquiry that harmony between the two was necessary for each, and for all Greece. Cimon, the pro-Laconian Athenian, had advised the Athenians at the time of the Spartan earthquake, 'do not allow Greece to go lame, nor Athens to lose its yoke-fellow' (Plut. *Cim.* 16). Herodotus agreed. Athens and Sparta should not be fighting for domination, but working together as two strong legs or a team of oxen to the benefit of all Greek cities, large and small.

FURTHER READING

General. Immerwahr (1966) 189–237 provides a good overall view, and can be supplemented by Gould (1989) and Lateiner (1989). On Herodotus' local sources, see especially Luraghi (2001b). For an ancient criticism of

Herodotus' presentation of the Greek cities, see Plutarch, *On the Malignity of Herodotus*, with Marincola (1994).

On Athens and Sparta, see Boedeker (1987), Fornara (1971a), Forrest (1984) and Moles (1996) and (2002), Munson (2001a) 52–66, 176–8, and Stadter (1992). On Aegina, see Figueira (1985). On Corinth and its tyrants, see Sourvinou-Inwood (1988) and Gray (1996).

NOTES

1. Apparently: his father Lyxes and uncle Panyassis bear Carian names.
2. For some of the implications of his residence in Thurii, see Munson's chapter in this volume.
3. Compare the references to Croesus' inquiry at 1.56.1, 1.59.1, 1.65.1, 1.69.1.
4. Compare other points of contact at 1.82, 1.152, 3.39–60, and 6.49–93.
5. Thuc. 1.118.2, cf. 1. 23.6, 1.86.5, 1.88.
6. Compare other significant references to fetters at 1.92 (Croesus sends his fetters to Delphi), 3.22.2, 23.4 (Cambyses sends gold chains to the Ethiopian king as necklaces) and 3.129.3, 130.4 (Darius rewards Democedes with gold chains), and 5.77.3–4 (Athens defeats the Chalcidians).
7. Hdt. 1.70, 77, 82–3, 3.57. Cleomenes resisted the temptation to fight in Asia, 3.148, 5.50. Cleomenes' general aggressiveness did not preclude restraint, just as Croesus held back from the Ionian islands (1.27). His half-brother Dorieus attempted to found a colony in Libya, then in Sicily, perhaps fighting at Sybaris as well: 5.42–7, cf. *CAH* (2nd edn) IV.751–2.
8. Cleomenes also tried to instal Isagoras as tyrant in Athens, 5.70–72.
9. Compare the specific reference to wartime invasions at 9.73.3.
10. The connection is common: cf. Athens' burning of the temples in Sardis (5.102.1) and Xerxes' wanton destruction.
11. Herodotus mentions another alternative, that they would have come to terms with Xerxes.
12. Demaratus' advice to Xerxes to seize Cythera, the island off the coast of Laconia (7.235), confirms Herodotus' opinion of the danger to the Peloponnese.
13. Compare 8.40, 49, 63, 71.
14. Herodotus was not certain that he 'wanted to become tyrant of Greece' (5.32), but Thucydides has no doubts of his perfidy (1.128–34).
15. Plut. *Cim.* 6.4–5, *De sera num. vind.* 555C.
16. Herodotus implies the Athenians will not fight vainly to the death, but he had suggested the same of Sparta (7.139.4).
17. Themistocles' later extortion from other islanders was for personal gain and not official (8.112).
18. The Athenians' ruthless suppression in 440–439 of the revolt of Samos, a major Ionian city (cf. Shipley [1987]) with an important role in the *Histories*, would have been foremost in the minds of Herodotus' audience.
19. Moles (1996). See also Friedman in this volume.
20. Pelling, however, above, pp. 113–14, sees the Athenian threat to join the Persians as a rhetorical gambit, not intended to be acted on.
21. Corcyra avoided Salamis, playing it safe, as it tried to do c. 433: cf. 7.168.

22. Thanks to a thirty-year peace with Sparta, Argos remained uninvolved during the first decade of the Peloponnesian War.

23. Thebes had supported Peisistratus (1.61), was vexed by Athens' alliance with Plataea (6.108), and angered again by the Athenians' victory over the Boeotians (5.77, although the Boeotians had attacked Athens first, 5.74). Soon it joined Aegina in raiding Attica (5.79–81).

24. Thucydides develops this irony in several points of his narrative of the siege and trial of the Plataeans.

25. The very fact of this notice is more indicative of Herodotus' interest than the slight disparity with Thuc. 2.2.3.

26. Herodotus thought the wealth of the Aeginetan merchant, Sostratus, exceeded all measure, 4.152.

27. Leotychidas' moving story of Glaucus indicates the injustice of the Athenian refusal, 6.86. Compare Immerwahr (1966) 213.

28. The Aeginetans also were present at Plataea, but missed the battle, and Herodotus thinks their tombs there were a false boast.

29. On some of the many themes in these stories, see Gray (1996), Sourvinou-Inwood (1988), Węcowski (1996), Dewald (2003).

30. Compare the table in Lateiner (1989) 172–9.

31. On Soclees' speech, see also Pelling's chapter in this volume.

32. Hdt. 7.137, 7.233.2, 6.131.2, and 6.71.2. Compare for Adeimantus, the Corinthian leader at Potidaea, Thuc. 1.60.2; for Eurymachus, who led, or managed, the attack on Plataea, Thuc. 2.2.3, 2.5.7.

33. Strasburger (1955), Stadter (1992), Moles (1996).

17

ROSARIA VIGNOLO MUNSON

An alternate world: Herodotus and Italy

Herodotus of Thurii

According to Aristotle, the first sentence of the *Histories* introduced it as the work 'of Herodotus of Thurii'.[1] Thurii was a panhellenic colony founded during Herodotus' lifetime (probably 444/443 BCE) under the guidance of Athens, initially by invitation of the Sybarites, on the site of the former Achaean city of Sybaris. It represented, to a great extent, a brilliant communal experiment. After the departure of the old Sybarites, the colony became, or at least strove to be, a *polis* for all Greeks, internally mixed, egalitarian and democratic.[2] If Aristotle is correct, Herodotus' identification with this project at the beginning of his work carries certain ideological consequences.

On the eve of the battle of Salamis, Themistocles declares to the uncooperative Greek allies that the Athenians might leave their home and move to Siris (8.62.2). If 'Herodotus of Thurii' is the first Italian reference in the work, Themistocles' threat is the last. In both passages, implicitly or explicitly, Italy is a place where one starts a new life. By travelling the distance between the one and the other, we will begin to derive from the scattered evidence in the *Histories* Herodotus' unified vision of the Italian West.[3]

Italy in the picture: selections and directions

Herodotus' *logos* is centred on Asia, mainland Greece and the space in between. The Italian peninsula, Sicily, Sardinia and Corsica are secondary to the plot. They appear and disappear frequently, however, in unexpected surroundings, and can be found in every book of the *Histories* except 2 and 9.[4] In many cases – and this is to some extent a separate issue – these passages suggest a Western setting for Herodotus' act of narration, and an audience particularly attuned to Western events and concerns.[5]

Herodotus reaches out to the West at many different levels of discourse. His version of the Lesbian and Corinthian tradition about the rescue of

Arion of Methymna by a dolphin includes Arion's trip to Italy and Sicily (1.24.2, 7). Incidentally inserted in the Scythian *logos* is a mysterious western legend about the appearance in Italian Metapontum of the ghost of the poet/ethnographer Aristeas of Proconnesus (4.14–15). Often the narrator himself in his own voice broadens the setting beyond the 'story': the grandeur of Polycrates of Samos was paralleled only by that of the tyrants of Syracuse (3.125.2); the Tauric Chersonese resembles not only the Attic Cape Sunium, but also the tip of Iapygia (4.99.4–5). At one point Herodotus explains that the Ionians of Panionium chose to form a league of twelve members just as the Achaeans in the Peloponnese have twelve cities (1.145); here he adds that one of these Achaean cities is on the 'always abundant river Crathis, which gave its name to the Italian Crathis' (the latter being a dry stream, as his western audience must have known).[6] In this passage we were speaking of Ionia, then jump to central Greece, then all of the sudden, for one brief moment, we are in the West as if this were home.

When it comes to this part of the world, perhaps because it is marginal but familiar, Herodotus appears especially free to say or not to say what he wants, and to give his narrative any direction he chooses. We notice first of all the peculiar way in which he treats the barbarians in this area. 'Indigenous' populations of Italy and Sicily (Umbrians, Oenotrians, Iapygians, Sicels, Sicans and Segestans) and more exotic inhabitants or newcomers (Etruscans, Western Phoenicians and Carthaginians) appear in the *Histories* as geographical terms or as historical agents. But there are no ethnographic descriptions to foreground their cultural distinctness.[7] More importantly, Herodotus' western barbarians also lack a distinct historical role.[8] The *Histories* as a whole may well be mainly about explaining historical conflicts and cultural differences between Greeks and non-Greeks. But in Herodotus' Italian narratives there is no sharp divide to discuss. The central problem, at any rate, is the political behaviour of Greeks.

Most of the important Greek cities of the West end up being featured in the *Histories*. But we find no reference – except in one case (7.153.1) – to their origins in the eighth and seventh centuries BCE. Most of the traditional features of such stories of early Greek settlements – crisis in the mother country, choice of the group of colonists, Delphic consultations, misinterpretations of oracles, false starts, hardships, encounters with native peoples, and foundation of cities – recur in Herodotus' Italian sections, as does the very vocabulary of colonisation.[9] Herodotus, however, transfers these elements to later journeys, at three crucial moments in the main 'story' of the *Histories*: the first Persian conquest of Ionia, the Ionian revolt, and Xerxes' invasion of Greece (1.161–70; 5.30–51, 6.1–25; 7.145–8.62). The resettlements he describes in these contexts stem from the Greeks' refusal to put up with political oppression at home and represent, therefore, a legitimate means of protection and defence.[10] Reinterpreted in this manner, the pattern of colonisation as escape from difficulties in the homeland also provides the main emplotment for Herodotus' Italian sections.[11]

Concerning the Greek cities of the West, Herodotus gives little information on a range of political issues: their ethnic identity (whether they are Ionian, Dorian, Chalcidian, Achaean and so on),[12] their civil struggles, legislators and constitutional forms of government.[13] Such omissions lend special visibility to a political phenomenon that appears frequently: tyrannical regimes. Throughout the *Histories*, of course, tyranny represents an overarching negative metaphor for immoral political action.[14] What is unique about western Greek tyranny is that it is still flourishing at the time when the central Greeks are free and warding off despotism in the Persian Wars.[15] In the West, moreover, the tyrannical model meets the model of colonisation that informs most of Herodotus' Italian sections. The two are in mutual competition, ideologically antithetical yet dangerously close. A flight to freedom may well become an expedition of conquest or result in the oppression of others.[16]

Getting out from under: the meaning of colonisation

Herodotus' first colonists to the West are not Greek. They are those Lydians who moved to Italy in the heroic age and became the Etruscans of Herodotus' day. Tormented by a famine, the Lydians drew lots to decide who should stay and who should go. Those who left colonised (*apoikisai*, 1.94.2) Umbria and changed their name to Tyrrhenians after their leader Tyrrhenus, the son of the king (1.94.5–7). The Lydian re-settlement in Italy occurred for the sake of 'land and livelihood', like many archaic Greek colonisations, including that to Cyrene, which Herodotus describes in Book 4. But the narrative context of this migration transforms it into an unintended journey to freedom. The Lydians of Lydia, as Herodotus reminds us at the end of the Tyrrhenian section, 'became enslaved to the Persians' (1.94.7).

The Lydians represent a broad paradigm for the Greeks of Asia, vulnerable to conquest by virtue of their geographical location.[17] After the first Persian conquest of Ionia, the sage Bias of Priene sees as the Ionians' only chance for freedom a unified expedition to Sardinia, where they should found (*ktizein*) a pan-Ionian city and 'be forever prosperous in the greatest of all islands, ruling over others' (1.170.1–2). By this time two Ionian communities, the Phocaeans and the Teans, have already left their homes, avoiding the political subjection that befell the others who stayed behind (1.169.1)

The colonising expedition of the Phocaeans, unlike its Lydian archetype, turns out to be problematic. Once upon a time the Phocaeans used to make

mercantile journeys to the remote West and enjoyed the hospitality and protection of Arganthonius, the king of Tartessus. That golden age, however,
gives way to harsher realities.[18] In the face of the Persian threat, 'indignant at
the thought of slavery' (1.164.2; cf. 169.1), the Phocaeans with their families
and cults (1.164.3) abandon their city. They attempt to purchase the Oenussae islands and settle close to home, but that project fails. They then join
their countrymen at Alalia in Cyrnus (Corsica).[19] That colony, however, does
not last long, because the Phocaeans use their famous penteconters (1.163.2,
164.3) to make piratical raids. These vicissitudes put into question the value
of Bias' 'most pragmatic' proposal of an autarchic island and the confusion
his advice reveals between colonisation and imperialism.[20] Bias had said that
the Ionians should settle in Sardinia 'in a single expedition' (*koinōi stolōi*)
and 'rule others' (1.170.2). The Phocaean colonists oppress their neighbours
in Corsica and are expelled by Etruscans and Carthaginians, united 'in a
single agreement' (*koinōi logōi*).[21]

This battle of Alalia is not, however, envisioned as a landmark in a struggle between Greeks and barbarians.[22] Herodotus is interested in what it
means for the Phocaeans. He calls it a 'Cadmean victory' because it represents a success that is really a failure, but also a failure that leads to
a success: the establishment of a legitimate, free and peaceful Greek *polis*
in the West. This is the city of Hyele (or Elea, or Velia), which the Phocaeans colonise in Oenotrian Italy.[23] In this part of Herodotus' narrative,
reparation and second chances make things right to the present day. The
Phocaeans find out that the Delphic oracle that had led them to Corsica
had not, really, promised to them the land of Cyrnus. It was rather telling
them to 'found Cyrnus', meaning a cult of the hero by that name.[24] On
the enemy side, the Etruscans of Agylla are directed by Delphi to expiate
the slaughter of the Phocaean prisoners and institute in their honour heroic
festivals they still celebrate (1.167.1–2). The parallel Delphic prescriptions
and heroic cults among Greeks and non-Greeks is an index of reconciliation. The earlier and perfectly successful story of the Lydian migration to
Etruria celebrates a resourceful people's escape from starvation and (eventual) enslavement. The mixed fortunes of the Phocaeans add a more specific
blueprint: the god of Delphi does not legitimise theft, colonisation is not an
act of aggression, and Italy – as opposed to her islands – is the appropriate
destination.

Getting out from under: individual ventures

The Phocaean resettlement in the West is a communal project, where no
single *oikistēs* (oikist or founder of a colony) or leader stands out. What

follows in the *Histories* is a number of individualistic initiatives that strike us for their moral ambivalence. First comes Democedes of Croton, who begins by travelling from west to east, where he is put in golden chains by Darius, then returns under escort to his native soil, escapes, and thumbs his nose at the king (3.129–38).[25] This outcome confirms that Italy is a place of freedom. But Democedes' journey of liberation is also the cause, as Herodotus interprets it (3.138.4), of the first Persian infiltration of Greece.[26]

Next comes the expedition of Dorieus (5.42–47). The Phocaeans, as we have seen, escape political enslavement, unlike the Ionians who *remain* (1.169.1). Dorieus goes to found a colony (*es apoikiēn*) because he cannot be king in Sparta – which he would have been, Herodotus says, if only he had *remained* (5.48; cf. 42.2). The Phocaeans fail in Corsica and succeed in Italy. Dorieus fails in Libya and meets with disaster in Sicily;[27] between these destinations he briefly passes through Italy, only to interfere (perhaps) in a local war, that of Sybaris against Croton (5.43–6). A coalition of barbarians expels the Phocaeans from Corsica. Similarly, Carthaginians and local Libyans drive Dorieus and his men out of Libya, while Phoenicians and Segestans defeat them in Sicily. In both cases, again, it is the Greeks' fault.[28] The Phocaeans misinterpret the oracle of Delphi; Dorieus fails to consult it, then asks the wrong question, then misinterprets the answer.[29] Just as the Phocaeans did not get the island of Cyrnus (the son of Heracles), so Dorieus does not get Eryx, though it supposedly belongs to Heracles and Heraclids like him.[30] After Dorieus and his companions are defeated, the enemy city of Segesta institutes a heroic cult for Philippus, one of those killed. As in the case of the Phocaean cult at Agylla, this barbarian replacement of the traditional cult of the founder achieves religious harmony after a failed colonising aggression by the Greeks.[31]

But unlike the Phocaean migration, the expedition of Dorieus is dangerous and misguided from beginning to end. Five other founders (*sunktistai*) appear in the narrative, all of whom Herodotus mentions by name, as reproducing Dorieus' destiny or illuminating for us his ambitions. The only one who does not die with Dorieus, Euryalus, captures the Greek city of Minoa, expels the sole ruler (*mounarchos*) of Selinus and is killed by the citizens of that city after he has seized the tyranny for himself (5.46). Among the other four, Philippus was an aristocrat from Croton, who had been banished from his city after becoming engaged with the daughter of Telys the tyrant of Sybaris, who started the war against Croton; he had then joined Dorieus in Libya when the marriage fell through (5.46–7). Herodotus' narrative about Dorieus is elliptical, derailed by the dispute of Sybarite and Crotoniate sources, and for us obscure. The affairs of all the cities involved are hard to reconstruct.[32] But one thing emerges which is perfectly clear: Dorieus and his carbon-copy companions are conquest-driven colonists, with tyrannical connections and tyrannical aims.[33]

Getting out from under: colonisation and tyranny

The Dorieus *logos* establishes the first explicit link between colonisation and the projects of despots. It is inserted within the narrative of the Ionian revolt – between the departure of Aristagoras for central Greece and his arrival at Sparta asking for help – and therefore it provides a fitting preliminary to the western repercussions of this eastern event. Both tyrannical leaders of the revolt make ridiculous plans concerning Sardinia, 'the greatest of islands'. Histiaeus promises to conquer it for the Persian king (5.106.6, 6.2.1);[34] Aristagoras considers it as a possible colony (*apoikiē*) and refuge for himself *from* the king (5.124.2). At the level of the discourse (the way Herodotus narrates events), the capture of Miletus triggers an optional reference to the destruction of Sybaris, also caused by its tyrant fifteen years before (6.21.1). At the level of the story (the sequence of events themselves), the defeat of the Ionians motivates freedom flights that mirror the most distasteful aspects of this ambivalent war.[35]

One fugitive is Dionysius of Phocaea: like his fellow-Phocaeans long ago in Corsica, this man becomes a pirate in Sicily (6.17). Some well-to-do Samians also go to Sicily, but as colonists (*es apoikiēn*, 6.22). It is a measure of Herodotus' irony in this section that the first venture is the more honest of the two. In preceding narratives, as we have seen, Sardinia and Corsica are the objects of unproductive Greek plans (the advice of Bias, the exploits of the Phocaeans, the machinations of Aristagoras and Histiaeus). Southern Italy represents an area where freedom is possible, if not guaranteed (Lydians, Phocaeans, Democedes). For Sicily a different picture has already started to emerge with the expedition of Dorieus. The Samian journey confirms that this part of the West – with Rhegium as a sort of appendage – is a breeding ground for tyranny on a notorious and unparalleled scale.[36]

The Samians respond to an invitation of the Zancleans to found (*ktisai*), a pan-Ionian city at Fair Shore (*Kalē Actē*), which 'belongs to the Sicels'.[37] They end up 'filching the very fair (*kallistē*) city of Zancle' (6.24.2), already established and Greek.[38] At the time of their departure, after the Ionian defeat at Lade, the Samians were indignant at the treasonous behaviour of their generals, and went to Sicily wishing to escape (political) slavery to the Persians and their native tyrant, Aeaces (6.22.1). Once in Sicily, however, they betray the city of Zancle in cooperation first with Anaxilaus, the tyrant of Rhegium, and then with Hippocrates, the tyrant of Gela, who sells the Zancleans into (literal) slavery (6.23.4).

Another character in this story is Scythes, the ruler of Zancle, who loses his job after the Samian take-over. Scythes reproduces in reverse the freedom journey of Democedes from Persia to Italy: he escapes from Hippocrates' jail in Sicily to the prosperity – and relative freedom – of Darius' court.[39] The son of this man or, at any rate, his close analogue is Cadmus of Cos, who will appear on the stage of the *Histories* in Herodotus' next western narrative. Cadmus, we learn, gives up his tyranny at home to come to Sicily where he appropriates, as Scythes had done, the city of Zancle (7.164).[40] He will become the shuttle diplomat of Gelon, the tyrant of Syracuse, with the king of Persia, going back and forth between the despotic West and the despotic East.

Sicilian tyranny and the Greek fight for freedom

We now come to Herodotus' narrative about Gelon of Syracuse, which is the longest and most elaborate western section in the *Histories*. As I have tried to show, in Herodotus' world-view, tyranny makes Sicily an inadequate place of refuge from political enslavement. Now we are about to see how tyranny also excludes Sicily as either an ally or as an analogue of Old Greece in its fight for freedom. In the imminence of Xerxes' invasion the confederate Greeks ask Gelon of Syracuse for his support in the resistance. Gelon promises he will send lavish help, but only if he is appointed supreme commander of the forces or at least general of the fleet. When the Greek envoys refuse, Gelon withdraws his offer and sends the Cadmus we have mentioned to Delphi ready to pledge allegiance to the Great King (7.157–63).[41]

Before the embassy scene and its aftermath, Herodotus' survey of Gelon's background (7.153–6) represents Sicilian Greek history from the most remote times as a prelude to his tyranny. Gelon himself emerges as the heir of the sort of policies we have seen Hippocrates pursue with the Samians at Zancle. As Hippocrates' officer, he distinguishes himself by helping, beyond Zancle, to enslave Callipolis, Naxos, Leontini, and to appropriate Camarina. At the death of Hippocrates, Gelon usurps power from his sons and crushes a revolt of the citizens of Gela. Next, he takes over Syracuse, which he makes the centre of his dominion. After performing this last trick (*heurēma*), he razes Camarina to the ground and deports the Camarinans to Syracuse. He also moves to Syracuse half of the inhabitants of Gela and the wealthy citizens of Sicilian Megara and Euboea. As for the common people of these last two cities, he sells them into slavery because he believed, Herodotus says (7.156.3), that the *dēmos* made for a 'most unpleasant cohabitation' (*sunoikēma acharitotaton*).[42]

The section I have just summarised begins by tracing Gelon's ancestry ultimately from a man from Telos who participated as associated colonist (*oikētor*) in the original Rhodian settlement of Gela (7.153.1). This reference to eighth-century Greek colonisation in the West is unique in the *Histories* and alludes to the fact that Hippocrates, Gelon and other Sicilian tyrants saw themselves as founders. They advertised their depopulations, purges, destructions, refoundations and other feats of social engineering in the light of the colonisation model, even expecting, and receiving, heroic honours as oikists after their deaths.[43] Though Herodotus reminds us of Gelon's claims by referring to his colonial ancestry (which no doubt facilitated his rise to power), he stops short of applying the vocabulary of colonisation to his or Hippocrates' policies. These he describes through the monarchical model, in terms that recall the conquests and deportations of the Persian kings.[44]

The identification of Sicilian tyranny with the despotic-barbarian rule that threatens the Greeks from the East is consistent with the secondary role Herodotus attributes to non-Greeks as their adversaries in the West.[45] Hippocrates and Gelon wage wars of aggression mostly against Greek cities, and secondarily against not fully identified Sicilian natives.[46] No other barbarians appear in Herodotus' narrative until Gelon himself brings them out of the blue in the negotiation scene (7.158.2): 'You Greeks', he complains, 'never gave me support in my war against the Carthaginians, when I begged you to help me to avenge the murder of Dorieus by the Segestans and liberate the *emporia* [trading posts] from which you yourselves derive much gain.' Gelon represents the expedition of Dorieus as a stage in a Greek–barbarian war which Gelon himself feels called upon to pursue.[47] Herodotus is here making Gelon indulge in the propaganda by which we know the Sicilian tyrants proclaimed themselves avengers and liberators of the Greeks in the West. But the text also makes such claims fall flat. The Greek ambassadors do not acknowledge Gelon's efforts, allegedly on their behalf. The barbarian wars he mentions are, at any rate, a thing of the past (7.158.3–5). And when the negotiations with the Greeks fail and Gelon sends Cadmus to Delphi, the Persians are clearly the only barbarians he is worried about (7.163.1).

Herodotus employs a similar distancing manoeuvre when he buries the mention of a major war between Gelon and the Carthaginians in a one-sentence *logos* told by the (presumably Greek) 'inhabitants of Sicily' to justify Gelon's absence from the Persian War (7.165–6).[48] The Sicilians describe a barbarian invasion by a large and multi-ethnic force (7.165), which was defeated, they say, on the same day as the Greeks defeated the Persians at Salamis (7.166.).[49] This parallelism with Xerxes' invasion reflects the over-evaluation of the victory of Himera by the fifth-century Sicilian tradition as an achievement equivalent or even superior to that of the other Greeks on the eastern front.[50] Herodotus' Sicilian sources, however, are extraordinarily inept, or so Herodotus makes them appear. They give few details on the decisive battle – not even its location – but have plenty to say on how the war began. Terillus, the tyrant of Himera, was expelled from his city by Theron, the tyrant of Acragas, and with the support of Anaxilaus the tyrant of Rhegium, who was his father-in-law, persuaded Hamilcar, to whom he was tied by guest-friendship, to invade Sicily. The pro-Gelonian Sicilians here undermine their own parallelism between what they call the victory 'of Gelon and Theron' in the west and that 'of the Greeks' in the east.[51] Unwittingly, they corroborate Herodotus' view of Sicily as a land of Greek tyrannical wars.[52]

Herodotus himself, in the Himera narrative, loses interest in Gelon and turns his attention to the defeated enemy commander, Hamilcar, and his mysterious disappearance after the battle or rather, as the Carthaginians say, his personal holocaust (7.166–7). Hamilcar was (we now learn) himself a Syracusan on his mother's side. Whatever his fate, all the Phoenician colonies (*apoikidōn*) have erected monuments and offer sacrifices to him. With a return to the vocabulary of colonisation, Herodotus here grants to Hamilcar the role of oikist he has denied to Gelon. He also underlines once again, as at the end of the Phocaean and Dorieus narratives, a barbarian religious victory, achieved with the establishment of a permanent cult.[53]

Colonisation and escape, tyranny and aggression, Greeks and non-Greeks – once again

Herodotus' devaluation of the battle of Himera becomes even clearer in the course of his account of the Greeks' next embassy asking for help against Xerxes, this time to Crete (7.169–71). Within the Gelon narrative the 'inhabitants of Sicily' talked about a victory over the barbarians by the western Greeks. Here the narrator himself goes far out of his way to record a western battle against the barbarians that led to the 'greatest *phonos* (slaughter) of Greeks'.

To the Cretans, who consult Delphi on whether or not to support the Greeks against the Persians, the Pythia's response goes back to events of the heroic age. Minos was killed in Sicania, she recalls, and the Cretans received no support in avenging his death. Nevertheless they participated with the Greeks in the expedition against Troy, exciting the anger of the spirit of Minos, who sent them a plague and a famine that practically depopulated the island. After the oracle reminds them of these events, the Cretans decline to join the Greek resistance against Xerxes so as not to anger the spirit of Minos again (7.169.1–2,171.1–2). This story of the Cretan embassy adds to the panorama of justifications brought forward by the medising Greeks. Herodotus' internal narrative, however, reshuffles familiar concerns of his western sections: colonisation, tyranny and the role of barbarians.

The narrator begins as if he were going to explain the reference of the Pythia to Minos' journey to Sicania in search of Daedalus and the circumstances of his violent death in that foreign land. But, just as he disregards the precedent of Heracles for the Phocaeans and Dorieus, so here he has no interest (it turns out) in the story of Minos in Sicily.[54] Out of that tradition, Herodotus rather spins out his own charter myth of colonisation, by focussing on the interesting outcome of the attempt the Cretans eventually made, urged by the god, to avenge their king. The Cretans sailed to Sicania with a great expedition (*stolōi megalōi*),[55] besieged Camicus for five years, then ran out of supplies, gave up and left (7.170.1). While on their way back home, a storm wrecked their ships and drove them to land in Iapygia. Here, they built (*ktisantas*) the city of Hyria and remained forever, becoming, Herodotus says, 'Messapian Iapygians instead of Cretans, and continentals instead of islanders' (7.170.2).

This reminds us of the Lydians who became Tyrrhenians at the beginning of the *Histories* (1.94.4). But even more than the Lydians, these Minoan Cretans, both as ancestors of present-day Cretans and as a non-Hellenic population in Italy, confuse the distinction between Greeks and barbarians.[56] As they become Iapygians of Messapia, moreover, they also become continentals instead of islanders. The Phocaeans, as we have seen, proceed from the Oenussae islands and Corsica to the stability of Hyele in Italy. Similarly, by settling in Italy, the Cretans give up their island home with its future expedition to Troy and subsequent troubles; they also give up Sicily, with the burden of avenging Minos' death there and the task of conquest.

To this positive barbarian paradigm, Herodotus adds a negative Greek one. The Minos tradition of a remote past (always in indirect discourse) gives the narrator a bridge for his own 'digression' (*parenthēkē*, as he apologetically calls it at 7.171.1), which mentions the latest of Herodotus' western events (7.170.3):

> From Hyria [the Cretans] founded other colonies (*oikisai*), which the people of Taras a long time afterwards tried to destroy, suffering a major defeat so that this was indeed the greatest slaughter of Greeks (*phonos Hellenikos megistos*) we know about.

In the neighbourhood of this episode of aggression, we predictably find a Greek tyrant of the 'Sicilian' brand. The 'greatest slaughter of Greeks' also involved 3,000 casualties of citizens from Rhegium who were compelled to fight the Iapygians by Micythus, a former retainer of Anaxilaus and regent in Rhegium for his sons. An aspirant oikist like the Sicilian tyrants, Micythus seems to have made his disastrous intervention on the side of Taras against the Iapygians in the hopes of emulating the victory which only one year before (474) Hieron, brother and successor of Gelon as tyrant of Syracuse, had won at Cumae against the Etruscans.[57] This was a feat which Pindar says liberated Greece and was equal to Salamis, Plataea and, first and foremost, the victory of Gelon at Himera (*Pyth.* 1.137–56). Herodotus does not care much for Himera, deliberately skips over Cumae, and does not mention a subsequent Tarentine victory against the Iapygians that was, once again, advertised with the usual panhellenic propaganda.[58] The *phonos Hellenikos megistos* in conjunction with the successful Cretan settlement in Iapygia is better suited to his message: no war, but colonisation; no Sicily, but Italy; no isolation but cohabitation, and parallel destinies for Greeks and non-Greeks in their new homes.

This is the last western narrative of the *Histories*, leading up the last western reference, mentioned at the beginning of our discussion. On the eve of the battle of Salamis, the Peloponnesians want to withdraw to the Isthmus, leaving Attica and central Greece to fend for themselves. Themistocles argues, cajoles and finally utters a threat (8.62.2): 'we Athenians will take up our families and go to Siris in Italy, which is ours already from ancient times and which prophecies say must be settled by us'. From the point of view of the Salamis narrative, these words insert the Athenians in the tradition of the Phocaean colonists, while also confirming the energetic mobility and boldness that are peculiar to the Athenians. But for Herodotus, relocation does not represent a productive solution in this case: 'if the Athenians had left their country', rather than strategically evacuating it for the purpose of the naval battle, the whole of Greece would have fallen to Persia (7.139.1).[59]

In relation to the extra-textual context of the times of Themistocles, his words probably reflect a theoretical interest in the West if not in 480, perhaps shortly afterwards, when Athens was organising the Delian League and represented itself as the mother country of all the Ionians. Siris was supposedly a foundation of Colophon, and therefore Ionian.[60] It lay, moreover, in the territory of Sybaris, an Achaean city but one tied particularly closely to Ionian Miletus (cf. 6.21); this connection is inherited by Athens, which now replaces Miletus as the leader of the Ionian Greeks.[61]

Finally, many years down the road, Themistocles' 'Italian plan' may have provided an illustrious precedent for some of the Athenian promoters of Thurii.[62] The early history of the colony – extremely hard to reconstruct – seems to have included changes of direction in several areas. A conflict with

Taras for the possession of Siris begun in 443 BCE ends at an unknown date in 'compromise and cohabitation'; from 434/433 Thurii distances herself from Athens, apparently goes back and forth from democracy to oligarchy, alternates friendship and hostility towards Croton, and makes alliances and war with different groups of barbarians.[63] Herodotus' political stance on these fluid and embattled issues is likely to have transcended a clear-cut polarisation, but it cannot be discerned. What we can say, in the light of Herodotus' overarching vision of the Italian West, is that the 'western' Themistocles of the Salamis narrative is not the ideological forerunner of the colonist historian. His pan-Ionian platform and proprietary claims on a piece of land on the basis of ancient *logia* recall the most unproductive aspects of the colonising projects described in the *Histories*. Themistocles is from Athens and an early representative of the Athenian will to power. Herodotus is altogether a more complex product: philo-Athenian and anti-Athenian, democratic and anti-imperialistic, panhellenic and *philobarbaros*. He is from Halicarnassus, and a citizen of Thurii.

FURTHER READING

There is no comprehensive study of the patterns and ideological concerns in the Italian passages of the *Histories*. The most useful representations of Herodotus' view of the Italian West emerge from the fascinating collection *Erodoto e l'occidente* (1999) and from Krings (1998). The latter examines all the Herodotean passages relevant to her topic with special literary sensibility, though in the service of a historical goal. Herodotus' treatment of non-Greeks in the West is surveyed by the separate contributions of Bondì and Nenci in Nenci and Reverdin (1990). Scholars have of course assiduously examined Herodotus' references to Italy and Sicily in their effort to determine their sources or to reconstruct events and realities, Greek and non-Greek, in southern Italy and adjacent islands in the eighth to fifth centuries BCE. See especially the following studies: Asheri (1998b) and (1992); Ciaceri (1927–32); Dunbabin (1948); Finley (1968); Lombardo (1993); Luraghi (1994a); Rutter (1973); and Vallet (1958).

NOTES

1. *Rhet.* 3.9, 1409a 34, against the unanimous reading of the manuscript tradition. But see Plutarch, *Mor.* 604F, 868A; Strabo 14.2.16. Jacoby (1913) 205 argues that *Thouriou* is the original reading.
2. Diod. 12.7–11, esp.12.10.3; 20.22.1; Str. 6.1.13–15. Ehrenberg (1948); Kagan (1969) 154–78; Malkin (1987) 97–101; Lombardo (1993). The exclusive behaviour of the Sybarites (other than the negative tradition about the city) may

explain overall derogatory portrayal of old Sybaris (5.44.1–2, 6.21.1; 6.127.1) in contrast with Siris (6.127.1) and especially Croton (5.44.1–2; 3.131.3, 137.1–5; 8.47). See Raviola (1999) 375–9.

3. By 'Italy' I here mean what we call 'Italy' today plus Corsica. Herodotus (3.136, 138) and Thucydides (1.12.4; 6.44.2; 8.91.2) defined *Italiē* as the Ionian coast of Italy beginning from Taras down to Rhegium; Ciaceri (1924–32) I.43–8.

4. Nenci (1990) 305; Bruno Sunseri (1999). There are 27 (or 28) passages, for a total of about 700 lines or 22 pages of Oxford text.

5. See, e.g., 4.99.4–5; Raviola (1999).

6. Compare 5.45.1; Str. 6.1.13 (263).

7. Nenci (1990), especially 308. On the barbarians of Italy, cf. Hecataeus, *FGrHist* 1 FF 38–72, 86–97, 100, and Thuc. 6.1–5 (Sicily). In Herodotus we find scattered ethnographic information about the origin of Tyrrhenians (1.94) and Messapian Iapygians (7.170); a custom of the Eneti of Illyria (1.196.1, if these are the same Italic population as the Eneti at 5.9.3); and, 'still in my time', heroic cults of the Tyrrhenians of Agylla (1.167), Segestans (5.47), Phoenicians (7.167.2). The Carthaginians appear as sources for Herodotus on Libyan matters at 4.43, 195, 196, and 7.167. Herodotus' vagueness about the geography and ethnography of the northwest and far west of Europe is of course a different phenomenon, implying lack of specific knowledge: Alonso-Núñez (1987); Nenci (1990) 301–2, 316.

8. They are on the offensive only at Himera, allied with other Greeks (7.165); on the defensive versus the Phocaeans (1.166), Dorieus (5.46), and various Greek cities and tyrants (6.17, 23, 7.154, 7.158.1–2, 7.170).

9. For the pattern of colonisation, see especially Dougherty (1993), Giangiulio (2001) 116–20. On the role of Delphi in colonisation, see Malkin (1987) 17–91. For words of the *ktizō* and *(ap)oikizō* families in Herodotus, see Casevitz (1985).

10. For withdrawal as a means of defence, see especially the Scythians and the Athenians: Hartog (1988) 35–8, 49–57; Krings (1998) 104; Munson (2001a) 212–13.

11. On the broader phenomenon of 'change of abode' (*metoikēsis*), see Demand (1988) and (1990).

12. Aside from fifth-century Ionian colonising projects (see especially 1.167.3 and 6.22.2), Herodotus only notes the ethnic origins of Gela (Rhodian: 7.153.1) and Croton (Achaean: 8.47). For the importance fifth-century sources attribute to the ethnic composition of western colonies, see especially Thuc. 6.1–5, 7.57; Graham (1964) 8–12; Antonaccio (2001).

13. For civil struggles, see Berger (1992). Herodotus only mentions one in Gela (7.153.1–2) and one in Syracuse (7.155.2). On the legislators Charondas of Catane and Zaleucus of Locris, see Pugliese Carratelli (1987a). Even though the story of Aristeas at Metapontum (4.15) is a Pythagorean tradition (see Bolton [1962] 142–83), Herodotus is silent about Pythagoras in the West from 530 BCE and Pythagorean oligarchies at Croton and other Italian cities. See Raviola (1999) 386–91.

14. The figure of the ruler is a prominent focus of the study by Immerwahr (1966). See also Lateiner (1989) 163–86; Corcella (1984) 163–77; Hartog (1988) 331–4; Gammie (1986); Munson (2001a) 49–73; the nuanced discussion of Dewald (2003).

15. Herodotus does not mention either the fall of tyrannies in Sicily and Rhegium in 471–461 (see Asheri [1992] 154–61) or western archaic tyranny (e.g. Phalaris of Acragas, Panaetius of Leontini); see Luraghi (1994a).

16. The founder-colonist and the tyrant are in fact related figures: McGlew (1993) 173–80.

17. Compare 9.106. For the Lydians as a paradigm for the Ionians, see Lombardo (1990) 202; Munson (2001a) 102–6.

18. Arganthonius is a western *tyrannos* (1.163.2) paradoxically in polar antithesis to the eastern *basileus* of the Persians: Krings (1998) 116–17. Compare the king of the long-lived Ethiopians (3.20–3). For the Phocaeans in the far West, see Bosch-Gimpera (1944).

19. Antiochus (*FGrHist* 555 F 8 = Str. 6.1.1 [C252]) and others mention Massalia, founded c. 600, as one of the destinations of the Phocaeans in 546. Herodotus' exclusion from this narrative of Massalia (cf. 5.9.3) keeps the focus firmly on the Italian West as a place of escape: Bats (1994); Sammartano (1999) 400–14.

20. Cusumano (1999), especially 165–79, on Bias' pragmatism vs. the usual Greek idealisation of Sardinia. On the Ionian idea on the desirability of islands, see Ceccarelli (1996); on the connection between imperialism and insularity in Athenian ideology, see Thuc. 1.143.5; [Xen.] *Ath. Pol.* 2.14.16; Mossé (1996).

21. Krings (1998) 121; Asheri (1988a) 359.

22. Krings (1998) 93–160, especially 96, and 149; Jehasse (1962) 242–3; *contra* Dunbabin (1948) 341–4; Bondì (1990) 280.

23. Krings (1998) 121. Strabo (6.1.1=252) comments on the *eunomia* of Hyele from the earliest times; cf. Diog. Laert. 9. 21. On the Phocaeans' renunciation of piracy after their move to Italy and the relations of Hyele with neighbouring Etrurians and Chalcidians, see Vallet and Villard (1966) 185–7.

24. The best discussion of this oracle is Lombardo (1972) 76–86 especially 82–4.

25. Griffiths (1987) 45.

26. Immerwahr (1957) 313–14. See Boedeker (1987) 191–2; Austin (1990) 299, and also Friedman in this volume.

27. Herodotus represents the expedition as a complete failure. In fact, the colonists may have managed to found a city named Heraclea in the land of Eryx (Diod. 4.23.3), or tried to resettle Minoa, which, according to Herodotus, Euryleon later captured, and was at some point called Heraclea Minoa: Asheri (1988b) 752; Malkin (1994) 215; Krings (1998) 169.

28. Dorieus encounters resistance by *local* populations. In Sicily, 'Phoenicians' does not mean the same as 'Carthaginians', who are mentioned instead by Diod. 4.23.3 (cf. also Justin 19.1.9, if this passage refers to Dorieus); see Krings (1998) 180, 183, 188.

29. 5.42.2; at 5.43 he consults Delphi not like a colonist but like a conquering king: Malkin (1987) 78–81, 22–3; (1994) 194. The Delphic response at 5.43 is ironic: see Macan (1895) I.185 and Pareti (1914) 14–15.

30. 5.43. On the adventures of Heracles in the West as charter myth for Greek colonisation, see Dunbabin (1948) 330, 335, 341; Nenci (1994) 216; Giangiulio (1983) 785–809; Asheri (1988b). On the story of Heracles' fight with the Elymian Eryx as a prelude to Dorieus' expedition, cf. Diod. 4.23.1–3, Paus. 3.16.4–5; cf. Apollod. 2.5.10.9. On Cyrnus, see Servius ad Verg. *Ecl.* 9.30.

31. The analogy is underlined by Dunbabin (1948) 335; Krings (1998) 177. The case of Philippus heroised by the Segestans (5.47.2) is thus fundamentally different from that of Leon of Salamis sacrificed by the Persians (7.180). For the heroic cult of the founder, see 1.168, 6.38.1; Malkin (1987) 188–266; McGlew (1993) 172–3.

32. For a good explanation, see Giangiulio (1989) 188–202.

33. For the tyrannical aspect of royal Spartans, see Munson (1993).

34. The ridiculousness is here enhanced by the pun between 'Sardinia' and 'Sardis': Macan (1895) I. 256.

35. For Herodotus' representation of the Ionian revolt, see especially Lateiner (1982); also Evans (1976). The plan of leaving Ionia is first formulated during the Ionian revolt by the Carians (5.119.2).

36. See already at 3.125.2 Herodotus' comparison with the Samos of Polycrates. On the tight connection of Rhegium and Zancle/Messana from 494, see Vallet (1958).

37. 6.22.2. The awkwardness of the gloss (Macan [1895] I.286) suggests the narrator's deliberate choice to specify the aggressiveness of the project. Compare 6.23.1.

38. For these events, see Vallet (1958) 335–54; Luraghi (1994a) 130–145. The Samians take Zancle 'empty of men' (6.23.2), as the Persians took Phocaea (1.164.3). Herodotus does not tell us that at some time between 493 and 476 BCE the Samians were driven out of Zancle by Anaxilaus (Thuc. 6.4.6), though at 7.164.1 he mentions incidentally the city's eventual change of name to Messana, which Thucydides associates with Anaxilaus' action. Compare Str. 6.2.3 (268); Paus. 4.23.6–10; Arist. *Pol.* 5.2.10, 1303a 35.

39. The parallel between Democedes and Scythes is explicit in Ael. *V.H.* 8.17.

40. Herodotus' narrative is again elliptical. On the issue of the identity between Scythes of Zancle and the father of Cadmus, and for reconstructions of Cadmus' role at Zancle, see Vallet (1958) 337, Luraghi (1994a) 134–44. Both Cadmus and Scythes are 'just men' close to tyranny and enablers for tyrants.

41. On this passage, see Pareti (1914) 115–27; Gauthier (1966) 14–25; Bravo (1993) 45–62; Luraghi (1994a) 337–8; Krings (1998) 270–84; Munson (2001a) 218–19.

42. This gloss has been taken as evidence for the difference between Sicilian fifth-century tyranny and its populist archaic counterpart all over the Greek world. Maddoli (1980) 41; Braccesi and Millino (2000) 54; see, however, Luraghi (1994a) 286–300, 370–3.

43. Hippocrates as oikist of Camarina: Thuc. 6.5.3; cf. Pind. *Ol.* 5.19. Anaxilaus as oikist of Messana: Luraghi (1994a) 213–214. Heroic honours for Gelon at Syracuse: Diod. 11.38.5; Luraghi (1994a) 298. Hieron as oikist of Aetna: Diod. 11.49.1–2. Hieron's heroic cult: Diod. 11.76.3; Strabo 6.2.3; Malkin (1987) 96–7, 239; Luraghi (1994a) 335–7; Braccesi (1998) 33.

44. For Sicilian tyranny inspired by the Persian model, see Asheri (1988b) 769–70; Braccesi (1998) ix; Demand (1990) 46; Luraghi (1994a) 377, 380.

45. Compare Asheri (1988b) 769–70: 'more than two generations before the first Carthaginian army destroyed a Greek city in Sicily, three had already been annihilated by a true "panhellenic" Greek tyrant'.

46. 7.154.2 ('several of the barbarians'); cf. the Sicels at 155.1. The Cyllirii at 7.155.2 are enslaved natives, probably Sicels: Macan (1908) I.217.

47. So do some modern historians, partly on the basis of Justin 4.2.6–7. See, e.g., Bosch-Gimpera (1944) 56; Maddoli (1980) 27–9, 36–7; Braccesi and Millino (2000) 96.

48. Krings (1998) 272, 278, 279, 280–2.

49. Compare Diod. 11.20–26, who compares Gelon to Themistocles and Pausanias, and Himera to Salamis and Plataea (23.1–3), while synchronising Himera with Thermopylae (24.1). The number of 300,000 (also in Diod. 11.20) matches that of the troops of Mardonius (Hdt. 8.100.5, 113.2; 9.32.2): How and Wells (1928) II.200.

50. Reflected by the poets of the tyrants' circles: Pind. *Pyth.* 1.137–56, composed in 470 BCE for Hieron, establishes a double parallel Himera/Plataea and Cuma/Salamis; see also Simonides, *FGE* XXXIV (Schol. *Pyth.* 1.152b). On the Sicilian tyrants' panhellenic propaganda, see Gauthier (1966); Krings (1998) 261–70, 279; Luraghi (1994a) 362–5.

51. In Herodotus, in other words, the alleged Salamis/Himera synchronism (factually impossible: see Pareti (1914) 124) bears no causal or moral significance, as Aristotle saw (*Poet.* 23, 1459a). Contrast the synchronism of Plataea and Mycale at 9.100: Gauthier (1966) 7; Krings (1998) 282.

52. Gauthier (1966) 24; Bondì (1980) 189–90. The role attributed to Terillus and Anaxilaus in the *casus belli* (unique to Herodotus), the participation of Theron (absent in the older sources), and the omission of Selinus as an ally of Hamilcar (Diod. 11.2.4–5; 13.55.1) all contribute to that representation.

53. Compare 1.167 and 5.47 (above, pp. 260 and 261). Krings (1998) 284 calls these three foundations of cults 'religious victories'.

54. Franco (1999), especially 205. See Strabo 6.2.6, 273; 6.3.2, 279; 6.3.6, 282; Diod. 4.79; cf. Luraghi (1994a) 37–44, 253–4.

55. Thereby leaving Crete almost empty (cf. 7.171.1): How and Wells (1928) II.204. This recalls the mass migration of the Phocaeans (1.164.3) and Bias' advice that the Ionians move to Sardinia *koinōi stolōi* (1.170.2). See above, pp. 259–60.

56. For the mutual integration between Greek and non-Greek elements in Iapygia, see Nenci (1978) 57. Nenci (1978) also argues that the tradition of the Cretan origin of the Iapygians (cf. Strabo 6.3.2 [279, 282]; Athen. 12.523a) was promoted by the Iapygians themselves in polemic with hostile Taras, and accepted by Athenian propaganda (cf. Plut. *Theseus* 16.2). Herodotus' favourable attitude towards the Iapygians may have something to do with their friendship with Thurii/Athens; cf. 4.99.4–5, Thuc. 7.33.3–4, and see Nenci (1976) 736–7, (1978) 46 n. 7, 49 n. 17.

57. Vallet (1958) 370–3. Luraghi (1994a) 227–9; cf. Maddoli (1980) 54–5. Micythus refounded Pyxus: Strabo 6.1.1 (253), Diod. 11.59.4. The numerous statues he later dedicated at Olympia, according to Herodotus (7.170.3; cf. Paus. 5.26.2–5), represent an index of prestige-seeking. Herodotus implies that Micythus was expelled, but cf. Diod. 11.66 for 466 BCE. On Hieron's victory at Cumae, see Diod. 11.52.2.

58. About 465 BCE: Paus. 10.13.10; Ciaceri (1927–32) II.284–6; Giangiulio (1987) 43.

59. Demand (1988) 422–3.

60. Raviola (1986) 13–23, 29–34, 59–71; see also Dunbabin (1948) 374. According to Plut. *Them*. 32.2, Themistocles named his two daughters Italia and Sybaris.
61. Athen. 12.523d citing Timaeus and Aristotle; cf. Strabo 6.1.14 (264); Ciaceri (1927–32) I.128–135, II.236–44.
62. Though perhaps not all: see Wade-Gery (1932) 218–19.
63. Thurii–Taras conflict: Str. 6.1.14 (264); also Diod. 12.23.2, 36.3; cf. Raviola (1986) 38–40 and Lombardo (1993) 315–22. For the Thurians' rejection of an Athenian oikist in favour of panhellenic Apollo in 434/433: Diod. 12.35.3. Constitutional changes: Arist. *Pol*. 5.7.8, 1307b6; cf. Plato, *Laws* 1.636b and Arist. *Pol*. 5.6.6, 1307a27. See Giannelli (1928) 21–2, 26–31; De Sensi Séstito (1993) 347–57. For Thurii and Croton, see Diod. 11.11.3, Iamb. V*it. Pyth*. 263–4, and perhaps Polyaen. 2.10.1 (war of Thurii against Terina, a Crotoniate colony). See also the interpretation of Polyb. 2.39.4–6 by Rutter (1973) 173–6. Polyaen. 2.10.4.5 talks about a Thurian war against the Lucanians, which according to Giannelli (1928) 25 began around 433–430 BCE. An alliance of Thurii with the Iapygians of Messapia seems certain at least until 432, in the city's pro-Athenian and anti-Tarentine period: see Thuc. 7.33.4.

18

MICHAEL FLOWER

Herodotus and Persia

In 546 BCE, when the Persians were laying siege to the Greek cities of Ionia following the defeat of Croesus, king of Lydia, the Spartans sent a single ship with a message for Cyrus the Great, the founder of the Persian empire (1.152–3). Cyrus was warned by a Spartan envoy not to harm any city of Greece, for the Spartans would not permit it. In reaction to this piece of effrontery, Cyrus asked other Greeks who were present: 'Who among men are the Lacedaemonians, and how many of them are there that they give such orders?' The modern reader of the text of Herodotus will have no trouble recognising the Spartans (here called Lacedaemonians), and might well know that there were not many of them, and that only 300 of them faced the Persians at the battle of Thermopylae in 480 BCE. But he or she is far less likely to know much about the Persians, other than that there were a whole lot of them and that they failed to conquer Greece and were themselves, at a much later date (334–331 BCE), conquered by Alexander the Great.

It may come as a surprise then that the *Histories* of Herodotus is as much about Persia as about Greece, and that individual Persians are given just as much narrative space as individual Greeks. In fact the Persian kings Cyrus, Cambyses, Darius, and Xerxes, as well as Xerxes' cousin Mardonius, figure even more largely in the narrative than the Athenian general Themistocles or the Spartan king Leonidas. On a larger scale, the whole structure of the *Histories* is built upon the birth, growth, and checking of the Persian empire. The Persians are the driving force of the history, and the advance of the narrative is inextricably linked to their efforts to expand their empire. It can hardly be a coincidence that both the first (1.1–4) and the last (9.122) narratives in this massive work are focalised through the eyes of the Persians.

Several questions arise. How accurate is Herodotus' account of Persian history and culture?[1] Are there Persian or other Greek sources that supplement, correct, or verify what Herodotus tells us? What is the relationship between the narrative of the growth of the Persian empire in Books 1–4 and that of the Persian invasions of Greece in Books 6–9?[2] Does Herodotus' depiction of the Persians coincide with that of other Greek literary texts or does he differ in important ways? What explanation, or nexus of explanations, does Herodotus himself give for the astonishing fact that the Persians, who possessed the greatest empire that the world had yet seen, suffered humiliation and defeat at the hands of the relatively poor and disorganised Greek cities? All of these questions, of course, cannot be fully answered within the brief compass of this discussion. In what follows, however, I will lay out some suggestions for how to approach the Persians in Herodotus.

The Persian empire was vast in extent and its resources dwarfed those of the Greeks. It was created by Cyrus, who overthrew the Medes and then conquered Lydia and Babylon. His son Cambyses added Egypt; Darius made further gains, pushing the borders to the river Indus. In Book 1 Herodotus narrates the birth, upbringing, conquests, and death of Cyrus the Great. In Book 3 Cyrus' son Cambyses conquers Egypt and shows increasing signs of madness, which include killing his sister-wife and ordering the execution of his brother Smerdis. While he is in Egypt, a *magus* impersonates Smerdis and seizes power. Cambyses dies before he can return to deal with the *coup d'état*, but seven Persian nobles put down this false Smerdis. One of the seven, Darius, then became the next king of Persia. Darius' ill-fated expedition against the Scythians forms the main subject of Book 4; his suppression of the Ionian revolt appears in Book 5; the battle of Marathon is narrated in Book 6. His son Xerxes' invasion of Greece is the subject of Books 7–9.

The impetus for Herodotus to have written a work on this scale and on such a topic may well have been the conviction that the Hellenes of the Persian Wars generation had done something as great as, or even greater than, the Achaeans who had fought the Trojan War. Nonetheless, Herodotus did not write what we might call 'triumphalist' history. The Persians are not depicted as weak and despicable rulers of an evil empire, who got their just deserts at the hands of morally and physically superior Greeks. Modern scholarship has emphasised recently that in the wake of the Persian Wars the 'barbarian' came to be seen as the generic opposite of the Greek in terms of ethnic identity.[3] This dichotomy between free and manly Greek/Athenian and servile and effeminate barbarian/Persian may be valid for some texts, such as Aeschylus' *Persians*,[4] but it does not correspond to the way that Persians are depicted in Herodotus. Or rather, if Herodotus' contemporaries shared a stereotype of the barbarian as weak, effeminate, and servile, he employs various narrative strategies to undercut it, challenge it, modify it, and subvert it. Perhaps one of his greatest virtues as an historian is that he can see 'self in other and other in self'.[5]

Yet this critical stance, the ability to see the enemy as just as human as oneself, is also an inheritance from Homer. It may be compared to Homer's sympathetic treatment of the shared humanity of Priam and Achilles in Book 24 of the *Iliad*. In the prelude to the great battle of Plataea, Herodotus describes a scene in which a Persian and a Boeotian shared a couch at a symposium (9.16). The Persian wept at the coming Persian destruction, expressing ideas about the human condition that were characteristically Greek and typically Herodotean. The distance between Greek and barbarian was not so great after all – human suffering binds all peoples. Yet the similarity between Persian and Greek in Herodotus is not as close as that between Trojan and Achaean in Homer.

Herodotus does not quite elide the differences to the degree that Homer can, because in the *Iliad* the Trojans and Achaeans are not viewed as being culturally distinct in any deeply significant way – both are governed by kings, worship the same gods, and practise the same customs.[6] For Herodotus, on the other hand, the Persians are culturally distinct from the Greeks, and that is why he includes a short ethnography of them in Book 1.[7] In Herodotus the reader is reminded at key moments (e.g. 7.11; 8.69; 9.41–2) that Persia is an autocracy in which men cannot express their views freely in open debate, but are subject to the arbitrary whims of an autocrat.

At the symposium mentioned above, the nameless Persian exclaims: 'This is the most hateful cause of pain among men, to know many things but to have power over nothing.' Those who disagreed with Xerxes, even his own uncle Artabanus (7.11.1), or his brother Masistes (9.111.5), aroused his wrath. In some contexts doing the King a favour could be just as deadly as doing him harm. When Cambyses asked Prexaspes what the Persians thought of him, he responded that they felt that he was too fond of wine. Cambyses, in order to demonstrate his sanity, then shot Prexaspes' son through the heart with an arrow (3.33–6). On occasion the king might take council and profit from it, as when the Greek general Coes of Lesbos advised Darius not to destroy the bridge over the Danube during the Scythian expedition (4.97), but there was no guarantee that the king would listen. Thus the Persians, even those most closely related to the reigning king, cannot be free in the same sense or to the same degree as are the Greeks.

Herodotus, of course, was not entirely independent of the biases of his own culture, and even if he were the plot line demanded that the Greeks be the defenders of liberty against Persian aggression. That explains why two different, but interlocking, lines of historical causation run though the *Histories*. One line sees the Persian invasion as retribution for the Athenian and Eretrian participation in the capture of Sardis and the burning there of the temple of Cybebe during the Ionian revolt of 499–494 BCE. The immediate consequence of the Ionian revolt was Darius' determination to punish Athens and Eretria (5.105), a determination inherited by his son and successor Xerxes. At the same time, however, Herodotus considers the burning of Sardis to have been a mere pretext used by the Persians for their invasions of Greece (5.102.1). He makes it clear in a number of passages that the Persians were intending to add Greece, indeed all of Europe, to their empire long before the Ionian revolt took place (3.133–8; 6.44, 48, 94; 7.138).

At this distance it is difficult for us to discern what Persian motives really were, but Herodotus' depiction of Persian foreign policy as being one of continual expansionism, with each king feeling the need to add to the empire, is confirmed in a general way by Persian royal inscriptions. Their custom (*nomos*), Xerxes says, is always to move forward and add to their empire (7.8). Herodotus, in effect, ascribes to Xerxes a notion that we would call 'manifest destiny', to wit, that it was the will of God that the Persians conquer the entire inhabited world: 'Thus God guides us, and we, by following his guidance, prosper greatly.'

As it happens, this sentiment meshes quite nicely with the rhetoric of the royal inscriptions of Cyrus, Darius and Xerxes. Those of the latter two kings regularly begin with the same standard formula:

> Ahura Mazda is a great god, who created this earth, who created that sky, who created man, who created happiness for man, who made Darius [Xerxes] king, one king of many, one lord of many. I am Darius [Xerxes], the Great King, king of kings, king of lands containing many men, king of this great earth far and wide, son of Hystaspes [Darius], an Achaemenid.[8]

Unfortunately, such documents cannot be taken completely at face value, for Assyrian royal inscriptions express similar claims to world rule by divine dispensation. Nonetheless, the ideology of manifest destiny makes sense in terms of the dynamics of empire over time and across cultures, and Herodotus was probably correct to distinguish short- and long-term causes for the Persian invasions. In this respect he anticipates Thucydides' notion of historical causation in his famous analysis (1.23) of the causes of the Peloponnesian War where he distinguishes the immediate complaints (the Athenian siege of Potidaea and alliance with Corcyra) and the truest cause (Spartan fear of the growth of Athenian power).

On the level of personal motivation, Herodotus gives a convincing analysis of the pressures that each Persian king after Cyrus must have felt to add to the empire. At some point before the Scythian expedition of 522, Darius sent a small party of Persians to investigate the coastal regions of Greece, with the Greek doctor Democedes of Croton acting as their guide. Democedes had arranged this by persuading Atossa, the daughter of Cyrus and wife of Darius, to point out to Darius that he needed to add to the empire in order to show the Persians that he was a man and to keep them too busy to plot against him (3.134). Interestingly, this foreshadows the debate about invading Greece at the beginning of Book 7. In that context, the naked truths that Atossa uttered in bed are dressed in more sophisticated terms. Mardonius points out that every other king has added to the empire, and the dream that appears to Xerxes in his sleep asserts that if he does not follow through with the invasion, 'just as you became great in a short time, so also shall you quickly be once again of low rank' (7.14). One suspects that the message of this dream, even if we are meant to understand it as a genuine communication from some divine power, represents simultaneously what was subconsciously weighing upon Xerxes' mind: if he backed down he might lose the support of the Persian nobility.

The modern reader of the *Histories* is likely to have one question fore-most in mind: is the history 'true'? Did the characters that fill the pages say what the historian has them say and do what he has them do? This question is more important to historians than it is to literary critics, but both realise that Herodotus' conception of 'historical truth' is unlikely to be exactly the same as ours. The modern distinction between fiction and non-fiction may not be precisely applicable to the writings of Herodotus. Certainly the narrative seems to be based on a core of hard facts: Persian documents from Persepolis confirm his names for the Persian high command and the Behistun inscription shows that he correctly gives the names of six of the seven conspirators who overthrew the false Smerdis.[9] Yet one could hardly claim that Dickens' *A Tale of Two Cities* is a work of history, rather than an historical novel, merely because there was a French Revolution, cities called Paris and London, and a French king named Louis XVI. In other words, the kind of deep corroboration of Herodotus' narrative that would confirm its status as non-fiction is unattainable. Speech and dialogue, as an inheritance from epic and tragic poetry, are certainly Herodotus' own free invention.[10] And so, for instance, it probably would not have surprised his ancient readers if Herodotus had taken the occasion of Xerxes' review of his troops at Abydus (7.44–52) as an appropriate set-ting for the king and his wise adviser (his uncle Artabanus) to engage in a fictional meditation on the shortness and sorrows of human life. There is a sense, however, in which one can transcend the modern obsession with dis-tinguishing between fact and fiction. As the above discussion has revealed, Herodotus' literary portrait of the Persians is based, to judge from Persian inscriptions, on their own self-projection as an imperial people. Herodotus has brilliantly manipulated his knowledge of Persian culture in order to fash-ion a literary account of a people and its rulers that is both compelling and profound.

Be that as it may, what sources lay behind Herodotus' account of Persian history and customs? It is possible that earlier Greek prose authors, whose works are no longer extant, had given brief accounts of Persian history and customs, or that an occasional documentary source forms the ultimate basis of Herodotus' account, as in the Persian tribute list (3.89–97) or the catalogue of Persian forces (7.61–98). The Persians themselves, it seems, did not write narrative history, although they kept administrative records and inscribed official documents for public view. During the excavation of the Persian ceremonial capital of Persepolis in the 1930s many thousands of clay tablets (written in Elamite) were discovered, but these are purely financial and administrative texts. A number of Persian royal inscriptions are also extant, but only one of these provides a narrative of events. That is the Behistun inscription, which is Darius' own version of how he disposed of the pretender and put down the subsequent revolt of subject peoples.

Herodotus' account of Darius' accession is close enough to that in the Behistun inscription to raise the possibility that he had access to an oral tradition that was derived from it.[11] For his account of Xerxes, Herodotus, theoretically at least, had access to eyewitness accounts. The grandson of a famous Persian named Zopyrus, the man who captured Babylon for Darius, deserted to the Athenians and Herodotus may have spoken with him (3.160). But the distance in time, space, and cultural milieu is so great, and the chain of transmission through which it is mediated so long and so varied, that Herodotus' account of the first three kings is not likely to correspond very closely to the words and deeds of the actual historical figures. The very fact that Herodotus twice insists (contrary, it would appear, to what many of his contemporaries were willing to believe: 3.80, 6.43) that Otanes urged the seven conspirators to abolish monarchy in favour of democracy, shows how little he understood the mentalité of sixth-century Persia.[12] And there are places where one suspects that Herodotus, or his source, has misunderstood the meaning of certain actions. In such cases it may be possible to infer other meanings on the basis of what we otherwise know of Near Eastern customs.[13]

Whatever Herodotus' sources may have been for his account of Persian history (that is, whether Greek or Persian, oral or written), many historians question its basic factual content. For instance, it is commonly argued that the false Smerdis truly was the son of Cyrus and brother of Cambyses, and that Darius denied this in order to legitimate his own seizure of the throne.[14] It has even been doubted that Persia was ever subject to the Medes since apparently there is no archaeological evidence for the existence of a unified Median state.[15] It is highly unlikely that Cambyses actually committed the transgressions against Egyptian religious cults and practices that so outraged Herodotus, and one strongly suspects that Herodotus was grossly misled by his Egyptian sources.[16] According to Herodotus, Cambyses' worst transgression was the fatal wounding of the sacred Apis bull (3.27–9). After he stabbed it, 'the priests buried the bull who died from his wounds in secret from Cambyses' (3.29.3). Yet the epitaph on the grave stele and the inscription on the sarcophagus of this very Apis survive, and they record that Cambyses buried the bull with elaborate funeral rites.[17] The reader should thus be aware that Herodotus' narrative cannot necessarily be taken at face value as a factual record of early Persian history. Modern historians are in the habit of trying to correct and rationalise Herodotus' version of events by employing a combination of probability (always a dangerous method) and documentary sources from Egypt and the Near East (although it should be remembered that official documents can misrepresent and distort events just like literary texts). Nor can later Greek authors (chiefly Xenophon, the fragments of the Greek doctor Ctesias of Cnidus, Diodorus Siculus, and Plutarch) straightforwardly be used to supplement Herodotus for the period that he treats, since Persian institutions and traditions are unlikely to have remained static, and subsequent Greek historians were not beyond turning to invention in the quest for originality.

Herodotus' brief survey of Persian customs and mores (1.131–40) constitutes a mixture of the idealised, the fairly accurate, and the somewhat misunderstood.[18] Herodotus has some knowledge of the ritual functions of the Median *magi*, but he nowhere mentions the prophet Zoroaster and he thinks that Mitra, a male deity, was the Persian version of Aphrodite (1.131).[19] To judge from his confident assertion that all Persian names end in the Greek letter sigma (1.139), which actually is only true in Greek transliteration, he apparently did not know the Persian language (although this may not be significant since the lingua franca of the Persian empire was Aramaic, not Persian).[20] On the other hand, his claim that the Persians hold other peoples in honour in relation to how close they dwell to themselves (considering those who live the farthest away to be the basest) finds corroboration in those Persian royal inscriptions that list the countries and peoples over which the King held sway: with only one exception, these lists begin with the peoples nearest Persia and then move progressively outwards.[21]

On occasion Herodotus uses Persian technical words (8.85.3; 9.110.2) and he cites Persian sources, but it by no means follows that he ever spoke to a Persian himself. When he cites 'the learned men among the Persians' (1.1), or uses phrases such as 'the Persians say' (1.5) or 'it is said by the Persians' (3.87; 7.12), or even when he claims that he knows four different versions of the story of Cyrus' birth and upbringing (1.95), such source citations could be secondhand or merely based on inference (which is not quite the same as being 'invented').[22] So too Herodotus claims to know different versions of Cyrus' death (1.214.5), and he gives two versions of the ruse whereby Darius' groom helped him to gain the kingship (3.87). Although Herodotus claims that in the case of Cyrus he is giving the most plausible version of his birth and death, we cannot be sure where these versions originated. It seems likely enough that the story that Herodotus does not believe to be true – that a bitch (*spako* in Median) reared Cyrus – was an authentic Persian tradition (1.110, 122). But the version that Herodotus prefers, that 'Spako' was a woman's name, sounds all too much like a Greek rationalisation of a Persian legend (perhaps assimilating it to the story of Oedipus' exposure). Nonetheless, for better or for worse, Herodotus remains the best and fullest source for Achaemenid history.

Herodotus' survey of Persian customs, quite apart from what it might or might not tell us about the historical reality of Persian life, is valuable because it can serve as a sort of litmus test for the actions of the Persians in the subsequent narrative. Their society is hierarchical (and there is an elaborate etiquette of greeting between individuals of different social ranks). The Persians are convinced of their own superiority to other peoples, they readily adopt foreign ways, and they are quick to indulge in new pleasures. Nevertheless, they are also truth-speaking and pious, and they consider bravery in battle the highest form of manly virtue. Herodotus explicitly praises some of their customs (1.137), and it is obvious that he approves of the fact that their youths are taught to do three things only, 'to ride, to shoot, and to tell the truth' (1.136). But one is also tempted to infer that some of the seemingly positive qualities of the Persians will actually contribute to the subsequent defeat of Xerxes' grand expedition: their confidence in numbers, their belief that the most inferior peoples are the ones who live the farthest from them, and their acquisitiveness in regard to pleasure and luxury. Clothing, in particular, becomes emblematic of the Persians in the subsequent narrative. Herodotus says that the Persians borrowed the attire of the Medes because it was 'more beautiful than their own'. Later on Aristagoras of Miletus ridicules men who fight 'wearing trousers and turbans' (5.49.3); and at Plataea it is their clothing that causes them the most harm (see below) and which the Greeks totally disregard as booty once the battle is over (9.80.2). At the end of the *Histories* the beautiful robe which his wife gave to Xerxes and which he in turn gave to his mistress brings destruction upon members of the King's family (9.109). Their fancy dress, an object of beauty in its own right, fails to support the Persians' own notions of the supreme importance of bravery and prowess in battle.

Cyrus is the Persian with whom no Persian ever thought it right to compare himself (3.160). The undoubted fact that he was a 'culture hero' for the Persians has left its mark on Herodotus' treatment of him; yet it is still the case that Herodotus has enough cultural distance to explain Cyrus' eventual undoing in terms of the Greek concept of hubris leading to a fall.[23] The first hint of his attitude is in his punishment of the river Gyndes by dividing it into 360 separate channels (1.189), an action which is referred to again in the context of Cyrus' ill-fated decision to attack the Massagetae who dwell beyond the river Araxes (1.202). But his hubris is especially manifested in his disregard of the lesson that he learned when he saved Croesus from the pyre, that he himself was a man like any other and thus subject to the same changes in fortune that affect all mortals (1.86.6). Impelled both by a belief that his birth was something more than human and by his unbroken chain of military successes (1.204), he attacked the nomadic Massagetae at the northeastern edge of the known world and came to an ignominious end (1.214).

His son Cambyses was mad, and that madness led him to transgress the customs of both Egyptians and Persians (3.16, 27–38). Yet perhaps Cambyses' last speech before his death is intended to elicit some sympathy on the part of the reader, as it did among his Persian audience (3.65–6): he laments the folly of killing his own brother, the impossibility of diverting 'what must be', and his own fortune in life. It is poignant indeed that on his deathbed the cruel and deranged tyrant should come to realise some of the core 'truths' about human existence that are embedded in the *Histories*.

Darius' actions in many ways foreshadow those of Xerxes. His bridging of the Danube, his slitting the throats of the three sons of the Persian Oeobazus (4.84), and his unsuccessful expedition against the Scythians prefigure Xerxes' bridging of the Hellespont, his killing of the son of Pythius under similar circumstances, and his disastrous expedition against Greece. In the Constitutional Debate Darius had maintained that monarchy was the best form of government when the best ruler was in power (3.82), and Darius does appear as the best and most successful of the Persian kings after Cyrus. Even so, there is something disquieting about Darius' unscrupulous grasping for power (3.71.5, 85–7) and his ruthlessness in maintaining it (3.118–19, 126–8), as well as in his sophistic assertion that lying and telling the truth are merely two different means of achieving the same goal, one's own profit (3.72.4).[24]

Xerxes is the Persian who receives the fullest treatment in the narrative, and indeed his invasion of Greece in 480 is the climax of the work. His behaviour falls short of the high standard of Persian ethical norms described in Book 1. His cutting in half of the son of the Lydian Pythius (7.39), his branding and whipping of the Hellespont (7.35), his burning of the temples on the Athenian acropolis (8.53), his mutilation of the body of the Spartan king Leonidas despite the latter's manifest courage, his affair with his son's wife and destruction of his brother's family all smack of the godless tyrant. We had specifically been told that the Persians hold rivers in reverence (1.138) and that not even the king can put a man to death for a single offence (1.137). The mutilation of Leonidas is particularly noteworthy since Herodotus claims that the Persians 'more than any other people I know of are accustomed to honour men who distinguish themselves in war' (7.238), and he twice mentions how Persians dressed the wounds of Pytheas of Aegina because of the courage he had displayed against them in battle (7.181; 8.92).

Nonetheless, even Xerxes is not wholly devoid of human feeling nor entirely an unsympathetic character. This marks a sharp difference between Aeschylus' *Persians* and Herodotus; for whereas Cyrus and Darius are noble figures in Aeschylus, the play stresses Xerxes' insolence, cowardice, and effeminacy.[25] The Xerxes of Herodotus is a far more complex figure. When he weeps for the brevity of human life while surveying his army and fleet at Abydus, he appears far from being a heartless tyrant.

Near the end of the *Histories*, Herodotus inserts a final story about Xerxes (9.108–13): he is still a tyrant, to be sure, but a weak man who is mastered by his passions and who transgresses established norms of proper conduct for a king, father, and brother.[26] After his return from Greece, he develops a passion for his brother Masistes' wife, and when his advances are unsuccessful, he turns his interest to Artaÿnte, the daughter of this woman and Masistes. The end result of the king's uncontrolled lust is the mutilation and death of Masistes' wife and the murder of Masistes. This passage, more than any other in Herodotus, brings out the weaknesses inherent in autocracy, and both looks back to and confirms Otanes' claim in the Constitutional Debate that a king 'interferes with ancestral customs, uses force on women, and puts men to death without trial' (3.80.5).[27] Yet at the same time the reader may feel that Xerxes is caught in a web of necessity and is more an object of pity than of fear or indignation.

Xerxes' wife, Amestris, was responsible for the mutilation of her sister-in-law, and this raises the issue of the depiction of Persian royal women. Herodotus does not discuss the political position of Persian women in his ethnography in Book 1; he merely mentions that Persian men have many wives (and a larger number of concubines) and that male children live with their female relations until the age of five. The political and social influence of women emerges rather in the course of the narrative. Such narratives of Persian royal women, it has been suggested, do not give us an accurate portrayal of their lives and influence but rather reflect the Greek tendency to construct an image of the Orient as female, decadent, and weak, and its royal women as cruel, violent, powerful, and vengeful. In other words, it is alleged that they have been constructed on the template of Medea or Clytemnestra, the sort of women whose unbridled power enables them to do bad things.[28]

Herodotus certainly believed that Atossa had 'complete power' at the court (7.3.4; cf. 3.133–4). Amestris, in addition to her mutilation of Masistes' wife, is a rather sinister figure: there is a brief allusion to her burying alive fourteen noble Persian boys 'as an offering in place of herself to the god said to be under the earth' (7.114.2). It would be rash, however, to dismiss this image of her as a mere Greek construction of the oriental female 'other'. Phaidime, the daughter of Otanes, upon her father's request, undertook the dangerous task of exposing the false Smerdis, and the wife of Intaphrenes (one of the seven conspirators who overthrew the false Smerdis) earned the admiration of Darius. When her husband and all her husband's relations were to be executed, save for the one she asked to have spared, like Antigone she requested the life of her brother (for she could acquire another husband and children, but not another brother since her parents were dead). Darius, 'because the woman seemed to him to speak well', gave her the life of her eldest son as well as that of her brother (3.118–19).[29] And most conspicuously there is Masistes' wife who rebuffed the advances of Xerxes. Comparative anthropology confirms that the political influence of royal wives, especially in traditional societies, can be considerable.[30]

It has been fashionable to attribute to Herodotus the view that the Persians failed to conquer Greece because the acquisition of an empire, with the immense wealth and foreign luxury that this brought them, had eroded their former toughness and made them soft.[31] Thus, just as Cyrus had been defeated by the Massagetae and Darius by the Scythians, they were once again worsted by a hardier and simpler people. It is true that the theme of hard and soft peoples runs throughout the *Histories*. Indeed Herodotus portrays Cyrus as inciting the Persians to win their freedom so that they may have 'countless good things' (1.126.5), and Herodotus himself claims that before the conquest of Lydia the Persians lived a simple life and had no luxuries of any kind (1.71, 89; cf. 1.207.6). Such statements, however, need to be seen in their particular context rather than forced into some overarching interpretative scheme. One should be wary of reducing a work as complex and as subtle as the *Histories* to a single and fairly banal explanatory formula. In any case, this is not an explanation that Herodotus gives for the Persian failure to conquer Greece in 480–479. In contrast to their Asiatic allies, who are often faulted for cowardice and who either need the spur of the lash or flee in terror, the Persians at Marathon (6.113), Plataea (9.62–3) and Mycale

(9.102) fight bravely and to the death.[32] Although the Persians attained a high degree of luxury as compared to the simpler and poorer Greeks (7.102.1; 8.26.3; 9.82), it is too simplistic to say, as many moderns have done, that Herodotus attributes their defeat to softness caused by luxury.

Throughout the *Histories*, the Persians, both individually and collectively, are capable of acts of outstanding courage. When we come to the decisive battle of Plataea in 479, in which the Persian and Spartan infantry finally meet head-to-head on equal terms, Herodotus nowhere suggests that either Mardonius himself or his Persian troops were not tough fighters; rather, he explains the defeat of the Persians at Plataea in terms of what we would call 'military technology' (9.62–3; cf. 7.211): 'In spirit and strength the Persians were not inferior [to the Spartans], but being without protective armour and in addition being inexperienced, they were not similar to their opponents in skill.' The Persians were not enfeebled by luxury: they threw themselves upon the Spartans, both singly and in groups of ten or more, grabbing hold of their opponents' spears and perishing in the process, but 'being light-armed soldiers they were contending against hoplites'.

No single Persian in the *Histories* puts on a greater display of boasting and hubris than Mardonius, the man who pushed Xerxes into invading Greece so that he could become the governor of the new province (7.6.1) and who disparaged the Spartans before the battle of Plataea (9.48, 58). Yet even he is not a cowardly barbarian despot: indeed, our last glimpse of him shows him fighting bravely and to the death upon his white horse with his thousand picked Persians (9.63). It was only when these fell that the Persian forces gave way to the Spartans.

So when all has been said and done, what final assessment is the reader to make about Greeks and Persians? The Persians, to be sure, are too confident in the strength of numbers (1.136; 7.48; 7.103) and they tend to underestimate their opponents, and some of them commit heinous acts.[33] Overall, however, they cut a noble figure in the *Histories*, both in terms of their imposing physical appearance and of their desire to accomplish great deeds.[34] The grandee Zopyrus took the extreme step of mutilating himself in order to capture Babylon for Darius (3.150–60), for, as Herodotus explains, 'among the Persians brave deeds are highly valued for the increase of one's prestige' (3.154.1).[35] In a very real sense, the dramatic power of the *Histories*, as of Homer's *Iliad*, depends on the enemy being worthy opponents of the Greeks. Yet, like the Trojans, the Persians are also morally the transgressors. And their transgressions must necessarily be of a severity and magnitude that justifies their defeat in terms of the moral sensibilities of Herodotus and his contemporary audience (cf. 8.109.3; 9.76.2). As he had said of the fall of Troy, 'the divinity brought it about that by their utter destruction the

Trojans should make it manifest to mortals that great wrong-doings incur great punishments from the gods' (2.120.5).

Nevertheless, the whole explanation for the Persian defeat cannot be found at the level of divine punishment for moral transgressions. For the narrative makes plain that the Persians, and Xerxes in particular, made gross strategic errors that cost them the war, while the Greeks made right decisions.[36] Herodotus himself was quite aware that the war was Xerxes' to lose. If only he had followed the advice of Demaratus (7.234–7) and Artemisia (8.68) and had sailed to the Peloponnese instead of engaging the Greek fleet off Salamis, the Hellenic alliance would have disintegrated without a blow. And even after Salamis, Mardonius was in a very strong position, with the powerful city of Thebes and all of central and northern Greece except Athens supporting him. If Mardonius had bided his time and used bribery to sow dissension in the Greek cities, as both the Thebans and the Persian Artabazus had suggested (9.2, 41), he might well have won without a fight, so fragile was Greek unity. Even though the Persian infantry was inferior to the Greek, and especially to the Spartan, in terms of military training and equipment, the Greek victory was by no means assured; one could even say that it was not very likely. The Persians had good reason to be confident of success. It was one man, Themistocles (a man who employed trickery and deceit), who did more than anyone else to bring the war to the point where the Greeks were able to fight at Salamis once Xerxes forced them to do so (7.143–4; 8.75).

Moreover, as some recent scholarship has been at pains to point out, by the end of the *Histories* the moral distance between Persian and Greek has become problematic.[37] After the victory at Plataea, the Spartan commander Pausanias had refused to impale the head of Mardonius, on the grounds that 'such things are more fitting for barbarians to do than for Greeks' (9.78–9). Indeed throughout the *Histories* impalement and crucifixion are typical Persian punishments.[38] Yet when the Athenian admiral Xanthippus (the father of Pericles) consents to the crucifixion of the Persian Artaÿctes, while his son is stoned to death before his eyes, the distinction between Greek and barbarian has become difficult indeed to discern (9.120). Even in Book 1 there are hints that Persians are in some ways more admirable than Greeks. In the passage with which this essay began (1.153), Cyrus declared to the Spartan herald that he had never yet feared men who gather in a market place and, swearing falsely, cheat each other. When the focalisation is that of truth-loving Persians, men who consider telling lies and owing money to be the two most disgraceful things (1.138), the Greeks seem like perjurers and cheats.

The final narrative of the *Histories* (9.122) is particularly relevant to the question of what kind of people the Persians are. Artembares once made a proposal to the Persians (at a time when they were 'ruling the whole of Asia'), which they in turn brought before Cyrus: namely, that the Persians should change their dwelling and exchange their harsh country for a better one. Cyrus says they can do that if they wish, but they must then prepare themselves no longer to rule but be ruled, since soft countries produce soft men. Hearing this, the Persians choose to keep their present land and be rulers.

This passage has received much scrutiny,[39] but the essential thing to realise is that Herodotus is not at the end of his *Histories* encoding an explanation of why the Persians failed to conquer Greece: they did in fact follow Cyrus' advice and did not move *en masse* into the plains. When Herodotus wrote this last scene (whether that was in c. 425 or c. 414) the future of the Greek world was far from certain and the Persian empire was still intact and powerful. Although the Persians lost control over the Aegean islands and the Greek communities in Asia Minor as a consequence of the Greek victory, they still posed a considerable threat to Greek liberty. Moreover, they still believed that the whole of Asia belonged to them (a point emphatically made by Herodotus at both the beginning and end of his history: 1.4.4 and 9.116.3). In 454 an Athenian armada of considerable size (between 40 and 200 war ships) was destroyed by the Persians in Egypt (Thuc. 1.104, 109), and there was an ever-present possibility that the Great King would side with either Athens or Sparta in the Peloponnesian War, as he eventually did in 412 by providing money to Sparta, or even attempt another invasion of mainland Greece (Thuc. 1.90 reflects such a fear). Cyrus' advice points a moral and gives a warning, but one whose full significance was yet to be realised. The *Histories* thus end with an image of the Persians as a tough people under a wise king. They could not and should not be underestimated in the future, a message no less relevant to the Greeks of the fifth and fourth centuries BCE than to posterity.[40]

NOTES

1. The most comprehensive history of the Persian empire is Briant (2002). Short but excellent accounts are Kuhrt (1995) ch. 13 and (2001). Brosius (2000) is a useful source book (cited below by document number). Also worth consulting are Cook (1983) and Wiesehöfer (1996), as well as *CAH* (2nd edn) IV, §§ 1 and 2.

2. This complex topic can only be touched on here; de Jong (2001b) makes some interesting suggestions.

3. See especially E. Hall (1989) and (1993); Hartog (1991). Cartledge (2002) ch. 3 is an accessible discussion.

4. Yet even Aeschylus does not really depict the Persians in a completely stereotypical way. Darius, for instance, stresses that Xerxes' actions have been un-Persian (*Pers.* 739–86).

5. The phrase comes from Greenblatt (1991) 127.

6. See Hall (1989) 19–47.

7. By contrast, the only Greek people to receive an ethnography are the Spartans (6.56–60), who were considered to be the most culturally distinct of the Greeks.

8. Brosius (2000) no. 47.

9. For the relevance of the Persepolis tablets to Herodotus, see Lewis (1984) and (1985); for the Behistun inscription, see n. 11 below.

10. On the speeches, see Pelling in this volume.

11. There are, however, some important differences. Herodotus (3.30) has Cambyses kill his brother Smerdis after his arrival in Egypt (not before he left), and (3.70) he has Darius slay the *magus*, who was pretending to be Smerdis, in Susa (rather than in Media). Köhnken (1980) sees these differences as being due to Herodotus' own compositional concerns. In general, see Balcer (1987) and the interesting discussions by Lenfant (1996) and Asheri (1999).

12. On this debate, see Pelling (2002) and Dewald (2003).

13. It is possible that Artabanus put on Xerxes' clothing and then sat on his throne and slept in his bed, not to test the King's bad dream, but as part of a Babylonian ritual of king substitution (Germain [1956]); that the Persian army marched between two halves of the son of Pythius not merely as a punishment, but as a rite of purification (Briant (2002) 243); that Xerxes burnt Greek temples, not because he was impious, but because he considered them to be inhabited by demons and thus in need of purification by fire (Georges [1994] 56–8); and that an attempted palace *coup* lies behind the story of Xerxes' passion for his brother's daughter (Sancisi-Weerdenburg [1983]). Also, there seem to be Indian and Near Eastern parallels for the 'ruse' of Darius' groom at 3.84–8 (see Briant [2002] 898).

14. See especially Briant (2002) 97–106; the modern consensus is challenged by Pelling (2002) 128.

15. Kuhrt (1995) 652–6, and Lanfranchi et al. (2003).

16. Briant (2002) 55–61.

17. Brosius (2000) nos. 21 and 22.

18. Note Immerwahr (1966) 184–8; Briant (1990); and Munson (2001a) 149–56.

19. Herodotus (1.101) alone calls the *magi* a Median tribe. See Cook (1983) 154–5; *CHI* 696–7; Briant (2002) 96, 245–6; Burkert (2004) 99–124.

20. I say 'apparently' because is it is possible that Herodotus is making a claim not about the spelling of Persian personal names, but about their pronunciation (as suggested by Legrand [1946] 155). His point may be that Persians do not realise that they pronounce their names with an 's' sound at the end, just as some Americans pronounce certain words (such as 'idea') with a final 'r'. I am grateful to Rosaria Munson for drawing my attention to this possibility.

21. Kuhrt (2002) 19–22.

22. The nature of Herodotus' source citations is much disputed by modern scholars. Most would reject the extreme position of Fehling (1989), esp. 12–86, that

the citations themselves are completely fictitious. The most compelling studies are Murray (2001a) and (2001b), Luraghi (2001b) and his contribution in this volume.

23. On Herodotus' characterisation of the Persian kings, see Immerwahr (1966) ch. 4; Evans (1991) ch. 2; Georges (1994) ch. 6; Dewald (2003). On Cambyses, see also Munson (1991) and on Xerxes, see Sancisi-Weerdenburg (2002).

24. At 3.89.3 this judgement is focalised through the Persians: 'The Persians say that Darius was a tradesman, Cambyses a master, and Cyrus a father.'

25. See especially lines 465–71, 739–86. Hall (1996) is an excellent commentary on this play.

26. See Wolff (1964) and Flower and Marincola (2002) 291–300.

27. Although Xerxes did not actually use violence against his sister-in-law, Herodotus says (9.108.1) that he only refrained from doing so out of respect for his brother.

28. See, in particular, Sancisi-Weerdenburg (1983) and Brosius (1996); cf. Dewald (1981).

29. On this story, see Dewald and Kitzinger in this volume.

30. For example, Mack (1991) on the Hausa women of Kano in Northern Nigeria.

31. Influential statements of this view are Cobet (1971) 172–6; Raaflaub (1987) 244–6 and (2002a) 171–2.

32. Flower and Marincola (2002) 15–16, 216–17, 312.

33. Oroetes, the governor of Sardis, ensnared and brutally murdered Polycrates of Samos (3.120–27); Artaÿctes deceived Xerxes himself into giving him the house of the Greek hero Protesilaus so that he could plunder it (9.116). It is important to note, however, that these men are represented as transgressing the moral standards of their own culture.

34. Herodotus never comments on the appearance of the Greek commanders, but Xerxes (7.187.2), Masistes (9.25.1), and Tigranes (9.96.2) are noteworthy for their 'size and beauty'.

35. So too thirty Persian nobles vied for the privilege of punishing Oroetes for Darius (3.128).

36. There are many historical studies of the Persian Wars, but the most sensible is Lazenby (1993). For a historiographical analysis, see Harrison (2002). See also Tritle in this volume.

37. Pelling (1997b) is a seminal study of this topic.

38. At its most extreme, Darius impaled the three thousand leading men of the Babylonians (3.159), but this cruel punishment is also dealt out on an individual basis.

39. Recent discussions include Moles (1996); Dewald (1997b); Pelling (1997b); and Flower and Marincola (2002) 311–14.

40. I would like to thank Harriet Flower, Christopher Pelling, and the editors for their comments and encouragement.

19

TIM ROOD

Herodotus and foreign lands

In the preface to his *Histories*, Herodotus promises to describe the great and wonderful deeds and monuments displayed both by Greeks and by non-Greeks as well as to explain why they fought against each other. He proceeds at once to what he claims is a Persian account of the origin of their disputes. The account attributed to the Persians turns out to be a sort of mythographic pastiche describing how enmity arose first when a Greek woman, Io, was seized by Phoenicians, and then from the seizure of three other women (Europa, Medea, and Helen). This Persian account of the origin of hostilities between Greeks and barbarians includes, among other notable features, the first ethnographic observation in Herodotus' *Histories* (1.4.4):

> The Persians say that while they, on the Asian side, took no account of it when their women were seized, the Greeks gathered together a great army for the sake of a Spartan woman and then came to Asia and destroyed the power of Priam; and they think that the Greeks have always been hostile to them from that time. For the Persians regard Asia and the barbarian people living there as their own, but think that Europe and the Greeks are separate.

According to these Persians, clashes of cultural attitudes lie at the heart of the hostility between different nations. This observation is the first hint that a study of foreign customs will play its part in Herodotus' attempt to explain why Greeks and barbarians fought each other. But as Herodotus' work progresses, it becomes clear that his inquiry into foreign lands and peoples does far more than just underpin his explanation of the cultural conflicts that culminate in the great Persian invasions of Greece. Herodotus' inquiry into other lands and customs proves to be as central to his project as his inquiry into the wars fought by Greeks and non-Greeks.

Herodotus describes the lands and customs of numerous peoples in the course of his work – among them the Lydians, Persians, Babylonians, Egyptians, Ethiopians, Scythians, and Libyans. The amount of space that Herodotus gives to descriptions of foreign lands and peoples would have been less surprising to his original audience than it is to modern readers accustomed to different notions of historiography. At the time Herodotus was writing, there was no rigid separation between genres such as geography, ethnography, and historiography. Herodotus built on the work of his predecessors, especially Hecataeus of Miletus (author of a geographical and a mythographic work), to produce something more substantial: a collection of empirical data that lets Herodotus and his (contemporary and future) audience examine both the variety and the constants of human behaviour.[1] Herodotus constructs both a cultural map and an image of the physical world that allow his Greek audience to read its own place within both grids, cultural and physical alike.

Where did Herodotus gain his information about so many little-known lands and peoples? Often he gives no indication about his sources. At times he attributes information to peoples: 'the Persians say', 'the Egyptians say'. These statements do not imply that the Persians or Egyptians gave the information to Herodotus himself: they merely indicate the existence of a tradition.[2] But occasionally Herodotus does claim that he has travelled and made inquiries and seen sights for himself. Such claims are particularly frequent in Herodotus' account of Egypt: he uses past tenses to imply that information was given directly to him when he was in Egypt (e.g. 'I heard this story', 2.43.1; 'after this the priests read out the names of another 330 kings', 2.100.1). Whether Herodotus did in fact travel to all the places he claims to have visited has been much doubted: there are many difficulties in making sense of what he claims to have seen, and some scholars have argued that nearly all of Herodotus' source-citations are fictional. In their most extreme form such claims do not make allowance for the literary and cultural context in which Herodotus was working, but it may be that we should not always equate Herodotus himself with the persona of the first-person narrator within the text.[3] Our concern here will in any case be with the way Herodotus' descriptions of foreign lands and peoples shape his audience's understanding of his narrative and of the world at large: what is important for this inquiry is to accept that Herodotus subjected to his own critical scrutiny the information that he transmits, whatever its source.

The Lydians, the first foreigners in the *Histories*

The first ethnographical section in the *Histories* – on the Lydians – shows many of the usual characteristics of Herodotus' descriptions of foreign lands and peoples: a concern for marvels (*thōmata*), great monuments (*erga*), and customs (*nomoi* or *nomaia*). The Lydian ethnography is placed after Herodotus has described how the Lydian king Croesus was defeated by the

Persians. Moving by a process of associative logic that can easily be mistaken for garrulity, Herodotus next describes some of Croesus' dedications at Greek sanctuaries, and then turns to Lydia itself: 'As for marvels, the land of Lydia does not have any in particular, compared at least with other lands, except for the gold dust brought down Mount Tmolus. It does offer one monument that is far the greatest except for the Egyptian and Babylonian monuments' – the tomb of Croesus' father Alyattes (1.93.1–2). It seems as if Herodotus is merely running through a list of categories – first marvels, then monuments. But the very slenderness of the textual motivation for this, the first description of a foreign land in Herodotus' work, is telling. Herodotus was writing for an audience for whom some description of marvels and monuments was an expected part of an account of a foreign land: when he mentions Alyattes' tomb Herodotus tempts his audience by alluding to the great man-made edifices that will appear in his descriptions of Babylon and Egypt. Indeed, the presence of such features partly explains the depth of coverage Herodotus gives in particular cases. At times, as in his description of Lydia, his account merely covers a page or two of modern text. Elsewhere – for instance in the case of the nomadic Scythians – his treatment is far more extensive. But nothing matches the hundred or so pages devoted to Egypt – a length of treatment that Herodotus justifies precisely on the grounds of its extraordinary features and monuments (2.35.1).

After describing the tomb of Alyattes, Herodotus turns to Lydian customs: 'the Lydians have customs similar to the Greeks, except that they prostitute their daughters' (1.94.1). Herodotus here explicitly measures foreign customs by Greek standards: it is because the Lydians are in other respects close to the Greeks that Herodotus does not describe their other customs. In some of his later, more detailed ethnographies, Herodotus will give far longer accounts of customs that differ from the Greek norm, focussing typically on features such as burial customs, religion, food, habitation, and clothing. His comment that the Lydians prostitute their daughters falls under another common heading, marriage customs: he has already described how Alyattes' tomb was built by traders and prostitutes, explaining that 'the daughters of the common people of the Lydians all work as prostitutes, gathering dowries for themselves, until they get married' (1.93.4).

Herodotus' account of Lydian customs also shows an awareness that customs are not static. He notes the inventions for which the Lydians were responsible (gold and silver coins, shopkeeping), and cites the Lydians themselves as saying that they invented all the games (except for draughts) that they share with the Greeks (1.94.1–2). His ethnographies are also lit up by vivid insights into social memory – that is, into how people interpret their present customs in the light of their past experiences: the Lydians, he explains, say that they invented games to relieve their sufferings during a famine (they would play games one day and eat the next). Similarly we later learn that the Athenians made their women change from Dorian to Ionian clothing to punish them for stabbing to death with their brooches the sole survivor of an Athenian force sent to Aegina (5.87.2: Ionian tunics did not need pins for fastening). In the story of the Lydian famine, ethnography even verges into what we understand as history: Herodotus proceeds to relate another expedient that the Lydians devised in addition to games – the emigration of half of their population, who eventually settled in Italy and became known as Tyrrhenians (Etruscans) after the name of their leader (1.94.5–7). This story of Lydian emigration seems to be an incidental addition (though we may recall it later in the *Histories* when the Athenians threaten to move to the West in response to the Persians' attack: 8.62.2). In the case of Egypt, by contrast, Herodotus includes a long historical survey, organised by kings, as well as his usual description of geographical and ethnographical features.

Ethnography and imperial expansion

While the ethnography of the Lydians establishes a pattern that is followed in many of Herodotus' later and longer accounts of foreign customs, it is in one way at odds with his usual practice. He describes Lydian customs *after* they have been subjugated by the Persians, while later in the *Histories* he tends to describe foreign lands and peoples when they first come into contact with or are attacked by the Persians. At one level, this difference reflects a shift in the broader structuring of Herodotus' work. He starts his history with the Lydian king Croesus because Croesus was the first foreign ruler to subject Greeks. After Croesus' downfall, and the Lydian ethnography that is appended to it, there is a strong sense of a new beginning (1.95.1): 'At this point our account seeks to find out who this Cyrus was who destroyed the rule of Croesus and how the Persians gained control of Asia.' Herodotus here marks the move from the question he had initially posed – who first subjugated Greeks? – to the story of Persian expansion, which will cover their conquest of many non-Greek peoples whom Herodotus will describe as the Persians conquer, or attempt to conquer, them. But Herodotus does not stick to this principle mechanically. When he describes Cyrus' desire to conquer the Massagetae, for instance, he gives some slight information about their habits and location at once (they are said to be populous and warlike, they live beyond the river Araxes), and more information (on their clothes and weapons, food and religion, marriage customs) later – as a sort of coda, after they have defeated and killed Cyrus (1.201–3, 215–16).

The way Herodotus integrates geographical and ethnographical information into his narrative of imperial expansion highlights the political aspects of scientific inquiry. While in the modern world inquiry into foreign lands has often gone hand in hand with imperial control, Herodotus was writing from the point of view of the invaded Greeks, not the invading Persians. It may seem significant, then, that Herodotus holds up his narrative of the Persians' imperialist march by lingering on the customs of those who succumb to or resist them.[4] It is as if his own narrative is opposing that relentless march. Indeed, Cambyses' ambition to conquer Egypt seems to be dwarfed by the vast account of Egyptian geography and history that Herodotus inserts – an account that is several times longer than the narrative of Cambyses' actual conquest of Egypt. Yet Herodotus is also highlighting the significance of Egypt to the Persians and putting this new conquest in the context of Egypt's long history – a history that is itself a tale of the expansive and monumentalising drive of kings. Herodotus indeed inserts into the Egyptian *logos* two stories that anticipate how Darius, Cambyses' successor, responded to the Egyptians' imperial past: an Egyptian priest refused to allow Darius to set up his statue in front of a statue of the Egyptian king Sesostris, since his conquests were no match for Sesostris'; and Darius completed the canal through to the Red Sea that another Egyptian king had started (2.110, 158).

Whatever the significance of Herodotus' arrangement, a clear understanding of the political impact of geographical and ethnographical information is shown by characters within the *Histories*. When Herodotus describes how Croesus sends envoys to find out which of the Greek states are the most powerful, he uses the same word for Croesus' inquiry that he uses of his own (*historiē*, 1.56.1). Other kings send scouts to gain geographical knowledge as a prelude to conquest.[5] Most revealing, however, is an episode that occurs just before the start of the Ionian Revolt in 499 BCE. Aristagoras, the tyrant of Miletus, gathers together his advisers to discuss whether Miletus should revolt against the rule of the Persian king Darius. All of his advisers recommend revolt – with one exception, the writer (*logopoios*) Hecataeus, who tries to deter Aristagoras from war 'by cataloguing all the nations and tribes subject to Darius and all his resources' (5.36.2). The wise adviser is ignored, and Aristagoras ventures abroad to Sparta to try to seek support for the revolt from the leading power in mainland Greece. Armed with a bronze sheet inscribed with the outline of the whole world, Aristagoras explains to the Spartan king Cleomenes how easy it would be to launch an expedition against Persia: the non-Greek inhabitants are feeble warriors who use bows and short spears, and wear trousers into battle. He then points to his map and gives a geographical sketch of Asia, describing the people who live along the route to Susa: the wealthy Lydians, the Phrygians who are extremely rich in flocks, and so on. Cleomenes postpones his decision until another meeting two days later, when he asks Aristagoras just one question: how far is the journey from the coast to Susa? Aristagoras replies that it is a three months' journey, and before he has the chance to elaborate on this Cleomenes dismisses him (5.49–50). Herodotus himself proceeds to give in his own person the description of the route (including the numbers of stages and parasangs) that Aristagoras was prevented from giving (5.52–4).

The presence of the geographer Hecataeus at Aristagoras' initial council is the first hint that this episode will offer insights into Herodotus' understanding of geographical and ethnographic knowledge. When he reports that Hecataeus gave an account of Persia's resources at the council at Miletus, Herodotus offers no further details (perhaps because he has already given a long account of the Persian empire on Darius' accession: 3.89–96). When Aristagoras gives a geographical discourse in his speech at Sparta, by contrast, Herodotus does include that speech in full. He also has Aristagoras use some of the mannerisms proper to the geographical style found in the fragments of Hecataeus and occasionally employed by the Herodotean narrator: the middle verb *echomai*, for instance, in the sense of 'be next to'. Aristagoras also moves from the coast over to an island, Cyprus, in the style of a *periplous* (a geographical description oriented from the point of view of a sailor voyaging along a coast). And his map with an outline of the whole world (*gēs hapasēs periodos*) echoes the title of Hecataeus' geographical work. But while Aristagoras adopts the Hecataean mode, he attempts to put geographical knowledge to a very different purpose. For Hecataeus, geographical knowledge is a deterrent; for Aristagoras, it is an incitement. Or rather, Aristagoras attempts to pass off as knowledge a rather crude version of ethnography, full of polysyllabic superlatives (*poluargutōtatoi, poluprobatōtatoi, polukarpōtatoi* – 'very rich in silver/flocks/crops') that he hopes will attract his rapacious listener. By contrasting the wise Hecataeus and the brash Aristagoras, Herodotus hints at the differing uses that readers could make of the geographical information that he himself imparts.[6]

Herodotus' own account of the journey inland against the king of Persia raises further questions about Aristagoras' speech. Herodotus employs more features of the proper geographical style when he describes the journey inland which Aristagoras never got the chance to describe: the dative of the participle (*diabanti*, 'for a person crossing') and a second person addressee ('you will pass through'). But Herodotus does not use the persona of the geographical inquirer in the same way as Aristagoras. We never get the chance to hear how Aristagoras would have described this journey, but what Herodotus' account stresses are the obstacles on the way to Susa: three gates, four forts, seven rivers. Perhaps Herodotus' account of the difficulties found along the course of the Royal Road was written in opposition to schemes of panhellenic conquest like Aristagoras'.[7] At any rate, Herodotus' treatment of geography here underlines one of the main messages of his work: the difficulty not just of acquiring knowledge, but also of using it intelligently.

Ethnography and Herodotus' Greek audience

Much as Aristagoras' presentation of Asia was moulded by what he thought would please Cleomenes, Herodotus' own presentation of foreign lands and peoples is inevitably constrained by the demands of his audiences and the restrictions of his own historical perspective. Writing for a Greek audience, Herodotus presents a geography and ethnography of difference: he focusses on what Greek listeners or readers would find strange. He says, for instance, that he will not explain to the Greeks the shape of a camel, since they know this, but he will describe what is not well known: that their genitals point backwards towards their tails (3.103). He makes the unfamiliar seem familiar by the use of analogy: he compares the shape of the Crimea with that of Cape Sunium near Athens or the southern coastline of Italy (4.99.4–5), or the journey from the coast of Egypt to Heliopolis with that from the Altar of the Twelve Gods in Athens to the temple of Olympian Zeus in Pisa (2.7.1); he writes that the Massagetae get drunk on the smoke of a certain plant just as Greeks get drunk on wine (1.202.2). It is not just in such overt ways that Herodotus' Greek perspective is apparent. In describing foreign lands, he gives most weight to two features in which Greece itself is deficient: rivers and vast man-made constructions. He is particularly fascinated by the river systems of Egypt and Mesopotamia: he expounds the system of irrigation in Mesopotamia (1.193), speculates on the reasons that the Nile floods in summer (2.19–27), and brings out how use of the flood waters is central to the Egyptians' agricultural production (2.14). As for monuments, it is enough to quote his striking remark about one of the great buildings that he claims to have seen in Egypt, the labyrinth at Lake Moeris (2.148.2): 'If one were to compare all the Greeks' forts and monuments, they would have taken less toil and expense than this labyrinth.' Herodotus's use of a Greek cultural matrix is also seen in his account of other people's customs. When he describes how the Persians sacrifice to their gods, he uses negatives to highlight what is different from Greek customs: they do not build temples, statues, or altars, or use libations or garlands when they sacrifice (1.131.1, 132.1). This Greek perspective also emerges in much less overt ways, as François Hartog in particular has brought out in discussing Herodotus' description of the spaces and customs of the nomadic Scythians, whose way of life seems utterly alien to the world of the Greek *polis*, yet whose strategy for resisting the Persians bears comparison in some ways with the Greeks' response later in the *Histories*.[8]

Another strand of Herodotus' ethnocentricity is revealed in a fascinating passage where he maps the world in terms of its marvels: 'the extremities of the inhabited world were allotted the finest features, just as Greece was allotted much the most finely mixed seasons' (3.106.1). Herodotus here suggests that there is a sort of cosmic balance, with Greece's finely mixed climate matching the extraordinary features found at the edges of the world (the point is underlined by verbal echoing: *kallista elachon* ~ *kallista . . . elache*). He goes on to describe those extraordinary features: the extremely large animals of India, the fragrant spices, winged snakes, and long-tailed sheep (with carts for their tails) found in Arabia, and the exceptionally handsome and long-lived men who inhabit Ethiopia. He also suggests that a similar balance operates in the animal world: savage predators like lions or those Arabian winged snakes produce very few offspring, while prey like hares can produce many. But while Herodotus explicitly attributes this balancing in the reproductive system of animals to divine providence (3.108.1), he offers no such explanation for the marvels found at the extremities of the earth – unless he is hinting at a climatic explanation: the seasons at the periphery are by implication far less finely mixed than in Greece. (He has earlier offered a climatic explanation for the good health of the Egyptians and Libyans, while also suggesting that the Ethiopians' longevity may be due to what they eat and drink [2.77.3, 3.22.4].)[9]

The end of Herodotus' account of the remote regions of the earth suddenly destabilises the picture he has earlier built up. After he has described the eastern and southern extremities of the earth, Herodotus admits that he knows far less the northern and western extremes of Europe (3.115–16). Poets describe an electrum-carrying river Eridanus, but Herodotus does not vouchsafe its existence. He also says that he has no eyewitness reports as to whether there is a sea at that end of Europe; he does not believe that the northern parts are inhabited by one-eyed men with natures in other respects like those of other men (presumably because he accepts that underlying different nations' contrasting customs there are some constant physiological elements). Such epistemological scepticism is found in a number of other passages where Herodotus matches increasingly uncertain information with increasing distance from the Greek centre. The interesting point here is that Herodotus adds (3.116.3): 'In any case the extremities, enclosing and bounding the rest of the world, are likely to have features that seem to us very fine and rare.' For all the cognitive distance, Herodotus keeps to the image of the exotic margins by using the criterion of what is probable (*to eikos*). But he also undermines that image by saying the features in the margins '*seem to us* very fine and rare'. That is, it is because the Greeks picture themselves in the centre and lands like Arabia and Ethiopia at the margins that they build up an image of the exoticism of the world's extremes. People living at the extremes may have different perspectives. From a Greek perspective, Ethiopia seems an extraordinarily rich land of gold. But, Herodotus has earlier explained, the Ethiopians value gold as other people value bronze, and *vice versa* (3.23.4). By exposing how the values given to metals are not dictated by anything intrinsic to them, Herodotus shows how Greeks and others are blinded by their limited perspective. He also uses the Arabians to demonstrate that people living at the extremities may themselves be blinded in a similar way. The Arabs, he claims, say that the whole world would be full of winged snakes, and human life impossible, were it not that those snakes produce very few offspring. But in fact, he explains, there are not so many winged snakes in the world, it just happens that they are all found in Arabia. The Arabs have made a false inference from the number of these creatures in their own land (3.109).

Far from pandering to Greek assumptions of cultural superiority, Herodotus' account of the earth's extremities encourages readers or listeners to think through and question their own preconceptions. Elsewhere, too, Herodotus relativises notions of superiority. He notes, for instance, that the Egyptians call all those who do not speak their own language 'barbarians' (2.158.5). His point is not that they use the same word as the Greeks, but that like the Greeks, they have a single word for those who do not speak their own language: Greeks are barbarians to Egyptians just as Egyptians are barbarians to Greeks. This insight is introduced incidentally, to explain the use of 'barbarian' in an Egyptian oracle. Precisely because it is so offhand, this remark illustrates how central a degree of cultural relativism is to Herodotus' world-view. He encourages Greeks to think about how other cultures view foreign peoples, and so how they as Greeks appear to others in much the same way that foreign peoples appear to Greeks.[10]

The trend towards relativism is nowhere clearer than in Herodotus' account of the madness of the Persian king Cambyses. After recording a number of instances of Cambyses' mad behaviour – committing incest with his sister, shooting the son of a loyal servant through the heart, mocking and even burning various cult statues at Memphis in Egypt – Herodotus justifies his claim that Cambyses was mad (3.38):

> It is altogether clear to me that Cambyses was mad in a big way – for he would not otherwise have gone in for mocking what was sacred and traditional. For if one were to give all peoples the chance to pick the best customs out of all customs, they would each consider and then choose their own: so much is each accustomed to regard their own customs as by far the best. It is not likely, then, that anyone other than a madman would mock at such things.

Herodotus then says that his claim that people think their own customs best could be illustrated by many different examples. He gives just one example: a cultural experiment carried out by Darius. Darius brought together some Indians from the Callatiae tribe and some Greeks who happened to be present at his court. He first asked the Greeks, whose custom was to burn corpses, what it would take for them to eat the corpses of their fathers; and then he asked the Indians, whose custom was to eat their fathers' corpses, what it would take for them to burn them. Both Greeks and Indians are horrified at his suggestion. That is, Greek practices are as repugnant to the Callatian Indians as Indian practices are to Greeks. No wonder Herodotus concludes by approving Pindar's famous maxim that 'custom (*nomos*) is king of all' (3.38).[11]

Herodotus' argument about Cambyses' madness does not show that he was a strict cultural relativist. He does not claim that all customs are equally valid, but rather that recognition that one's own perspective on others' customs is culturally determined should lead to tolerance. Elsewhere he does occasionally assess different customs himself, praising some (Babylonian marriage auctions, 1.196) and criticising others (all Babylonian women have to sit in a sanctuary of Aphrodite and have sex with a stranger, 1.199). It is not clear whether Herodotus thought that he had somehow freed himself from the rule of Greek custom when he made such judgements. At any rate, when he discusses Cambyses' madness, Herodotus' commitment to tolerance for other customs emerges from a glaring leap in his argument. Cambyses' mocking of Egyptian cult could have been taken not as a proof of his madness, but simply as a sign that people regard their own customs as best. Herodotus presumes that people will first be aware that they perceive their own customs as best; then be aware that everyone shares this perception; and finally understand that their own perception of superiority is culturally conditioned. Far easier proof of Cambyses' madness was available earlier, when Cambyses burnt the corpse of the Egyptian king Amasis: burning corpses, Herodotus noted, was impious both for Persians and for Egyptians (3.16).

Darius' cultural experiment makes its point particularly well because it turns on the emotive issue of the disposal of parents' corpses. Yet the message

Herodotus draws from this experiment seems to be undermined by the way the Greeks and Indians respond to Darius' question. While the Greeks simply reply that no amount of money would make them eat their parents, the Indians shout out loud and tell Darius to keep an auspicious silence (*euphēmeein*: the word has a religious connotation). By contrasting the restrained Greek response with the emotional Indian shout, is Herodotus inviting his Greek audience to admire their own stiff upper lip and look down on the primitive Indians? Not necessarily. Greek readers and listeners did not need the narrator to prod their emotions at the thought of eating their parents. They did need to be made to re-think their own habits. Far from pandering to Greek assumptions, the Indians' profound disgust at what seems natural to Greeks in fact reinforces Herodotus' message of tolerance.

Darius' experiment also tells us something about Darius himself. In his account of Persian customs, Herodotus claims that the Persians respect most those living closest to them, and least those living furthest away (1.134.2) – another hit at the Greeks' own ethnocentric assumptions. Here we see a Persian king summoning representatives from the furthest regions of Persian influence – Greece and India. He is putting them in their place with a display of his own power: once more we see how ethnographic inquiry may be interlinked with imperial domination. Later Herodotus shows how Darius himself became king in part at least thanks to Persian custom. After the overthrow of the *magi*, when the Persian grandees were debating what sort of a constitution to adopt, Darius appealed to Persian custom (*nomos*) in support of a monarchy (3.82.5). This argument bears the hallmark of a man who had earlier claimed that people tell lies or speak the truth as it suits them (3.72.4) – even though the Persians themselves were supposedly trained to tell the truth (1.136.2). Custom may be king of all, but Darius himself becomes king thanks to his manipulation of custom.

Herodotus and the anthropological model

Herodotus may have invited his Greek audience to think through their own preconceptions by the way he relates the customs of other peoples, but for all that, his ethnographical descriptions have disappointed some modern readers. Herodotus' perspective, it has been felt, is not that of the modern anthropologist, trying to understand a foreign culture in its own terms, but that of a curious onlooker who gets no further than a rich description and gridding of particularities.[12] Indeed, the very category of custom (*nomos*) seems to provide a convenient stopping point to Herodotus' inquiry. By using a similar grid (burial and marriage customs, food) to approach different customs, Herodotus points both to differences and similarities between different peoples: their customs can simply be read against each other. (There is one Libyan tribe – the Androphagi, or 'Man-Eaters' – which lacks *nomos* altogether [4.106], but here Herodotus is using the word in the more restricted sense of 'law'.) But Herodotus does in fact provide some explanations for foreign customs. He links, for instance, the Persians' failure to set up statues of gods with their rejection of anthropomorphism (1.131.1); and he mentions the rationale (*noos*) behind the Massagetae custom of sacrificing horses to the sun, the only god they worship (1.216.4): 'They offer the swiftest of mortal beings to the swiftest of the gods.' Still, explanations of this sort do not quite amount to a sense of a cultural system.

Herodotus does have an eye for one sort of system: coherent and self-regulating modes of social organisation such as the Babylonian marriage auctions which he overtly praises (1.196). Herodotus describes how every year all the women to be married are gathered and auctioned; the best-looking women are auctioned first, and the money gained is used to provide dowries for the ugliest. That is, the Babylonians achieve a neat balancing act, and it is this that attracts Herodotus' admiration – even if we may suspect that the whole account is a play of fancy, a projection on to a foreign people of the concerns of Greek political theory (concerns about equality and the social order, for instance).[13] Elsewhere Herodotus shows a keen sense for how different peoples adapt to their physical environments. He describes, for instance, how merchants carrying goods down to Mesopotamia use boat frames covered with skins, and then, since the current is too strong to sail up river, they dismantle the boats and journey back upriver by donkey with the skins; and that is why they make their boats out of skins rather than wood (1.194). The contrast with Greek practice is explained by local conditions. The same interest in a cultural system regulated by its environment pervades Herodotus' account of the inhabitants of Lake Prasias in Thrace (5.16): they live on platforms in the lake, and each man collects three posts for each woman he marries. They also tie their babies by the ankle to stop them falling in to the lake, and live off fish from the lake. The inhabitants of this lake, Herodotus notes, were the only Thracians able to resist the Persians: that is, they provide a model of self-sufficiency, a lesson on how to survive against an invasion. The way of life of the nomadic Scythians provides the same sort of model on a grander scale.[14] These various barbarian peoples show precisely the sort of practical intelligence that Herodotus admires (and exemplifies in his own inquiries).

The sense of a cultural system is strongest in Herodotus' account of the topsy-turvy life of the Egyptians. The Egyptians' customs, Herodotus writes, are the reverse of all other peoples': women go out and shop while men stay at home and weave; men carry burdens on their heads, women on their shoulders; women urinate standing up, men urinate squatting; priests shave their heads instead of wearing their hair long (2.35–6). It is not to assert Greek cultural superiority that Herodotus attributes to the Egyptians habits that are the opposite of those of the Greeks (and in any case he says that Egyptian customs invert those of all other peoples). Rather, he draws his audience's attentions to a pattern in Egyptian society: the topsy-turvy nature of Egyptian customs is their defining mark. Herodotus also seems to provide an explanation for their unusual customs when he writes that their climate and river are different from others (2.35.2). Egypt itself is a 'gift of the Nile' thanks to silting (2.5.1: Herodotus took the phrase from Hecataeus), and the character of the inhabitants is somehow homologous to their unusual physical environment. Herodotus later maps out a series of oppositions between the Egyptians, who live in a hot southern land, and the Scythians, who live in a cold northern land: Egypt is dominated by the Nile, while Scythia has many rivers, which are compared with the channels of the Nile (4.47.1); Egypt is unusual because the Nile floods in summer, Scythia is unusual because it rains in summer (4.28.2); the Egyptians thought that they were the oldest of all peoples, while the Scythians regard themselves as the youngest (2.2.1, 4.5.1); and so on. Here too we may suspect that Herodotus is hinting at a geographical explanation for these differences: the contrast between Scythia and Egypt (and Libya) was established in contemporary scientific writers.[15]

The neat schematism of the Egypt–Scythia polarity can be traced elsewhere in Herodotus' perception of the world, but it also reflects a mode of thought that Herodotus at times attacks (notably in his attack on overly symmetrical ideas about the division of continents, 4.36). And in general a sense of particularity is the dominant note in his account of foreign lands. He reports, for instance, that the Eneti in the northern Adriatic have the same marriage auctions as the Babylonians (1.196.1). Much later he mentions that the Sigynnae, whose territory comes close to that of the Eneti, wear Median clothing and are said to be descended from the Medes – themselves near-neighbours of the Babylonians (5.9). Perhaps the Eneti learnt their Babylon-style marriage customs from the Median Sigynnae? Herodotus does not make the link. All he says is that he cannot imagine how the Sigynnae could be Median colonists – but he adds that anything can happen in the long run.

Greeks and non-Greeks

Herodotus may have constructed a cultural map of the differing customs of Greeks and non-Greeks, but this does not mean that he was working with static ethnic categories. Herodotus' text does famously define the Greeks as sharing the same blood, language, religious rites, and way of life (8.144.2). But this definition is offered in a speech, when the Athenians are parading before the Spartans their refusal to join the Persians – an offer that had been made through the Macedonian king, whose own claim to Greekness Herodotus has earlier accepted (5.22). Elsewhere differences among the Greeks emerge. Herodotus himself offers a description of the Ionians which stresses that they do not all speak quite the same language (1.142). And in his account of Spartan kingship (an ethnography of sorts), he explicitly points to similarities with non-Greek practices (6.59–60): the Spartans emerge as an internal Other.[16] Herodotus also uses an evolutionary perspective, describing how the Greeks were 'separated off' from the barbarians (1.60.3): here he uses the same verb (*apokrinesthai*) that cosmologists used for the separation of elements out from an undifferentiated mass. The implication is that Greeks have developed from the same basis as barbarians.

Herodotus' model of cultural interaction and diffusion also blurs the boundaries between different peoples: peoples change as they come into contact with others and learn their habits (as the Greeks learnt much from the Egyptians). Changes happen for other reasons too, as can be seen within the temporal scope of the *Histories*. Towards the start of the work, one of Herodotus' wise advisers, Sandanis, warned Croesus against attacking the Persians because there was nothing to gain from conquering them: they are primitive, living in a rugged land that gives them a meagre livelihood – and Herodotus comments: 'until they conquered the Lydians, the Persians had nothing delicate or good' (1.71.4). Later we get hints that the Persians have been softened by success: they are no longer the strong men who emerge from a rugged country (cf. 1.126, 9.122). Yet even so at the battle of Plataea Herodotus still insists that the Persians were let down not by a lack of courage but by the limitations of their armour (9.62.3).[17] He does not cling to an overly simplified polarity of soft and slavish Asiatics against hardy and free Greeks.

*

Herodotus' rich and varied ethnographic descriptions cannot be reduced to the simple aim of bolstering the Greeks' sense of their own cultural identity: rather, they form an important part of the monumental intellectual endeavour represented by the *Histories* as a whole. Throughout the work, the juxtaposition and interlinking of stories point to similarities, as well as differences, between Greeks and non-Greeks; at the same time, the development of the narrative overturns many overhasty oppositions. Herodotus was also concerned to explain cultural differences in various ways (by reference to political systems and to climate, for instance), and to analyse how cultural differences arise and change with time. He announced in his preface that he was interested in causation: his ethnographical descriptions themselves are part of his attempt not just to explain why Greeks and barbarians fought each other, but also to increase his audience's understanding of how human behaviour is moulded by culture and environment and to encourage reflection on how difficult it is for one people to read another people's set of different cultural assumptions with any certainty.

FURTHER READING

Herodotus' ethnography has been treated at length in two recent books in English: Thomas (2000) explores the scientific background of Herodotus' speculations, while Munson (2001a) looks in particular at the modes of his ethnographic discourse. Munson develops and refines the study of Herodotus' 'rhetoric of alterity' in Hartog (1988), a very influential study that focusses particularly on Herodotus' portrayal of the Scythians. There is also a wide-ranging recent book in German (Bichler [1999]) and an Italian study that analyses the presentation of ethnography within the narrative sections (Dorati [2000]). For good briefer discussions of the ethnographic sections, see the final chapter of Immerwahr (1966); Redfield (1985); Gould (1989) ch. 5; and Lateiner (1989) ch. 7. On Herodotus' blurring of the boundaries between East and West, Pelling (1997b) is especially suggestive. Humphreys (1987) and Selden (1999) offer interestingly different discussions of the conceptions of culture exemplified in the 'custom is king of all' anecdote; this is also one of the episodes exploited by Kurke (1999) in her ambitious attempt to use Herodotus' ethnographies as evidence for competing elite and civic ideologies within the Greek world. Useful short treatments devoted to Herodotus' portrayal of a specific region can be found in Bakker, de Jong, and van Wees (2002) chs. 18–21, while more detailed studies include Rollinger (1993) on Babylon and Lloyd (1975–88) on Egypt. For other approaches to Herodotus' treatment of Egypt, see Marincola (1987) on the distinctiveness of Herodotus' persona in this section, and Moyer (2002) on the need to take account of ideological manipulation of the past by Herodotus' informers. These studies bear on the broader issue of Herodotus' narratorial presence: Fehling (1989) is the most important and controversial advocate for the fictionality of Herodotus' 'source citations'; but see the suggestive re-interpretation of Fehling's perceptions advanced by Luraghi (2001b).

NOTES

1. See Fowler's chapter in this volume.
2. See Luraghi's chapter in this volume.
3. Compare Blakesley (1854) I.xlv, comparing Herodotus with Defoe; West (1991) 151.
4. Compare Payen (1995) 337.
5. Christ (1994) discusses royal inquirers within the *Histories*.
6. Compare Dewald (1998) 669. On this episode, see further Romm's chapter in this volume. Munson's chapter on Italy and the connection between the language of tyranny and that of colonisation is also relevant.
7. Compare Flower (2000) 70–3.
8. Dewald (1990) offers a helpful review of Hartog (1988).
9. Compare Immerwahr (1966) 306–26 on Herodotus' conception of the order of nature. On ancient accounts of the edges of the earth, see Romm (1992), and on natural history Romm's chapter in this volume.
10. On Herodotus' cultural grid, see Pembroke (1967); Rosselini and Saïd (1978); Gould (1989) 86–109.
11. On the religious aspect of this episode, see Scullion's discussion in this volume.
12. Compare Redfield (1985).
13. Compare Fehling (1994) 14–15 and especially Kurke (1999) 227–46.
14. See Hartog (1988) 34–60 on how the Scythians' self-sufficiency matches the Athenians' naval strategy for resisting the Persian invaders.
15. Compare Redfield (1985) 106–9; Thomas (2000) 42–74, 130–1. On polarity in Greek thought generally, see Lloyd (1966). See also Thomas in this volume for Herodotus' connection with the medical writers.
16. Compare Cartledge (2002) 80.
17. Compare Pelling (1997b); Flower and Marincola (2002) 15–16 and 312, and Flower in this volume.

20

SIMON HORNBLOWER

Herodotus' influence in antiquity

Charming beyond all other ancient authors, Herodotus surely never sank from view.[1] His home city in Asia Minor was always proud of him: a recently discovered long poem, inscribed on stone and dating from the second century BCE, celebrates the glories of Halicarnassus, including the 'prose Homer, Herodotus'.[2] And his statue stood in the royal library of Hellenistic Pergamum.[3] Did his work continue to be recited in later centuries as it certainly was in his lifetime?[4] We can be certain only of literary reception, but we should not forget that Greek culture continued to be oral long after the arrival of widespread literacy and that this most memorable of historians may have exerted influence in informal ways as well as via the written papyrus roll. The only specific mention of Hellenistic public recitation of Herodotus, in the theatre at Alexandria, is not usable if we adopt the standard emendation to 'Hesiod'.[5] The other author there said to have been recited is Homer, who is the reason for emending the other name; but it is tempting to keep 'Herodotus' and juxtapose the poetic and the prose Homer, as above.

The fifth century BCE

The story of Herodotus' literary reception begins right back in the middle of the fifth century with Sophocles (Aeschylus' most obviously relevant play the *Persians* was produced in 472 so that any influence must have run in the opposite direction, and the same is true of the Persian Wars poetry of Simonides). A famous passage of the *Antigone* (904–20) of about 443 BCE makes the heroine use arguments for saving her brother which are notoriously more at home in another sort of story, one where a woman is being given a 'Sophie's choice' of saving husband, son or brother. Only the last is strictly irreplaceable if the parents are dead. Just such a story and argument are found in Herodotus (3.119). Therefore, most readers have concluded that the poet borrowed from the historian. Stephanie West, in a recent study of Sophocles' *Antigone* and Herodotus Book 3, not only accepts this but speaks more generally of 'the less obvious (because better integrated) evidence of pervasive Herodotean influence on this play'.[6] She brings out well the similarities between the portrayal of the Sophoclean Creon and such Herodotean tyrants as Cambyses, Periander and Polycrates, rulers of Persia, Corinth and Samos respectively. But Sophocles' alleged borrowings are not only from Book 3 of Herodotus.[7]

Euripidean parallels and therefore possible borrowings are harder to find. The idea of weeping for the newly born and rejoicing for the dead is found in both authors.[8] But is it much more than an elaboration of the thoroughly Sophoclean idea that not to be born is best of all? Fornara, as part of his case for a late 'publication date' for Herodotus, argues that the phantom Helen in *Electra* of ?414 (1280–3) and in *Helen* itself (412) derives from Herodotus (2.112–20), and that Herodotus' account of the Taurian cult of Iphigenia (4.103) was the inspiration for another late play *Iphigenia among the Taurians*. But 414 is by no means agreed as the date of *Electra* and neither the Egyptian Helen nor the Taurian Iphigenia were uniquely or originally Herodotean. Talk of Euripides' 'sudden awareness of Herodotus' is much too strong.[9] If the closer affinity is between Herodotus and Sophocles, that might prompt us to reflections about Sophoclean piety and pessimism, and about the sort of material which Sophocles found congenial. But any such speculation must be highly provisional in view of the number of lost plays of both tragedians. For instance the *Tereus* of Sophocles, of which we have substantial fragments, was evidently a revenge tragedy with macabre features which made it quite unlike any of the surviving seven plays; it is anybody's guess what detailed relation this might have to Herodotus, but I would be surprised if there were none.

Aristophanes was as fascinated by Herodotean despots as was Sophocles, and the conventions of his plays permitted him, unlike Sophocles, to make direct allusions by name. The exploits of Artemisia, queen of Halicarnassus, in the battle of Salamis (8.87–8) are the subject of just such clear allusions in two plays of 411 BCE (*Lys.* 675, cf. *Thesm.* 1200). Otherwise the highest concentration of plausible references is in *Birds* of 414.[10] So far, everything is compatible with a fairly late 'publication date' for Herodotus. More controversial are the supposedly Herodotean passages near the beginning of *Acharnians* of 425.[11] Little weight can be put on these,[12] but the account later in the play of the causes of the Peloponnesian War in terms of abduction of women (525ff.) does seem to me to presuppose Herodotus' opening four chapters with their sequence of mythical rape and counter-rape, and this is not refuted by the simultaneous likelihood that Euripides' *Telephus* is being parodied.

The authors so far considered are all Athenians and this alone makes it scarcely credible that their contemporary Thucydides the Athenian historian could have been unaware of Herodotus' history, of which he was in a sense the continuator. In fact its influence on him was surely profound and pervasive.[13] Influence can, and in the history of ancient historiography often does, take the form of reaction and rejection. Even before Thucydides started writing but had chosen his theme, he had already parted company with Herodotus. One of the main messages of his introductory section (1.1–21, the so-called 'Archaeology') is that the Peloponnesian War is a greater upheaval than any predecessor, including the Persian Wars. This rebuke is directed at many authors other than Herodotus, and at much popular opinion and artistic celebration as well, but it certainly represents a distancing from Herodotus, whatever else it represents. And yet Thucydides is not consistent because when in his narrative he wants to compare Thermopylae (480) with Pylos (424) he apologises for 'comparing great with small'; the little Herodotean word *atrapos* in the relevant sentence (4.36.3) gracefully turns the allusion into something close to a quotation. Elsewhere too, the distancing is not carried through ruthlessly. Not for Thucydides an explanation of the main Peloponnesian War in terms of women (see above), but he does tell us that the Sicilian disaster of 415–413 had its origins in a quarrel between Segesta and Selinus over 'marriage matters' (6.6.2). So too the story which forms the closure to Book 2 (the matricide and pollution of the mythical Alcmaeon) is an unexpected touch from an author who had apologised in advance for the absence of *to mythōdes* or fairy-tale element (1.22). Sometimes Thucydides adopts a Herodotean manner to suit the context; thus in one chapter only (2.97, two occurrences) does he measure distance by the amount of ground that could be travelled in a day by a 'man travelling light' (lit. 'well-girt'). The context is ethnographic – and so is the expression. Again, the incident of the old Spartan who shouts criticism at King Agis (5.65.2) is an unusual example of a piquant anecdote of the Herodotean type, and is told in a Herodotean manner: the old man says that the king is curing ill with ill (cf. Hdt. 3.53.3) and Thucydides himself rounds the story off by giving a double explanation 'whether because of the old man's shout or because it struck Agis himself as a better course of action'. And whatever the explanation for the excursus about the Athenian tyrannicides Harmodius and Aristogiton (6.54–9), the handling is detailed and Herodotean, with an uncharacteristic sexual element, as suits a story set a century earlier, in a 'Herodotean' period. Thucydides may have disapproved of Herodotus' methods and outlook, but he was not above showing off how well he could 'do a Herodotus' when he felt like it.

On the classic view of F. Jacoby,[14] the final strand of influence exerted by Herodotus in his own century was that he generated local history, a sub-category with a long and rich future. In his great collection of the fragments (quotations) of lost historians, the historians of individual Greek cities, lands and islands take up nos. 297–607, over three hundred names, almost all post-classical. Even specialists in Greek history must feel humbled by their own ignorance when they turn over the pages of the volume containing this huge assembly of scarcely-known historians. Just one text, the so-called 'Lindian *anagraphē*', a very interesting local religious record inscribed on a stone 100 BCE and found on Rhodes a century ago, gives an idea both of the sheer number of these local historians and of the way they supplemented Herodotus.[15] Thus the *anagraphē* makes the Persian commander Datis in 490 visit and make dedications at the temple of Athena Lindia (Herodotus [6.118] had told us about a visit to Apollo's temple at Delos only). Jacoby's view was that local history of this sort grew out of Herodotus, not the other way round, but Robert Fowler has challenged this in an important study.[16] What Fowler, whose title is 'Herodotus and his *contemporaries*', offers is altogether messier, 'rather than thinking of a step-by-step development, we would be wise to think in terms of a long and mutually beneficial exchange of work and ideas between Herodotus and his contemporaries'.[17] Fowler is right that the dates of figures like, say, Charon of Lampsacus, systematically pushed down by Jacoby, can just as well be pushed up again. But I would still want to make a stand on behalf of one important figure (because of his use by Thucydides for the local Sicilian history at 6.3–5), and one area of coverage: Antiochus of Syracuse (*FGrHist* 555) and Sicily/Italy. We know that his Sicilian history, written in the Ionic Greek of Herodotus, not the Dorian Greek of his home city, terminated in 424, the year of the conference of Gela described by Thucydides.[18] It still seems to me an excellent conjecture that Antiochus 'intended from the first to supplement Herodotus' work of local history in regard to the West'.[19] Herodotus, though he emigrated to Thurii in south Italy, had much less to say about the West than we might have expected and hoped.[20] Antiochus, we may say, was to Herodotus what Timaeus of Tauromenium, the first Greek historian to think seriously about Rome, would be to the Alexander historians. The vogue for Ionic Greek as the medium for ethnography was not initiated by Herodotus – Hecataeus of Miletus before him had used it as a matter of course – but Antiochus' less natural decision to use it was surely conditioned by Herodotus. We shall see that, after Antiochus, it became the normal medium for such writing, even in the Hellenistic period when its use was more obviously literary and artificial.

The fourth century

After this, things get easier. None of the main writers so far considered (Sophocles, Euripides, Aristophanes, Thucydides, Antiochus) actually name their coeval Herodotus at all, but after his death that changes, and we are mostly dealing with specific mentions and quotations.[21] From now on we have explicit references – which tend to be disparaging. A passing remark of Jacoby is worth quoting here for its general validity as regards Greek historiography: 'polemic usually names its object, borrowings are anonymous'.[22] Ctesias, the author of a work about Persia, roundly called Herodotus a liar (*FGrHist* 688 T 8), but his own versions often presuppose him.[23] He is the first writer in more or less explicit dialogue with Herodotus. It has been suggested that Ctesias' Ionicisms 'may be intended to emphasise a link with his predecessors, Herodotus and, before him, Hecataeus'.[24] Again, Aristotle once disparagingly called Herodotus a *mythologos* or mythologiser (*de gen. An.* 756b), but the Aristotelian *Constitution of the Athenians* used Herodotus, and most probably without an intermediary.[25]

There are two exceptions to the generally dismissive treatment of Herodotus in the fourth century before Alexander. One is Ephorus, dealt with below; the other is more controversial. It was long thought that Theopompus of Chios wrote an epitome (précis) of Herodotus (*FGrHist* 115 FF 1–4), which if true would be a salute of a pioneering sort – nothing less than the first known epitome of a classical author. But perhaps (it has been suggested) the epitome was not really a separate work but merely formed part of Theopompus' main historical production, the *Philippika*: Theopompus could merely have incorporated Herodotean material extensively in the section on the western satrapies of the Persian empire. On this view Theopompus was not so much displaying deference to Herodotus as seeking aggressively to show that he could improve on him.[26] A doubt remains: if as is possible the epitome was a juvenile work, it is not all that surprising that Dionysius of Halicarnassus should have overlooked it when summarising Theopompus' output (to call T 20 a 'detailed list' begs the question). And other big names in fourth-century historiography helped themselves freely from Herodotus without having epitomes attributed to them. That is true of Callisthenes, author of an important Greek history (the *Hellenica*) and of a *Deeds of Alexander* which for the early years of Alexander's campaign was the ultimate source behind all accounts. Not only did Callisthenes follow Herodotus closely on at least one complicated geographical point; he even described the Athenian fining of the tragedian Phrynichus for his play about the fall of Miletus without making reference to Herodotus at all, although he is the palpable source.[27]

Jacoby's remark about anonymous borrowing certainly holds for the non-polemical Xenophon, who rates only a few words in Jacoby's own excellent account of Herodotus' reception in antiquity.[28] The reason for the neglect is presumably that Xenophon's borrowings are not so much factual as stylistic and narratological. But the debt is great.[29] The starting point has to be the ancient literary critic Dionysius of Halicarnassus, who said that Xenophon modelled himself on Herodotus in subject-matter, language and organisation of material – though Dionysius concludes that he fell short of his model (*Letter to Gnaeus Pompeius* 4). Such ancient theories of imitation and rivalry should not necessarily be read biographically but as a lively and personalised way of making comparisons which are often acute. The key feature which Xenophon has in common with Herodotus is the stress on moral and praiseworthy behaviour. This is most obviously true of the *Hellenica*, but Herodotus lies behind other Xenophontic writings too: the *Anabasis*, a very important source for normal Greek religious attitudes,[30] breathes the atmosphere of Herodotus not Thucydides; and the ethical dialogue between the wise Simonides and the tyrant Hiero in the *Hiero* has its ancestor in the imaginary exchanges between the Herodotean Solon and the Lydian king Croesus (1.29–33). In the fictional *Education of Cyrus* (*Cyropaedia*) this fantasy element is taken much further but Herodotus is often presupposed, for instance in the meeting between Cyrus and Croesus (1.87–90).[31] Between them Herodotus and Xenophon are thus important predecessors of the Greek novel (see below in section 'Romans, and Greeks under Roman rule'). From the *Hellenica* we may single out the story (*Hell.* 3.1) of the sub-satrap Mania, whose murder and replacement by her son-in-law Midias is menacingly disapproved by the Persian satrap Pharnabazus. Midias sent Pharnabazus conciliatory gifts, but Pharnabazus told him to keep them and look after them well because he would not wish to live without avenging Mania. Herodotus might well have ended the story there, or rather with a spectacular punishment of Midias by Pharnabazus, and then some remark on the lines of 'so did *tisis* (requital) overtake Midias'. Xenophon's treatment is, however, more involved and straggly: the Spartan Dercylidas, in the vicinity campaigning against the Persians, gets possession of Midias and his property which he regards as belonging to Mania and so to Pharnabazus. But by right of conquest they now belong to the Spartans since Pharnabazus is their enemy; as for Midias, Dercylidas tells him to live in his native city of Scepsis in his father's house. The story owes a debt to Herodotean stories of requital and revenge, and it inverts ethnic and gender stereotypes in good Herodotean style (the Persian satrap and the woman behave honourably, the Greek Midias despicably), but it lacks Herodotus' satisfying snap. There is closure of a sort (the put-down about Scepsis and the father's house), but also loose ends: any child will ask: 'What did Pharnabazus do now?' His promise of revenge is after all not fulfilled, and this is unsatisfying as narrative. Dionysius was right to perceive a certain falling-off.[32]

One of the most popular and widely read Greek historians of any age was Ephorus, whose enormous universal history was used by Diodorus Siculus in the late first century BCE for his *Bibliothēkē* or *Library*, another universal history but a derivative one, as its give-away title implies. Ephorus too was derivative. Unfortunately there is a long gap in our texts of Diodorus for the archaic period before the Persian Wars, so the true extent of his indebtedness to Ephorus cannot be calculated precisely, but only with the help of fragments of Diodorus Books 7–10, which, however, have plenty of non-Herodotean material as well. As with the reception of Thucydides,[33] we cannot always be certain whether proven knowledge of Herodotus' subject-matter on the part of a post-Ephoran author was obtained directly or via Ephorus. But Herodotus' Greek was not difficult like that of Thucydides, at any rate in his speeches, so that there seems little reason for us to invoke the readable Ephorus. Ephorus himself was, unusually for a Greek historian, polite about his predecessor: he apologises for a digression by saying that he does not wish to criticise Herodotus (Diod. 10.24.1). That did not stop him from diverging from Herodotus both on points of detail and by moralising more insistently.

The Alexander historians and the Hellenistic period

That Herodotus came into his own with the Alexander historians and in the early Hellenistic period was brilliantly demonstrated by Oswyn Murray.[34] The conquests of Alexander opened new lands, or more often made accessible to Greek schematising curiosity some very old civilisations. A characteristic Greek response to such novelty was promptly to render the unfamiliar in familiar terms. So the island of Icarus in the Aegean sea to the west of Samos (modern Icaria) gave its name, on Alexander's own instructions, to the island now called Failaka in the Persian Gulf (Arr. *Anab.* 7. 20).[35] For people who thought in this sort of way, Herodotus' *Histories* provided a mechanism of interpretation; the old fourfold ethnographic scheme geography–customs–marvels–political history could be re-applied endlessly. In a way, Greek historians were merely re-discovering the categories of traditional ethnography (below), but there is a strong case for going further and saying that they looked specifically to Herodotus.

Of the Alexander historians themselves, Nearchus in his '*paraplous* of India' (that is, his voyage from the Indus to the Euphrates)[36] is the most spectacular pupil of Herodotus, whose Egyptian as well as Indian material was a powerful influence. But we must be careful: our knowledge of this work is largely derived from the use made of it in the *Indikē* of Arrian, a stylist from a self-consciously literary age (the second century CE), who made his own contribution. For instance, Arrian's treatise is in Ionic Greek, which has been taken to be a gesture by Nearchus himself to emphasise the Herodotean connection (cf. above for Ctesias).[37] But this is not agreed or certain: for another distinguished modern authority, Ionic was 'surely A[rrian]'s choice',[38] though it is possible to have things both ways and hold that both Nearchus and Arrian (in this work) used Ionic.[39] As for detail, Nearchus does not (at any rate as transmitted to us by Arrian and Strabo, a necessary qualification) seem to have cited Herodotus by name; but there is no doubt who lies behind his discussion (F 8) of the gold-digging ants 'of the sort which some writers have described as native to India' (see Hdt. 3.102 and 105). Nearchus merely says of these creatures that he himself has not seen them, a mild rebuke indeed. (For what Greek historians could do when they got the polemical wind in their sails see Book 12 of Polybius.)

Other early Hellenistic historians reverted to the old combination of explicit abuse and silent exploitation, thus Hecataeus of Abdera, whom Diodorus drew on in Book 1 for Egypt, is probably the real author of Diodorus' denunciation of 'Herodotus and certain writers on Egyptian matters' who put truth second to myths and *paradoxologein*, the recounting of marvels (1.69.7).[40] As usual Hecataeus' show of independence did not deter him from what would now be called plagiarism ('the whole section on the history of Egypt . . . is in fact for the most part taken with only the smallest alterations from Herodotus'[41]). The motive of Hecataeus is also different from that of Herodotus, namely to show that Egyptian civilisation was older and better, and thus to praise the new Ptolemaic kingdom.[42] The difference is important. Historiography and geography in Ptolemaic Alexandria have a definitely political motive which is absent from Herodotus; thus the exaggeratedly long lists of Alexander's city foundations have, in an outstanding recent study, been ingeniously and plausibly traced to a lost 'book of the cities of Alexander' which had its genesis in Alexandria and was designed polemically to minimise the solid urbanising achievements of the rival Seleucid kingdom.[43] Again, the greatest of the political historians of the first century of the Hellenistic era, Hieronymus of Cardia (whose account can be retrieved with satisfying fullness from Diodorus Books 18–20), included a long ethnographic excursus, in the Herodotean manner, on the Nabataean Arabs (Diod. 19.94ff.) This is not just there for fun; there is a political sub-text hinted at by the introductory sentence 'it will be useful to describe the customs *by which it is thought that they preserve their freedom*'. Hieronymus is here issuing a veiled plea to his patron, the

Antigonid Macedonian king Antigonus Gonatas, not to go too far in suppressing Greek freedom: 'couched in the language of utopian theory and dressed in the exotic colours of the barbarian east, Hieronymus . . . gave his warning'.[44] Herodotus has supplied the presentational model, but advising and warning autocrats is not at all how Herodotus saw the purpose of history.

There is an intriguing trio of early Hellenistic writers who wrote from the inside, or at any rate with first-hand knowledge, about India, Egypt and Babylonia. They are Megasthenes, Manetho and Berossus.[45] Plenty of Megasthenes has come down to us via Diodorus, Strabo and Arrian, but the other two are harder to evaluate with confidence. All of them are likely to have been strongly influenced by Herodotus in their general handling, though we should not forget that some of the features of ethnographic writing had already been fixed when Herodotus wrote. Manetho is said to have convicted Herodotus specifically in his Egyptian material of 'making many mistakes through ignorance' (609 F 7a, from Josephus). This is the tone of Hecataeus of Abdera again (though there is a hint of patronising charity in the word 'ignorance'), but Manetho as a priest with access to priestly records may have had better justification for making his corrections.[46]

Polybius is one of the three most important successors of Herodotus as a political and military historian, the others being Thucydides and Hieronymus. It has been noted that there is no reference to Herodotus anywhere in Polybius,[47] but we cannot safely build on this absence because so much of Polybius is lost. At any rate Herodotus escapes abuse in Book 12, where Callisthenes and Timaeus are the chief targets. Nor is there any reason to think that Polybius had Herodotus specially in mind in his attacks on 'tragic history'(though he would not I think have regarded Herodotus as being as much of a 'pragmatic' historian, i.e. one with first-hand experience of war and politics, as Thucydides – whom, however, he also disregards as far as our surviving text allows us to say – or even as Hecataeus of Miletus, who advised his fellow-Ionians at the time of their contemplated revolt from Persia). But this is not the same as proof that Polybius was ignorant of Herodotus. In his (fragmentary) book on geography, Polybius says he deliberately 'passes over the older authors' (34.5.1), and it has been observed that he does much the same with historians.[48] Nobody who had thought hard about how to do history or geography, as Polybius certainly did, could fail to have assimilated Herodotus almost with his mother's milk. Similarly Polybius' continuator, the important but badly preserved Posidonius (FGrHist 87), addressed many geographical problems to which Herodotus had made a contribution – along with many others from Homer on.[49] 'Influence' at this level, and on so fragmentary an author, is exceptionally hard for us to pin down now, but it may have been no less real for that. At least Agatharchides (a second-century historian and geographer, and model for Posidonius), had the grace to call Herodotus a 'tireless researcher and an experienced historian' (*FGrHist* 86 F 19 = Diod. 1.37.4). The context is that chestnut of ancient geographical discussion, the river Nile.

Romans, and Greeks under Roman rule

By the time of Dionysius of Halicarnassus and Livy, that is to say the time of the emperor Augustus, Herodotus was a classic who could be argued with on his own terms, pillaged, and adapted freely; it was no longer so necessary to prove one's own independence by declaring Herodotus to be a fool or a liar. Apart from the respect which Dionysius shows him in his literary treatises, he takes him seriously in his own history, the *Roman Antiquities*: Dionysius' complicated account (1.26–30) of the Etruscans rejects Herodotus' notion (1.57) that they were Lydian by origin.[50] Livy is more frivolous. For example, his account of the capture of Gabii (1.53) combines – naturally without acknowledgement – two separate picturesque Herodotean stories: that of Zopyrus and the capture of Babylon, and the exchange between Thrasybulus of Miletus and Periander of Corinth (Hdt. 3.154 and 5.92). But was this Livy himself or some much earlier, perhaps even third-century, historian?[51] So many centuries after Herodotus, similar problems of *layering*, as we may call it, arise frequently. A century after Livy, Tacitus sorted the possible constitutions into democracy, oligarchy and one-man rule (*Annals* 4.33) and we naturally think of Herodotus' debate in Persia as the undeclared model (3.80–82). But the threefold classification was already there in Pindar a generation before Herodotus (*Pythian* 2.86–8) – and in how many others after Herodotus? Greek novels of the Roman period look back to Herodotus and Xenophon as we have already briefly seen. The adoption of deliberately Herodotean décor was one elegant way of acknowledging the debt, thus the *Metiochus and Parthenope* is set in the court of that most Herodotean figure, Polycrates of Samos. But Herodotus is not uniquely flattered in this way: Chariton set his *Chaereas and Callirhoe* in the Syracuse of Thucydides. The novelists were well-read and eclectic and many influences came together in their writings.

One important Greek writer of the imperial Roman period went to Herodotus direct, imitated him frequently and took material from him without citation on (it has been calculated) at least 82 occasions. This was Pausanias in his *Guide to Ancient Greece*, written in the second century CE. He is 'as close to, and as fond of, Herodotus as the separation of some six hundred years allows'.[52]

Three Greek works from the second century CE engage with Herodotus directly and unequivocally. Two of them are extended virtuoso treatises in Herodotus' own style – parodies, pastiches, or clever but serious efforts to wrestle with Herodotean subject-matter in suitably Herodotean style (we saw that it was Thucydides who began this process). They are the *Indikē* of Arrian, already considered above in connection with Nearchus, and the *de dea Syria* of Lucian. Neither of these is a mere *jeu d'esprit*, so that talk of parody and pastiche is to that extent misleading – though the intention behind the Lucianic treatise, unlike that of Arrian, is surely humorous in part because certain Herodotean mannerisms are imitated so well. Lucian is describing the sanctuary of Atargatis at Hierapolis, and his account has been confirmed in significant respects by archaeology as well as by other literary sources. The Herodotean dress has the effect of conferring quasi-Hellenic status on what was certainly a barbarian religious phenomenon.[53]

The third and last treatise, actually slightly earlier in date, is Plutarch's *de malignitate Herodoti* (*On the Malice of Herodotus*). The title says it all; it is a strange work, not least because it seems so out of character for the 'kindly Plutarch' as he has been called.[54] We should make a good deal of allowance for the patriotic motive so candidly declared at the outset (*Mor.* 854E-F): Plutarch wishes, he says, to rescue the Boeotians (and Corinthians) from Herodotus' spite against them because it is only right to do so 'on behalf of my ancestors and of the truth', in that order. The point is that Plutarch was a citizen of (Boeotian) Chaeronea and Herodotus had made very clear that in the Persian Wars some of the Boeotians (not all) medised, that is they were traitors to Greece. But why, after so many centuries, should this have still been a live issue? The answer is to be found in the longevity of what has been called the 'Persian Wars tradition' in ancient Greece – and Rome.[55] The Parthians were redefined as the new Persians, and not just by poets such as Horace. Herodotus' *Histories* had particular relevance in the first three centuries CE. It was topical not just because of the appeal of its literary qualities (acknowledged by Plutarch in his first sentence) in a very self-conscious literary age, but because of the appeal to educated Greek provincials like Plutarch of the Persian Wars which were after all Herodotus' main theme.

FURTHER READING

Apart from the works cited above for specific points (especially Busolt [1895], Jacoby [1913] and Murray [1972]), there is a thorough treatment of Herodotus' reception in Riemann (1967). This Munich dissertation deals with literary texts not covered in the above chapter, such as the fourth-century military writer Aeneas Tacticus (pp. 44–5), paradoxography, i.e. collections of marvels (60), and Hellenistic poetry such as Apollonius Rhodius and the Herodotus-inspired tragedy about King Gyges of Lydia, found on papyrus (*P. Oxy.* 2382) in the last century (64–5). For the general topic of the interrelationship between the historians of antiquity see Marincola (1997). Drews (1973) has a useful chapter (4) on 'Herodotus' Successors'. See also Momigliano (1990), ch. 2, 'The Herodotean and the Thucydidean Tradition', but there are many good remarks on Herodotus' reception scattered throughout Momigliano's *Contributi*, i.e. the nine volumes of his collected papers: Momigliano (1955–92).

NOTES

1. The essential account of Herodotus' reception is Jacoby (1913) cols. 504–20. See also Busolt (1895) 615.
2. *SEG* 48. 1330, line 43. Later writers such as Longinus also make the Homeric comparison; for more see the contribution of Marincola in this volume.
3. *Inschriften von Pergamon* no. 199; cf. Murray (1972) 204 and Parsons (1993) 161.
4. Momigliano (1980).
5. Jason, *FGrHist* 632 F 1 = Ath. 620D.
6. West (1999) 131.
7. With Hdt. 1.108, the dream of Mandane, cf. *El.* 417: Pelling (1996) 69; with Hdt. 2.35 on Egypt cf. *OC* 337ff. On Herodotus and Sophocles see also Dewald and Kitzinger in this volume.
8. With Hdt. 5.4 cf. Eur. *TGF* F 449, from the *Kresphontes*.
9. Fornara (1971b) 31.
10. Aristoph. *Birds* 552ff. with Hdt. 1.179 (walls of Babylon); 1142 with Hdt. 2.136 (boast of personal measurement); 488, the Persian king as 'great and mighty'. Compare Busolt (1895) 615 n.2.
11. *Acharn.* 85–7 and 92, cf. Hdt. 1.1–4.
12. Fornara (1971b), arguing against Wells (1923) ch. 9.
13. Hornblower (1996) 137–45 for a list of 139 parallel passages; cf. 122–37. See also Rood (1999).
14. Jacoby (1909) 118 and (1913) 506.
15. The 'Lindian Chronicle' is at *FGrHist* 532; for text, translation and commentary see Higbie (2003).
16. Fowler (1996), especially 69.
17. Compare Thomas (2000), with – again – a revealingly non-committal title, 'Herodotus *in Context*'.
18. For the terminal date see Antiochus, *FGrHist* 555 F 3 = Diod. 12. 71. 2.
19. Jacoby (1949) 118.
20. 5. 42–8, the Dorieus of Sparta episode, and 7.170 are two conspicuous exceptions. See also the contribution of Munson in this volume.
21. Not completely, however: thus 'certain historians' at Diod. 11.15.1, referring to the equivocal attitude of the Corcyraeans in 480, evidently means Herodotus

(cf. Hdt. 7.168); Diodorus' source here, by the way, is presumed to be the fourth-century Ephorus. And we shall see that Xenophon owes much to Herodotus without ever naming him.

22. Jacoby (1913) 508.
23. Several instances are cited by Jacoby (1922) 2049–52.
24. Stevenson (1997) 8; for examples see Jacoby (1922) 2064.
25. Rhodes (1982) 20 and n.122.
26. Christ (1993).
27. For the first point see *FGrHist* 124 F 38, from Strabo. For Phrynichus, F 30, also from Strabo, cf. Hdt. 6.21.2.
28. Jacoby (1913) 509.
29. This has been well demonstrated by Gray (1989) 3–9, 14–16, 74, etc.
30. Parker (2004).
31. Tatum (1989) 154.
32. See Griffiths in this volume for Herodotean storytelling habits.
33. Hornblower (1995).
34. Murray (1972).
35. Papalas (2002) 139–43.
36. See *FGrHist* 133, especially the enormous F 1.
37. Murray (1972) 206.
38. Brunt (1983) 541, observing that Nearchus was 'not a literary man by profession'.
39. Pearson (1960) 112.
40. Nevertheless Diodorus must be taken to endorse the rebuke and this is a good moment to point out that Diodorus avoided direct use of Herodotus anywhere; see above for his preference for Ephorus (and thus mediated Herodotus) as a source for Greek history up to the Persian Wars.
41. Murray (1972) 207.
42. Fraser (1972) I.504.
43. Fraser (1996).
44. Hornblower (1981) 144–53 and 178.
45. *FGrHist* nos. 715, 609 and 680, respectively.
46. Fraser (1972) I.506.
47. Murray (1972) 211. Walbank (1972) 38 n.30 says more or less the same thing but more cautiously: 'There is no firm evidence that he [Polybius] was acquainted with Herodotus.'
48. So rightly Walbank (1979) 588.
49. Kidd (1988) 1020 (index locorum) has eighteen separate citations of Herodotus, usually adduced for this sort of indirect reason.
50. Gabba (1991) 112.
51. Ogilvie (1965) 195, 205.
52. Habicht (1998) 3 n.7; cf. 97 and n.7.
53. Jones (1986) 41–3; on parody and pastiche elsewhere in Lucian see 19. For text, translation and commentary on the *de dea Syria* see Lightfoot (2003).
54. Meiggs (1972) 192; Russell (1973) 60 notes that Plutarch does not, in the *Parallel Lives*, draw on Herodotus as much as we should have expected, so Plutarch is at least consistent to that extent.
55. Spawforth (1994) and (1996).

GLOSSARY

aitiē	reason; charge; grounds for complaint
akoē	hearsay; oral tradition
dēmiourgos (pl. *dēmiourgoi*)	craftsman; public worker
gnōmē	a judgement; reasoned judgement
historiē	inquiry, investigation
logos (pl. *logoi*)	something spoken, speech; argument; reason; account. We often speak of the various *logoi* of Herodotus' work, e.g. the Egyptian *logos*, the Scythian *logos*, etc. Herodotus sometimes personifies *logos*, e.g. 1.95, 'Our *logos* now examines who this Cyrus was who destroyed the power of Croesus, etc.'
metoikēsis	a change of abode, either voluntary or compulsory
nomos (pl. *nomoi*)	custom, i.e., the established way of doing something; law; sometimes contrasted with *physis*
opsis	the act of eyewitness
physis	nature, the natural world; sometimes contrasted with *nomos*
sophiē	wisdom, but also the sense of 'cleverness' both for good and bad
sophos (pl. *sophoi*)	wise man
technē	a skill or craft
thōma (pl. *thōmata*)	marvel

TIMELINE

The Greek World	The Non-Greek World
c. 1200 Trojan War	
c. 750–700 Homer's *Iliad* and *Odyssey*	
	c. 700 Deioces founds Median dynasty
	664–526 Twenty-sixth (Saite) dynasty in Egypt:
	664–610 Psammetichus I
	610–595 Nekos II
	595–589 Psamettichus II
	589–570 Apries
	570–526 Amasis
c. 657–627 Cypselus tyrant in Corinth	
c. 627–587 Periander tyrant in Corinth	
	c. 620 Greek settlement at Naucratis in Egypt
	612 Fall of Assyrian capital Nineveh
c. 600–570 Tyranny of Cleisthenes of Sicyon	
594/3 Archonship of Solon at Athens	
	585–550 Astyages king in Media
c. 560–550 Long struggle between Sparta and Tegea ends in alliance	

c. 561–510 Peisistratid tyranny at Athens:
 	
  561–527 Peisistratus (from 561–546 intermittent success) rules
  527–510 Hippias rules	

	c. 560 Croesus become king of Lydia
	c. 550 Cyrus defeats Astyages and the Medes
c. 546 Sparta defeats Argos	546 Cyrus defeats Croesus; Fall of Sardis
	530 Death of Cyrus; Cambyses becomes king of Persia
	525 Cambyses conquers Egypt
	522 Revolt of the Magi; death of Cambyses; Darius and Persian nobles put down revolt; Darius becomes king of Persia
520–490 Cleomenes king at Sparta	
514 Assassination of Hipparchus at Athens	
	c. 513 Darius' unsuccessful expedition against the Scythians
	512–510 Megabazus conquers Thrace for Darius
510 Spartans assist Athenians in ousting Hippias Dorieus in Italy; Croton destroys Sybaris in S. Italy	
c. 510–481 Intermittent war between Athens and Aegina	
c. 500 Hippias at Persian court encourages attack on Athens	

499–494 Ionian Revolt
499 Aristagoras asks for Athenian and
Spartan help
498 Ionians with Athenians and
Eretrians burn Sardis; Athens abandons
alliance in aftermath
494 Ionian defeat at the battle of Lade;
sack of Miletus

c. 491 Gelon becomes tyrant at Syracuse

c. 491 Cleomenes' plots against
Demaratus; Demaratus flees to Persia

491 Darius demands submission of
Greek states

490 Persians attack Greece; enslave
Eretria; (September) battle of Marathon

c. 490 Death of Cleomenes; Leonidas
becomes king at Sparta

489 Death of Miltiades

486 Darius dies; Xerxes becomes king
of Persia

484–481 Xerxes prepares for invasion
of Greece

481 Greek League formed to fight
Persia; Athens and Aegina end
hostilities

480 Persians attack Greece;
(September) battles at Artemisium and
Thermopylae; Athenians abandon
Athens; Xerxes takes Athens, burns the
city; (end of September) battle of
Salamis; Xerxes returns to Persia

480 Gelon of Syracuse defeats
Carthaginians at Himera

479 Persian commander Mardonius
winters in Thessaly; makes overtures to
Athens; (spring) invades Greece, burns
Athens again; Persians defeated at
Plataea and retreat; Persians defeated at
Mycale; Ionians join Greek league

479/8 (Winter) Athenians besiege
Sestos, expel Persians

472 Aeschylus' *Persians*

465 Xerxes dies in palace intrigue

c. 444/3 Foundation of Thurii

BIBLIOGRAPHY

Aarne, A. and S. Thompson (1961) *The Types of the Folktale* (Helsinki).

Alcock, S. (2002) *Archaeologies of the Greek Past: Landscape, Monuments and Memories* (Cambridge).

Alonso-Núñez, J. M. (1987) 'Herodotus on the Far West', *AC* 56. 243–9.

Alter, R. (1981) *The Art of Biblical Narrative* (New York).

Althoff, J. (1993) 'Herodot und die griechische Medizin', in K. Döring and G. Wörrle, eds., *Antike Naturwissenschaft und ihre Rezeption* (Bamberg), 1–16.

Aly, W. (1921/1969) *Volksmärchen, Sage und Novelle bei Herodot und seinen Zeitgenossen*; 2nd edn., with additions by L. Huber (Göttingen).

Antonaccio, C. (2001) 'Ethnicity and Colonization', in Malkin (2001) 113–57.

Appadurai, A. (1981) 'The Past as a Scarce Resource', *Man* 16. 201–19.

Asheri, D. (1988a) *Erodoto: La Lidia e la Persia. Libro I delle Storie* (Milan).

— (1988b) 'Carthaginians and Greeks', in *CAH* (2nd edn) IV. 739–80.

— (1990) *Erodoto: La Persia. Libro III delle Storie* (Milan).

— (1992) 'Sicily, 478–431 BC', in *CAH* (2nd edn) V. 147–70.

— (1993) 'Erodoto e Bacide', in M. Sordi, ed., *La profezia nel mondo antico* (Milan), 63–76.

— (1999) 'Erodoto e Bisitun', in E. Gabba, ed., *Presentazione e Scrittura della Storia: Storiografia, Epigrafi, Monumenti* (Atti del Convegno di Pontignano, Aprile 1996, *Biblioteca di Athenaeum* 42) (Como), 101–16.

Assmann, J. (1992) *Das kulturelle Gedächtnis. Schrift, Erinnerung und politische Identität in frühen Hochkulturen* (Munich).

Austin, M. M. (1990) 'Greek Tyrants and the Persians 546–479 BC', *CQ* 40. 289–306.

Austin, N. (1975) *Archery at the Dark of the Moon* (Berkeley and Los Angeles).

Bakhtin, M. (1968) *Rabelais and His World* (Cambridge, Mass.), trans. by H. Iswolsky of Russian original (Moscow 1965).

Bakker, E. J. (1991) 'Foregrounding and Indirect Discourse: Temporal Subclauses in a Herodotean Short Story', *Journal of Pragmatics* 16. 225–47.

— (1993) 'Topics, Boundaries, and the Structure of Discourse: An Investigation of the Ancient Greek Particle *Dé*', *Studies in Language* 17. 275–311.

— (1997) *Poetry in Speech: Orality and Homeric Discourse* (Ithaca and London).

— (1999) 'Homeric OYTOΣ and the Poetics of Deixis', *CPh* 94. 1–19.

— (2002) 'The Making of History: Herodotus' *Historiēs Apodexis*', in Bakker, de Jong and van Wees (2002), 3–32.

Bakker, E. J., I. J. F. de Jong, and H. van Wees, eds. (2002) *Brill's Companion to Herodotus* (Leiden, Boston and Cologne).

Balcer, J. M. (1987) *Herodotus and Bisitun* (*Historia* Einzelschriften, 49; Stuttgart).

Balot, R.K. (2001) *Greed and Injustice in Classical Athens* (Princeton).

Bassi, K. (1998) *Acting Like Men: Gender, Drama and Nostalgia in Ancient Greece* (Ann Arbor).

Bats, M. (1994) 'Les silences d'Hérodote ou Marseille, Alalia et les Phocéens en Occident jusqu'à la fondation de Vélia', in *Apoikia: Scritti in onore di Gorgio Buchner* (Naples), 133–48.

Beekes, R. (1986) 'You Can Get New Children . . .', *Mnemosyne* 34. 225–39.

Benardete, S. (1969) *Herodotean Inquiries* (The Hague).

Berger, S. (1992) *Revolution and Society in Greek Sicily and Southern Italy* (Stuttgart).

Bergson, H. (1940) *Le Rire. Essai sur la signification du comique* (Paris); trans. as 'Laughter', in Sypher (1956) 61–190.

Bernabé, A. (1988) *Poetae Epici Graeci* I (Teubner).

Bertelli, L. (2001) 'Hecataeus: From Genealogy to Historiography', in Luraghi (2001c) 67–94.

Bichler, R. (2000) *Herodots Welt. Der Aufbau der Historie am Bild der fremden Länder und Völker, ihrer Zivilisation und ihrer Geschichte* (Berlin).

Binder, G. (1964) *Die Aussetzung des Königskindes: Kyros und Romulus* (Beiträge zur klassischen Philologie, Heft 10; Frankfurt am Main).

Bischoff, H. (1932) *Der Warner bei Herodot* (Marburg), partly repr. in Marg (1982) 302–19 and 681–8.

Blakesley, J. W. (1854) *Herodotus, with a Commentary*, 2 vols. (London).

Blok, J. (2000) 'Phye's Procession: Culture, Politics and Peisistratid Rule', in H. Sancisi-Weerdenburg, ed. (2000) 17–48.

Blundell, M. (1989) *Helping Friends and Harming Enemies: A Study in Sophocles and Greek Ethics* (Cambridge).

Boedeker, D. (1987) 'The Two Faces of Demaratus', *Arethusa* 20. 185–201.

— (1988) 'Protesilaos and the End of Herodotus' *Histories*', *CA* 7. 30–48.

— (1993) 'Hero Cult and Politics in Herodotus: the Bones of Orestes', in C. Dougherty and L. Kurke, eds., *Cultural Poetics in Archaic Greece: Cult, Performance, Politics* (Cambridge), 164–77.

— (2000) 'Herodotus' Genre(s)', in M. Depew and D. Obbink, eds., *Matrices of Genre: Authors, Canons and Society* (Cambridge, Mass.), 97–114.

— (2001) 'Heroic Historiography: Simonides and Herodotus on Plataea', in Boedeker and Sider (2001) 120–34.

— (2002) 'Epic Heritage and Mythical Patterns in Herodotus', in Bakker, de Jong and van Wees (2002) 97–116.

— (2003) 'Pedestrian Fatalities: The Prosaics of Death in Herodotus', in Derow and Parker (2003) 17–36.

Boedeker, D. and D. Sider, eds. (2001) *The New Simonides: Contexts of Praise and Desire* (New York and Oxford).

Boegehold, A. and A. C. Scafuro, eds (1994) *Athenian Identity and Civic Ideology* (Baltimore).

Bolton, J. D. P. (1962) *Aristeas of Proconnesus* (Oxford).

Bondì, S. F. (1980) 'Penetrazione fenicio-punica e storia della civiltà punica in Sicilia', in Gabba and Vallet (1980) I.163–87.

— (1990) 'I Fenici in Erodoto', in Nenci and Reverdin (1990) 255–86.

Booth, W. (1974) *A Rhetoric of Irony* (Chicago).

Bosch-Gimpera, P. (1944) 'The Phokaians in the Far West. An Historical Recontruction', *CQ* 38. 53–9.

Bowen, A. J. (1992) *Plutarch: The Malice of Herodotus* (Warminster).

Bowie, E. (1986) 'Early Greek Elegy, Symposium and Public Festival', *JHS* 106.13–35.

— (1993) 'Lies, Fiction and Slander in Early Greek Poetry', in C. Gill and T. P. Wiseman, eds., *Lies & Fiction in the Ancient World* (Exeter and Austin).

— (2001) 'Ancestors of Historiography in Early Greek Elegiac and Iambic Poetry?' in Luraghi (2001c) 45–66.

Braccesi, L. (1998) *I tiranni di Sicilia* (Rome and Bari).

Braccesi, L. and G. Millino (2000) *La Sicilia Greca* (Rome).

Branham, B., ed. (2002) *Bakhtin and the Classics* (Evanston, Il.).

Branham, R. (1989) *Unruly Eloquence: Lucian and the Comedy of Traditions* (Cambridge, Mass. and London).

Bravo, B. (1993) 'Rappresentazioni di vicende di Sicilia e di Grecia degli anni 481–480 a.C. presso storici antichi. Studi di racconti e discorsi storiografici', *Athenaeum* 81. 39–99, 441–81.

Briant, P. (1990) 'Hérodote et la société perse', in Nenci and Reverdin (1990) 69–104.

— (2002) *From Cyrus to Alexander. A History of the Persian Empire*, trans. by P. T. Daniels (Indiana; French original, Paris 1996).

Brock, R. (2003) 'Authorial Voice and Narrative Management in Herodotus', in Derow and Parker (2003) 3–16.

Brosius, M. (1996) *Women in Ancient Persia, 559–331 BC* (Oxford).

— (2000) *The Persian Empire from Cyrus to Artaxerxes I* (Lactor 16; London).

Bruno Senseri, G. (1999) '*Moira toi tes Hellados ouk elachiste meta archonti ge Sikelies*: Erodoto e l'occidente coloniale', in *Erodoto e l'occidente* (Rome), 51–65.

Brunt, P. A. (1983) *Arrian: History of Alexander and Indica*, vol. 2 (Loeb Classical Library; Cambridge, Mass. and London).

Bulman, P. (1992) *Phthonos in Pindar* (Berkeley, Los Angeles and Oxford).

Burke, P. (1992) *History and Social Theory* (Cambridge).

Burkert, W. (1965) 'Demaratos, Astrabakos und Herakles: Königsmythos und Politik zur Zeit der Perserkriege', *MH* 22. 166–77, repr. and trans. in Burkert (2001).

— (1985) 'Herodot über die Namen der Götter: Polytheismus als historisches Problem', *MH* 42. 121–32.

— (1990) 'Herodot als Historiker fremder Religionen', in Nenci and Reverdin (1990) 1–39.

— (2001) *Savage Energies*, trans. by P. Bing (Chicago) of German original, *Wilder Ursprung. Opferritual und Mythos bei den Griechen* (Berlin 1990).

— (2004) *Babylon, Memphis, Persepolis: Eastern Contexts of Greek Culture* (Cambridge, Mass.).

Burn, A. R. (1977) 'Thermopylai Revisited and some Topographical Notes on Marathon and Plataiai', in K. H. Kinzl, ed., *Greece and the Eastern Mediterranean in Ancient History and Prehistory* (Berlin), 89–105.

— (1984) *Persia and the Greeks: The Defense of the West, 546–478 B.C.* (2nd edn) (London and New York; first edn 1962).

Busolt, G. (1895) *Griechische Geschichte*, vol. 2 (Gotha).

Cagnazzi, S. (1975) 'Tavola dei 28 Logoi di Erodoto', *Hermes* 103. 385–423.

Cairns, D. L. (1996) '*Hybris*, Dishonour, and Thinking Big', *JHS* 116. 1–32.

Calame, C. (1986) *Le récit en Grèce ancienne* (Paris).

— (1995) *The Craft of Poetic Speech in Ancient Greece* (Ithaca and London), trans. by J. Orion; a revised version of Calame (1986).

Carpenter, R. (1966) *Beyond the Pillars of Heracles: The Classical World Seen through the Eyes of its Discoverers* (New York).

Carrière, J. (1966) 'Démon tragique', *Pallas* 12. 7–20.

Cartledge, P. A. (1995) ' "We are all Greeks"?: Ancient (especially Herodotean) and Modern Contestations of Hellenism', *BICS* 40. 75–82.

— (2002) *The Greeks. A Portrait of Self and Others* (2nd edn) (Oxford; first edn 1993).

Cartledge, P. and E. Greenwood (2002) 'Herodotus as a Critic: Truth, Fiction, Polarity', in Bakker, de Jong and van Wees (2002) 351–71.

Cary, M. and E. H. Warmington (1963) *The Ancient Explorers* (2nd edn) (Baltimore).

Casevitz, M. (1985) *Le vocabulaire de la colonisation en grec ancien: étude léxicologique* (Paris).

Ceccarelli, P. (1996) 'De la Sardaigne à Naxos: le role des îles dans les Histoires d'Hérodote', in Letoublon (1996) 41–55.

Charles, R. H. (1913) *The Apocrypha and Pseudepigrapha of the Old Testament in English* (Oxford).

Chiasson, C.C. (1980) *The Question of Tragic Influence on Herodotus* (diss. Yale).

— (1986) 'The Herodotean Solon', *GRBS* 27. 249–62.

Christ, M. (1993) 'Theopompus and Herodotus: A Reassessment', *CQ* n.s. 43.47–52.

— (1994) 'Herodotean Kings and Historical Inquiry', *CA* 13. 167–202.

Ciaceri, E (1927–32) *Storia della Magna Grecia*, 3 vols. (Milan and Rome).

Clay, J. S. (2003) *Hesiod's Cosmos* (Cambridge).

Cobet, J. (1971) *Herodots Exkurse und die Frage der Einheit seines Werkes* (Historia Einzelschriften 17) (Wiesbaden).

— (1988) 'Herodot und mündliche Überlieferung', in von Ungern-Sternberg and Reinau (1988) 226–33.

Cole, T. (1983) 'Archaic Truth', *QUCC* 13.7–28.

Connor, W. R. (1987) 'Tribes, Festivals and Processions: Civic Ceremonial and Political Manipulation in Archaic Greece', *JHS* 107. 40–50.

— (1993) 'The *Histor* in History', in Rosen and Farrell (1993) 3–15.

Conybeare, F. C. et al. (1898) *The Story of Ahikar from the Syriac, Arabic, Armenian, Ethiopic, Greek and Slavonic Versions* (London).

Cook, J. M. (1983) *The Persian Empire* (London).

Corcella, A. (1984) *Erodoto e l'analogia* (Palermo).

— (1993) *Erodoto: La Scizia e la Libia. Libro IV delle Storie* (Milan).

Coulmas, F. (1984) 'Reported Speech: Some General Issues', in F. Coulmas, ed., *Direct and Indirect Speech* (Berlin), 1–28.

Cowley, A. E. (1923) *Aramaic Papyri of the Fifth Century B.C.* (Oxford).

Cropp, M. (1997) 'Antigone's Final Speech (Sophocles' *Antigone* 891–928)', *G&R* 44.137–60.

Cusumano, N. (1999) 'Biante e la Sardegna: libertà, dominio e felicità in Erodoto', in *Erodoto e l'occidente*, 139–96.

Darbo-Peschanski, C. (1987) *Le discours du particulier. Essai sur l'enquête hérodotéenne* (Paris).

— (2000) 'Rire et rationalité: le cas de l'historiographie grecque', in Desclos (2000) 203–13.

David, E. (1989) 'Laughter in Spartan Society', in A. Powell, ed., *Classical Sparta. Techniques Behind Her Success* (London and Norman, Ok.), 1–25.

de Jong, I. (1989) 'The Subjective Style in Odysseus' Wanderings', *CQ* n.s. 42. 1–11.

— (1999) 'Aspects narratologiques des *Histoires* d'Hérodote', *Lalies* 19. 217–75.

— (2001a) *A Narratological Commentary on the Odyssey* (Cambridge).

— (2001b) 'The Anachronical Structure of Herodotus' *Histories*', in S. J. Harrison, ed., *Texts, Ideas, and the Classics* (Oxford), 93–116.

— (2002) 'Narrative Unity and Units', in Bakker, de Jong and van Wees (2002) 245–66.

De Sensi Séstito, G. (1993) 'Da Thurii a Copia', in Stazio and Ceccoli (1993) 329–78.

de Souza, P. (2003) *The Greek and Persian Wars, 499–386 BC* (Oxford).

Deffner, A. (1933) *Die Rede bei Herodot und ihre Weiterbildung bei Thukydides* (Munich).

Del Corno, D. (1993) 'L'immagine di Sibari nella tradizione classica', in Stazio and Ceccoli (1993), 9–18.

Demand, N. (1988) 'Herodotus and *Metoikēsis* in the Persian Wars', *AJPh* 109. 416–23.

— (1990) *Urban Relocation in Archaic and Classical Greece* (Norman, Oklahoma).

Demont, P. (1988) 'Hérodote et les pestilences. Note sur Hdt. VI 27; VII 171 et VIII 115–117', *Rev. Phil.* 62. 7–13.

— (1993) 'Die *Epideixis* über die *Techne* im V. und IV Jh.', in W. Kullmann und J. Althoff, *Vermittlung und Tradierung von Wissen in der griechischen Kultur* (Tübingen), 181–209.

— (1994) 'Le *Protagoras* de Platon, Hérodote et la providence', in *Actas del VIII Congreso Español de Estudios Clásicos* (Madrid), 145–58.

Denniston, J. D. (1952) *Greek Prose Style* (Oxford).

Derow, P. (1995) 'Herodotus Readings', *Classics Ireland* 2. 29–51.

Derow, P. and R. Parker, eds. (2003) *Herodotus and his World: Essays from a Conference in Memory of George Forrest* (Oxford).

Desclos, M.-L., ed. (2000) *Le rire des Grecs. Anthropologie du rire en Grèce ancienne* (Grenoble).

Detienne, M. (1995) *The Masters of Truth in Archaic Greece* (New York), trans. by J. Lloyd of French original, *Les maîtres de vérité dans la Grèce archaïque* (Paris 1967).

Detienne, M. and J. Svenbro (1989) 'The Feast of the Wolves, or the Impossible City', in M. Detienne and J.-P. Vernant, eds., *The Cuisine of Sacrifice*, trans. by P. Wissing (Chicago), 148–63.

Dewald, C. (1981) 'Women and Culture in Herodotus' *Histories*', in H. P. Foley, ed., *Reflections of Women in Antiquity* (New York), 91–125.

— (1985) 'Practical Knowledge and the Historian's Role in Herodotus and Thucydides', in M. Jameson, ed., *The Greek Historians: Literature and History. Papers . . . A. E. Raubitschek* (Sarasota, California), 47–63.

— (1987) 'Narrative Surface and Authorial Voice in Herodotus' *Histories*', *Arethusa* 20. 147–70.

— (1990) Review of Hartog (1988), *CPh* 85. 217–24.

— (1993) 'Reading the World: The Interpretation of Objects in Herodotus' *Histories*', in Rosen and Farrell (1993), 55–70.

— (1997) 'Wanton Kings, Pickled Heroes, and Gnomic Founding Fathers: Strategies of Meaning at the End of Herodotus's *Histories*', in D. H. Roberts, F. M. Dunn, and D. Fowler, eds., *Classical Closure. Reading the End in Greek and Latin Literature* (Princeton), 62–82.

— (1998) 'Introduction and Notes', in R. Waterfield, trans., *Herodotus: The Histories* (Oxford).

— (1999) 'The Figured Stage: Focalizing the Initial Narratives of Herodotus and Thucydides', in Falkner, Felson and Konstan (1989), 221–252.

— (2002) ' "I Didn't Give My Own Genealogy": Herodotus and the Authorial Persona', in Bakker, de Jong and van Wees (2002), 267–89.

— (2003) 'Form and Content: The Question of Tyranny in Herodotus', in K. Morgan, ed., *Popular Tyranny* (Austin), 25–58.

— (forthcoming) 'Paying Attention: History as the Development of a Secular Narrative', in S. Goldhill and R. Osborne, eds., *Rethinking Revolutions through Ancient Greece*.

Dickey, E. (1996) *Greek Forms of Address* (Oxford).

Dihle, A. (1962a) 'Herodot und die Sophistik', *Philologus* 106.207–20.

— (1962b) 'Aus Herodots Gedankenwelt', *Gymnasium* 69.22–32.

— (1981) 'Die Verschiedenheit der Sitten als Argument ethischer Theorie', in G. B. Kerferd, ed., *The Sophists and their Legacy* (*Hermes* Einzelschriften 44; Wiesbaden), 54–63.

Diller, H. (1950) *Göttliches und menschliches Wissen bei Sophokles* (Kieler Universitätsreden II; Kiel), repr. in H. Diller, *Kleine Schriften zur antiken Literatur* (Munich 1960), 255–70.

Dillery, J. (1996) 'Reconfiguring the Past: Thyrea, Thermopylae and Narrative Patterns in Herodotus', *AJPh* 117. 317–54.

Dodds, E. R. (1973) *The Ancient Concept of Progress and other Essays on Greek Literature and Belief* (Oxford).

Dorati, M. (2000) *Le Storie di Erodoto: etnografia e racconto* (Pisa and Rome).

Dougherty, C. (1993) *The Poetics of Colonization: From City to Text in Archaic Greece* (Oxford).

— (1994) 'Archaic Greek Foundation Poetry: Questions of Genre and Occasion', *JHS* 114.35–46.

— (2001) *The Raft of Odysseus: The Ethnographic Imagination of Homer's Odyssey* (New York and Oxford).

Douglas, M. (1975) 'Jokes', in M. Douglas, *Implicit Meanings: Essays in Anthropology* (London), 94–114.

Dover, K. J. (1986) 'Ion of Chios: His Place in the History of Greek Literature', in J. Boardman, C. E. Vaphopoulou-Richardson, eds., *Chios: A Conference at the Homereion in Chios 1984* (Oxford) 27–37; repr. in Dover (1988) 1–12.

— (1988) *The Greeks and their Legacy* (Oxford).

Drews, R. (1973) *The Greek Accounts of Eastern History* (Cambridge, Mass.).

Duchemin, J. (1968) *L'agon dans la tragédie grecque* (Paris).

Dunbabin, T. J. (1948) *The Western Greeks* (Oxford).

Edelstein, E. J. and L. Edelstein (1945) *Asclepius. A Collection and Interpretation of the Testimonies* (Baltimore).

Edwards, A. (2002) 'Historicizing the Popular Grotesque: Bakhtin's *Rabelais and His World* and Attic Old Comedy', in Branham (2002) 27–55.

Ehrenberg, V. (1948) 'The Foundation of Thurii', *AJPh* 59. 149–70, repr. in V. Ehrenberg, *Polis und Imperium. Beiträge zur alten Geschichte* (Zurich and Stuttgart 1965), 298–315.

— (1950) 'Origins of Democracy', *Historia* 1. 515–48.

Emerson, C. (2002) 'Coming to Terms with Bakhtin's Carnival: Ancient, Modern, sub Specie Aeternitatis', in Branham (2002) 5–26.

Erbse, H. (1992) *Studien zum Verständnis Herodots* (Berlin and New York).

Erodoto e l'occidente (1999) (no ed.) Atti del Convengo 'Erodoto e l'occidente', Palermo, Aprile 1999. Supplement to *Kokalos* 15 (Rome).

Erskine, A. (2001) *Troy Between Greece and Rome* (Oxford).

Evans, J. A. S. (1976) 'Herodotus and the Ionian Revolt', *Historia* 25. 31–7.

— (1991) *Herodotus, Explorer of the Past: Three Essays* (Princeton).

Falkner, T., N. Felson, and D. Konstan, eds. (1999) *Contextualizing Classics: Ideology, Performance, Dialogue. Essays in Honor of John J. Peradotto* (Lanham–Boulder, New York and Oxford).

Fehling, D. (1972) 'Erysichthon oder das Märchen von der mündlichen Überlieferung', *RhM* 115. 173–96.

— (1989) *Herodotus and his 'Sources': Citation, Invention and Narrative Art*, trans. J. G. Howie (Leeds), of German orig. *Die Quellenangaben bei Herodot. Studien z. Erzählkunst Herodots* (Berlin and New York 1971).

— (1994) 'The Art of Herodotus and the Margins of the World', in Z. R. W. M. von Martels, ed., *Travel Fact and Travel Fiction: Studies on Fiction, Literary Tradition, Scholarly Discovery, and Observation in Travel Writing* (Leiden), 1–15.

Fentress, J. and C. Wickham (1992) *The Social Memory* (Oxford).

Figueira, T. J. (1985) 'Herodotus on the Early Hostilities between Aegina and Athens', *AJPh* 106. 49–74; repr. in T. J. Figueira, *Excursions in Epichoric History* (Lanham, Md. 1993), 35–60.

Finkelberg, M. (1995) 'Sophocles *Tr.* 634–639 and Herodotus', *Mnemosyne* 48.146–52.

Finley, M. I. (1968) *A History of Sicily: Ancient Sicily to the Arab Conquest* (London and New York).

Fisher, N. R. E. (1992) *Hybris* (Warminster).

— (2002) 'Popular Morality in Herodotus', in Bakker, de Jong and van Wees (2002) 199–224.

Flory, S. G. (1978a) 'Laughter, Tears, and Wisdom in Herodotus', *AJPh* 99. 145–53.

— (1978b) 'Arion's Leap: Brave Gestures in Herodotus', *AJPh* 99. 411–21.

Flower, H. I. (1991) 'Herodotus and Delphic Traditions about Croesus', in M. A. Flower and M. Toher, eds., *Georgica: Greek Studies in Honour of George Cawkwell* (*BICS* Supplement 58) (London), 55–77.

Flower, M. A. (1998) 'Simonides, Ephorus, and Herodotus on the Battle of Thermopylae', *CQ* 48. 365–79.

— (2000) 'From Simonides to Isocrates: The Fifth-Century Origins of Fourth-Century Panhellenism', *Classical Antiquity* 19. 65–101.

Flower, M. A. and J. Marincola, eds. (2002) *Herodotus: Histories Book IX* (Cambridge).

Fohl, H. (1913) *Tragische Kunst bei Herodot* (diss. Rostock).

Foley, H. (2001) *Female Acts in Greek Tragedy* (Princeton and Oxford).

Ford, A. (1991) *Homer. The Poetry of the Past* (Ithaca and London).

Fornara, C. W. (1971a) *Herodotus: an Interpretative Essay* (Oxford).

— (1971b) 'Evidence for the Date of Herodotus' Publication', *JHS* 91. 25–34.

— (1983) *The Nature of History in Ancient Greece and Rome* (Berkeley, Los Angeles and London).

Forrest, W. G. (1984) 'Herodotus and Athens', *Phoenix* 38. 1–11.

Forsdyke, S. (1999) 'From Aristocratic to Democratic Ideology and Back Again: the Thrasybulus Anecdote in Herodotus' *Histories* and Aristotle's *Politics*', *CPh* 94. 361–72.

— (2001) 'Athenian Democratic Ideology and Herodotus' *Histories*', *AJPh* 122. 329–58.

— (2002) 'Greek History c. 525–480 BC', in Bakker, de Jong and van Wees (2002) 521–49.

— (2005) *Exile, Ostracism and Democracy. The Politics of Expulsion in Ancient Greece* (Princeton).

Fowler, R. L. (1996) 'Herodotos and his Contemporaries', *JHS* 116.62–87.

— (1997) 'Polos of Akragas: Testimonia', *Mnemosyne* 50. 27–34.

— (1998) 'Genealogical Thinking, Hesiod's *Catalogue*, and the Creation of the Hellenes', *PCPS* 44. 1–19.

— (2000a) *Early Greek Mythography*, vol. I: *Text and Introduction* (Oxford).

— (2000b) 'P. Oxy. 4458: Poseidonios', *ZPE* 132. 133–42.

— (2001) 'Early *Historiē* and Literacy', in Luraghi (2001c) 95–115.

— (2003a) 'Herodotus and Athens', in Derow and Parker (2003) 305–18.

— (2003b) 'Pelasgians', in E. Csapo and M. Miller, eds., *Poetry, Theory, Praxis: the Social Life of Myth, Word, and Image in Ancient Greece* (Oxford), 2–18.

Franco, A. (1999) 'Erodoto e i centri sicani tra propaganda siceliota e ateniese di V sec.', in *Erodoto e l'Occidente* (Rome), 197–212.

Fraser, P. M. (1972) *Ptolemaic Alexandria*, 3 vols. (Oxford).

— (1996) *The Cities of Alexander the Great* (Oxford).

Freeman, E. A. (1891–94) *History of Sicily*, 4 vols. (Oxford)

Freud, S. (1963) *Jokes and their Relation to the Unconscious*, trans. by J. Strachey. (New York).

— (1966) *Wit and Its Relation to the Unconscious*, in *The Basic Writings of Sigmund Freud*, trans. by A. Brill (New York), 633–803.

Freudenburg, K. (1993) *The Walking Muse. Horace on the Theory of Satire* (Princeton).

Friedman, R. (1997) 'Home and Displacement in Herodotus' *Histories*' (diss. Columbia).

Frisch, P. (1968) *Die Träume bei Herodot* (Beitr. zur klass. Phil. 27; Göttingen).

Gabba, E. (1991) *Dionysius and the History of Archaic Rome* (Berkeley, Los Angeles and London).

Gabba, E. and G. Vallet, eds. (1980) *La Sicilia Antica*, 2 vols. in 5 parts (Palermo).

Galligan, E. (1984) *The Comic Vision in Literature* (Athens, Ga.).

Gammie, J. G. (1986) 'Herodotus on Kings and Tyrants: Objective Historiography or Conventional Portraiture?', *JNES* 45. 171–95.

Gauthier, Ph. (1966) 'Le parallèle Himère–Salamine au Ve et au IVe siècle av. J.-C.', *REA* 68. 5–32.

Gehrke, H.-J. and A. Möller (1996) *Vergangenheit und Lebenswelt: Soziale Kommunikation, Traditionsbildung und historisches Bewusstsein* (Tübingen).

Gentili, B. (1988) *Poetry and its Public in Ancient Greece: From Homer to the Fifth Century* (Baltimore and London), trans. by T. Cole of Italian original, *Poesia e pubblico nella Grecia antica* (Rome 1984).

Georges, P. (1994) *Barbarian Asia and the Greek Experience* (Baltimore and London).

Germain, G. (1956) 'Le songe de Xerxès et le rite babylonien du substitut royal: Étude sur Hérodote VII 12–18', *REG* 69. 303–13.

Giangiulio, M. (1983) 'Greci e non Greci in Sicilia alla luce dei culti e delle leggende di Eracle', in *Forme di contatto e processi di trasformazione nelle società antiche*. Atti del convegno di Cortona, 24–30 maggio 1981 (Pisa and Rome), 785–846.

— (1987) 'Aspetti di storia della Magna Grecia arcaica e classica fino alla guerra del Peloponneso', in Pugliese Carratelli (1987b) 9–53.

— (1989) *Ricerche su Crotone arcaica* (Pisa).

— (2001) 'Constructing the Past. Colonial Traditions and the Writing of History: the Case of Cyrene', in Luraghi (2001c) 116–37.

— (forthcoming) 'Tradizione storica e strategie narrative nelle *Storie* di Erodoto: il caso del discorso di Socle corinzio', in M. Giangiulio, ed., *Formazione e trasmissione delle tradizioni storiche in Grecia. Erodoto e il 'modello' erodoteo*.

Giannelli, G. (1928) *La Magna Grecia da Pitagora a Pirro* (Milan).

Gigante, M. (1966) 'Il logos erodoteo sulle origini di Elea', *PP* 21. 295–310.

Gill, C. (1996) *Personality in Greek Epic, Tragedy, and Philosophy: the Self in Dialogue* (Oxford).

Gilula, D. (2003) 'Who was Actually Buried in the First of the Three Spartan Tombs (Hdt. 9.85.1)? Textual and Historical Problems', in Derow and Parker (2003) 73–87.

Goldhill, S. (1991) *The Poet's Voice: Essays on Poetics and Greek Literature* (Cambridge).

— (2002) *The Invention of Prose* (*Greece & Rome* New Surveys in the Classics, 32; Oxford).

Gomme, A. W. (1954) *The Greek Attitude to Poetry and History* (Berkeley).

Gould, J. (1973) 'Hiketeia', *JHS* 93. 74–103; repr. (with addendum) in J. Gould, *Myth, Ritual, Memory, and Exchange* (Oxford 2001), 22–77.

— (1989) *Herodotus* (London and New York).

— (1994) 'Herodotus and Religion', in S. Hornblower, ed., *Greek Historiography* (Oxford), 91–106.

Graham, A. J. (1964) *Colony and Mother City in Ancient Greece* (Manchester).

— (1982) 'The Western Greeks', *CAH* (2nd edn) III. 163–5.

Grant, M. (1924) *The Ancient Rhetorical Theories of the Laughable* (University of Wisconsin Studies in Language and Literature, 21; Madison).

Gray, V. (1989) *The Character of Xenophon's Hellenica* (London and Baltimore).

— (1996) 'Herodotus and Images of Tyranny: The Tyrants of Corinth' *AJPh* 117. 361–89.

— (1997) 'Reading the Rise of Peisistratus: Herodotus 1.56–68', *Histos* 1. Electronic publication: http://www.dur.ac.uk/histos.

— (2001) 'Herodotus' Literary and Historical Method: Arion's Story', *AJPh* 122.11–28.

— (2002) 'Short Stories in Herodotus' *Histories*', in Bakker, de Jong and van Wees (2002) 291–317.

Green, P. (1996) *The Greco-Persian Wars* (Berkeley, Los Angeles and London).

Greenblatt, S. (1991) *Marvelous Possessions* (Oxford and Chicago).

Griffin, J. (1980) *Homer on Life and Death* (Oxford).

— (1990) 'Die Ursprünge der Historien Herodots', in W. Ax, ed., *Memoria Rerum Veterum. Festschrift . . . C. J. Classen* (Stuttgart), 51–82.

— (2004) 'The Speeches', in R. Fowler, ed., *Cambridge Companion to Homer* (Cambridge), 156–70.

Griffiths, A. (1987) 'Democedes of Croton: a Greek Doctor at Darius' Court', in Sancisi-Weerdenburg and Kuhrt (1987) 37–51.

— (1995) 'Latent and Blatant: Two Perspectives on Humour in Herodotus', in S. Jäkel and A. Timonen, eds., *Laughter Down the Centuries* (Turku), II. 31–44.

— (1999) 'Euenios the Negligent Nightwatchman (Herodotus 9.92–6)', in R. Buxton, ed., *From Myth to Reason? Studies in the Development of Greek Thought* (Oxford), 169–82.

— (2001a) 'Behind the Lines: the Genesis of Stories in Herodotus', in F. Budelmann and P. Michelakis, eds., *Homer, Tragedy and Beyond: Essays in Honour of P. E. Easterling* (London), 75–88.

— (2001b) 'Kissing Cousins: Some Curious Cases of Adjacent Material in Herodotus', in Luraghi (2001c) 161–78.

Grundy, G. B. (1901) *The Great Persian War and its Preliminaries* (London).

Gurewitch, M. (1975) *Comedy. The Irrational Vision* (Ithaca and London).

Guthrie, W. K. C. (1971) *The Sophists* (Cambridge) = *A History of Greek Philosophy* III (Cambridge 1969), 3–319.

Habicht, C. (1998) *Pausanias' Guide to Ancient Greece* (Berkeley, Los Angeles and London).

Hall, E. (1989) *Inventing the Barbarian. Greek Self-Definition through Tragedy* (Oxford).

— (1993) 'Asia Unmanned: Images of Victory in Classical Athens', in J. Rich and G. Shipley, eds., *War and Society in the Greek World* (London), 108–33.

— (1996) *Aeschylus: Persians* (Warminster).

Hall, J. M. (1997) *Ethnic Identity in Greek Antiquity* (Cambridge).

— (2002) *Hellenicity. Between Ethnicity and Culture* (Chicago).

Halliwell, S. (1991) 'The Uses of Laughter in Greek Culture', *CQ* 41. 279–96.

— (2002) *The Aesthetics of Mimesis: Ancient Texts and Modern Problems* (Princeton and Oxford).

Hanson, V. D. (1989) *The Western Way of War* (New York).

— (1991) *Hoplites. The Classical Greek Battle Experience* (London).

Harrison, T. (2000) *Divinity and History. The Religion of Herodotus* (Oxford).

— (2002) 'The Persian Invasions', in Bakker, de Jong and van Wees (2002) 551–78.

Hartog, F. (1988) *The Mirror of Herodotus. An Essay on the Interpretation of the Other* (Berkeley, Los Angeles and London), trans. by J. Lloyd of French original, *Le miroir d'Hérodote* (1st edn) (Paris 1980).

— (1989) 'Écriture, généalogies, archives, histoire en Grèce ancienne', in A. de Pury, ed., *Histoire et conscience historique dans les civilisations du Proche-Orient Ancien*. Actes du colloque de Cartigny 1986 (Cahiers du Centre d'Étude du Proche-Orient Ancien 5; Leuven), 121–32.

— (1991) *Le miroir d'Hérodote. Essai sur la représentation de l'autre* (2nd edn) (Paris).

— (2001) *Memories of Odysseus: Frontier Tales from Ancient Greece*, trans. by J. Lloyd (Chicago and London).

Hasford, G. (1979) *The Short-Timers* (New York).

Havelock, E. A. (1972) 'War as a Way of Life in Classical Culture', in E.A. Gareau, ed., *Classical Values and the Modern World* (Ottawa), 19–78.

Heinimann, F. (1945) *Nomos und Physis* (Basel).

Hellmann, F. (1934) *Herodots Kroisos-Logos* (Neue Philologische Untersuchungen 9; Berlin).

Heni, R. (1976) *Die Gespräche bei Herodot* (Heilbronn).

Herr, M. (1978) *Dispatches* (New York).

Higbie, C. (2003) *The Lindian Chronicle and the Greek Creation of their Past* (Oxford).

Hignett, C. (1963) *Xerxes' Invasion of Greece* (Oxford).

Hohti, P. (1974) 'Freedom of Speech in Speech Sections in the *Histories* of Herodotus', *Arctos* 8. 19–27.

— (1976) *The Interrelation of Speech and Action in the Histories of Herodotus* (*Commentationes Humanarum Litterarum* 57; Helsinki and Helsingfors).

Holladay, A. J. (1982) 'Hoplites and Heresies', *JHS* 102. 94–103.

Hornblower, J. (1981) *Hieronymus of Cardia* (Oxford).

Hornblower, S. (1991) *A Commentary on Thucydides*, vol. I: *Books I–III* (Oxford).

— (1995) 'The Fourth-Century and Hellenistic Reception of Thucydides', *JHS* 115. 47–68.

— (1996) *A Commentary on Thucydides* vol. II: *Books IV–V.24* (Oxford).

— (2002) 'Herodotus and his Sources of Information', in Bakker, de Jong and van Wees (2002) 373–86.

— (2003) 'Panionios of Chios and Hermotimos of Pedasa (Hdt. 8.104–106)', in Derow and Parker (2003) 37–57.

How, W. W. and J. Wells (1928) *A Commentary on Herodotus*, 2 vols. (Oxford).

Huber, L. (1965) 'Herodots Homerverständnis', in *Synusia. Festgabe . . . W. Schadewaldt* (Pfullingen), 29–52.

Humphreys, S. (1987) 'Law, Custom and Nature in Herodotus', *Arethusa* 20. 211–20.

Hunt, P. (1998) *Slaves, Warfare, and Ideology in the Greek Historians* (Cambridge).

Hussey, E. (1990) 'The Beginnings of Epistemology: From Homer to Philolaus', in S. Everson, ed., *Epistemology* (Cambridge), 11–38.

Huxley, G. L. (1969) *Greek Epic Poetry from Eumelos to Panyassis* (London and Cambridge, Mass.).

— (1975) *Pindar's Vision of the Past* (Belfast).

— (1989) *Herodotos and the Epic* (Athens).

Immerwahr, H. R. (1954) 'Historical Action in Herodotus', *TAPA* 85. 16–45.

— (1957) 'The Samian Stories of Herodotus', *CJ* 52. 312–22.

— (1960) '*Ergon*: History as a Monument in Herodotus and Thucydides', *AJPh* 81.261–90.

— (1966) *Form and Thought in Herodotus* (APA Philological Monographs 23; Cleveland).

Isager, S. (1999) 'The Pride of Halikarnassos', *ZPE* 123. 1–23.

Jacoby, F. (1909) 'Über die Entwicklung der griechischen Historiographie und den Plan einer neuen Sammlung der griechischen Historikerfragmente', *Klio* 9. 80–123, repr. in F. Jacoby, *Abhandlungen zur griechischen Geschichtsschreibung* (Leiden 1956), 16–64.

— (1913) 'Herodotos', *RE* Suppl. II. 205–520.

— (1922) 'Ktesias', *RE* 11. 2032–73.

— (1945) 'Some Athenian Epigrams from the Persian Wars', *Hesperia* 14.157–211, repr. in F. Jacoby, *Kleine Philologische Schriften* (Berlin 1961) I. 456–520.

— (1947) 'Some Remarks on Ion of Chios', *CQ* 41.1–17, repr. in F. Jacoby, *Abhandlungen zur griechischen Geschichtsschreibung* (Leiden 1956) 144–68.

— (1949) *Atthis: The Local Chronicles of Ancient Athens* (Oxford).

Janko, R. (1997) 'The Physicist as Hierophant: Aristophanes, Socrates and the Authorship of the Derveni Papyrus', *ZPE* 118. 61–94.

Jehasse, J. (1962) 'La victoire Cadméenne d'Hérodote (1.166) et la Corse dans les courants d'expansion grecque', *REA* 64. 241–86.

Jones, C. P. (1986) *Culture and Society in Lucian* (Cambridge, Mass.).

Jouanna, J. (1992) *Hippocrate* (Paris).

Kagan, D. (1969) *The Outbreak of the Peloponnesian War* (Ithaca).

Kazazis, J. N. (1978) *Herodotus' Stories and History: a Proppian Analysis of his Narrative Technique* (Urbana).

Keegan, J. (1976) *The Face of Battle. A Study of Agincourt, Waterloo, and the Somme* (Harmondsworth).

Kent, R. (1953) *Old Persian: Grammar, Texts, Lexicon* (New Haven).

Kerferd, G. B. (1981) *The Sophistic Movement* (Cambridge).

Kermode, F. (1979) *The Genesis of Secrecy* (Cambridge, Mass.).

Kidd, I. (1988) *Posidonius*, vol. II: *The Commentary*, 2 vols. (Cambridge).

Kiesling, E. C. (2003) 'The Oldest "New" Military Historians: Herodotos, W. G. Forrest, and the Historiography of War', in Derow and Parker (2003) 88–100.

Kirchberg, J. (1964) *Die Funktion der Orakel im Werke Herodots* (Hypomnemata 11; Göttingen).

Kleinknecht, H. (1940) 'Herodot und Athen. 7.139/8.140–4', *Hermes* 75. 241–64, repr. in Marg (1982) 541–73.

Knox, B. (1964) *The Heroic Temper: Studies in Sophoclean Tragedy* (Berkeley and Los Angeles).

Köhnken, A. (1980) 'Herodots falscher Smerdis', *WJb* 6a. 39–50.

Konstan, D. (1987) 'Persians, Greeks and Empire', *Arethusa* 20. 59–73.

Kraus, C., ed. (1999) *The Limits of Historiography. Genre and Narrative in Ancient Historical Texts* (Leiden, Boston and Cologne).

Krings, V. (1998) *Carthage et les grecs c. 580-480 av. J.-C.* (Leiden).

Kuhrt, A. (1995) *The Ancient Near East*, vol. II (London and New York).

— (2001) 'The Achaemenid Persian Empire (c. 550–c. 330 BCE): Continuities, Adaptations, Transformation', in S. E. Alcock, T. N. D'Altroy, K. D. Morrison, and C. M. Sinopoli, eds., *Empires* (Cambridge), 93–123.

— (2002) *'Greeks' and 'Greece' in Mesopotamian and Persian Perspectives* (J. L. Myres Memorial Lecture, Oxford 2002).

Kurke, L. (1999) *Coins, Bodies, Games and Gold. The Politics of Meaning in Archaic Greece* (Princeton).

Lane, W., and A. Lane (1986) 'The Politics of Antigone', in P. Euben, ed., *Greek Tragedy and Political Theory* (Berkeley and Los Angeles), 162–82.

Lanfranchi, G., M. Roaf and R. Rollinger (2003) *Continuity of Empire (?): Assyria, Media, Persia* (Padua).

Lang, M. L. (1984) *Herodotean Narrative and Discourse* (Cambridge, Mass.).

Lasserre, F. (1976a) 'L'historiographie grecque à l'époque archaïque', *QS* 4.113–42.

— (1976b) 'Hérodote et Protagoras: le débat sur les constitutions', *MH* 33. 65–84.

Lateiner, D. (1977) 'No Laughing Matter: A Literary Tactic in Herodotus', *TAPA* 107. 173–82.

— (1982) 'The Failure of the Ionian Revolt', *Historia* 31. 129–60.

— (1985) 'Limit, Propriety and Transgression in the *Histories* of Herodotus', in M. H. Jameson, ed., *The Greek Historians. Papers Presented to A.E. Raubitschek* (Saratoga), 87–100.

— (1986) 'The Empirical Element in the Methods of Early Greek Medical Writers and Herodotus: A Shared Epistemological Response', *Antichthon* 20. 1–20.

— (1987) 'Nonverbal Communication in the *Histories* of Herodotus', *Arethusa* 20. 83–107.

— (1989) *The Historical Method of Herodotus* (Toronto, Buffalo and London).

Lattimore, R. (1939a) 'The Wise Advisor in Herodotus', *CPh* 34.24–35.

— (1939b) 'Herodotus and the Names of Egyptian Gods', *CPh* 34. 357–65.

Lazenby, J. F. (1993) *The Defence of Greece, 490–479 B.C.* (Warminster).

Le Goff, J. (1977/1992) *History and Memory* (New York), trans. by S. Rendell and E. Claman of Italian original, *Storia e memoria* (Turin 1977).

Lefkowitz, M. (1992) *First-Person Fictions: Pindar's Poetic 'I'* (Oxford).

Legrand, Ph.-E. (1946) *Hérodote: Histoires Livre I* (Paris).

— (1966) *Hérodote: Introduction* (Paris).

Lendle, O. (1992) *Einführung in die griechische Geschichtsschreibung* (Darmstadt).

Lenfant, D. (1996) 'Ctésias et Hérodote, ou les reécritures de l'histoire dans la Perse achéménide', *REG* 109. 348–80.

Lesky, A. (1953) 'Das hellenistische Gyges-Drama', *Hermes* 81.357–70 = A. Lesky, *Gesammelte Schriften* (Bern 1966), 204–12.

Letoublon, F., ed. (1996) *Impressions d'îles* (Toulouse).

Levine, J. (1969) *Motivation in Humor* (New York).

Lewis, D. (1984) 'Postscript 1984', in Burn (1984) 587–609.

— (1985), 'Persians in Herodotus', in M. H. Jameson, ed., *The Greek Historians: Literature and History. Papers presented to A.E. Raubitschek* (Saratoga, Cal.), 101–7, repr. in Lewis (1997) 345–61.

— (1997) *Selected Papers in Greek and Near Eastern History*, ed. P. J. Rhodes (Cambridge).

Lewis, S. (1996) *News and Society in the Greek Polis* (London).

Lightfoot, J. (2003) *Lucian: de dea Syria* (Oxford).

Linforth, I. M. (1926) 'Greek Gods and Foreign Gods in Herodotus', *UCPCP* 9. 1–25.

— (1940) 'Greek and Egyptian Gods', *CPh* 35. 300–1.

Lloyd, A. B. (1975–88) *Herodotus: Book II*, 3 vols. (Leiden).

— (1990) 'Herodotus on Egyptians and Libyans', in Nenci and Reverdin (1990) 215–53 (with discussion).

Lloyd, G. E. R. (1966) *Polarity and Analogy* (Cambridge).

— (1979) *Magic, Reason and Experience. Studies in the Origin and Development of Greek Science* (Cambridge).

— (1987) *The Revolutions of Wisdom. Studies in the Claims and Practice of Ancient Greek Science* (Cambridge).

Lloyd, M. (1992) *The Agon in Euripides* (Oxford).

Lloyd-Jones, H. (1999) 'The Pride of Halicarnassus', *ZPE* 124. 1–14.

Lombardo, M. (1972) 'Le concezioni degli antichi sul ruolo degli oracoli nella colonizzazione greca', *ASNP*, 3rd series, 2. 63–89.

— (1993) 'Da Sibari a Thurii', in Stazio and Ceccoli (1993) 255–328.

Long, T. (1987) *Repetition and Variation in the Short Stories of Herodotus* (Frankfurt).

Lopez Eire, A. (2000) 'À propos des mots pour exprimer l'idée de "rire" en grec ancien', in Desclos (2000) 13–43.

Loraux, N. and C. Miralles, eds. (1998) *Figures de l'intellectuel en Grèce ancienne* (Paris).

Luraghi, N. (1994a) *Tirannidi arcaiche in Sicilia e Magna Grecia* (Florence).

— (1994b) 'Erodoto tra storia e fantasia: la parola alla difesa', *Quaderni di storia* 40. 181–90.

— (2001a) 'Introduction', in Luraghi (2001c) 1–15.

— (2001b) 'Local Knowledge in Herodotus' *Histories*', in Luraghi (2001c) 138–60.

— ed. (2001c) *The Historian's Craft in the Age of Herodotus* (Oxford).

— (2002) 'Antioco di Siracusa', in R. Vattuone, ed., *Storici greci d'Occidente* (Bologna), 55–89.

Macan, R. W. (1895) *Herodotus: The Fourth, Fifth and Sixth Books*, 2 vols. (London; repr. in 1 vol., New York 1973).

— (1908) *Herodotus: The Seventh, Eighth and Ninth Books*, 3 vols. (London; repr. in 2 vols., New York 1973).

Mack, B. (1991) 'Royal Wives in Kano', in C. Coles and B. Mack, eds., *Hausa Women in the Twentieth Century* (Madison), 109–29.

Mackie, H. (2003) *Graceful Errors: Pindar and the Performance of Praise* (Ann Arbor).

Macleod, C. W. (1983) *Collected Essays* (Oxford).

Maddoli, G. (1980) 'Il VI e il V secolo a.C.', in Gabba and Vallet (1980) II.3–102.

Malkin, I. (1987) *Religion and Colonization in Ancient Greece* (Leiden).

— (1994) *Myth and Territory in the Spartan Mediterranean* (Cambridge).

— ed. (2001) *Ancient Perceptions of Greek Ethnicity* (Cambridge, Mass. and London).

Marg, W. (1982) *Herodot. Eine Auswahl aus der neueren Forschung* (3rd edn) (Darmstadt).

BIBLIOGRAPHY

Marincola, J. (1987) 'Herodotean Narrative and the Narrator's Presence', *Arethusa* 20.121–42.
— (1994) 'Plutarch's Refutation of Herodotus', *AncW* 25. 191–203.
— (1997) *Authority and Tradition in Ancient Historiography* (Cambridge).
— (1999) 'Genre, Convention and Innovation in Greco-Roman Historiography', in Kraus (1999) 281–324.
— (2001) *Greek Historians* (*Greece & Rome* New Surveys in the Classics, no. 31; Oxford).
— (forthcoming) 'Odysseus and the Historians: Ancient Historiography and the *Odyssey*'.
Martin, R. (1992) 'Hesiod's Metanistic Poetry', *Ramus* 21.11–34.
Matthaiou, A. P. (2003) 'Ἀθηναίοισι τεταγμένοισι ἐν τεμένεϊ Ἡρακλέος (Hdt. 6. 108.1)', in Derow and Parker (2003) 190–202.
Matthews, V. J. (1974) *Panyassis of Halicarnassus* (Leiden).
Maurice, F. (1930) 'The Size of the Army of Xerxes in the Invasion of Greece 480 B.C.', *JHS* 50. 210–35.
Mauritsch, P. (2000) 'Lüge oder Wahrheit – ein alltägliches Problem?', in C. Ulf, ed., *Ideologie – Sport – Aussenseiter. Aktuelle Aspekte einer Beschäftigung mit der antiken Gesellschaft* (Innsbruck), 29–50.
McGlew, J. F. (1993) *Tyranny and Political Culture in Ancient Greece* (Ithaca and London).
Meiggs, R. (1972) *The Athenian Empire* (Oxford).
Meredith, G. (1956) 'An Essay on Comedy', in Sypher (1956) 3–57.
Mikalson, J. (2002) 'Religion in Herodotus', in Bakker, de Jong and van Wees (2002) 187–98.
Milanezi, S. (2000) 'Indications bibliographiques', in Desclos (2000) 591–623.
Möller, A. (2001) 'The Beginnings of Chronography: Hellanicus' *Hiereiai*', in Luraghi (2001c) 241–62.
Moggi, M. (1972) 'Autori greci di *Persiká*. I: Dionisio di Mileto', *ASNP* (3rd series) 2. 433–68.
Moles, J. L. (1996) 'Herodotus Warns the Athenians', *PLLS* 9. 259–84.
— (2002) 'Herodotus and Athens', in Bakker, de Jong and van Wees (2002) 33–52.
Momigliano, A. (1955–92) *Contributi alla Storia degli Studi classici e del Mondo Antico*, 9 vols. in 11 parts (Rome).
— (1966) 'The Place of Herodotus in the History of Historiography', in A. Momigliano, *Studies in Historiography* (London), 127–42; also in A. Momigliano, *Secondo Contributo alla Storia degli Studi Classici* (Rome 1960), 29–44; orig. *History* 43 (1958), 1–13.
— (1980) 'The Historians of the Classical World and their Audiences', in A. Momigliano, *Sesto Contributo alla Storia degli Studi Classici e del Mondo Antico* (Rome) 361–76; orig. in *ANSP* (3rd series) 8 (1978) 59–75.
— (1990) *The Classical Foundations of Modern Historiography* (Berkeley, Los Angeles and London).
Moniot, H. (1970) 'Les sources de l'histoire africaine', in H. Deschamps, ed., *Histoire générale de l'Afrique noire* (Paris) 1. 123–47.
Montiglio, S. (2000) 'Wandering Philosophers in Classical Greece', *JHS* 120. 86–105.
Morreall, J., ed. (1987) *The Philosophy of Laughter and Humor* (Albany, NY).
Mossé, C. (1996) 'Athènes comme île', in Letoublon (1996) 95–101.

Moyer, I. S. (2002) 'Herodotus and an Egyptian Mirage: The Genealogies of the Theban Priests', *JHS* 122. 70–90.

Müller, D. (1981) 'Herodot – Vater des Empirismus?', in G. Kurz, D. Müller and W. Nicolai, eds., *Gnomosyne. Festschrift . . . Walter Marg zum 70. Geburtstag* (Munich), 299–318.

Munson, R. V. (1988) 'Artemisia in Herodotus', *ClAnt* 7. 91–106.

— (1991) 'The Madness of Cambyses (Herodotus 3.16–38)', *Arethusa* 24. 43–65.

— (1993) 'Three Aspects of Spartan Kingship in Herodotus', in Rosen and Farrell (1993) 39–54.

— (2001a) *Telling Wonders: Ethnographic and Political Discourse in the Work of Herodotus* (Ann Arbor).

— (2001b) '*ANANKE* in Herodotus', *JHS* 121. 30–50.

Murnaghan, S. (1986) '*Antigone* 904–920 and the Institution of Marriage', *AJPh* 107.192–207.

Murray, O. (1972) 'Herodotus and Hellenistic Culture', *CQ* 22. 200–13.

— (1993) *Early Greece* (2nd edn) (London and Cambridge, Mass.).

— (2001a) 'Herodotus and Oral History', in Luraghi (2001c) 16–44; orig. in H. Sancisi-Weerdenburg and A. Kuhrt, eds. *Achaemenid Studies*, vol. II: *The Greek Sources* (Leiden 1987), 93–115.

— (2001b) 'Herodotus and Oral History Reconsidered', in Luraghi (2001c) 314–25.

Murray, P. (1981) 'Poetic Inspiration in Early Greece', *JHS* 101. 87–100.

Myres, J. L. (1953) *Herodotus. Father of History* (Oxford).

Nagy, G. (1987) 'Herodotus the *Logios*', *Arethusa* 20. 175–84.

— (1989) 'Early Greek Views of Poets and Poetry', in G. Kennedy, ed., *The Cambridge History of Literary Criticism*, vol. I: *Classical Criticism* (Cambridge), 1–77.

— (1990) *Pindar's Homer: The Lyric Possession of an Epic Past* (Baltimore and London).

Neitzel, H. (1980) 'Hesiod und die lügenden Musen', *Hermes* 108. 387–401.

Nenci, G. (1976) 'Il *barbaros polemos* fra Taranto e gli Iapigi e gli *anathêmata* tarentini a Delfi', *ASNP* (3rd series) 6.719–38.

— (1978) 'Per una definizione della *Iapygia*', *ASNP* (3rd series) 8. 43–58.

— (1990) 'L'occidente barbarico', in Nenci and Reverdin (1990), 301–18.

— (1994) *Erodoto: la rivolta della Ionia. Libro V delle Storie* (Milan).

Nenci, G. and O. Reverdin (1990) *Hérodote et les peuples non grecs* (Entretiens sur l'antiquité classique 35; Fondation Hardt, Vandoeuvres-Geneva).

Nestle, W. (1908) *Herodots Verständnis zur Philosophie und Sophistik* (Schöntal).

— (1942) *Vom Mythos zum Logos* (2nd edn) (Stuttgart).

Neuberg, M. (1990) 'How Like a Woman: Antigone's Inconsistency', *CQ* 40. 54–76.

Notopoulos, J.A. (1949) 'Parataxis in Homer: A New Approach to Homeric Literary Criticism', *TAPhA* 80.1–23.

Ober, J. (1989a) *Mass and Elite in Democratic Athens. Rhetoric, Ideology and the Power of the People* (Princeton).

— (1989b) 'The Nature of Athenian Democracy', *CPh* 84. 322–34, repr. in J. Ober (1996) 107–22.

— (1996) *The Athenian Revolution. Essays on Ancient Greek Democracy and Political Theory* (Princeton).

— (1998) *Political Dissent in Democratic Athens. Intellectual Critics of Popular Rule* (Princeton).

Ogilvie, R. M. (1965) *A Commentary on Livy Books 1–5* (Oxford).

Oost, S. (1972) 'Cypselus the Bacchiad', *CPh* 67. 10–30.

Osborne, R. (2002) 'Archaic Greek History', in Bakker, de Jong and van Wees (2002) 497–509.

Ostwald, M. (1991) 'Herodotus in Athens', *BICS* 16.137–48.

Otterlo, W. A. A. van (1944) 'Untersuchungen über Begriff, Anwendung und Entstehung der griechischen Ringkomposition', *Mededelingen der Nederlandse Akademie van Wetenschappen, Afdeeling Letterkunde* (Niewe Reeks 7.3).

Oudemans, C. W. and A. Lardinois (1987) *Tragic Ambiguity: Anthropology, Philosophy and Sophocles' Antigone* (Leiden).

Page, D. L. (1951) *A New Chapter in the History of Greek Tragedy* (Cambridge).

Papalas, A. (2002) *Archaia Ikaria* (Ikaria; English edn. *Ancient Icaria*, New York [1992]).

Pareti, L. (1914) *Studi siciliani ed italioti* (Florence).

Parker, R. (2004) 'One Man's Piety: The Religious Dimension of the *Anabasis*', in R. Lane Fox, ed., *The Long March: Xenophon and the Ten Thousand* (New Haven and London), 131–53.

Parsons, P. (1993) 'Identities in Diversity', in A. W. Bulloch et al., eds., *Images and Ideologies: Self-definition in the Hellenistic World* (Berkeley, Los Angeles and London), 152–70.

Payen, P. (1995) 'Comment résister à la conquête? Temps, espace et récit chez Hérodote', *REG* 108. 308–38.

Pearson, L. (1939) *Early Ionian Historians* (Oxford).

— (1942) *The Local Historians of Attica* (Philadelphia).

— (1960) *Lost Histories of Alexander the Great* (Philadelphia).

— (1987) *The Greek Historians of the West* (Atlanta).

Pearson, L. and F. Sandbach (1965) *Plutarch's Moralia*, vol. 11 (Cambridge, Mass. and London).

Pelling, C. B. R. (1991) 'Thucydides' Archidamus and Herodotus' Artabanus', in M. A. Flower and M. Toher, eds., *Georgica: Greek Studies in Honour of George Cawkwell* (*BICS* Suppl. 38; London), 120–42.

— (1996) 'The Urine and the Vine: Astyages' Dreams at Herodotus 1. 107–8', *CQ* 46. 68–77.

— (1997a) 'Aeschylus' *Persae* and History', in C. Pelling, ed., *Greek Tragedy and the Historian* (Oxford), 1–19.

— (1997b) 'East is East and West is West – Or Are They? National Stereotypes in Herodotus', *Histos* 1, electronic publication, http://www.dur.ac.uk/Classics/histos.

— (2000) *Literary Texts and the Greek Historian* (London and New York).

— (2002) 'Speech and Action: Herodotus' Debate on the Constitutions', *PCPhS* 48. 123–58.

— (2006) 'Educating Croesus: Talking and Learning in Herodotus' Lydian *logos*', to appear in *Classical Antiquity* 25.1.

Pembroke, S. (1967) 'Women in Charge: The Function of Alternatives in Early Greek Tradition and the Ancient Idea of Matriarchy', *JWCI* 30. 1–35.

Perry, B. E. (1965) *Babrius and Phaedrus* (Cambridge, Mass. and London).

Plass, P. (1988) *Wit and the Writing of History. The Rhetoric of Historiography in Imperial Rome* (Madison).

Powell, J. (1937) 'Puns in Herodotus', *CR* 51. 103–5.

— (1939) *The History of Herodotus* (Cambridge).

Pratt, L. (1993) *Lying and Poetry from Homer to Pindar. Falsehood and Deception in Archaic Greek Poetics* (Ann Arbor).

Prins, G. (2001) 'Oral History', in P. Burke, ed., *New Perspectives on Historical Writing* (2nd edn) (Cambridge), 120–56.

Pritchett, W. K. (1965–85) *Studies in Ancient Greek Topography* (Berkeley).

— (1971–91) *The Greek State at War*, 5 parts (Berkeley).

— (1995) *The Liar School of Herodotus* (Amsterdam).

Puelma, M. (1989) 'Der Dichter und die Wahrheit in der griechischen Poetik von Homer bis Aristoteles', *MH* 46. 65–100.

Pugliese Carratelli, G. (1970) 'La nascita di Velia', *PP* 25. 7–18.

— (1987a) 'Primordi della legislazione scritta', in G. Pugliese Carratelli (1987b) 99–102.

— ed. (1987b) *Magna Grecia: lo sviluppo politico, sociale ed economico* (Milan).

Pulleyn, S. (1997) *Prayer in Greek Religion* (Oxford).

Purdie, S. (1993) *Comedy: The Mastery of Discourse* (Toronto and Buffalo).

Raaflaub, K. A. (1987) 'Herodotus, Political Thought and the Meaning of History', *Arethusa* 20. 221–48.

— (1988) 'Athenische Geschichte und mündliche Überlieferung', in von Ungern-Sternberg and Reinau (1988) 197–225.

— (2002a) 'Philosophy, Science, Politics: Herodotus and the Intellectual Trends of his Time', in Bakker, de Jong and van Wees (2002) 149–86.

— (2002b) 'Herodot und Thukydides: Persischer Imperialismus im Lichte der athenischen Sizilienpolitik', in N. Ehrhardt and L.-M. Günther, eds., *Widerstand – Anpassung – Integration. Die griechische Staatenwelt und Rom. Festschrift für Jürgen Deininger zum 65. Geburtstag* (Stuttgart), 11–40.

Raviola, F. (1986) 'Temistocle e la Magna Grecia', in L. Braccesi, ed., *Tre studi su Temistocle* (Padua), 13–112.

— (1999) 'Erodoto a Turii', in *Erodoto e l'Occidente* (Rome), 373–92.

Redfield, J. (1985) 'Herodotus the Tourist', *CPh* 80. 97–118.

Regenbogen, O. (1961) 'Herodot und sein Werk', in O. Regenbogen, *Kleine Schriften* (Munich), 57–100; orig. in *Die Antike* 6 (1930), 202–48; also repr. in Marg (1982) 57–108.

Reinhardt, K. (1960) 'Herodots Persergeschichten', in K. Reinhardt, *Vermächtnis der Antike: Gesammelte Essays zur Philosophie und Geschichtsschreibung* (Göttingen), 133–74; orig. in *Geistige Überlieferung: ein Jahrbuch* (Berlin 1940), 138–84; repr. also in Marg (1982) 320–69.

— (1979) *Sophokles*, trans. H. and D. Harvey (Oxford).

Rhodes, P. J. (1982) *A Commentary on the Aristotelian* Athenaion Politeia (Oxford).

Richardson, S. D. (1990) *The Homeric Narrator* (Nashville).

Rieks, R. (1975) 'Eine tragische Erzählung bei Herodot (*Hist.* 1, 34–45)', *Poetica* 7. 23–44.

Riemann, K. (1967) *Das herodoteische Geschichtswerk in der Antike* (diss. Munich).

Rösler, W. (1990) '*Mnemosyne* in the Symposium', in O. Murray, ed., *Sympotika: A Symposium on the Symposion* (Oxford), 230–7.

— (2002) 'The *Histories* and Writing', in Bakker, de Jong and van Wees (2002) 79–94.

Rollinger, R. (1993) *Herodots Babylonischer Logos. Eine kritische Untersuchung der Glaubwürdigkeitsdiskussion an Hand ausgewählter Beispiele* (Innsbruck).

Romm, J. S. (1989) 'Herodotus and Mythic Geography: The Case of the Hyperboreans', *TAPA* 119.97–113.

— (1992) *The Edges of the Earth in Ancient Thought* (Princeton).

— (2002) Review of Harrison (2000), *AJPh* 123.122–6.

Rood, T. (1999) 'Thucydides' Persian Wars', in Kraus (1999) 141–68.

Root, M. C. (1979) *The King and Kingship in Achaemenid Art* (Leiden).

Rosen, R. M. and J. Farrell, eds. (1993) *Nomodeiktes: Greek Studies in Honor of Martin Ostwald* (Ann Arbor).

Rosenmeyer, T. (1982) 'History or Poetry? The Example of Herodotus', *Clio* 11. 239–59.

Rosselini, M. and S. Saïd (1978) 'Usages des femmes et autres *nomoi* chez les "sauvages" d'Hérodote: essai de lecture structurale', *ASNP* (3rd series) 8. 949–1005.

Roux, G. (1963) 'Kypselé: Où avait-on caché le petit Kypselos?', *REA* 65.279–89.

Rudhardt, J. (1992) 'Les attitudes des Grecs à l'égard des religions étrangères', *RHR* 209. 219–38.

Ruschenbusch, E. (1995) 'Eine schriftliche Quelle im Werk Herodots (*FGrHist* 3, Pherekydes von Athen)', in M. Weinmann-Walser, ed., *Historische Interpretationen Gerold Walser zum 75. Geburtstag dargebracht von Freunden, Kollegen und Schülern* (Stuttgart), 1321–49.

Russell, D. (1973) *Plutarch* (London and New York).

Rusten, J. (1982) *Dionysius Scytobrachion* (Papyrologica Coloniensia 10; Cologne).

Rutherford, I. (2001) 'The New Simonides: Towards a Commentary', in Boedeker and Sider (2001), 33–54.

Rutter, N. K. (1970) 'Sybaris: Legend and Reality', *G&R* 17.168–76.

— (1973) 'Diodorus and the Foundation of Thurii', *Historia* 22.155–76.

Saïd, S. (2002) 'Herodotus and Tragedy', in Bakker, de Jong and van Wees (2002) 117–45.

Ste. Croix, G. E. M. de (1975) 'Aristotle on History and Poetry (*Poetics* 9, 1451a36–b11)', in B. Levick, ed., *The Ancient Historian and his Materials: Essays . . . C.E. Stevens* (London) 45–58; repr. in A. O. Rorty, *Essays on Aristotle's* Poetics (Princeton 1992), 23–32.

Saki [Munro, H. H.] (1914) 'The Seventh Pullet', in Saki [H. H. Munro], *Beasts and Superbeasts* (London).

Sammartano, R. (1999) 'Erodoto e la storiografia siceliota', in *Erodoto e l'Occidente* (Rome), 393–429.

Sancisi-Weerdenburg, H. (1983) 'Exit Atossa. Images of Women in Greek Historiography of Persia', in A. Cameron and A. Kuhrt, eds., *Images of Women in Antiquity* (London), 20–33.

— (2000) *Peisistratos and the Tyranny: a Reappraisal of the Evidence* (Amsterdam).

— (2002) 'The Personality of Xerxes, King of Kings', in Bakker, de Jong and van Wees (2002) 579–90.

Saxonhouse, A. (1996) *Athenian Democracy: Modern Mythmakers and Ancient Theorists* (South Bend, Ind.).

Schadewaldt, W. (1934) 'Herodot als erster Historiker', *Die Antike* 10. 144–68; repr. in Marg (1982) 109–21.

Schepens, G. (1975) 'Some Aspects of Source Theory in Greek Historiography', *Anc. Soc.* 6. 257–74.

— (1980) *L' 'autopsie' dans la méthode des historiens grecs du Ve siècle avant J.-C.* (Brussels).

Schmid, W. and Stählin, O. (1934) *Geschichte der griechischen Literatur*, vol. I.2: *Die griechische Literatur in der Zeit der attischen Hegemonie vor den Eingreifen der Sophistik* (Munich).

Scodel, R. (1998) 'Bardic Performance and Oral Tradition in Homer', *AJPh* 119. 171–94.

— (2001) 'Poetic Authority and Oral Tradition in Hesiod and Pindar', in J. Watson, ed., *Speaking Volumes: Orality and Literacy in the Greek and Roman World* (Leiden, Boston and Cologne), 109–37.

Selden, D. L. (1999) 'Cambyses' Madness or the Reason of History', *MD* 42. 33–63.

Shapiro, S. (1996) 'Herodotus and Solon', *CA* 15. 348–64.

Shay, J. (1994) *Achilles in Vietnam* (New York).

Shipley, G. (1987) *A History of Samos 800–180 B.C.* (Oxford).

Shrimpton, G. (1997) *History and Memory in Ancient Greece* (Montreal).

Sinos, R. (1994) 'Divine Selection. Epiphany and Politics in Archaic Greece', in C. Dougherty and L. Kurke, eds., *Cultural Poetics in Archaic Greece* (New York and Oxford), 73–91.

Slings, S. R. (1990) *The Poet's 'I' in Archaic Greek Lyric* (Amsterdam).

Solmsen, F. (1974) 'Two Crucial Decisions in Herodotus', *Mededelingen der Koninklijke Nederlandse Akademie van Wetenschappen, Afd. Letterkunde. Nieuwe Reeks,* 37.6, 139–70, repr. in F. Solmsen, *Kleine Schriften* III (Hildesheim, Zurich and New York 1982), 78–109.

Solmsen, L. (1943) 'Speeches in Herodotus' Account of the Ionian Revolt', *TAPA* 64. 194–207; repr. (in German) in Marg (1982) 629–44.

— (1944) 'Speeches in Herodotus' Account of the Battle of Plataea', *CPh* 39. 241–53, repr. (in German) in Marg (1982) 645–67.

Sourvinou-Inwood, C. (1988) ' "Myth" and History: On Herodotus III. 48 and 50–53', *Opuscula Atheniensia* 17. 167–82; repr. in C. Sourvinou-Inwood, *Reading Greek Culture: Texts and Images, Rituals and Myths* (Oxford 1991), 244–83.

— (forthcoming) 'Reading a Myth, Reconstructing its Constructions', in S. des Bouvrie, ed., *Myth and Symbol*, vol. II: Proceedings of the Symposium on Myth and Symbol 2000 and 2002 (Papers from the Norwegian Institute at Athens 7; Athens).

Spawforth, A. (1994) 'Symbol of Unity? The Persian-Wars Tradition in the Roman Empire', in Hornblower (1994) 233–47.

— (1996) 'Persian-Wars Tradition', *OCD* (3rd edn) 1147.

Spiegel, G. M. (1997) *The Past as Text: The Theory and Practice of Medieval Historiography* (Baltimore and London).

Stadter, P. (1992) 'Herodotus and the Athenian *Arche*', *ASNP* (3rd series) 22. 781–809.

Stahl, M. (1983) 'Tyrannis und das Problem der Macht. Die Geschichten Herodots über Kypselos und Periander von Korinth', *Hermes* 110. 202–20.

Stahl, H.-P. (1968) 'Herodots Gyges Tragödie', *Hermes* 96. 385–400.

Stazio, A. and S. Ceccoli, eds. (1993) *Sibari e la sibaritide. Atti del trentaduesimo Convegno di studi sulla Magna Grecia: Taranto-Sibari 7–12 Ottobre 1992* (Taranto).

Stern, J. (1991) 'Scapegoat Narratives in Herodotus', *Hermes* 119. 304–11.

Stevenson, R. (1997) *Persica* (Edinburgh).

Stoddard, K. (2004) *The Narrative Voice in Hesiod's Theogony* (Leiden).

Strasburger, H. (1955) 'Herodot und das perikleische Athen', *Historia* 4. 1–25, repr. in H. Strasburger (1982) 592–626; repr. also in Marg (1982) 574–608.

— (1972) *Homer und die Geschichtsschreibung*, SHAW 1 (Heidelberg), repr. in H. Strasburger (1982) 1057–97.

— (1982) *Studien zur alten Geschichte*, 2 vols. (Hildesheim and New York).

Svenbro, J. (1976) *La parole et le marbre* (Lund).

Sypher, W., ed. (1956) *Comedy* (New York).

Tatum, J. (1989) *Xenophon's Imperial Fiction: On the Education of Cyrus* (Princeton).

Thomas R. (1989) *Oral Tradition and Written Record in Classical Athens* (Cambridge).

— (1997) 'Ethnography, Proof and Argument in Herodotus' *Histories*', *PCPhS* 43. 128–48.

— (2000) *Herodotus in Context: Ethnography, Science and the Art of Persuasion* (Cambridge).

— (2001) 'Herodotus' *Histories* and the Floating Gap', in Luraghi (2001c) 198–210.

Thompson, N. (1996) *Herodotus and the Origins of the Political Community: Arion's Leap* (New Haven).

Tod, M. N. (1985) *A Selection of Greek Historical Inscriptions* (Chicago; reprint of Oxford 1951 edn with new material).

Tritle, L. A. (2000) *From Melos to My Lai. War and Survival* (London and New York).

Vallet, G. (1958) *Rhégion et Zancle: histoire, commerce et civilisation des cités chalcidiennes du détroit de Messine* (Paris).

Vallet, G. and F. Villard (1966) 'Les Phocéens en Méditérranée Occidentale à l'époque archaïque et la fondation de Hyèle', *PP* 21. 166–90.

van der Veen, J. E. (1996) *The Significant and the Insignificant: Five Studies in Herodotus' View of History* (Amsterdam Studies in Classical Philology 6; Amsterdam).

van Wees, H., ed. (2000) *War and Violence in Ancient Greece* (London and Swansea).

— (2002) 'Herodotus and the Past', in Bakker, de Jong and van Wees (2002) 321–49.

Vandiver, E. (1991) *Heroes in Herodotus* (Frankfurt am Main).

Vannicelli, P. (1993) *Erodoto e la storia dell'alto e medio arcaismo* (Rome).

— (2001) 'Herodotus' Egypt and the Foundations of Universal History', in Luraghi (2001c) 211–40.

Vansina, J. (1961) *De la tradition orale. Essai de méthode historique* (Tervuren).

— (1985) *Oral Tradition as History* (Madison).

— (1994) *Living with Africa* (Madison).

Vegetti, M. (1999) 'Culpability, Responsibility, Cause: Philosophy, Historiography, and Medicine in the Fifth Century', in A. A. Long, ed., *The Cambridge Companion to Early Greek Philosophy* (Cambridge), 271–89.

von Fritz, K. (1967) *Die griechische Geschichtsschreibung*, 2 vols. (Berlin and New York).

von Leyden, W. (1949/50) 'Spatium Historicum', *Durham University Journal* 11. 89–104.

von Ungern-Sternberg, J. and H. Reinau, eds. (1988) *Vergangenheit in mündlicher Überlieferung* (Stuttgart).

Wade-Gery, H. T. (1932) 'Thucydides the Son of Melesias: A Study of Periclean Policy', *JHS* 52. 205–27.

— (1933) 'Classical Epigrams and Epitaphs: The Cimonian Age', *JHS* 53.71–104.

Wageningen, J. van (1913) 'Tibulls sogenannte Träumereien', *Neue Jahrbücher* 31. 350–55.

Walbank, F. W. (1972) *Polybius* (Berkeley and Los Angeles).

— (1979) *Commentary on Polybius*, vol. 3 (Oxford).

Walcott, D. (1990) *Omeros* (New York).

— (1993) *The Odyssey: A Stage Version* (New York).

Wankel, H. (1976) *Demosthenes: Rede für Ktesiphon über den Kranz*, 2 vols. (Heidelberg).

Waters, K. H. (1966) 'The Purpose of Dramatisation in Herodotus', *Historia* 15. 157–71.

— (1971) *Herodotus on Tyrants and Despots. A Study in Objectivity* (Historia Einzelschriften 15; Wiesbaden).

Węcowski, M. (1996) 'Ironie et histoire: le discours de Soclès (Hérodote V 92)', *Anc. Soc.* 27. 205–58.

Wells, J. (1923) *Studies in Herodotus* (Oxford).

West, M. L. (1978) *Hesiod: Works and Days* (Oxford).

— (1985) 'Ion of Chios', *BICS* 32. 71–8.

— (2003) *Greek Epic Fragments* (Cambridge, Mass. and London).

West, S. R. (1985) 'Herodotus' Use of Inscriptions', *CQ* 35. 278–305.

— (1991) 'Herodotus' Portrait of Hecataeus', *JHS* 111. 144–60.

— (1999) 'Sophocles' Antigone and Herodotus Book Three', in J. Griffin, ed., *Sophocles Revisited: Essays Presented to Sir Hugh Lloyd-Jones* (Oxford), 109–36.

Whatley, N. (1964) 'On the Possibility of Reconstructing Marathon and Other Ancient Battles', *JHS* 84. 119–39.

White, H. (1973) *Metahistory: the Historical Imagination in Nineteenth-century Europe* (Baltimore and London).

— (1987) *The Content of the Form: Narrative Discourse and Historical Representation* (Baltimore and London).

Whitman, C. (1958) *Homer and the Heroic Tradition* (Cambridge, Mass.).

Wiesehöfer, J. (1996) *Ancient Persia* (London).

Wilkins, J. (1993) *Euripides: Heraclidae* (Oxford).

Winnington-Ingram, R. P. (1980) *Sophocles: An Interpretation* (Cambridge).

Winton, R. (2000) 'Herodotus, Thucydides and the Sophists', in C. Rowe and M. Schofield, eds. *The Cambridge History of Greek and Roman Political Thought* (Cambridge), 89–121.

Wiseman, T. P. (1983) 'The Credibility of the Roman Annalists', *LCM* 8.2. 20–22.

Wohl, V. (2002) *Love among the Ruins. The Erotics of Democracy in Classical Athens* (Princeton).

Wolff, E. (1964) 'Das Weib des Masistes', *Hermes* 92. 51–8, repr. with alterations in Marg (1982) 668–78.

Woodman, A. J. (1988) *Rhetoric in Classical Historiography: Four Studies* (London and Portland).

Yunis, H. (2001) *Demosthenes: On the Crown* (Cambridge).

INDEX OF PASSAGES

Theopompus
(FGrHist 115)

T 20	310
FF 1–4	310

Thucydides

1.1	44
1.21	308
1.22	308
1.22.1	118
1.22.4	22, 72
1.23	277
1.23.6	238, 255
1.40.5	43
1.41.2	43
1.60.2	256
1.67–87	108
1.68–71	229
1.70	229
1.73.2	57
1.86.1	235
1.86.5	255
1.88	255
1.88.1	238
1.90	287
1.95.1	246
1.101.2	245
1.104	287
1.109	287
1.114.2	245
1.118.2	238, 255
1.119	269
1.128–34	255
1.130	232
1.140.1	253
1.143.5	270
2.2.3	256
2.5.7	256
2.8.4	253, 254
2.27	252
2.36.1–3	230
2.41.4	230, 231
2.62	239

2.63.2	239
2.67	74, 206
2.97	308
3.42	240
5.65.2	308
5.72.1	223
5.84–111	74
6.1–5	269
6.3–5	309
6.4.6	271
6.5.3	271
6.8–26	240
6.44.2	269
6.54–9	308
7.33.3–4	272
7.33.4	273
7.57	269
8.91.2	269

Tyrtaeus

F 11.31–4	209

Xenophanes
(VS 21)

A 33	62
B 1.13	201–2
B 10	207
B 11	207
B 11–12	207
B 14–16	207
B 23	202
B 23–4	201
B 34	207
B 34.4	207

Xenophon
Anabasis

2.6.2–6	223

Hellenica

3.1	311

[Xenophon]
Ath. Pol. 2.14.16   270

INDEX

rationalisation 38, 147, 280
rationalism 60, 78, 87
readerly involvement 116
recitation 306
reliability of Herodotus 3, 4, 88
religion, and Herodotus 61, 192
retribution 8, 84
revenge 48–9
revisionism 21
Rhampsinitus 85, 137, 138, 143, 149, 153, 207
rhetoric of history 4
ring-composition 93, 141
rivalry of Athens and Sparta 242
rivers 296
Royal Road 296

Said, Edward 5
Saki 144
Salamis, battle of 20, 22, 47, 54–6, 85, 110–12, 119, 155, 214, 216–18, 240, 245, 248, 250, 257, 267, 272, 286
Samos and the Samians 149, 153
Sandanis 116, 303
Sappho 26
scorched-earth tactics, of Lydians 213
Scylax 34, 39
Scythes 263
Scythia and the Scythians 6, 63, 65, 67, 70, 141, 158, 189, 202, 242, 276, 277, 282, 284, 290, 292, 301, 302
seer 168
Self and Other 226
Semonides 25
Sesostris 138, 189, 294
Sicinnus 112
Simonides 16, 18, 25, 26, 306, 311; his poem on Plataea 16
Simonides the Genealogist 41
Siris 267, 268
Smerdis 157, 275, 278, 279
social memory 9, 226, 292
'social surface' 90
Socle(e)s 106–8, 111, 117, 135, 252
Solon 26, 42, 52, 54, 59, 104–6, 109, 156, 167, 173, 174, 183, 195, 197, 240, 249, 311
Sophanes 136
Sophocles 11, 46, 306–7; and Herodotus 122–7
  Alexandros 49

Ajax 52, 53, 57
Antigone 57, 125–7
Electra 49
Oedipus at Colonus 57
Oedipus Tyrannos 49, 51, 52, 53
Trachiniae 52, 57
sophiê 7, 65, 69, 167, 189, 190, 221
sophists 60, 67–70, 202, 225, 227
sophos 73
Sosibius 162
Sostratus 256
source-citations 3, 4, 37, 77, 83–4, 87, 131, 136–7, 281, 291
sources 71
Sparta and the Spartans 65, 133, 134, 149, 242, 243–4, 247, 253, 254, 303
speeches, in Herodotus 103–17
'spurious akribeia' 143
stereotypes 111
Stesichorus 21
Stesimbrotus 41, 45
stichomythia 54
stories and story-telling 38, 83, 98, 101, 130–42, 203–4, 224
Strabo 314
structuralism 5, 10
structure, of Histories 3, 135, 242
style of Herodotus 92–101, 132, 295
suntaxis 94–101, 102
supplication, motif of 48, 115
Sybaris 257
syntactic style 97

Tacitus 161, 315
technê 10, 30, 75, 169, 171, 172
Tegea 244
tekmêria 72
'text as stream' 132–4
Thales 62, 63, 179–80, 189
The Thousand Nights and a Night 137
Thebes and the Thebans 242, 250–1, 253, 286
thematic patterning 11
Themistocles 20, 23, 48, 55, 68, 104, 110–12, 114, 174, 194, 203, 208, 217, 220, 232, 240, 247, 248, 251, 252, 253, 257, 267–8, 272, 273, 274, 286
Theognis 17
Theophrastus 34, 160, 179, 181
Theopompus 310
theoriê 167, 168, 173
Thera 80, 82

CAMBRIDGE COMPANIONS TO LITERATURE

The Cambridge Companion to Greek Tragedy edited by P. E. Easterling

The Cambridge Companion to Roman Satire edited by Kirk Freudenburg

The Cambridge Companion to Old English Literature edited by Malcolm Godden and Michael Lapidge

The Cambridge Companion to Medieval Women's Writing edited by Carolyn Dinshaw and David Wallace

The Cambridge Companion to Medieval Romance edited by Roberta L. Krueger

The Cambridge Companion to Medieval English Theatre edited by Richard Beadle

The Cambridge Companion to English Renaissance Drama, second edition edited by A. R. Braunmuller and Michael Hattaway

The Cambridge Companion to Renaissance Humanism edited by Jill Kraye

The Cambridge Companion to English Poetry, Donne to Marvell edited by Thomas N. Corns

The Cambridge Companion to English Literature, 1500–1600 edited by Arthur F. Kinney

The Cambridge Companion to English Literature, 1650–1740 edited by Steven N. Zwicker

The Cambridge Companion to English Literature, 1740–1830 edited by Thomas Keymer and Jon Mee

The Cambridge Companion to Writing of the English Revolution edited by N. H. Keeble

The Cambridge Companion to English Restoration Theatre edited by Deborah C. Payne Fisk

The Cambridge Companion to British Romanticism edited by Stuart Curran

The Cambridge Companion to Eighteenth-Century Poetry edited by John Sitter

The Cambridge Companion to the Eighteenth-Century Novel edited by John Richetti

The Cambridge Companion to Gothic Fiction edited by Jerrold E. Hogle

The Cambridge Companion to Victorian Poetry edited by Joseph Bristow

The Cambridge Companion to the Victorian Novel edited by Deirdre David

The Cambridge Companion to Crime Fiction edited by Martin Priestman

The Cambridge Companion to Science Fiction edited by Edward James and Farah Mendlesohn

The *Cambridge Companion to Virgil* edited by Charles Martindale
The *Cambridge Companion to Ovid* edited by Philip Hardie
The *Cambridge Companion to Dante* edited by Rachel Jacoff
The *Cambridge Companion to Cervantes* edited by Anthony J. Cascardi
The *Cambridge Companion to Goethe* edited by Lesley Sharpe
The *Cambridge Companion to Dostoevskii* edited by W. J. Leatherbarrow
The *Cambridge Companion to Tolstoy* edited by Donna Tussing Orwin
The *Cambridge Companion to Chekhov* edited by Vera Gottlieb and Paul Allain
The *Cambridge Companion to Ibsen* edited by James McFarlane
The *Cambridge Companion to Flaubert* edited by Timothy Unwin
The *Cambridge Companion to Proust* edited by Richard Bales
The *Cambridge Companion to Baudelaire* edited by Rosemary Lloyd
The *Cambridge Companion to Thomas Mann* edited by Ritchie Robertson
The *Cambridge Companion to Kafka* edited by Julian Preece
The *Cambridge Companion to Brecht* edited by Peter Thomson and Glendyr Sacks
The *Cambridge Companion to Walter Benjamin* edited by David S. Ferris
The *Cambridge Companion to Lacan* edited by Jean-Michel Rabaté
The *Cambridge Companion to Nabokov* edited by Julian W. Connolly

The *Cambridge Companion to Chaucer, second edition* edited by Piero Boitani and Jill Mann
The *Cambridge Companion to Shakespeare* edited by Margareta de Grazia and Stanley Wells
The *Cambridge Companion to Shakespeare on Film* edited by Russell Jackson
The *Cambridge Companion to Shakespeare Comedy* edited by Alexander Leggatt
The *Cambridge Companion to Shakespeare on Stage* edited by Stanley Wells and Sarah Stanton
The *Cambridge Companion to Shakespeare's History Plays* edited by Michael Hattaway
The *Cambridge Companion to Shakespearean Tragedy* edited by Claire McEachern
The *Cambridge Companion to Christopher Marlowe* edited by Patrick Cheney
The *Cambridge Companion to Ben Jonson* edited by Richard Harp and Stanley Stewart
The *Cambridge Companion to Spenser* edited by Andrew Hadfield
The *Cambridge Companion to Milton, second edition* edited by Dennis Danielson
The *Cambridge Companion to John Dryden* edited by Steven N. Zwicker
The *Cambridge Companion to Aphra Behn* edited by Derek Hughes and Janet Todd
The *Cambridge Companion to Samuel Johnson* edited by Greg Clingham
The *Cambridge Companion to Jonathan Swift* edited by Christopher Fox
The *Cambridge Companion to Mary Wollstonecraft* edited by Claudia L. Johnson
The *Cambridge Companion to William Blake* edited by Morris Eaves
The *Cambridge Companion to Wordsworth* edited by Stephen Gill
The *Cambridge Companion to Coleridge* edited by Lucy Newlyn

The Cambridge Companion to Byron edited by Drummond Bone
The Cambridge Companion to Keats edited by Susan J. Wolfson
The Cambridge Companion to Mary Shelley edited by Esther Schor
The Cambridge Companion to Jane Austen edited by Edward Copeland and Juliet McMaster
The Cambridge Companion to the Brontës edited by Heather Glen
The Cambridge Companion to Charles Dickens edited by John O. Jordan
The Cambridge Companion to George Eliot edited by George Levine
The Cambridge Companion to Thomas Hardy edited by Dale Kramer
The Cambridge Companion to Oscar Wilde edited by Peter Raby
The Cambridge Companion to George Bernard Shaw edited by Christopher Innes
The Cambridge Companion to Joseph Conrad edited by J. H. Stape
The Cambridge Companion to D. H. Lawrence edited by Anne Fernihough
The Cambridge Companion to Virginia Woolf edited by Sue Roe and Susan Sellers
The Cambridge Companion to James Joyce, second edition edited by Derek Attridge
The Cambridge Companion to T. S. Eliot edited by A. David Moody
The Cambridge Companion to Ezra Pound edited by Ira B. Nadel
The Cambridge Companion to W. H. Auden edited by Stan Smith
The Cambridge Companion to Beckett edited by John Pilling
The Cambridge Companion to Harold Pinter edited by Peter Raby
The Cambridge Companion to Tom Stoppard edited by Katherine E. Kelly

The Cambridge Companion to Herman Melville edited by Robert S. Levine
The Cambridge Companion to Nathaniel Hawthorne edited by Richard Millington
The Cambridge Companion to Harriet Beecher Stowe edited by Cindy Weinstein
The Cambridge Companion to Theodore Dreiser edited by Leonard Cassuto and Claire Virginia Eby
The Cambridge Companion to Willa Cather edited by Marilee Lindemann
The Cambridge Companion to Edith Wharton edited by Millicent Bell
The Cambridge Companion to Henry James edited by Jonathan Freedman
The Cambridge Companion to Walt Whitman edited by Ezra Greenspan
The Cambridge Companion to Ralph Waldo Emerson edited by Joel Porte and Saundra Morris
The Cambridge Companion to Henry David Thoreau edited by Joel Myerson
The Cambridge Companion to Mark Twain edited by Forrest G. Robinson
The Cambridge Companion to Edgar Allan Poe edited by Kevin J. Hayes
The Cambridge Companion to Emily Dickinson edited by Wendy Martin
The Cambridge Companion to William Faulkner edited by Philip M. Weinstein
The Cambridge Companion to Ernest Hemingway edited by Scott Donaldson
The Cambridge Companion to F. Scott Fitzgerald edited by Ruth Prigozy
The Cambridge Companion to Robert Frost edited by Robert Faggen
The Cambridge Companion to Ralph Ellison edited by Ross Posnock
The Cambridge Companion to Eugene O'Neill edited by Michael Manheim

The Cambridge Companion to Tennessee Williams edited by Matthew C. Roudanée
The Cambridge Companion to Arthur Miller edited by Christopher Bigsby
The Cambridge Companion to David Mamet edited by Christopher Bigsby
The Cambridge Companion to Sam Shepard edited by Matthew C. Roudané
The Cambridge Companion to Edward Albee edited by Stephen J. Bottoms

CAMBRIDGE COMPANIONS TO CULTURE

The Cambridge Companion to Modern German Culture edited by Eva Kolinsky and Wilfried van der Will
The Cambridge Companion to Modern Russian Culture edited by Nicholas Rzhevsky
The Cambridge Companion to Modern Spanish Culture edited by David T. Gies
The Cambridge Companion to Modern Italian Culture edited by Zygmunt G. Baranski and Rebecca J. West
The Cambridge Companion to Modern French Culture edited by Nicholas Hewitt
The Cambridge Companion to Modern Latin American Culture edited by John King
The Cambridge Companion to Modern Irish Culture edited by Joe Cleary and Claire Connolly